Investment Withholding Tax

Palgrave Macmillan Finance and Capital Markets Series
For information about other titles in this series please visit the website
http://www.palgrave.com/business/finance and capital markets.asp

Also by Ross McGill:

GLOBAL CUSTODY AND CLEARING SERVICES (*with Naren Patel*)

SARBANES OXLEY – Building Working Strategies for Compliance (*with Terence Sheppey*)

TECHNOLOGY MANAGEMENT IN FINANCIAL SERVICES

THE NEW GLOBAL REGULATORY LANDSCAPE – Impacts on Finance & Investment (*with Terence Sheppey*)

Investment Withholding Tax

Best Practice and Strategies for Intermediaries and Investors

ROSS MCGILL

palgrave
macmillan

First published 2009 by
PALGRAVE MACMILLAN

Palgrave Macmillan in the UK is an imprint of Macmillan Publishers Limited, registered in England, company number 785998, of Houndmills, Basingstoke, Hampshire RG21 6XS.

Palgrave Macmillan in the US is a division of St Martin's Press LLC, 175 Fifth Avenue, New York, NY 10010.

Palgrave Macmillan is the global academic imprint of the above companies and has companies and representatives throughout the world.

Palgrave® and Macmillan® are registered trademarks in the United States, the United Kingdom, Europe and other countries.

ISBN: 978–0–230–22162–8 hardback

This book is printed on paper suitable for recycling and made from fully managed and sustained forest sources. Logging, pulping and manufacturing processes are expected to conform to the environmental regulations of the country of origin.

A catalogue record for this book is available from the British Library.

A catalog record for this book is available from the Library of Congress.

10 9 8 7 6 5 4 3 2 1
18 17 16 15 14 13 12 11 10 09

Printed and bound in Great Britain by
CPI Antony Rowe, Chippenham and Eastbourne

For Marty

Contents

PART 3 TECHNOLOGY

PART 4 PERFORMANCE

PART 5 THE FUTURE

Figures

Tables

Abbreviations and Acronyms

AUM	Assets under management
ARAS	Advanced Relief at Source
DTA	Double Tax Agreement
PDF	Portable Document Format
ADBIC	Additional Destination Bank Identifier Code (see also BIC)
ADR	American Depositary Receipt
APC	American Power Conversion Company
ASCII	American Standard Code for Information Interchange
BGP	Border Gateway Protocol
BIC	Bank Identifier Code
BEI	Business Entity Identifiers
CAA	Credit Advice Authorization
CEO	Chief Executive Officer
CSD	Central Securities Depositary
DR	Depositary Receipt
DTCC	Depositary Trust & Clearing Corporation
ECB	Euroclear Bank
EFTPS	Electronic Federal Tax Payment System
EU	European Union
EUCLID	Euroclear proprietary system
FFS	Fact Finding Study
FI	Financial Institution
FISCO	Fiscal Compliance Group
FTP	File Transfer Protocol
HTTP	Hyper Text Transfer Protocol
HTTPS	Hyper Text Transfer Protocol Secure
ICG	Informal Consultative Group on Taxation of Collective Investment Vehicles
ICSD	International Central Securities Depositary

IDS	Intrusion Detection Systems
IMI	Investment Management Institution
IRS	US Internal Revenue Service
ISIN	International Securities Identifying Number
ISO	International Standards Organization
KYC	Know Your Customer
LOA	Letter of Authority
LOB	Limitations of Benefit
MCC	Martinsburg Computer Center
MDPUG	Market Data Providers' User Group
MT	Message Type
NAT	Network Active Translation
NQI	Non-Qualified Intermediary
NYRS	New York Registry Share
OECD	Organisation for Economic Cooperation & Development
QI	Qualified Intermediary
QFI	Qualified Financial Intermediary
RAS	Relief At Source
RFP	Request for Proposal
SD	Stamp Duty
SDRT	Stamp Duty Reserve Tax
SEC	US Securities & Exchange Commission
SI	Specified Intermediary
SICAF	Societe d'Investissement a Capital Fixe
SICAV	Societe d'Investissement a Capital Variable
SLA	Service Level Agreement
SMTP	Simple Mail Transfer Protocol
STP	Straight Through Processing
SWIFT	Society for Worldwide Interbank Financial Telecommunication
TRA	Tax Reclaim Agent
TRSB	Tax Reclaim Service Bureau
UPS	Uninterruptible Power Supply
V-STP	Virtual Straight Through Processing (see also STP)

Preface

When investments are made cross border, income derived from those investments is taxed both in the source country (country of investment) at a high (statutory) tax rate, before being remitted to the investor where it is typically subject to taxation also under the recipient's tax rules. Such double taxation is clearly harmful to the free movement of capital and so double tax agreements between pairs of countries provide principles and mechanisms so that such income is taxed only once and at a mutually agreed (treaty) rate.

To be realised, such entitlements must be claimed either before (relief at source) or after (long form) the date that the taxable income is distributed. However, each jurisdiction operates its own systems with many variables, forms, deadlines and information and reporting constraints which make it extremely difficult for investors and their financial services intermediaries to efficiently maximise returns on investment. Such is the world of international withholding tax.

Currently, there is nearly $1.6 trillion of tax that is recoverable, an amount that is increasing by over $300 billion every year. Of this, it is expected that less than 7% will ever get back to those who have the entitlement. Many factors go towards making this figure as small as it is. However, the largest single factor is awareness of the issue and its complexity. Only with a greater understanding by all those in the investment chain between issuer and investor, can effective strategies be devised to improve performance.

This book, the third I have written on this general topic, is written for the full range of professional investors, their advisors and for financial intermediaries, to bring such awareness to a higher level and to bring together the various threads of the issue into focus. Much has changed since my previous works were published:

- Cross-border investment has been consistently rising at over 16% a year;

- The number of Double Tax Treaties signed to engender inward investment has increased by over 400;
- Confidence in the financial services community has plumbed to all-time lows and is struggling to regain trust with its clients;
- Trading strategies have become more complex;
- Tax authorities are increasingly questioning claims from the market in greater detail;
- Regulatory authorities are clamouring for a wholesale reform of the withholding tax landscape to increase controls and also to create a more harmonised playing field for cross-border investors;
- Custodians are under more pressure than ever to reduce costs while delivering a better service in order to maximise custody fee income;
- Investors are becoming far more aware of the potential damage to performance from inappropriate tax strategies and sensitive to the need for solutions;
- New tax processes are being formulated which require additional processes including tax information reporting and audit oversight.

These are merely the outward signs of more fundamental changes including changes in attitude and political will within major trading blocks. To that extent, this book has become more important than its predecessors as a practical repository for aggregated information. It's not enough any longer for professionals in the industry to know the practical issues in a global context, although in this edition, all of these issues are enumerated, discussed and updated from the original works. They must also know of the strategic shifts taking place. These include changes in paradigms of processing, the advent of Virtual Straight Through Processing as the precursor for full STP in withholding tax, which I estimate still to be at least a decade away. Also of importance are the views of major groups on the commercial side such as G30 as well as Giovannini and FISCO on the political side. The work of the OECD is also valuable to understand. So, in this edition, you will find more extensive references to the work of these bodies and in some cases, reproduction of important tracts. Since I take some time to discuss the context and relevance of the work of these bodies, it is useful to be able to reference the significant parts of their work in one place.

In the previous editions, I gave scale and scope to the effects withholding tax, so it's apposite to review the situation five years on. Global assets under management (AUM) in 2008 exceeded US$108 trillion. Of this 27.7% (US$30 trillion) were held cross border. At a 5% yield, the tax imposed by foreign governments on the income from these assets was around US$300 billion. This figure is compounded to over US$1.56 trillion when statutes of limitation are included.

Since the global financial markets are founded on cross-border trade, it's clearly in the interests of each market to balance its need for tax revenue with the need to stimulate and maintain inward investment in the face of strong global competition. This has been brought into clearer focus by the upheaval in the financial markets in late 2008 followed by general global recession in 2009. As companies struggle to survive, dividends will decrease in number and size. So tax revenues will decrease both from corporate taxation and the taxation of investment distributions. With linked economies, attracting inward investment will become more important providing a driver for more efficiencies in withholding tax processes while at the same time, increased regulation will make the job of financial services firms more complex and more costly.

In my work around the globe, it used to be common for fund managers to be sanguine about a 2.5% performance improvement available from having an active tax reclamation policy in place, since overall performances were typically already at 20% to 30%. Now, that situation has changed. Funds are closing at an unprecedented pace, new market strategies are developing and regulation requires a greater transparency between investor and fund manager and 2.5% is now very material to performance.

From whichever perspective you view it, withholding tax optimisation has never been more important for the investment world and I therefore believe that this book is important for everyone in the investment chain.

Of the $1.6 trillion in extant tax mentioned earlier, less than 7% ever actually gets recovered back to its rightful owners. This is a lamentable performance which is a compound effect of many factors some of which are outside the control of the industry. However, many factors are within our concerted grasp. If we could make the processes of assessing and calculating entitlements for all clients in all investment structures; if we could engage with tax authorities and help them develop more automated, non-paper-based processes; if we can agree on common principles of control that will satisfy tax authorities, then substantial improvements in performance are possible.

For example, if the industry could recover 93% of the tax over-withheld by foreign governments, instead of the 7% it currently achieves, the money put back into client's investment accounts would:

- offset *all* the sub-prime write-offs and losses which characterised the financial crisis of 2008;
- improve funds' performance by around 2.5%;
- increase custody fees (which are based on the increased performance of these funds) by around $4.2 billion a year.

All in all, not a bad return for making one process more efficient. The object of this book is to give as wide an audience as possible to all the issues that need to be addressed in the hope that some momentum can be gained to improve industry performance.

That said, there are a large number of people out there who have knowledge of the withholding tax issue readily at hand. Most financial firms have at least one person, and often many more, who deal directly with these issues on a daily basis. Many more in each firm have indirect contact with the issue, whether it's the messaging function moving withholding tax messages between firms, compliance officers dealing with meeting regulatory requirements or lawyers dealing with liability issues. A great deal of information about withholding tax is also available on the world wide web. Most tax authorities now have web sites and indeed most custodians and several industry utilities, such as DTC, SWIFT, DALI, GlobeTax and CREST have web sites where the pieces of the jigsaw can be identified, if not brought together. In addition, there are many suppliers to the industry whether they be solutions providers or advisors, such as the major accountancy practices.

There are also various forums and resource centres where withholding tax issues, and in particular the operational aspects, are discussed. These include both on-line forums as well as the more traditional conferences, seminars and training courses. The International Bureau for Fiscal Documentation is an excellent resource centre, but by no means the only one. Finally, there's experience. I've spent 12 years now meeting and talking with people ranging from tax operations specialists all the way to senior members of tax authorities and management in the key utilities. My value in this book is the ability to bring it all this together in one place so that the reader has the opportunity to think about the issues in a more holistic way and perhaps find a better way of doing things.

In writing this book, I have drawn on all these public sources to try to bring together a more integrated picture of withholding tax which goes beyond just the facts about the tax itself. I've tried to explain the impact of the tax on financial firms operations as well as on their customers – the investors and also the top of the chain – the income distributing corporations. This means taking the many thousands of words in things like double tax agreements or regulatory documents and asking the question "So what does this mean in practice?"

So the question is, who should actually read this book and why? This book can, and should, be read by a wide variety of professionals interested or involved with cross-border investment or royalty income. The nature of a book with such a wide audience is of course that some parts will be common knowledge to some readers, whilst to others will be entirely new. Hopefully, however, this book has value for most of the professionals who are likely to have to come into contact with international withholding tax.

In my experience in the industry, I have rarely found anyone, in any of the categories mentioned below, who has a full and working knowledge of all the process and operational impacts described, let alone the many ways in which these issues inter-relate. Knowledge of the tax rates and regimes in itself is not difficult to research, but it *is* long winded and expensive in time and resource. Institutional investors, fund managers, broker dealers, private banks, major corporations and custodians all need to understand not only the tax implications but also the operational framework within which the tax is administered if funds are to perform to their best. Within these firms, compliance officers, risk management, tax operations management, institutional sales management, corporate finance directors and accountants all have a vested interest in understanding the scope of this issue and specifically the operational impacts of it, to maximise their business interests. Tax authorities themselves need to understand the industry better to better prepare themselves for the changes that will be asked of them.

INSTITUTIONAL INVESTORS

Institutional investors are one of the key groups which has a multiplicity of needs to satisfy, all driven by the need to generate return on investment at minimum risk. While many have historically taken an arms length attitude to their investments, today's uncertain world has led, through corporate mis-governance, financial and political upheaval, to a need for a greater degree of knowledge and involvement in the delivery of returns. Institutional investors have, until now, few if any tools to understand this arcane area of tax, yet it can make a big difference. The needs fall into three categories:

- understanding the basics of the different tax regime types and the scale and scope of the effects this can have on portfolio spread, risk reduction and return on investment;

- understanding the structural and operational issues faced by their custodians so that they can adopt complementary internal processes to minimise the effects of withheld tax on investment income;

- Applying benchmarks of the process to Service Level Agreements to assure compliance and best practice and assert liability for risk reduction or indeed using them as a competitive assessment tool.

FUND MANAGERS AND BROKER DEALERS

It is in this area that the knowledge of the issue of withholding tax is most fragmented and most misunderstood. The lines between custody and brokerage are becoming more blurred as many broker dealers, primarily due to their increasing spend on process automation, take up some custody elements in order to enhance their service offerings. Fund managers, in the face of increasing custody fees, are more often looking to in-source those elements of custody which add most value or at least they are becoming more discerning of the real cost-benefit of custody services provided to them. In the face of this partial homogenisation, both fund managers and broker dealers must have enough information, knowledge and understanding to assess withholding tax as a significant value service to investors, in the light of the complexities and particularly the liabilities of undertaking the process.

PRIVATE BANKS

Private banks thrive predominantly on quality of service and attention to detail that the larger firms are not positioned to deliver in quite the same way. Whether outsourced or in-sourced, this issue is of critical value to private banks. As will be seen later, a solid understanding of the withholding tax arena can easily be converted into added competitive value and exceeding client expectations. In comparison to the major global and country custodians, private banks are relatively small and thus the cost effects of dealing with this issue are significant. On the other hand, their client base is much more likely to be invested cross border and therefore they need a clear strategy to get the greatest possible return from portfolio spread.

COMPLIANCE OFFICERS AND RISK MANAGEMENT STAFF

Most people only consider one dimension of this issue, the tax issue. Compliance and risk management staff have a duty to understand not just the tax issues themselves but also the relationships between the issue and how it is handled within an organisation. There are clear risks and consequent liabilities that can be demonstrated. The lack of globally accepted benchmarking in this area highlights not only risk but also the requirement for proper assessment in order to correctly manage the risk. The scale of liability can, in some cases, reach millions of dollars should a custodian for instance, have failed to have performed any or all its potential tax reclaims without ensuring that its clients are aware of the fact and have explicitly understood that this value enhancing activity is not taking place. That liability can in theory aggregate historically for several years in some cases. The wording of service level agreements may not protect some firms who could be deemed to be experts in the area and thus have an obligation to explain the size of the issue to clients or at least explain any form of limitation of scope in which they undertake operations in this area.

TAX OPERATIONS MANAGEMENT

Whilst they should be more knowledgeable on the tax issues and even the operational issues, there are clearly opportunities for improvement for tax operations professionals. Benchmarking, as well as opportunities for increased automation and risk reduction, are discussed here. Tax operations departments can be the least well served and least included in strategic, operational or sales discussions (or budgeting). They thus suffer from one of the lowest levels of investment in resources yet they are one of the highest deliverers of value to the custody and investment chain. Their input and experience is invaluable and hopefully a wider readership of this book will help them gain the status they deserve.

INSTITUTIONAL SALES MANAGEMENT

It is in sales management's interests to place a best case for their own institution. Only recently has it become clear that sales management needs to have a more holistic understanding and knowledge of the elements of the custody back office. As investors become more aware and educated about these issues sales management, unable to answer questions, place their firms at a disadvantage against more enlightened and knowledgeable custodians. I often run courses for financial services firms helping them "join the dots" between back office value and what an institutional investor wants to see in a proposal or response to tender. Commonly a sales function will provide a potential customer with no real reasons for choosing them over another institution, other than their size, geographical spread and credit rating. There's very little differentiation and, in my experience, precious little attention to what the customer actually needs to hear. Rather, custodians have a tendency to become introspective and focused on telling institutional investors how good they are without connecting the feature of themselves with the benefit it delivers to the investor. I recently ran a course for five firms and gave them the challenge of making a pitch to me as a potential institutional client. Not one mentioned how much money they could make for me or why their size or their geographical spread made them any different to their (similarly sized and similarly spread) competitors. Any one of them could have used the withholding tax issue as a prime example of how and why they were the best choice. If they had it would, to me as an investor, have seemed a very direct and positive example of how they could benefit me. From an understanding of the issues, this book should allow institutional sales professionals to connect the issues with their own firm's activities and transform internal benchmarks of performance into benefits they can use to differentiate themselves from their competitors, with their clients.

FINANCE DIRECTORS

General knowledge of the tax is already likely to be widespread amongst finance directors. However, the operational processes undertaken by a corporation's bankers or custodians may not be well understood. The Double Tax Treaties which encode this global issue cover more types of income that just dividend income. The US 1441 NRA regulations have nearly twenty different types of US-source income that could be paid to a non-resident alien (individual or corporation etc.) and which would be subject to withholding tax. Undoubtedly, for many readers, dividend income will constitute the vast majority of their concerns, but its well to be aware of the broader applicable base of the tax. Cross-border royalties are an example of income subject to withholding tax and therefore liable, in the same way as dividends, to over-withholding. Indeed, as an example, the Australian government statistics (available at their web site) show that they withheld about the same in dividend withholding tax as in royalty withholding tax. Corporations generally will rate the costs of dealing with this tax as very high because there are few tools or experts available to simplify the process or make it more cost effective. On the other hand, the custodian banks, who already probably deal with the dividend announcement and distributions parts of the corporation's affairs do have this knowledge, technology and experience. Finance directors with a knowledge of the overall process will be able to judge more effectively whether their cross border income streams can be improved.

ACCOUNTANTS

Ask most finance directors and they will say that their accountant deals with the issues of withholding tax. From experience, this is not always the case. Where the financial services industry, with a level of knowledge, skill and automation is only addressing a fraction of this tax, the corporate market is unlikely to have anything like the same level of application. This book is of interest therefore, not because it will give any insight into the details of the tax legislation, but because it will provide a valuable information tool to understand the operational issues surrounding withholding tax. It is not enough to know the tax rates or treaty details between countries if you have no knowledge of the process constraints and costs involved in dealing with the issue once identified.

It must be made clear at the outset that this book is not about the minutiae of taxation for any particular country or any particular kind of income. This book is about the administrative processes whose general application is to all countries and most types of cross-border income.

IT STAFF

This book will also be valuable to IT management in the financial services sector, as a foundation of key issues in this area. Enterprise wide projects are common at the trading floor and cross-functional collaboration is high and generally effective. In the back office however, due primarily to the historically manual and arcane nature of the administration processes, there is a very low level of cross-disciplinary understanding or communication.

As will be described in more detail later, knowledge of these processes will, for the first time, give these interest groups an ability to select and set appropriate benchmarks to achieve best practice in order to reduce operational risk and, as a result, maximise fund values and returns.

So, withholding tax remains generally a fragmented, knowledge-based, often manual, resource-intensive, error-prone, inefficient and costly process. The ability and ultimate success of these different departments, each with their own agendas, priorities and budgets, to make substantial improvements, can be enhanced by each having a common basic understanding of the processes involved.

Included in the appendices to this book are a range of support materials. These have two levels of relevance. Firstly, they are referred to within the body of the book as referents to particular issues. In that context they are intended to exemplify larger principles. However, secondly, they have relevance as stand-alone documents. For example, the standard OECD Tax

Convention Articles, as amended in 2008, provide not only good background reading on the complexities of withholding tax as perceived and codified by the governments that adopt this model, but also because they are increasingly being used as the base model for new double tax conventions; the appendix is a good reference source in and of itself.

Acknowledgements

I would like to acknowledge the following for their support:

Martin S. Foont, Len A. Lipton, William Treut, Jose Bisono, Harold Shapero, Robert Weiss, John Niblo and Andrew Stephens at GlobeTax for their help in providing background material;

Charlotte McGill for helping with large tracts of reformatting of the basic manuscript;

Andrew Stephenson of globalcustody.net for his permission to use asset data; and

Terence Sheppey of Precision Texts Ltd for his work in indexing the manuscript.

Although the author has made every effort to ensure the complete accuracy of the text, neither he nor Palgrave accept any legal responsibility whatsoever for consequences that may arise from errors or omissions or any opinions or advice given.

Nothing in this book is or is intended to constitute the provision of taxation or investment advice. Readers are strongly advised to take professional independent advice on these matters.

About the Author

Ross McGill entered the withholding tax industry in 1996 and has since become a recognised authority at both strategic management and tactical levels. He acts as a member of numerous industry bodies including an ISO 20022 Securities Evaluation Group and the International Capital Markets Services association. He has also maintained close relationship with many tax authorities including the United States Internal Revenue Service where he co-chaired the Operational Impact Committee for Section 1441 NRA regulations. He is currently Managing Director of GlobeTax, the largest independent provider of withholding tax processing and data services and CEO of TConsult Ltd, a training organisation focused on regulatory compliance and tax issues. Ross is also the author of several financial services reference works including:

- *International Withholding Tax – A Practical Guide to Best Practice & Benchmarking*
- *International Withholding Tax – Relief at Source*
- *Sarbanes Oxley – Strategies for Compliance* co-authored with Terence Sheppey
- *The New Global Regulatory Landscape* co-authored with Terence Sheppey
- *Global Custody & Clearing Services* co-authored with Naren Patel
- *Technology Management in Financial Services*

PART 1

Essentials

Withholding tax is an incredibly easy concept to understand. Unfortunately when the concept is put into practice by over 230 different tax jurisdictions each with its own concerns, language, drivers for inward investment and so on, the result is a minefield of custom and practice and one which is currently undergoing its greatest rate of change in several decades.

In the Preface, I mentioned some quite staggering statistics regarding the amount of tax that could be recovered, and the amount that actually ever will be – around 7%. The big questions are – (i) is the number valid and (ii) why is this number so low?

The 7% figure is actually a derived number because there is no reliable industry wide research in this area of sufficient scope to accurately define the issue. In 2004 I did some "research of research". Across multiple sets of securities industry research, performed between 2000 and 2004, I identified some common metrics and tabulated these and then compared them to overall assets under management, including cross-border AUM. From my experience in the industry since 1996, I'd say that the 7% figure is a reasonable measure. Even if its error margin were 100%, the message it sends is clear.

It's low because there are a number of factors that can cause a claim not to be filed. The following are some *examples* of why entitlements might not get recovered:

- Lack of awareness (custodian and beneficial owner). There may be an entitlement but no-one ever does anything about it.

- Choice of non-disclosure. Some beneficial owners choose not to claim in order to avoid disclosing their identity either to a foreign tax authority or to another financial institution

- Failure to meet deadlines. In markets where there is only a RAS process with no long form process, documentation can be very specific and time delimited. Many beneficial owners and their custodians struggle to meet them.

- Claims falling outside statute. Custodian and beneficial owner inefficiencies mean many claims that are identified are never filed because FIs have too large a backlog.

- Type of intermediary. Some types of intermediary do not offer tax services to clients, for example, brokers and prime brokers, so their clients, unless they engage a third party, lose out on all entitlements.

- Lack of service offering. If the custodian does not provide a service, *all* the possible claims on all their clients holdings go into the "not claimed" pot.

- Threshold. Claim values below a certain threshold never get filed. The threshold varies per custodian.

- Lack of scope of offering – income type. Many custodians do not claim on particular types of income, for example, ADRs for perceived complexity reasons.

- Lack of scope of offering – beneficial owner type. Some beneficial owners types are very expensive and complex to process.

- Lack of scope of offering – by market. Above all things, the cost of research is a critical factor, not least because it must be relative to the client and investment bases and be used only after independent verification from at least two sources. Key main markets are often the limitation of custodians.

- Type of client base. A custodian's client base has an important impact. If there are many retail investors compared to institutional, it may be that only the institutional investors are offered a service thus disintermediating part of the customer base, and their entitlements, for simple commercial reasons.

- Lack of scope of offering – structure. Some custodians will not do claims for clients with complex structures because the risk is too high and the cost is too high.

- Structure. Some investment structures, for example complex Trusts, are deemed transparent. The claim at the fund level would be viable, but with thousands of investors, claims at the investor level are just not worth filing (cost is too high), and so they never get done.

- Lack of scope of offering – systems limitations. Some custodians cannot process certain types of claims because their systems are not structured to aggregate data in the right way.

- Claims filed incorrectly. Many tax authorities reject claims if the correct paperwork is not completed accurately. Sometimes, they even tell the claimant!

- Location. Some investors, who would have an entitlement if they invested directly, choose to invest via a specific market structure, for example Cayman corporate. They lose out on entitlements because of that choice as their entitlement is subsumed by the investment vehicle which has no entitlement.

...I could go on, but I'm sure you see the problem both of scaling the issue and even describing it. Many of the players in the list above are unlikely to admit to any of the relevant "misses" let alone the scale and scope of their potential client entitlements.

So, while the concept might be very simple to understand, clearly the message is not getting received or applied somewhere along the line.

Investors have an unambiguous interest in the subject – where they have any knowledge of it at all. Financial intermediaries have a rather more subtle interest. That interest borders on the one hand at the level of fiduciary duty – the responsibility to act on your specialist knowledge in the best interests of your customers; and on the other hand, the self-interest driven by the fact that the more tax credited back into your client's accounts, the higher your custody fees will be.

Essentially withholding tax must be understood in terms of the principles and the context in which they apply. To try to apply knowledge of only one of these areas leads to failure.

In this first part of the book, we will look at Principles, Context and Primary factors. These three issues will set out what withholding tax is, how the issue is currently addressed by the various interested parties in the investment chain and some of the key factors that are affecting change in the industry, of which both investors and financial intermediaries should be cognisant.

Principles establish the broad issues to be addressed. For instance, the principle of withholding tax establishes that an investor can be entitled to a lower rate of tax than would otherwise perhaps be applied. However, *having* an entitlement doesn't do an investor very much good if they don't *exercise* that entitlement. The only way to exercise the entitlement is to understand the context in which the principle applies. The context, in this case for example, establishes that there are three broad operational processing regimes under which an entitlement might be obtained – relief at source, long form claim or combination. This is just one of many contextual issues that must be understood alone and in concert and both under the over-arching principles that guide them.

This part of the book seeks to explain the principles and associated contexts in such a way that subsequent parts of the book are more easily understood and integrated.

CHAPTER 1

Principles

Whether you're reading this book as a private investor, institutional investor or as a custodian or other financial intermediary or firm, this book is important because its subject can significantly affect the value of investment portfolios which equally affects returns, fees and wealth.

DOUBLE TAX PRINCIPLE

When income is generated across borders, the tax authority in the country of generation (country of issue) requires of withholding agent banks that, unless they have reason to know otherwise, they must tax the income distributions to non-resident investors at a specified rate (the statutory rate). Under normal circumstances, the recipient of such income would also be required, under their own domestic law, to declare the income for domestic income tax purposes in his country of residence. There are two effects that flow from this. Clearly there is a potential for double taxation of a single item of income to occur. Worse, the consequential effect, if left unaddressed would be that inward investment to that market could be significantly damaged. Even just looking at statutory rates, why would you invest in Switzerland and be taxed at 35% when you could invest in France and be taxed at 25% or Germany and be taxed at 21.1%? See Figure 1.1.

To avoid these effects, pairs of countries with common economic interests enter into Double Taxation Agreements or DTAs. By this means they establish a Treaty Rate of withholding. This enables the issuer of the income to withhold a smaller amount (based on the lower treaty rate) as long as the recipient is eligible for that lower rate. This is known as an entitlement.

Figure 1.2 shows how the world of tax is not as static as one might at first suppose for such a process bound up in administration and inter-governmental negotiation. There are, on average 70 to 80 new treaties brought into force

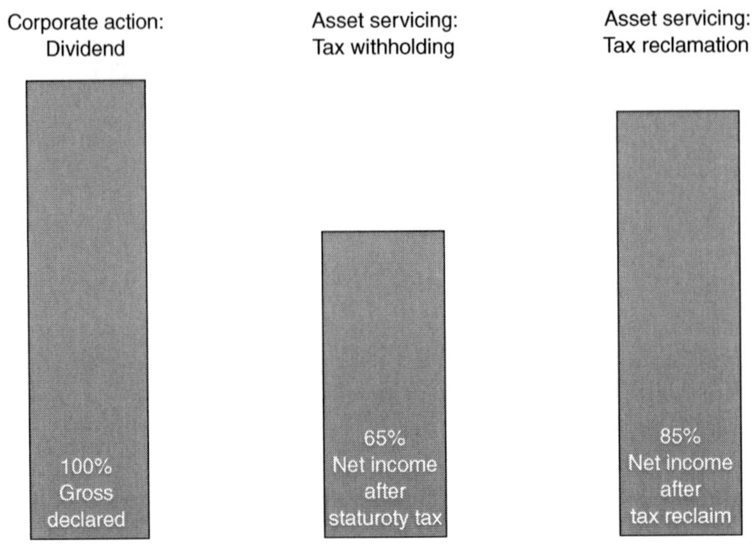

Figure 1.1 The withholding tax effect

Source: Author.

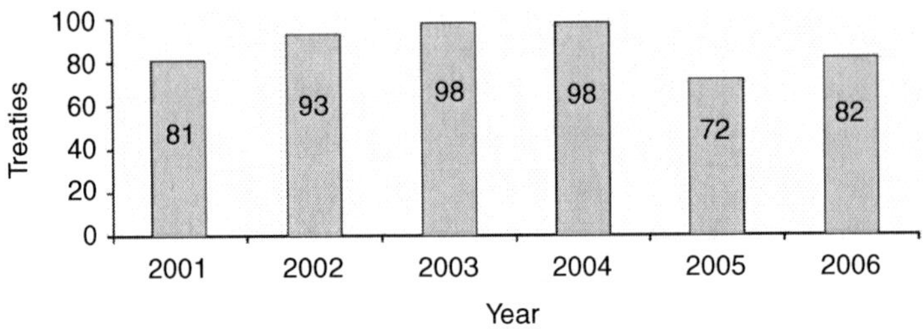

Figure 1.2 Tax treaties enacted 2001–2006

Source: GlobeTax.

each year. These figures do not include changes to existing treaties. The combination of new treaties and changes to existing ones means that large swathes of the investment community are subject to changes and potentially beneficiaries of new entitlements each year.

However, it's one thing to have an entitlement and quite another to gain the benefit of that entitlement. Treaties commonly do not prescribe the process by which entitlements can be realised. Instead, this is left to the taxation authorities within each market to define. As we'll see later, the variation of processes and procedures causes a great deal of cost and risk for investors and intermediaries alike.

Even at this top level, we see the "it depends" effect at work. This statutory and treaty tax-rate principle would be good if it weren't for the fact that there is not always one statutory rate in all markets of issue. For example, one eastern European country has a statutory rate of 20% applied to non-resident aliens *except* if the company making the distribution is an oil company in which case the statutory rate is 25%.

JURISDICTIONAL PRINCIPLE

So, as a given, we have a situation where an investment made across border is about to generate a distribution. This might be a cash dividend on a long equity position or it might be a coupon payment on a bond. Technically, the treaty would provide the basis for an entitlement based on the residence and legal form of the investor, the nature of the income and the year in which the income is to be paid. Local law would provide for the statutory rate that would be applied and the treaty would establish the treaty rate that might apply, the difference being the entitlement. When it comes to obtaining the entitlement, there are different ways this can be done. All are based on two things – data and documentation.

There are three broad categories of process:

- Relief at Source claim (RAS)
- Quick Refund
- Long Form Claim

Relief at source is a pre-pay-date process. If the beneficial owner can prove their entitlement prior to the pay-date, according to the correct procedures, the correct *treaty* rate of tax will be deducted. Clearly, relief at source is a preferable taxation method because it ensures that investors receive correct distributions in the fastest possible way. The problem is that, unlike long form claims, the time frame in which this documentation needs to be provided can be very tight. The result is that, although preferable, it's not always feasible.

Quick refund is a process offered commercially by withholding agents mainly to other custodian banks and brokers. Essentially, the withholding agent will usually make payments to the tax authority on a regular basis, as opposed to every time a payment is distributed. So, in some cases, the withholding agent offers to make a book adjustment to the tax it has if the beneficial owner or intermediary provides enough documentation to prove eligibility for a treaty rate. The tax is therefore remitted to the claimant by the withholding agent not the tax authority. As a result, quick refund processes are very fragmented in the nature of the rules, dates and types of documentation required. Once the quick refund window has passed, the withholding agent will pass the tax to the tax authority.

Long form claims are a post-payment process. The beneficial owner is taxed at the Statutory Rate for that market and, within a certain given period (statute of limitations), if a retrospective claim is filed, the over-withheld tax is remitted back to the beneficial owner. In some cases, tax authorities also pay interest on amounts that take longer than expected to remit.

Even so, the way in which the availability of these processes is delivered to market varies. Some jurisdictions permit only a relief-at-source mechanism. If the beneficial owner fails to apply for it, there is no long form process. At the other end of the spectrum are jurisdictions like Switzerland where there is no relief-at-source process, only the long form process. In between, there are jurisdictions that allow both. So if the beneficial owner does not make the deadline for relief at source, they still have an opportunity to file long form claims. These are called *combination* jurisdictions.

These latter are important because they are likely to form the basis of any harmonisation that takes place in the market. Fiscal Compliance Group (FISCO), G30 and the Giovannini committee have already indicated that a combination approach would be the preferred common process for all jurisdictions. This nicely sidesteps the thorny and all but impossible alternative interpretation of harmonisation, that of the tax rates themselves. All the actors in the market agree that individual states should retain the rights to tax as they see fit both for the benefit of domestic tax payers and also for non-resident aliens (in-bound investors).

TRANSPARENCY PRINCIPLES

The entitlement we have spoken about so far has been created from the existence of the treaty and the wish of governments to encourage inward investment and to avoid double taxation. However, in a complex financial world, there are different ways in which investors can group themselves in order to make investments across border. Some of those mechanisms are viewed suspiciously by tax authorities and give rise to limitations on the benefits that some investors may be entitled to, merely because of the way they invest. At worst, this can mean that the investor loses any entitlement at all. At best it means that he would be no worse off. Good examples of these groupings include pension funds, hedge funds, Societe d'Investissement a Capital Variable (SICAVs) and Societe d'Investissement a Capital Fixe (SICAFs), unit trusts and so on. A pension fund for example would typically be exempt from withholding tax, as investing directly would be able to claim the whole of an entitlement to bring it up to 100% of a distributed dividend. However, if the pension fund invested in the market by being an investor in a unit trust, as far as a foreign tax authority is concerned, the unit trust may well be the ultimate beneficial owner who can only access a treaty rate, say of 15%. In such a case, the pension fund loses out on 15% tax that it cannot recover simply because of the way in which it invested in the market. The unit trust in that case was "fiscally opaque" that is, the tax authority did not need to penetrate any deeper than the fund level, but the investors in the fund lost out equally. A US hedge fund that invests across border is typically viewed as a partnership. Tax authorities generally view partnerships as flow through or fiscally transparent entities that is, the fund is not the actual ultimate beneficial owner, the individual partners are. To that end the transparency principle may seem to make the situation simpler as the entitlement will be at the partner level (based on the partner's residency and legal form as opposed to that of the fund). However, when combined with the process and procedure principles we will discuss next, as far as tax is concerned, the hedge fund has an enormous administrative load placed upon it, if it wants to provide its investor partners with good value. The result is that most US hedge funds never attempt to recover tax.

Even where these entitlements exist and the nature of the transparency principle makes it clear where the entitlement is within a collective investment vehicle, there is also an issue of disclosure. Many high net worth and ultra high net worth individuals are not always too happy about disclosing their income to a foreign government. This does not so much affect corporate entities like pension funds and so on, who are regulated anyway. However, it's an important part of the transparency principle that in order to get tax back from a foreign government, to which you are entitled, you have to disclose yourself to that government or to an entity that that government has contracted with for that purpose (cf. US 1441 NRA regulations).

PROCESS AND PROCEDURE PRINCIPLES

So, now we understand that there is a double taxation effect, and in principle that effect can be mitigated through the application of treaties to generate an entitlement. Access to those entitlements is mitigated in part by transparency issues. Now, depending on the market, an investor may be able to realise that entitlement in one of several ways.

The first myth to *bust* is the offset principle. Many beneficial owners are of the opinion that any tax they over-pay abroad can be taken as a tax credit against their domestic tax liability, effectively an offset process. In most cases this is not true. In most jurisdictions, the rules are that you can only take a credit for the *irrecoverable* portion of foreign tax overpaid. Since there are recovery procedures in place, albeit complex, in most jurisdictions, the offset concept is not usually a legal one.

With the offsetting myth put in context, the key ways in which these entitlements can be realised is through process and procedure. Unfortunately, the processes and procedures are different for each market of investment. However, they do share some common characteristics. They all require the claimant to provide evidence of their legal form and residency for tax purposes. However, the particular forms of evidence that are required by each market, of each claimant type – also varies. Also, once evidence of legal form and residency are established, for long form claims, all markets have a form on which the details of the income on which tax was over-deducted, must be provided. These forms are also the basis of the tax authority asking common questions of claimants to assure themselves that a false claim is not being filed, for example the length of time that a security was held by the claimant prior to the pay-date, the reason for the claimant's ownership of the security, the answers to both of which, might indicate dividend washing or treaty shopping. The forms vary by year sometimes and also vary in many cases depending on the type of income received. So, for example, the form to recover tax on dividends in Austria is different from the form needed to claim tax back on interest. The questions asked on each of these forms are also different.

Finally, in addition to evidence of the claimant's status and details of the claim, the claimant must also provide evidence that the income was in fact received by them and also that it was over-taxed. In classical terms this would be done with a tax voucher. For custodians however, electronic records, including copies of SWIFT (Society for Worldwide Interbank Financial Telecommunication) messages, are also increasingly accepted by tax authorities.

On the procedural front, life is not much easier, as we'll see in more detail later. For some markets the claim, once compiled, can be filed directly to the tax authority. In others however, for example France, the claim must be filed with an agent bank, who undertakes to review the claim's validity and process it through to the tax authority, for which of course they charge a fee. This is jurisdictional procedure. There are also different procedures for some income types, irrespective of the market concerned. A good example is American Depositary Receipts (ADRs) which are generally "sponsored" by one of four (at the time of writing) ADR sponsoring banks – Citi, JPMorgan Chase, Bank of New York Mellon and Deutsche Bank. Claims on ADR positions cannot be filed to a tax authority or an agent bank because they are not recognised as securities, they are derivative products. The claim must be filed back to the depositary that sponsored the issue. More on that later.

AUTOMATION PRINCIPLES

The reader will have undoubtedly noticed by now that while the concept of withholding tax is simple, its implementation in a global financial market is anything but simple. It will also not have escaped most people's attention that the means by which all these principles are delivered would seem to be manual that is, paper-based. This leads us to another principle – automation. At present, taking the initial announcement of a cash dividend as the beginning of the process and crediting a client's account with recovered tax as the other; the process of withholding tax is at least 60% manual for a custodian and almost 100% manual for an investor even at the institutional level. The variation in process and procedure also means that there is little or no standardisation in the industry. The combination of the two over the years has led to a black hole of performance only slightly different from the black hole of risk assessment associated with the market collapse of 2008. Standardisation and automation are the pre-requisites for improvement in performance as all investors want to be able to maximise their portfolio value and all custodians want to reduce cost and risk. Behind those pre-requisites however lies the need for the will to make it happen and the ability to think of new business models to get us all there. The advent of Virtual Straight Through Processing (V-STP) in 2007 pioneered by independent firm GlobeTax in the United States highlighted a trend in automation that brought these two factors together. Prior to 2007, tax authorities, who represent a significant proportion of the manual processing elements, had indicated that they were in favour of automation "in principle" but had critically left it to individual states to define what was meant by "automation". This led to one or two authorities making valiant, though uncoordinated efforts to improve things. In Germany, spreadsheets were defined as "automation" although at first, you could only get paid on an electronic claim filed by spreadsheet after you'd filed the back-up paperwork. In Switzerland bar-codes were put on forms so that the information on a form could easily be read. In the United States, electronic tax information reporting was made mandatory on withholding amounts under section 1441 NRA regulations, initially in 2001 using magnetic tape or floppy disk, to a file format that took over hundred pages to describe, and which had to be accompanied by a paper form to make the submission. As you can see, what constitutes electronic had neither consistency nor efficacy as founding principles.

Frankly, while there remain variations even at the highest level between jurisdictions, automation can only go so far. The work of Alberto Giovannini establishing barriers to efficient operation of markets was a good start, although his remit was, and is, only the European Union States. The establishment of a working operational model founded on a standard relief-at-source process combined with a long form tax reclaim process, is yet to be widely accepted. The foundation of the relief-at-source element of that process is already fundamentally flawed by recommending the US model which, with 800 pages to describe it, has already created massive cost for the industry with little or no benefit for either the IRS or the industry. Recent reports indicate that tax information reporting, which is a new facet of the process connecting deposits to a reporting and reconciliation system saw rejection and failure rates as high as 70%.

INTERESTS PRINCIPLE

This principle asks the question – who has an interest in knowing about the issues and doing something about them. This, again, is not as simple as it sounds at first. The market generally has several levels where interests of different types exist. The nature of those interests can change with time and also where the interested party sits in the investment chain.

Issuers

Issuers are the listed corporate entities in which investors make their investments. Many large corporations have institutional investments in-bound from many different sources some of which are resident in other countries. If an issuer wants to attract investment money, it's in its interests to make some efforts not to disadvantage its future shareholders. Yet until recently, in prospectuses it was common to see legal wording about tax issues that put the entire responsibility for tax on investment income squarely on the investor's shoulders. "Not our problem" is essentially what the Issuers were saying to the market. In 2006, the institutions that brought together institutional investor power – the proxy voting agencies – started to take cognisance of this issue. Proxy voting companies provide their customers with guidelines and policies with respect to voting on matters at annual general meetings. In recent times there has been increased interest in including voting policies related to the actions of the board on withholding tax. Essentially, the feeling is that C-level personnel, particularly the CFO and CEO, if they want to be seen to be encouraging inward investment from what is likely to be cross-border sources, should explicitly include policies that either educate investors as to the tax implications, or better, provide access to optimisation services.

Intermediaries

Intermediaries clearly have a role to play and an interest. For most investors, the effort of finding out, understanding, researching and filing claims is too much. Intermediaries thus fall into three categories: those who advise investors, those who provide safekeeping services – custodians – and those who provide clearing and post settlement – the (international) central securities depositories (I)CSDs. Much of the rest of this book will highlight issues of withholding tax primarily from a custodian's perspective because it is here that the main weight both of responsibility (contractual and fiduciary) and opportunity lie. Any intermediary who provides safekeeping services must assess the degree to which they offer withholding tax processing services. This will be a complex decision because the cost of providing a service is proportional to a number of factors including

- the size of the custodian's client base,
- the residencies of beneficial owners represented in the client base,
- the types of beneficial owner or pooling of assets by investment vehicle represented in the client base,
- the number and type of markets into which investments are made,
- the expertise available to the custodian,
- the availability of external expertise via an agent bank network or upstream global custodian network and
- competitive offerings by other custodians

Of course, these factors must be taken into account with the cost associated with providing a service. This leads to a limitation principle. Custodians essentially cut their cloth according to their perceived need. However custodians also derive, on the surface at least, financial benefit from provision of these services. Most custodians make money by charging custody fees based on the value of assets they manage. Ergo, if they recover extra tax, the value of assets goes up and the fees they charge increases. Unfortunately, while this is a simple principle to understand, most custodians provide their services on a pooled or bundled basis. In other words it's often difficult, if not impossible, to extract either the cost or the revenue associated with the provision of a service.

Advisors

Advisors have a key role to play. In this category I also include trustees and administrators. The latter two have not only a financial interest but also a fiduciary interest. As we will see later, this fiduciary interest creates the potential for a longer term risk. For the banking community this is critical. In 2008, the market crash was, in the most part, the result of banks engaging in activity, the risk of which was not properly understood. When the reality was understood in Q4 of that year, the global financial crisis of the century began. One of the questions that went unasked at the time, surprisingly, was if we didn't anticipate the way in which banks were acting with respect to debt risk, what else do we not know about their activities?

Vendors

Many of the interested parties have different views of what they should be doing, what they can be doing and what they will do on behalf of their clients. For administrators of funds for instance, this may include advising fund managers and trustees of the withholding tax issue at one end and supporting any claims made at the other. In many cases, fiscally transparent funds making claims cannot succeed without providing a list of underlying beneficial owner investors. This is so that the receiving tax authority can be assured that the claim being made at the fund level would essentially be the same as that made by the investors were they to have invested directly, that is, they would in effect be subject to the same entitlement. To that extent non-custodial intermediaries have more need of information tools than of processing tools.

For custodians, the issue is different. They are more likely to be filing the claims and therefore have need of both informational tools and processing tools or access to them.

The net result is that there is a small but important support industry focusing on providing the information and processing tools to a variety of the other interested parties. Generally speaking any fees incurred in the provision of those tools is usually either paid for by the investor directly out of optimised tax or indirectly through custody fees.

Investors

And finally, we get to the most important interested party – the investor. For most private, retail-level investors with a few hundred shares, it's unlikely that there will ever be a realistic way to gain access to their entitlements. On the one hand, they lack the knowledge, skill and experience (and time) to do the job and equally, the amount of time spent on such activity would not equal the likely return. It falls to the institutional investors to have the most interest because once assets are pooled in any way, the value of tax recoverable does make the recovery financially viable.

On the other hand, once assets are pooled, it makes the claim process more complex because one of the key concerns of tax authorities is that the pooling is done for the purpose of avoiding tax as opposed to optimising it. Thus many claims are straightforward when filed for a simple direct beneficial owner, but become subject to greater scrutiny when filed at a pooled level. Much of the un-recovered tax extant today exists because it has been deducted from the income to a pooled asset vehicle and the underlying beneficial owners have no way to either claim their portion directly or force their asset vehicle manager to do so.

With so many interested parties, many of whom have a financial interest in increasing the return of tax refunds to investors, it does therefore seem counter-intuitive that so little is actually achieved.

CHAPTER 2

Context

Having established the broad principles under which withholding tax works, we now move on to consider the context in which these principles operate. There are many aspects to context, which will be discussed in this chapter. These include

- materiality,
- value of assets under management,
- tax reclaim statistics and market share,
- growth in cross-border AUM,
- regulation and peer groups and
- corporate governance – issuers and investors.

All of these issues give flavour to the principles underlying withholding tax.

MATERIALITY

There's a saying that when times are good, no-one pays much attention to withholding tax. When times are bad *everyone* pays attention to withholding tax. The reason from a capitalist perspective is easy to understand, although more difficult to empathise with if you're an investor. In the period 2006–2007 fund performances in the range of 20% to 30% growth were common. In that context, explaining to someone that they could add another

1.5% to that performance by engaging in a really difficult, long-winded, complex process where that return might be a year down the line generally meets with a negative response. However, when fund values are falling or may be wiped out in any 24-hour period, as was the case in late 2008, suddenly that 1.5% to 2.5% can make a significant difference and, as a proportion of fund performance, becomes material.

There's also a case to consider in the larger context when we look at the overall trends in investment and the absolute amounts involved.

Whilst this area is relatively poorly researched from an investor perspective, as we've seen, there are published articles that indicate that as much as $300bn of tax could be over-withheld each year globally. Taking into account the effects of Statutes of Limitations, this figure would give rise to an extant tax value of nearer $1.6tn a year on a rolling basis. Of this, only a fraction is ever reclaimed. It's important to note here that estimates of withheld tax and reclaimed amounts do vary widely depending on the source. What is consistently agreed by all observers of the industry however is that there is a large amount of tax over-withheld each year, that a large dollar value goes un-recovered each year and that Statutes of Limitations compound this value. Here's how this number is arrived at:

Assets under management	$113,069tn
Average proportion held cross-border	37.13%
Cross-Border assets under management	$41.982tn
Average long-term yield	5%
Yield subject to tax	$2.1tn
Average reclaim (statutory rate–treaty rate)	15%
Annual claim value	$314.9bn
Average statute of limitations	5.2 years
Extant recoverable tax	$1.64tn

So, it's self-evident that those receiving cross-border income streams, and the industry in general, have an issue to address, unless of course they are confident that they fall completely inside the recovered element or are eligible and gain relief or exemptions.

For institutional investors, who have substantial assets invested internationally, and who therefore derive significant income streams liable to be subject to withholding, it is critical to know enough about the management of their investments and the economic, regulatory and political environment in which they exist, to make intelligent decisions. In particular the way in

Table 2.1 Comparative market performance

Country	*Dividend*	*Taxes withheld (%)*	***Dividend received (%)***	*Recoverable taxes (%)*	***Dividend received (%)***
Australia	100	30	**70**	15	**85**
Austria	100	25	**75**	10	**85**
Canada	100	25	**75**	10	**85**
Finland	100	28	**72**	13	**85**
France	100	25	**75**	10	**85**
Germany	100	21.1	**78.9**	6.1	**85**
Italy	100	27	**73**	12	**85**
Netherlands	100	25	**75**	10	**85**
New Zealand	100	30	**70**	15	**85**
Spain	100	18	**82**	3	**85**
Sweden	100	30	**70**	15	**85**
Switzerland	100	35	**65**	20	**85**

Source: e-TaxData Online. GlobeTax.

which an investment portfolio is deployed, managed and maximised must include a serious concern with the effects of withholding taxation and appropriate benchmarking of this activity.

While every portfolio is different, a typical valuation of a portfolio of investments across just five countries can show a difference of up to 30% dependent on whether this issue is addressed correctly or not. Most funds these days are invested in between 13 and 25 countries. Table 2.1 shows the effect on a portfolio spread. The effect of understanding this issue can clearly be seen.

These last two years have seen more movement in taxation rates than many others in the last twenty years. The data in the table above was correct at the time of research, but may have changed since then.

Figure 2.1 shows the effect of these new treaties combined with changes to existing treaties. There are two noteworthy aspects to this chart. First, most changes take place in January each year. Second, given a database of tax rates that must contain the changes as they may apply to types of beneficial owner, types of income, year of income (the change may be retrospective), any given single change is likely to affect more than one data point. The combination of these effects on custodians and other intermediaries

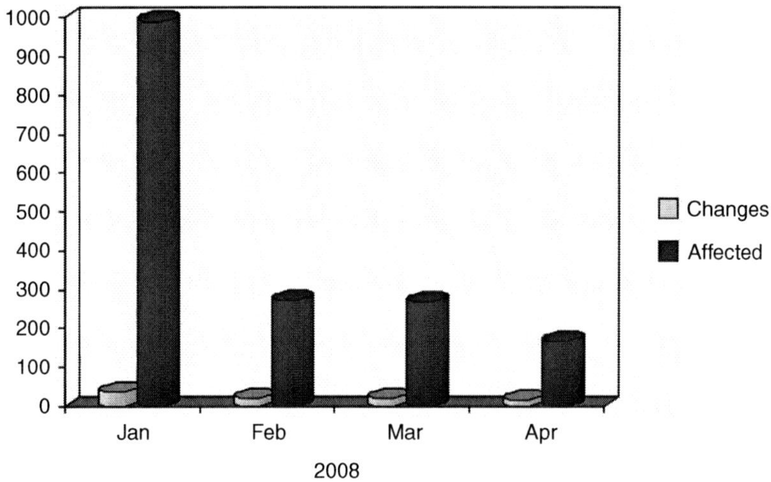

Figure 2.1 Changes to tax treaties and their effects

Source: e-TaxData Online. GlobeTax.

is that resources need to be increased in December and January to assess and implement the changes to internal databases and more importantly assess the effects on clients. A single change by a single country can mean several hundred changes to database points and again several hundred impacts on clients.

Despite this, the effects of taxation in this regard have, for many years been ignored or, at best, treated as a necessary evil involving complex administration, much form filling and long-winded follow-ups with tax authorities. However, more recently, following some notable changes, withholding tax been rising up the investment and, as a result, the management and custodial agenda. These changes fall into three categories commercial, geo-political and technological.

Commercial

Two major commercial factors have been at work to bring withholding tax issues to the fore. They are

- Increasing proportions of portfolios invested across border and
- Increasing pressure on custody margins

Recent years have seen major increases in the degree to which funds are invested cross-border. In 2000 a typical fund would have invested between 15% and 25% of its value across international boundaries. The most recent

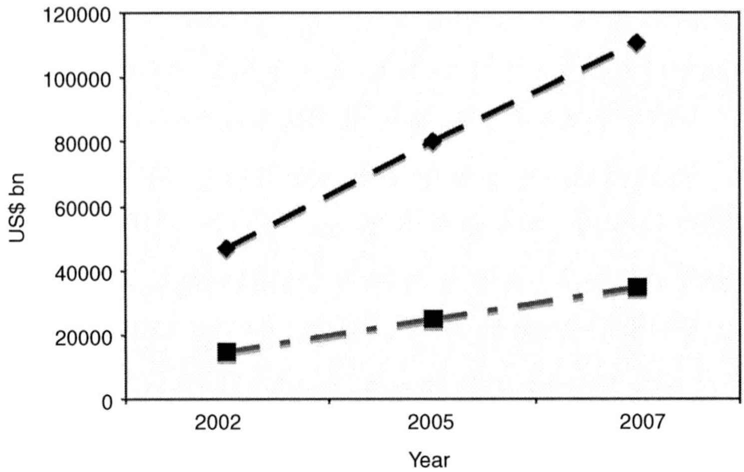

Figure 2.2 Growth in cross-border assets under management

Source: Author.

research shows that this figure is now above 33% average. Figure 2.2 shows the rate of increase in investment across border. The darker line shows the total assets under management, while the lighter line shows the value of cross-border assets. It's key to note that between 2002 and 2007 while the absolute value of assets increased, the proportion held cross border also increased but at a lower rate. Since 2007 and in particular 2008 and 2009, these trends have changed. The value of assets has been hit hard by the global recession, while the proportion held across border has increased as a percentage since many investors are increasing the spread of their portfolio to mitigate and spread risk.

Of course, most of those assets are held by custodians in safekeeping accounts or with (International Central Securities Depository) ICSDs. So, it's equally important to understand not just that the market is growing but where the assets are held. Table 2.2 below shows the top 10 custodians in terms of their cross-border portfolios.

As we can immediately see, data on withholding tax is fragmented even at the custodial level. However, if we assume that the general proportion of cross-border business, for those who report both numbers, is consistent for those who don't then we see that across 54 custodians who reported global assets under management of $113,069 bn, the value of cross-border assets under custody at the beginning of 2009 can be estimated at $41,982 bn or nearly $42 tn – 37.13%.

The reality is however that there are over 25,000 financial firms worldwide managing assets, some of which are cross-border. If we assume that those data available from the top 54 custodians represent 80% of the market, which seem reasonable since they are the largest custodians, then the total

Table 2.2 Break-down of assets under custody by custodian

Rank	*Bank*	*Assets ($bn)*	*$bn across border*
1	BNY Mellon	22,385	8,966
2	JP Morgan	15,614	5,264
3	State Street	15,299	3,507
4	Citi	13,088	N/A
5	HSBC SS	6,097	2,818
6	BNP Paribas	5,595	2,617
7	Northern Trust	4,100	1,912
8	Societe Generale	3,925	2,035
9	UBS AG	3,800	N/A
10	CACEIS IS	3,120	N/A

Source: © 2009 globalcustody.net
No reproduction without consent. Extract from www.globalcustody.net used with permission. The above extract depicts data from globalcustody.net as on 12August 2009. Service providers can submit their latest figures in real-time, so please refer to globalcustody.net for the most up-to-date and comprehensive data.

estimate for assets under management globally would be in the region of $141 tn of which $52.5 tn would be held across border. Under that scenario, using the same assumptions as before of a 5% yield and 15% reclaim, the annual tax recoverable would be in the region of $393.6 bn and the total extant at any one time, around $2.05 tn.

These are very rounded numbers. I have taken into account and balanced the mitigating factors that some pairs of countries in which the assets are held will have no treaty and therefore the claim values will drop. On the other hand, there will be many investor types that are entitled to much more than the average 15% recoverable. Either way, the numbers are truly enormous and the area worthy of close scrutiny.

The majority of the above-listed custodians do have relatively sophisticated processes in place for minimising tax, from relief-at-source services to outsourced or semi-automated tax recovery systems. It is likely therefore that much of it will be reclaimed or have been subject to relief at source. Even so, whilst this book has value for those custodians who are not reclaiming at all, I hope it will still serve as a useful source of ideas for those already fully engaged in the process. As cross-border trade increases year by year, and new markets emerge, the scale of this issue will continue to rise.

Increasing volatility in markets and massive drops in fund performance have also led to increasing risk and focus on previously "marginal" added value issues. Put simply, when the times get tight and the yield from the fund decreases, the proportionate impact of tax becomes a statistically significant factor. This has also led to a more intense focus on portfolio planning based on the relative friendliness of the tax regime in the invested country.

Secondly, increasing pressure on custodial margins has led to a business focus by fund managers and custodians alike, on ways in which to add value for investor clients and thus exploit opportunities for enhancing margin delivery and remain competitive. This pressure has created new services for investors including, for example, contractual tax, where the fund manager/custodian agrees to pay income gross (for a small fee), based on his knowledge of the tax reclaim market and his ability to reliably predict his receivables from those markets. When I first entered the industry contractual tax was very much the exception. In recent months I've come across custodians offering contractual tax in up to fifteen markets as a matter of normal business practice. The complexity and cost of the process itself has also led to a degree of "unbundling" of fees from fund managers and custodians so that they can clarify the added value they are providing over and above normal custody operations and maximise their profit potential.

Geo-political

Increasing levels of inter-governmental liaison, fuelled by concern over abuses of tax law increases and anti-terrorist activities, has led to (i) an increasing acceptance of the need to share information about citizens across international borders and (ii) recognition by tax authorities of the long-term benefits of moves to electronic handling of data.

The market is also not homogenous across the globe. The mature markets of investment, where over 95% of claims are currently filed have historically been the key focus. But today, the emerging markets are becoming more important. Financial power is seen to be moving towards China. The Asia Pacific region generally is more likely to have short and shallow recessions. Its historic trend has been to invest predominantly intra-regionally, but it is starting to see major fund flows inwards. However, the number of treaties, on which almost all tax reclamation depends, is relatively small. There are currently just over 5,000 treaties globally. Table 2.3 shows the number of treaties that Asia Pacific markets have with other jurisdictions. With a total of just 700, the region represents, currently, only 14% of the active global treaties.

Increasing regulatory pressure on compliance and risk management functions together with recent spiralling of global corporate mismanagement

Table 2.3 Treaties of the Asia Pacific Region

Country	*Outbound Treaties*
India	77
Singapore	58
Hong Kong	4
China	88
Australia	42
New Zealand	34
North Korea	8
South Korea	69
Vietnam	37
Taiwan	16
Indonesia	57
Malaysia	67
Thailand	52
Phillipines	35
Japan	56
Total	700

Source: GlobeTax.

scandals, has increased current and historical legal exposure of custodians to investors, for failure to adopt (or have adopted) best practice or to explicitly communicate gaps in service which an investor may reasonably have presumed were being performed. It has even been seen as questionable whether a custodian or fund manager can rely on a Service Level Agreement (SLA) with an institutional investor which specifically excludes or limits responsibility for tax reclaims. The argument is that these exclusions or limitations are usually hidden away in the small print of an SLA. The scale and scope of the effect of withholding tax is so fundamental and potentially large that, in the absence of the investor knowing about the issue, the fund manager or custodian must make the investor more explicitly aware of the implications of his decision simply because the fund manager's or custodian's role so fundamentally revolves around maximising fund value.

Technological

Increasing availability of technology-driven or specialist solutions has meant that previously very high administrative costs have, or can be, reduced significantly.

Industry moves towards Straight Through Processing (STP) and shorter trade cycles (T + 1) have, overall, demonstrated a clear business model for trade settlement and clearance. The industry is now beginning to address "back-office" administrative functions in order to truly deliver STP. Yet even now, the ISO standards for messaging between custodians related to this important area are very fragmented and have yet to be integrated into an effective model. In its research findings, SWIFT consistently reports that corporate actions automation is one of the key topics and perceived benefits of automation, yet in the same surveys it is clear that efforts to deliver it are not just fragmented, they have been lamentably slow to pick up any momentum.

Technology has been applied however not just to the movement of withholding tax information and to the ISO standards which will underpin it. Technology has increasingly been deployed by a variety of interests to improve the efficiencies of most, but not all parts of the process. There are basically four ways in which technology can be deployed in this area either directly or indirectly. They are

- Buy – third party software solutions;
- Outsource – to third parties who have technology solutions and significant operational experience;
- Build – an internal system to automate processes; or
- Bureau – buy solutions to those parts of the process that are either difficult or expensive to handle in-house.

There are some commercial companies offering technology solutions in this area. Custodians will also, for a variety of often internal political or policy reasons, choose to build their own system in-house and many have done so in recent years. Bureau solutions have offered custodians the ability to selectively buy those elements of the process that are either the most expensive to perform internally or the most difficult, leaving the remainder of the process to be integrated internally. Finally, outsourcing allows custodians to "focus on core business" whilst ensuring that someone else, who has integrated their systems, takes on the full role. There are ups and downs to all these technology-based solutions, which I will discuss later, but the fact remains that technology has the capacity to make these tax processes more efficient. The degree to which it has succeeded has been influenced by history and by the various commercial interests involved. Its future capability to address this issue is becoming more clear as the tools available begin to encompass the full breadth of the taxation process rather than elements of it. Figure 2.3 shows a Venn diagram to explain a common occurrence. There are certain elements of the tax process which are more amenable to automation than others. At the same time, financial firms tend to treat their tax operations in different ways. Often one branch or arm of the firm will have automated processes whilst another, operating almost independently, will deal with the issues manually or not at all. On top of that, there may be an internal decision or strategy which provides the solution only to selected accounts, perhaps proprietary versus client accounts or large versus small accounts. The effect of this complexity is that, for any given firm, parts of that same firm, in different places, may have any one or more of the available solutions in place working simultaneously. Whether this is the result of a deliberate and well-thought-out risk management strategy, or more likely the result of historical development will be specific to the firms concerned.

The issue with all technology-based solutions is that of cost, a factor that, internally must be weighed against the return provided through fees (as any

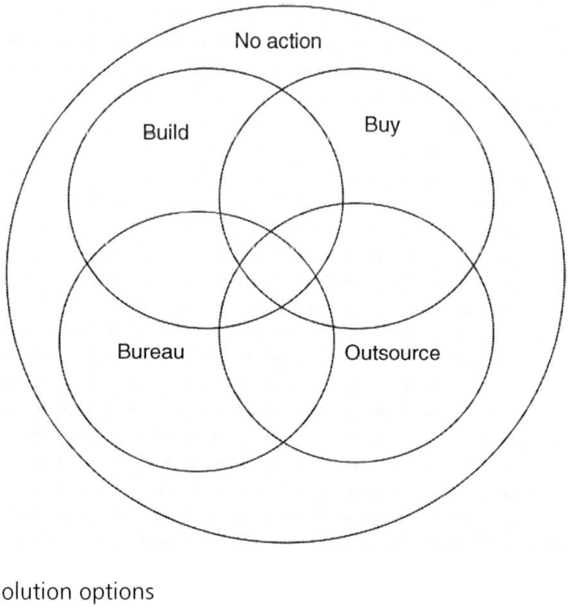

Figure 2.3 Solution options

Source: Author.

reclaim value or minimization of tax is of course the property of the investor).

WHY SHOULD WE CARE?

We should care because it's important, because it is an entitlement. This is not some application for a benefit or, like class actions, an attempt to get part of a legal claim. The sums involved are the rightful property of the investors and anyone or any firm that chooses to manage assets should have a clear and customer-facing view of their attitude to maximising returns for investors.

All these factors, alone and in concert, have contributed to a much more focused attitude by many, but by no means all, investors and custodians to leverage every possible piece of value.

Technically, the cost/benefit for the withholding tax issue has now become firmly established on the benefit side, not least because of the scale of difference that can be achieved in yield when different attitudes to tax are considered. A UK higher rate taxpayer receiving income from a Swiss investment, without any attention to the tax issue, could see a massive drop in net income after tax from his investment (Swiss withholding tax is 35% and the recoverable could be either 20% or even the full 35%.) However, knowledge of the general business principles and appreciation of the importance of the issue are still extremely fragmented at all but the highest levels of custody.

It is clear that there are many investors who are not receiving the benefits of professional attention to this issue. The problem is that many don't even know that they are missing out, or have a problem. Most of the texts available to date are highly technical or are not aimed at the investor or concerned custodian from an operational perspective. They assume a level of knowledge of the tax systems involved that most investors, fund managers and custodians at the business point of contact do not have.

As a result there has been no explanatory text in this area to date which brings the threads of this important issue together so that investors and custodians can consider all the factors in one place.

Institutional investors in particular, often outsource or contract either indirectly or directly with third parties – fund managers, custodians et al., to undertake some or all of the "back-office" or "corporate actions" activities that flow from their original investments (e.g., dividend announcements, bonds, rights issues, proxy voting). So, to a large extent, institutional investors are often unaware of withholding tax, or if they are aware of it, it's only to the extent of knowing basically what it is and that someone else purportedly does it for them. The question is – who? See Figure 2.4.

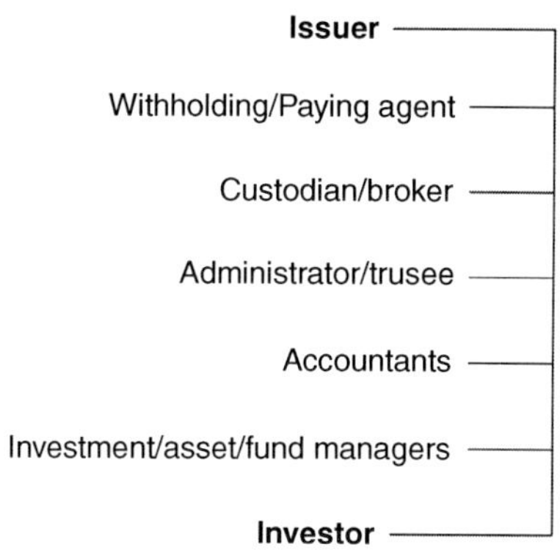

Figure 2.4 The investment chain
Source: Author.

However, these first-line fund managers also often outsource upwards what they consider to be "non-core" elements of their service. The primary investor may not even know that this has been done as the fund manager/ custodian may have contracted to perform the function, but has a "back to back" vanilla contract with a third party. So there comes into existence a chain of assumption about who is taking on the ultimate responsibility, and thus liability for this issue.

Even knowing that your custodian does actually perform tax processing should not be enough to satisfy investors. Many custodians apply a "lower threshold" to their tax operations based on their own internal estimates of cost of administration. This means that any recoverable amount below the threshold will not usually be reclaimed because the cost of doing so is administratively more than the reclaim itself. The more enlightened investor would be aware that some custodians, for these small reclaims, will credit the reclaim value to the investor anyway as a customer relations benefit even though they do not pursue the reclaim itself. Others would be aware that some markets allow aggregation of small reclaims together. These are the types of issues discussed in this book, allowing the investor to ask pertinent questions and gauge more accurately, the efficiencies or otherwise that lie behind the statement "yes we do tax reclaims".

Institutional investors actually often believe that this is a non-issue. It seems obvious that the scale of the benefit of dealing with withholding tax is so great that everyone must know about it and deal with it as fundamental to their service offering. It goes to the issue of what is "management" and what is "custody" and what I can reasonably expect from my fund manager or custodian in this area.

The business reality is that a great deal of over-withheld tax goes un-reclaimed. Ipso facto not all fund managers and custodians are maximising their investor's fund performance. An investor needs to be in a position to assess the performance of his incumbent custodian (and also competitive submissions by custodians) in terms of whether or not a custodian understands and/or deals with taxation.

Custodians in the most general sense, for their part, operate in a thin margin, highly competitive business. They have to make commercial decisions about their product and service offering and they are being increasingly driven by technology and the need to make economies of scale and reduce transactional costs. In this environment, tax, as a labour-intensive, predominantly manual activity, is an area not usually focused on for adding value.

However, in any commercial and marketing environment, its important for those at the business end of custody to understand enough of the back-office detail and of the investor issues, to make intelligent decisions about the value any of their services might bring to an investor. Some custodians, for example, exclude tax reclaims from custody contracts or limit the extent of their services in this area because of the perceived complexity and cost. What should concern the investment community is the extent to which the custodian has explicitly informed the investor of this extent and if so, what the likely loss in funds will be based on the mix of the portfolio.

In 2001 *Global Investor* published an article in which a hypothetical example of two managers in different institutional investment firms was cited to show the effect. Both invest their own money in pension funds as well as professionally manage the funds of their firms. They both retire on the same day and compare notes about the value of their respective personal retirement funds, only to find that one is 30% larger than the other, even though the investment portfolio and spread were both pretty much the same. The article successfully personalised the issue – how would you feel if your pension fund dropped 30%, because you didn't reclaim or minimise withholding tax. Whether it's your own money or your firms, or your client's, that scale of difference deserves serious attention. Of course the example was hypothetical, since the assumption made was that all of the investments of the fund were across border whereas in most cases the proportion of funds held across border is actually nearer to 30%, but the principle is still valid. We also now know the reaction that people have to a 30% drop in fund values from the collapse of 2008.

If that isn't enough, given the global economic slow-down it seems self-evident that, in the absence of significant market growth, maintaining the value of what growth *is* generated becomes increasingly important. At core, this book is about three things:

- understanding what withholding tax is;
- the business and process issues that surround it and the impact it can have; and most importantly

- giving both investors and custodians enough information about the process to define, in their own framework, best practice and performance benchmarks.

This book is not written as a detailed technical description of any individual regime, in terms for instance of the rates applicable to various types of income in different circumstances. It's more concerned with increasing the level of general knowledge of the process in terms that a non-expert will find useful. Those who should be concerned to read this book are those that are in the chain of responsibility for ensuring best practice. Ultimately the investor bears the ultimate responsibility – it's his money after all.

While this book primarily focuses on withholding tax from a custodial and investment perspective, there are a number of different scenarios under which this tax is applied. One important one, discussed later, is withholding tax on cross-border royalties. This is not an insignificant area and most obviously would concern those accountants dealing with sectors such as pharmaceuticals, music, literature, publishing and tobacco. If major investors and custodians, whose specialty is to know and apply best practice in the financial arena, only manage to reclaim a fraction of reclaimable tax, it is more than likely that corporate enterprises and their accountancy firms may need to be more aware of the issue also.

We've spoken so far about some of the contextual issues relating to the overall market in terms of size. However, the most interesting thing about withholding tax is the dichotomy between its simplicity as a concept on the one hand and its complexity in delivery on the other.

Figure 2.5 makes this point eloquently.

In order to understand this diagram, we must first understand that an entitlement endowed by treaty is based on a number of variables. How long it takes to get back an entitlement will also depend on a number of variables as will the process that must be followed. All these variables can act alone or in concert with one or more of the other variables. The result may be a failure or inability to recover at all, a successful recovery or a delayed recovery. These factors are discussed in more depth in Chapter 3. However, to give some flavour, Table 2.4 shows the market average recovery time and statutes for a range of jurisdictions.

Of course for most investors the key variable is the length of time it will take to get money back and many are surprised to learn that it can take week, months and even years, up to ten years in some cases to get claimed funds back. There are however two edges to this sword, the other being the Statute of Limitations. This is the amount of time after the pay-date of the original income, that you have before you essentially make a free donation of your money to a foreign government.

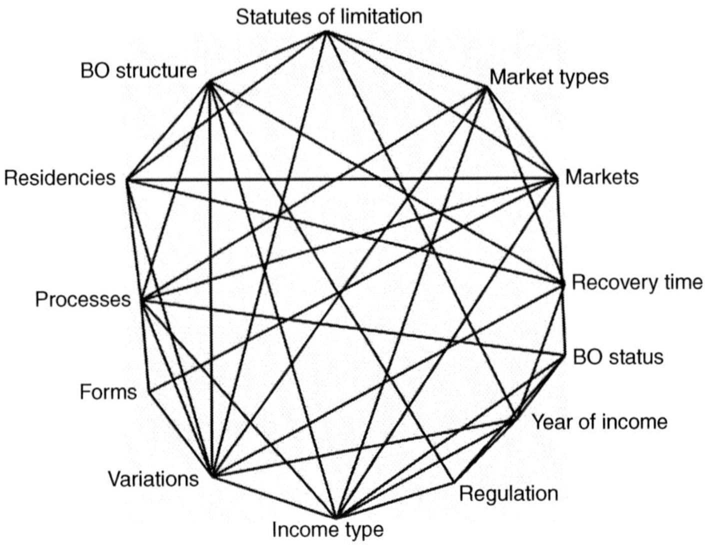

Figure 2.5 The tax cat's cradle

Source: Author.

NON-TREATY-BASED ENTITLEMENTS

In most cases, withholding tax optimisation is based on the existence of a treaty. The principle is that if there is no treaty, there is no claim since there is no entitlement. Well, it depends! In some cases, even where there is no treaty, there can be an entitlement under domestic law. Typically this will be where the jurisdiction concerned has enacted law that essentially promises to treat all investors equally, irrespective of whether they are resident or non resident.

Process and procedure

That cat's cradle diagram hides still more complexity. Each jurisdiction has both a given process or processes and different procedures. As these will be discussed in much more detail in subsequent chapters, its enough for the present to understand that there can be different processes, even within one jurisdiction, that may apply.

Documentation and forms

The basis of all withholding tax lies in documentation and forms. In order to establish an entitlement, a beneficial owner, or their intermediary will have to provide evidence of that entitlement. While there is a core of information that is common across jurisdictions, many tax authorities have different ways of structuring the information.

Table 2.4 Statutes and recovery times

Country of issue	*Deadline for filing claims*	*Indicative times to recovery*
Australia	No Deadline	9 Months
Austria	5 years from end of year div. was paid	6 Months
Belgium	3 years from end of year div. was paid	2 Years
Canada	2 years from end of year div. was Paid	14 Months
Denmark	20 years from pay-date	3 Months
Finland	5 years from pay-date	3 Months
France	2 years from end of year div. was paid	1.25 Years
Germany	4 years from end of year div. was paid	10 Months
Ireland	10 years from pay-date	6 Months
Italy	4 years from pay-date for div. With record date after 7/1/99	5 Years
	Prior div. 1 year from end of year div. was paid	
Luxembourg	2 years from pay-date	6 Months
Mexico	5 years from pay-date	6 Months
Netherlands	3 years from end of year div. was paid	2 Months
New Zealand	8 Years from end of year div. was paid	6 Months
Norway	3 years from pay-date	2 Years
Spain	2 years from pay-date	1.25 Years
Sweden	5 years from pay-date	3 Months
Switzerland	3 years from end of year div. was paid	14 Months
Uniled Klngdom	6 years from end of lax year (ending April 5) that the div. was paid	6 Months

Source: GlobeTax.

Proof of residency establishes that the claimant is resident in a treaty country and that therefore one of the two required elements of entitlement exists. This can be done either using a self-certification of residency (e.g., W-8BEN form for the USA), a formal residency certificate issued by the claimant's local tax authority or it can be a stamp put onto the claim form by the claimant's local tax authority. Different jurisdictions, different requirements. It is also true that this type of documentation will be naturally included in an account set-up package of a custodian or broker under its domestic Know-Your-Customer (KYC) rules. Some authorities will not accept a self-certification of residence unless the KYC rules of the beneficial owner's jurisdiction have been pre-approved by the foreign jurisdiction.

Proof of income will usually be generated by a custodian on behalf of a beneficial owner in the form of a tax voucher or credit advice. SWIFT messages, where the beneficial owner is another financial institution and receives confirmations by this method, are also acceptable.

Forms are the acts of claim. Some of the information above, such as certification, can be included on these forms, but, as always, it depends. The forms vary by jurisdiction and within a jurisdiction, may vary depending on the type of income. Some will allow multiple income items on one form, some are even in English – but some are not. Most have multiple parts or copies which must be distributed correctly. An increasing number of foreign tax authorities also require a tax identification number to be issued for their own jurisdiction before they will accept a claim. For example, a Swiss claim can't be filed unless the beneficial owner has applied for and been granted a Swiss SRD number. This also supports the principle of cross-governmental information sharing. Some tax authorities will require a list of underlying investors to be attached for many pooled investment vehicles. Finally, the forms can vary by year as tax authorities change the fundamental information requirements for their forms.

Corporate governance

This area has received little attention in the past and we deal with this later in this book. However, from a contextual perspective corporate governance has two aspects. The first and the more obvious is the responsibility of issuers to their shareholders. Typically on tax matters, issuers, those corporations making corporate distributions of dividends or coupon payments of interest, have maintained a discreet distance from their shareholders. Their usual stance is that a shareholder's tax affairs are just that – the shareholder's affair. However, it is becoming more obvious that issuers have not just a moral obligation but a rapidly increasing commercial interest in trying to leverage the funds of investors. In the same way that governments have established treaties to encourage inward investment rather than just tell foreign investors that the tax is their problem, issuers also have the opportunity if not the commercial requirement to create a better inward investment profile for their business. Not only do they now have to compete with other issuers in the same industry sector or market for investor's funds, but also they can no longer rely on the banks for loan funding which has, historically, been the counterpoint of their fiscal planning. It's likely therefore that issuers will be launching more aggressive investor relations programs in the future and that these will include some provision of either education or facilitation for shareholders.

The second area of corporate governance is not so obvious and relates to those financial institutions that are also listed businesses. It applies also to those which are private, but the latter is more difficult to regulate on this topic. The issue is similar to the Sarbanes–Oxley scenario where the market has an expectation that anything about the firm's business that could affect the share price should be made known to the market under the principle of full disclosure, which prevents, to a certain extent, insider trading and fraud. While this may not have made many waves in the past, tightening of finances at many funds is making institutional investors much more aware of the tax problem. There is also an issue of banks not informing their customers in an appropriate way, of the degree to which their operations support their client. This is called proportionality and is based on both the legal and commercial presumption that the role accepted by a custodian has, at its core, the idea of having the interests of the client as paramount. If I have a tax entitlement to $150 and I find that my custodian knew about it but failed to make a claim, I might be disappointed but not upset. If I have an entitlement to $500,000 and I find that no claim was filed, even though my custodian knew that such an entitlement existed, now I'm upset, especially if someone shows me some small print that gives the bank a disclaimer. If it's not a legal issue, it's certainly a commercial one. I expect my financial advisor to keep an eye on such issues and at least keep me informed. That information should at least be in proportion to the effect on my portfolio value. This occurs also at the fund level. I've seen many fund managers dismiss an entitlement without considering that they may have an obligation to inform their investors, based on the size of the entitlement and whether the entitlement is at the fund level or at the investor level. Both these issues are likely to come to the fore in the form of regulation in the not too distant future, requiring a fuller disclosure of "material failure". We are already seeing this from the United States both in terms of Sarbanes–Oxley and the current proposed changes to the US Non-Resident Alien Regulations (NRA) Section 1441 withholding tax regulations.

So, now after understanding the guiding principles of withholding tax, hopefully its contextualisation has given the reader a good enough understanding of the complexity involved to see that while this is an extremely valuable and important subject, the industry and investors are very far away from addressing it sufficiently well and that a deeper understanding will hopefully give people enough ideas to make changes that can transform that 7% recovery figure to something more like 93%.

CHAPTER 3

Primary Factors

In this chapter, having established the basic principles and context of the issue, we come across the first "it depends" scenario that pervades the industry. How do various factors impact on any given decision or entitlement?

Some of those factors affect whether a claim is ever made, especially if the factor concerned makes the process so complex that the cost of obtaining the entitlement is more than the value of the entitlement. Others affect the efficiency of a claims process.

To set the scene, Figure 3.1 shows a typical withholding tax process as used by most custodians. Since we'll be thinking about automation later in the book, I've shaded those activities that are essentially manual in grey, and marked those processes that are manual as dotted lines.

DOCUMENTATION

The single biggest factor that affects entitlement to a favourable rate of tax is documentation. Documentation sits at the heart of the process, irrespective of whether it's relief at source, quick refund or long form. Documentation has three segments to it which all investors need to be aware of and all Financial Institutions (FIs) need to follow. Within each area, documentation is necessary to allow other parts of the process to take place efficiently.

Relationship

This form of documentation establishes the relationship between investor and financial firm. Most often it will set the price for any service offered as well as, in some cases, the service benchmarks. Even if the price is "bundled" into a single fee for the whole of custody, there will be an element that

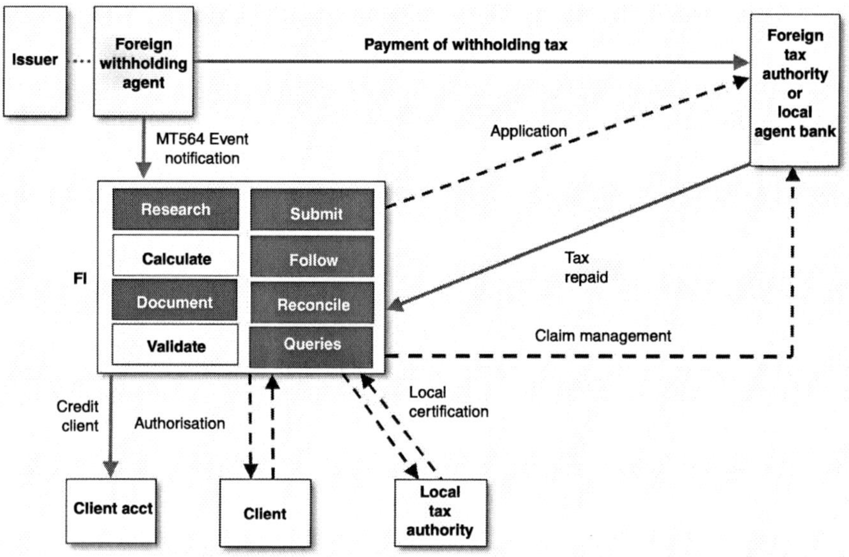

Figure 3.1 Typical withholding tax process
Source: Author.

is attributable to withholding tax processing. More of that later. For investors, the primary document is a service level agreement (SLA) which sets out what is promised and should be delivered. Yet, in many cases, the custodian will have no way to know what proportion of their custody fees is actually attributable to the withholding tax function – which leads to bad decisions on scale and scope of services. Also, the investor will have little or no way to hold the custodian or broker to account for any failure in service levels, since most custody agreements do not have any detail in this area.

Treaty

Many people forget about the treaties as documents, even though they are fundamental to the process in most, but not all cases (it depends!). The treaty is the source of the entitlement for many investors. There are, at present 234 tax jurisdictions in the world. If each had a treaty with each other jurisdiction, there would be a potential 54,522 treaties. There are actually around 5,000 to 6,000 treaties in existence. As many of the forms needed to file claims require the investor to assert the particular treaty Article under which they are claiming, there is a need to have up-to-date and historical research on treaties, when they came into force and what their terms are.

Many custodians have this information in soft assets – people – employed because they have knowledge and experience of market practice. This is a risk as people leave or, in current time, are made redundant, and the knowledge base under which a particular institution is able to maintain its expertise can be degraded severely.

It's true that many treaties now follow a common model – the OECD model a copy of which is provided in Appendix 2 to this book. That said, several treaties have variances based on local law and intent. One such is the US treaty which with all countries includes a limitation of benefits clause or LOB. So, it's important not just to have copies of all the relevant treaties on hand, or to have people who know what's in them. It's important to have the treaty documents available in an automated way (searchable) to allow the right decisions and updates to be made.

Status

We now move into the core of documentation. In order to establish an entitlement, there are two basics that a foreign tax authority is interested in. Can the claimant prove that they are who they say they are and can they prove residency (see below)?

As far as status is concerned, there are a number of ways in which this can be done. The documentation that a foreign tax authority will accept as evidence of a beneficial owner's status varies by market. In many, but not all, cases beneficial owners or their appointed agents can obtain a certificate of residency from their own local tax authority. Equally, many, but not all foreign tax authorities will accept these certificates as evidence of the beneficial owner's status as a tax payer in their local market. This is generally a key factor for a tax authority receiving a claim. However, usually a foreign tax authority will require additional documentation where the beneficial owner is not an individual. For a corporate this may be the company's certificate of incorporation. For other types of non-individual entity, the documentation requirement helps the receiving tax authority understand and decide whether the claimant is, for their purpose, the beneficial owner. This introduces the concept of fiscal transparency and opacity.

Fiscal transparency can be exemplified in the case of a US resident hedge fund. For the most part, US resident hedge funds, unlike most of their non-US counterparts, are deemed to be fiscally transparent. The documentation of the hedge fund at the top of this structure makes it immediately obvious to foreign tax authorities that the fund is, to all intents and purposes, a partnership. From an operational perspective this means that one of three possible claim models might be appropriate, depending on the market concerned. The tax authority might choose to allow claims at the fund level, even though the fund is actually a partnership. The tax authority might allow the claim at the fund level, but require additional information about the investors in the fund, typically their names and confirmation that they are all, or predominantly of the same residency as that of the fund itself. Finally the tax authority may decide that the fund itself is not the beneficial owner at all and require that any claims made are filed at the underlying partner level.

This same principle applies to many of the more exotic investment vehicles. Any form of collective investment vehicle is currently subject to additional scrutiny so as to avoid "treaty shopping". As new types of vehicle emerge, the tax authorities have to make judgements on a case-by-case and market-by-market basis as to the real nature of these vehicles, their purpose and ultimately a decision on who the real beneficial owner is.

For the most part of course, many of these documents will have been obtained when the account was opened. That in itself can cause compliance issues. In current times the degree of compliance required in documentation is set out in KYC rules which most markets now have. The problem is that these rules are changed and the documentation requirements amended from time to time as, usually, stricter controls are identified as being necessary. So, you may have an account opened some time ago using KYC rules valid at the time, but which may now be out of date and inadequate to the task of evidencing status to a foreign tax authority. However, it gets more complex still when we consider the changes currently being discussed at trading block level. The US 1441 NRA regulations are based on documentation which includes not just KYC level documents but also assumes additional documentation designed by the tax authority themselves. In the case of the United States this is the W-8 or W-9 series of documents which are essentially self-certifications of residency, status and claim of entitlements. If the Qualified Intermediary (QI) regime is extended, it's likely that there will need to be some discussion about the degree to which self-certifications are acceptable, since, by definition, the new tax rules are aimed at finding those investors who are engaged in treaty shopping. It's not entirely unreasonable to expect an investor engaged in treaty shopping, essentially tax evasion, to file a self-certification which supports that activity. While the US regulations are clear that a custodian should use both the W-8/W-9 documentation *and* KYC documentation, this adds yet more burdens to the document management requirements.

Residency

As noted above, residency can often be determined by the use of a certificate of residency, however, this is not, as one might have presumed, the ultimate panacea for this issue. In some markets the certificate will not be accepted and only the original tax reclaim form, stamped by the beneficial owner's local tax office will suffice. For custodians this can cause a major problem. Of all the potential elements in the processing chain, the weakest is the link between the custodian and the beneficial owner. Part of this is due to the low level of awareness at the beneficial owner level of the importance of the documentation requested, the impact it can have on their portfolio value and finally the impact that any delay can have on their custodian's operations. Suffice it to say that any one client being a bit tardy in getting his tax forms stamped by the local tax authority would be annoying but not of major concern. When you're running a department processing 20,000 claims in fifteen markets for several thousand beneficial owners resident in several markets, this issue can create major systemic problems. New systems for tracking and monitoring claims at different stages are required which for the most part are dealt with using spreadsheets.

Authority

I touched indirectly above on the issue of who has the responsibility to make certain process elements happen. Clearly, for a custodian or broker or third party provider to do an efficient job, they need to be in control of as many aspects of the process as possible, even the manual ones. To that extent, many custodians require their clients to sign powers of attorney granting the custodian legal rights to act as the agent of the beneficial owner. These powers of attorney can be used at several points in the tax reclamation process. Sometimes they can be used to obtain certificates of residency and sometimes they can be used to file claims to foreign tax authorities. The trick is to know which markets allow delegated authorities to be used. But that's not the end of the story as far as creating an efficient process is concerned. I have mentioned on several occasions that one of the biggest issues blocking an automated process is the lack of standardisation. The issue of whether any given market accepts delegated authority is only one half of the problem. The other half is whether the beneficial owner is prepared to give that delegated authority. In my travels, I have found that the percentage of clients providing delegated authority to their custodians varies from 40% to 60% but is rarely above 70%. Again, this creates a problem when constructing or managing a tax reclaim function. The custodian now has to manage a matrix as shown below.

Power of attorney (POA) from client	*Market accepts POAs*
Yes	No
Yes	Yes
No	Yes
No	No

To make matters worse of course, this matrix can change over time giving the custodian a major headache for tracking systems. This also affects the time to recovery since if the market does not accept delegated authority *or* if the client refuses to provide one, the time needed to process the claim can increase significantly.

It's also important to know that each tax authority has the ability to decide whether the wording of any particular delegated authority is, in its opinion, sufficient to allow the agent to act on behalf of the beneficial owner in a claim. So, it's important to have verified and to maintain knowledge of what wording is acceptable to each tax authority.

There is also little consistency across types of beneficial owner. A greater proportion of individuals are likely to agree to such delegated powers however, the more complex corporate types of beneficial owner are often more sensitive about such delegation of powers and some even have constitutions that forbid such delegation. Custodians are therefore faced with a very difficult and complex task of document management.

Validity

Finally, if the above is not enough to exemplify the difficulties involved in documentation, many of the documents required have definite periods of validity. This of course is a core part of the custody process and so most custodians have established processes to monitor and re-validate account documentation.

STATUTES OF LIMITATION

Another key factor, unfortunately as we'll see, is the "time bar" or statute of limitations. In relief-at-source processes, the statute of limitations is essentially the pay-date. For all other entitlement types, each market has its own time-period during which a claim can be filed. These vary from months to many years and in once case, currently, a market with no statute of limitations.

The effect of a statute of limitations is that, for any given payment made net of statutory rate tax, the jurisdiction concerned will allow a certain period of time during which any claim can still be filed and paid (if valid). This may sound simple, but there are several issues surrounding this principle.

Of course the most obvious is that the scale of managing the issue, for a custodian or broker is directly proportionate to the number of markets in which they file claims.

Some markets have more than one statute of limitations, usually varying by claimant type.

By far the largest issue surrounding statutes of limitation of course is what happens when the statute is approached or breached. The latter is simple, once the statute has been passed, the claim will probably not be honoured by the receiving tax authority. In Chapter 12 I identify the benchmark: Statute Risk. This benchmark exists because, in manually driven processes used by most custodians, there is a risk that the identification and preparation process may take up a significant proportion of the statute period. As the statute is approached, the risk increases that a claim even if filed, may not get there in time to be allowed by the receiving authority. This leads to the practice of "protective claims", frowned upon when abused.

What's more important, but less obvious is the implication of the statute of limitations on investors where custodians are operating in a manual environment. A manual environment is inherently inflexible. Changes in trading volumes or in the coverage of investment markets are difficult to respond to quickly. The natural inclination of operations and HR staff is to staff minimally most of the year and staff up for critical periods, typically the dividend seasons. The problem with that approach is that you have to have greater monitoring in place on relatively untrained staff which results in a build-up of claims. In other words, for any significant custodian, the number of possible claims builds up far faster than their resource is able to manage. The net result is that most custodians operate in a backlog. Some of those backlogs are extremely large. Departments often end up in a major scramble at year end trying to get claims filed that are about to go out of statute that is, and this is important to understand, claims that could have been filed many, many months ago but weren't. This is brinkmanship of a scary kind when you consider that it's client money at stake. But that's not all. There is another consequence of approaching but not breaching the statute of limitations. Tax authorities are also very manual, but they know that banks do have more technologically advanced resources. When it comes to paying money out again, their approach can easily be one of "well if they took 2 years before they filed their client's claim, they can't be that worried about it" which has the effect of putting your client's claim to the bottom of the pile while they service the people who were on top of their game.

To make matters worse, there are also three types of statute of limitation. The effect of this is that custodians must not only look to the date-based validity of their documentation of client's residency and status, but also to the dates on which they were the recipients of taxed income. It's a generally accepted if unwritten rule that if a client gets to within 90 days of a statute, the chance of preparing and filing all the documentation, with relevant approvals, successfully, is almost nil. The different statute types are:

- Pay-date-based – a given number of years calculated from the actual date on which payment was made to the beneficial owner;

- Tax year-based – a given number of years calculated from the end of the tax year in which the income was received (e.g., 5 April); and

- Calendar year-based – a given number of years calculated from the end of the calendar year in which the income was received (i.e., 31 December).

Year of income

Following on from statutes of limitation both literally and figuratively is the issue of the year in which the income is received. Investors rarely look backwards, but they do change their advisors and agents from time to time (more frequently recently of course). The degree to which any given investor was having their income analysed and optimised for tax purposes can mean that at any given time, there are entitlements in existence that are not current but historic that is, the income was received at some point in the past but either no claim was identified or no claim was filed. If the statute of limitations has not run out, that entitlement is still technically valid. Of course, operationally, there is a greater risk that if any given custodian did not spot or file a reclaim historically, that it will not spot it in current trading. So the issue of which year the income was received, in this context usually, only comes about either when an investor finds out from some other source that there is a potential entitlement or when they change custodian, or third party agent, to one who spots the "miss".

Of course the other impact directly on custodians is that while they may lose customer at one end of the pipe, they will usually be gaining them at the other. So, the so-called legacy claims are an issue for everyone. The operational difficulty is not just identifying if your client has entitlements from income received in previous years, it's also in determining what the relevant statutory and treaty rates were at the time they received the income and what other rules of the time may apply to any claim lodged after that year. Tax authorities are, and do, change their procedures on almost an annual basis and such changes rarely apply retroactively. So a claim for a legacy entitlement will generally have to be filed under the rules that applied at the time the income was received. This of course puts intermediaries under an enormous burden of research and is also why the cost of such research is so high.

Types of income

Type of income received is also a factor because the processes and calculations are different. In the world of equities, straightforward dividend payments on ORD shares represent around 90% of the withholding tax market. Although it's expected that bond income as a percentage of the whole will increase in the coming years as the amount of government debt (gilts) in the form of bonds, issued to offset the global economic downturn, increases.

Generally ORDs are treated by either applying for relief at source, quick refund or long form claim, but the actors concerned are primarily the tax authorities or agent banks (e.g., France) where claims are filed directly to the market. Following some of the concerns of tax authorities about trading strategies, it is an increasing requirement, as with bonds, that claimants must show that they owned the ORDs for a set length of time before receiving the dividend. This is to try to counteract the activity known as dividend washing.

Derivative products, particularly Depositary Receipts or DRs are treated differently. There are many kinds of DR, but they generally represent a number of underlying securities, often ORDs. The difference is that foreign tax authorities often don't recognise the DR as a security on which a claim can exist, only the underlying security. So the market process for DRs differs in that any claim from the market must be made to the bank that issued the DR in the first place, as they hold the underlying securities. For American Depositary Receipts, these are JPMorgan Chase, Bank of New York Mellon, Deutsche Bank and Citi.

Bond, or fixed, income is treated differently with many more complex calculations being necessary both because the security is a more complex instrument and also because there has always been concern over the use of tax arbitrage – the trading of securities on the basis of tax advantages as the basis for profit.

Forms

If the foregoing is not enough to indicate to investors that this is a complex area, or to custodians that the process is fundamentally more risky that one might at first think; the issue of forms takes us to an entirely new level. So far, we have talked about factors that affect whether a claim can be filed and if so when. Forms addresses the issue of how claims get made. The forms are the primary communication that establishes a claim of entitlement between one party and the tax authority concerned. For custodians the problem is that each jurisdiction has its own forms and within each jurisdiction those forms can change dependent on time as well as the type of income. Custodians need to make sure that they file the correct forms for the correct year of income and for the correct type. Notwithstanding all this, some of the forms may not be in English especially if the two jurisdictions concerned do not have English as a primary language.

The forms used also differ in the information that is required. All have a common core of information of course, albeit it will be in different places and different formats for different forms. That will be the position in the security, amount paid and amount claimed. Each jurisdiction however has other information that is requested and this varies by market making it virtually impossible to create a standardised model.

Adding to complexity, custodians need to be aware that some jurisdictions allow multiple claim items to be included on one form. Some allow a separate "schedule" of claims to be appended to a form up to a given limit. Others do not allow aggregation of claims per beneficial owner at all.

It's also well known that tax authorities are very particular about the accuracy of forms. Anecdotally, some tax authorities will reject claims for even minor typographical errors or missing information.

As you can imagine, for custodians this is going to be difficult enough to manage with their resources, even when scaled up to take account of a large number of markets. For investors themselves, this issue is pretty much impenetrable.

Recovery time

I've spoken a lot about identifying claims and filing them. Getting the money back is of course what it's all about. Tax claims are not like claims under securities class actions suits. In the latter, a claim for damages is being made and the amount of any award is not certain, nor is the proportion of the distribution attributable to any given claimant. In the case of a tax claim, there is an entitlement created by the treaty between a pair of jurisdictions. So there is certainty, as long as the claim is identified correctly, filed within the statute of limitations and there were no other factors that might cause the tax authority to believe that the claim was false, duplicate, protective or otherwise should not be paid.

That leads us, and of course all investors, to ask the obvious question: How long will it take to get my money back? The answer always surprises people, that claims payments will take different amounts of time to get paid, even within one jurisdiction. In other words – it depends.

Some of these delays are caused by the fact that most tax authorities are much more manually oriented than the custodians. So they are dealing with paper from a large number of sources, completed to different quality levels (many are handwritten). They are not generally, as many people think, trying to hold the money, they are generally genuinely trying to meet their treaty obligations since the benefit of meeting those obligations is to encourage inward investment. That's a much bigger prize than payment of any one claim.

It's also important to make sure that we understand what we mean by recovery time. As I mentioned earlier, and is explained in more depth in Chapter 12, most of the figures quoted for recovery time start the process from the point at which the claim is filed to the tax authorities. Relief-at-source claims of course have a zero recovery time since the correct provision of documentation results in payment of income at the correct rate on pay-date. For long form claims the real start of the process starts when the income is paid net of statutory rate tax – the pay-date. If one wanted to be even more accurate, for a custodian who has good documentation systems in place, the point at which they know that a claim will exist is on the record date, usually a few days before the actual pay-date. The reason that recovery times are not cited from this earlier base is because it would highlight the differences between custodian's performance. Since custodians have very different approaches to an equally manual process and different allocations of resource and money, each custodian can take very different amounts of time to get from knowing that a claim exists for one of their clients, to actually filing the claim to the tax authorities. I have seen management reports of major custodians that show backlogs of over three years. In other words, they still have claims that were identified internally over three years ago, that have not yet been filed to the market. So, if the market average were 6 months, while the tax authority might take 6 months to repatriate tax, the reality is that it has taken 3 years and 6 months for that process to take place. This is one of the hidden inefficiencies in tax reclamation that investors are rarely told about.

TAX INFORMATION REPORTING AND AUDIT OVERSIGHT

The United States as an investment market has created a new paradigm since 2001 when Section 1441 of US NRA regulations came into force. Prior to that year, the relief-at-source processes, with the exception of Depository Trust Company's (DTC's) Elective Dividend Service (EDS) system, and long form reclaim processes were all relatively stand-alone. In other words, the activities of a custodian or other intermediary on behalf of their customers did not have any reporting requirements associated with the activity in the preceding year. Nor were there any oversight constraints, again with the exception of DTC Participant banks, imposed by tax authorities on financial institutions, other than on a case-by-case basis.

The 1441 NRA regulations changed all that. The basic QI contract between an institution and the US Internal Revenue Service (IRS) laid out certain benefits, in return for which the institution had to submit to certain new oversights. The two primary ones being the requirement for aggregated tax reporting at the FI level, plus an oversight requirement defined in terms of two audits of compliance undertaken during the 6-year term of the QI contract.

Two issues flow from this new paradigm. First, the net effect after 7 years of this single-market regime, is that the IRS is proposing to further enhance the constraints of both reporting and oversight, as we'll see later on. Second is that the European Union (EU), in the guise of Mr Giovannini, as well as other groups such as FISCO and G30 have adopted the principle of the 1441 NRA regulations (i.e., documentation-backed relief at source) as the model for addressing Giovannini's Barrier 11 – withholding tax across the whole of the EU. So, where before, we could restrict ourselves to operational factors that affect our industry, we now have also to consider broader regulatory factors that will have an enormous impact on custody costs.

The implied costs of tax information reporting and audit oversight cannot be underestimated. The IRS alone expects fines on non-US financial institutions to rise to over $300 million in the next few years for non-compliance. Already there has sprung up a new industry sector aimed at helping firms deal with these additional burdens because it's clear from the results of the past 7 years of the US regulations, that "foreign" (in this case non-US) banks have and continue to experience major problems in compliance that not only impact themselves as banks but also their customers.

The essence of the two factors is described below, although there is a longer explanation of the detail and implications in Chapter 5 as well as reference to the same issue in Part V "the future of withholding tax". The reader may infer from this the level of importance that should be attached to these factors when thinking about how to structure withholding tax services and/or solutions for the next decade.

Tax information reporting is a consequence of a tax authority delegating the job of documenting and assessing a client's entitlement to a favourable rate of tax in a relief-at-source environment. Essentially, in many regimes, such documentation must flow up or include the tax authority themselves in some way, before any investor can access a relief-at-source process. In the qualified intermediary system, the role of documentation is entirely adopted by the QI, however, the tax authority as a result requires the QI to provide some end-of-year reporting that enables the tax authority to reconcile the amounts withheld under the system, to the amounts of tax actually deposited. In the case of the United States as an investment market, it is primarily a regulatory requirement to report all US persons using forms 1099 which are a series classified by income type, for example,1099-DIV reports dividends paid to a US person whereas a 1099-INT reports interest. For non-US persons who are customers of a QI, reporting is "pooled" and within the 1042 series of forms, for example,. 1042-S, 1042-T and 1042 each having a different function, with the 1042-S being created based on different variables for example, withholding-rate pool, income type, and so on. It quickly becomes easy for a QI to exceed 250 of these forms, at which point the operational imperative is for the QI to file such forms electronically, which is a whole different process subject to its own compliance and penalties. Reporting is also complicated by the way in which the tax authority manages such reporting. In the case of 1099 reporting for example, forms cannot be downloaded from the internet (www.irs.gov) but must be requested directly, whereas the forms 1042 series can be downloaded.

The reason for describing these issues, which are only a very small part of the picture, is that tax information reporting as an activity, is new to most financial institutions in the way that the IRS, and presumably many other tax authorities in future, envisage. What's happening in the industry at the moment, which is very frustrating, is not that institutions are not responding to the changes, but that the response is neither integrated nor consistent. In the face of knowledge that tax information reporting will almost certainly extend beyond the US QI regime, there is no real way that institutions can develop new systems to cope with the generality of tax information reporting (TIR); they must perforce react individually to each new set of rules as they come out. Clearly, this is not optimal for the industry, but it seems that until tax authorities work more effectively to design and implement regulation in an integrated way, custodians and therefore investors, will be impacted by the costs associated with fragmented change.

The audit oversight is also an outgrowth of the principle of having the industry be the implementer of relief-at-source procedures. In addition to the processes themselves for documentation, withholding, deposits and reporting, the IRS has oversight capability indirectly through the contractual requirement for QIs to undergo audits. In their latest consultation paper, they propose to increase the controls on QIs by having audits performed not by one auditor, but by two, one of which must be in the United States, each taking joint and several liability for the results of the audit. When taken in conjunction with the procedures and new tax information reporting requirements, it's clear that costs will rise significantly.

If the basic QI type regime is adopted across Europe, to say nothing of the Middle and Far East, Scandinavia and so on, and TIR and multiple audit oversight are also implemented, the average custodian managing investments into say 13 core markets, would be compiling over 26 sets of tax information reporting and undergoing over 52 audits in each 6-year rolling period. With the banks in their current financial position, the cost of complying with these types of regulation will become disproportionate to the benefits to clients. This will manifest itself in higher thresholds, meaning that more investors will lose out on entitlements and in a consolidation of service offerings into a small number of banks that can afford the compliance costs for given markets. The latter will also mean less choice for investors. Together, while they may help tax authorities with an increasing burden of outsourcing administration of withholding tax, it's likely that there will be a "sea-change" in investment activity as the tax advantages of investment wither away.

So, in this chapter we have seen that there are a number of primary factors. The key word here is "primary". There are actually a great many more factors to consider and we'll come across many of these in subsequent chapters. They all however share a common trait – that the application of the factor has many twists and turns. These are not simple rules or "on/off" switches that can be applied scientifically to come to the perfect solution. Each, as we've seen, has elements which complicate and add cost for everyone in the investment chain.

PART 2

Practice

The next four chapters deal with real-life withholding tax processing. They explain in detail, the different types of processing environment – relief at source, long form claims which together account for over 95% of all withholding tax processing, together with chapters showing how these processes sit in context to current practice as well as some optimisation issues that custodians should be aware of if not deploying.

Part of the issue with real-life practice is that it does not always follow theory. It depends on the perspective from which we view the issue. For example, if we described withholding tax from an investor's viewpoint the picture would look like this:

Exemption ⟶ Relief at source ⟶ Quick refund ⟶ Long form claim

The difficulty with this view is that it mixes several different issues in a way that makes the process *look* homogenous. Exemption will be a market specific opportunity available on a case-by-case basis and derived from treaty, custom and practice. Relief at source will available in those markets where the tax authority has established this as an available process. Quick refunds may only be available in markets where the investor's particular custodian supports such a process commercially, which in turn will depend on the payment requirements imposed by tax authorities on their domestic withholding agents (see later). Long form claims again are a tax authority-based processing (as opposed to treaty-based) opportunity.

So, the problem that an investor has, is not just to establish what his or her portfolio's tax position might be, but also to establish what tools are available to mitigate tax and from where. It does not stop there however, and this is usually where the communications problems start. If the investor is not aware of the source of a given market practice, they naturally assume that all elements of available process are theirs to choose from or worse, theirs by right. For example, I meet regularly with investors who claim that, in given markets, they are entitled to a quick refund. They are surprised to hear that “it depends”. It depends on whether, in that market, there is a process and also who is responsible for that process – it’s not always the tax authority – and whether they have a relationship with that institution. To make matters worse, one would naturally expect that if there’s a treaty, there would be a process and vice versa. This is not so. There are some markets where there is a treaty between two jurisdictions, but no process. In these cases there’s no official documented way to get your money back.

So, again we see that most investors do not understand the difference between having an entitlement under treaty and the act of getting that entitlement in the most efficient way possible.

The largest chapter by far in this section is related to relief-at-source processing. This is only partly due to the fact that relief at source is set to become, for a large part of the world, the default primary withholding tax process. It is also a common fallacy, certainly in the investment community, that relief at source is a simpler process than the other available processes. These chapters will hopefully disavow readers of this belief. While in some cases (but by no means all) relief at source may be easier in processing element terms, relief at source suffers from different and particularly stringent timing requirements. To a large extent transparent to investors, this makes a huge difference to custodian’s costs and infrastructures. The latest expected developments in terms of adding tax information reporting to the mix will also see relief at source as not only as complex, but also more complex than other processes.

To that extent, I make no apology for spending a significant portion of this section, if not the book, on this topic. The first chapter in this section, on current context will add detail to this.

CHAPTER 4

Current Status

As was outlined in the preface, most over-withheld tax is never returned to its rightful owners. Different people may have different views on the amounts, but all are in agreement that the numbers are extremely significant. If my research is anything to go by, the amount of un-recovered tax would, if actually recovered, more than cover the losses declared by all the FIs in 2008. It would also increase custody fees by over $4.2 billion a year, making those same FIs more stable as well as more competitive. Fund performance would rise by between 150 and 250 basis points at a conservative estimate. While in 2007, those 250 basis points were often derided by fund managers as "of no consequence" or "not material", today we see those same fund managers scrabbling for every basis point they can find.

In addition, as has hopefully been amply demonstrated, the processes currently in place are 60% manual. Individuals have virtually no chance of understanding the issues let alone getting tax recovered by themselves. That leaves the custody, brokerage and advisory community with a moral, if not fiduciary or contractual obligation to educate investors as well as put programs in place to change that 7% into something substantially higher.

Even without the global financial turmoil of 2008, the world of withholding tax, stagnant for many years, is seeing an enormous amount of change that was set in motion in the last 5 years. To what extent the events of 2008 will exacerbate those changes already in progress or change their direction or create the need for new changes, is unclear, although, if history is anything to go by, we can make some educated guesses. But that's for a different chapter of this book.

Today, we have a massive legacy of unclaimed tax, an increasing number of pairs of jurisdictions entering into double tax agreements or amending existing ones – in order to mitigate global financial issues. We have a range of procedures which have mostly manual elements to them that create cost, risk and liability for intermediary institutions. We have a radically more educated and aware global institutional investor base who are more active on behalf of their underlying investors. Several of these forces lend themselves to a common objective of making the process more efficient and this book seeks to explain and contribute to some of these, not least the issue of automating filing processes so that many of the obstacles can be removed and the markets allowed to work for the benefit of investors.

However, the question before us at this stage of the book, before we try to fix the problem, is to understand where we are now. The next chapters in this book focus on specific types of process – relief at source and long form claims as the most prevalent ways to mitigate tax. However there are other issues we need to consider, for their effects on our current status.

ENTITLEMENTS AND THEIR PLACE IN THE MACRO ECONOMIC CYCLE

At the global level entitlements establish the principle of an entitlement. See Appendix 2. The reason for the entitlement is a recognition at governmental level, that differential and double taxation of investors is not conducive to cross-border trade and in particular for the countries concerned, to inward investment. What started in the US domestic debt markets as "the sub-prime crisis" rapidly spread to the general global debt market, which in turn lowered the confidence of the banks (and confidence in them) and subsequently hit the equity markets, evidenced in increasing market volatility in late 2008. The failure of some FIs also heralded a reduction in lending and borrowing which, on top of already excessive personal debt, triggered the global recession. The recession as it bit deeper, also affected the foreign exchange markets with differentials between the Euro and Sterling being extremely marked. Also a resultant from these factors is an anticipated change of emphasis between yield delivered by equities and those delivered by fixed income instruments. As companies see the global recession bite, fortress mentality is already setting in. This was evidenced first by the banks as they scrambled to borrow from their governments, but failed to pass on these borrowings to customers (as loans) as was the intention. Instead, in the face of unknown levels of risk purchased in a loosely principles-based regulatory environment, they took the money at low interest and put it straight onto their balance sheets to improve their capital adequacy. Similarly, we are already seeing this fortress mentality in the open market. The number of companies declaring or intending to declare dividends is dropping substantially. So even where firms do declare dividends, it's likely that the dividends will be much smaller than before. Asset allocations are also changing in favour of the fixed interest instruments, although, one of the results of the enormous amounts of money being pumped into the system by governments is a massive increase in government debt instruments (gilts). The problem here is that, because of low confidence in governments (to understand, let alone deal with such issues), the risk associated with government debt has risen above that of corporate debt as has the price. One of the key questions for 2009/2010 is whether the headline amounts governments are pledging to solve the economic crisis, are sustainable from debt they are able to acquire in the markets. The reality is that it is a knife edge as to whether anyone is going to invest in government debt when the risk is high and the price is high.

All of this of course is a self-fulfilling prophecy. These are the signs of recessionary forces still gathering pace but equally, it's clear that taxation in absolute amounts of money, as well as a percentage of income, is going to become increasingly important in the performance mix.

PROCEDURES

As has been referred to, each jurisdiction has many rules and procedures which determine how any given entitlement can be realised.

Exemption is clearly the most efficient model, but this option is open really only to a select few types of investor, normally where there is a state-based "interest" in allowing an exemption. Common occurrences of this are pension funds. Another less common occurrence is with types of investor known "sovereign immunes". These are typically governments themselves or funds controlled by governments which can, due to their status, negotiate immunity from tax with specific partners. There is no general model here and each such immunity agreement is negotiated between the parties. It's likely that, outside the parties and their close advisors, no-one even knows that such an arrangement exists. That said, unless the withholding or paying agent has specific knowledge of the arrangement, they would normally have to apply the normal rules. In a practical sense of course, exempt entities are aware that they are exempt, sovereign immunes make their own specific arrangements, but in both cases, the amounts that they are investing are typically in a relatively small number of instruments but in very large amounts. Such entities therefore make sure that they have in place specific arrangements so that, in addition to having the entitlement, they are often not taxed at all on the income. Relief at source Relief at source comes in many flavours ranging from the extremely simple "address rule"-based models through to the extremely complex "qualified intermediary" model. The address rule-based model is generally falling rapidly out of favour since it presents too many opportunities for abuse. In today's paranoiac world of identity and fraud concerns, assessing someone's entitlement to a favourable tax rate-based solely on an address on a utility bill is just not a sustainable model. However, the alternative currently being presented, as will be discussed later, is almost equally unsustainable in terms of being overly prescriptive on documentation and deadlines whilst adding significant new onerous obligations on the custody community for tax information reporting and audit oversight. Relief at source is the presentation up the chain of custody of either documentation or confirmation that any given beneficial owner is evidenced to an entitlement for a favourable rate of taxation and that this evidence or confirmation is provided before the income distribution is made.

Quick refund

Where a domestic withholding agent has deducted tax at a statutory withholding rate, but has an agreement with its tax authority to remit those funds in aggregate at specified times and frequencies, rather than item by item, this leads the path open to a quick refund process. While the tax has not yet been remitted to a tax authority, a claimant can, if the withholding agent offers such a service make what is essentially a market claim that is, a claim to a market participant such as a financial institution, rather than a claim to a tax authority. The times for payment, documentary requirements, the terms and the procedural requirements are then set by the withholding agent on a commercial basis. As such, for example, an investor with accounts at two Italian institutions may be offered quick refunds through one institution but not through the other. So, from that perspective it's difficult to describe quick refunds as a market level procedure.

Long form claims

Long form claims are really the back stop procedure of the industry. They are used in two circumstances. Either they are the only method to get back an entitlement for example, in Switzerland *or* they are a secondary process supporting a primary relief-at-source procedure for example, in France. The number of occasions where this process has to be used in either methodology is extremely large.

Inter-relationship

Of course, at present most tax authorities apply one or more of the preceding models to their relationship between themselves and other jurisdictions. Most people expect that a given tax authority will have a given "position" on procedure with respect to another jurisdiction. Would that it were that simple. Some tax authorities will allow relief at source for some investor types but not for others. On the other hand some tax authorities agree special procedures with certain custodians based on the number of claims the custodian represents. This in turn of course varies by market depending on the number, residency and type of customer the custodian has on its books at any one time. The fact is that each tax authority makes case-by-case judgements based on a number of factors. One of the principles to which interest groups such as FISCO and G30 are working, is the concept of a single homogenous model. While laudable, the fact is that even with a homogenous model, even with some level of automation and standardisation, the proportion of procedures that are "special" and outside the general rules, may be significant either in volume and/or value.

In addition to the above, some tax authorities offer "combination processing". In other words, there may be a relief-at-source process which is expected to be the most prevalent, but if the deadlines for relief at source are not met and statutory rate tax is actually deducted, the jurisdiction concerned has a post-payment long form process that can be used to obtain the entitlement.

STANDARDS, AUTOMATION

Standards are noticeably lacking in the industry. The ISO guardian for the industry, SWIFT, has a few ISO15022 level MT messages that contain some tax qualifiers, but there is no consistent business process within ISO15022 to allow for the development of such a message set. ISO20022 has the capacity to establish such business processes but has not yet addressed this corporate action sub-type. While related distantly, there is also very little automation surrounding withholding tax. There are one or two software companies that have created solutions for some parts of the process, but by no means all. Custodians who historically designed and built their own systems are rapidly diversifying out of this model as the true complexity of an in-house solution becomes clear (quite apart from their need to reduce costs). Technology solutions generally work best when automating complex processes within a set of pre-determined rules. While this sounds like what withholding tax is, it's actually so complex, with so many variables that the even the pre-determined rules have variables. The tax authorities are only recently starting to engage in the concept of automation having been for many years, and most still are, reliant on manual processes based on different forms and data for each market. Without standards, automation has no real chance to succeed. Without automation, the number variables and paper processes can't be eradicated and thus without these two issues "in-play" in the community, there is no real short-term efficiency solution deliverable in-house.

LEGAL INITIATIVES

As I noted, there are some initiatives that are changing the face of withholding tax. Initiatives of course implies some guiding force or thought process with a defined objective. However, most of the initiatives surrounding withholding tax are either accidental, reactive to a given set of circumstances or the result of a narrowly focused group of players in the market. There is recent legal activity, brought by some institutional investors, to try to force a favourable rate of tax even when the treaty entitlement does not allow it. In these circumstances the investor cites domestic law rather than the treaty to establish that; under domestic (European) law, an investor must be treated the same way irrespective of which EU State they are resident in. Under those circumstances, if the domestic law provides an exemption from tax, then a non-resident of one EU State can claim the same exemption when investing in another EU State. This kind of application of law is currently not widespread.

Firstly, there are no truly global initiatives when it comes to withholding tax. It may seem like it sometimes but apart from the United States in 2001 and the EU currently, there are many areas where there is no major change. It's true that historically the EU markets and the United States represented 95% of all the long form claims made on an annual basis, but with economic power moving towards Asia Pacific, these regions are now entering a new phase. Historically their investments have been more oriented to intra-Asian markets where the number of treaties is much smaller. However, there is currently a significant increase in interest in withholding tax.

So, our current status in the industry is that

- most investments *are* subject to over-taxation;
- entitlements to a lower treaty-based rate of tax are commonplace;
- the issue, scale and scope means that the amounts, concerned typically up to 250 basis points, will continue to become proportionately more "material" for investors;
- jurisdictions, complex enough in the past, maintain a variety of possible models for returning entitlements of in-bound investors;
- the inconsistency and unfairness inherent in having so many disparate rules and processes is currently being challenged either through the international courts, to assure homogenous treatment of domestic and non-resident investors, or through the efforts of a small number of

pressure groups, some commercial for example, G30; some governmental for example, FISCO.

- Despite the long history of withholding tax in a commercial environment that spends over $1 trillion a year on automation, there are currently no standards for communicating tax-related issues between counterparties and little or no automation that could leverage such standards.

CHAPTER 5

Relief at Source

In this chapter, we will look at the first of the two broad types of processing used by tax authorities. Remember that the existence of a treaty only generates an entitlement. The way in which that entitlement is delivered to the market, and to the investor, is in the purview of each tax authority. Despite many years of words like "harmonisation", we have yet to see any really effective attempt deliver the goods. As this book is written, there is a more concerted effort being made through the efforts of Alberto Giovannini, G30, OECD and FISCO. However, even these groupings have a hard and long task ahead.

The most common comment I hear in the market is that relief at source or RAS is easier than long form claiming. While it's true, to an extent that the documentary requirements are often more simplistic, these are far outweighed by the processing requirements which have much tighter time deadlines. Appendix 1 shows the relief-at-source procedure required by the ICSDs (Euroclear and Clearstream) in order to obtain relief at source on Spanish Eurobond coupon distributions. I doubt, having read it, that anyone would think that this process is easier than the long form claim process.

So, in this chapter, I describe several types of relief-at-source jurisdiction ranging from the simple to the very advanced. From systems that have been developed commercially (e.g., DTC's EDS system) to those which have been developed at governmental level for example, US 1441 NRA regulations. Also, to show how these latter regulations are beginning to be adopted and adapted by other jurisdictions, I have described both the Japanese and Irish systems for comparison.

PRIMARY DIFFERENCE TO RECLAIM REGIMES

In basic terms RAS is simple. If, when an income event occurs, enough is already known about the beneficial owner to decide that he is eligible for treaty rate benefits, and the market concerned allows relief at source, then, subject to the appropriate procedures, the withholding agent can withhold the correct amount of tax due in the treaty thus removing the need for long form reclaims.

This may sound simple and indeed in theory it is. In practice however, different jurisdictions take a different view on what they require to evidence a relief-at-source claim. Fundamentally the problem is that investors change, many things change and someone who may be eligible on one day, may not be the next. So tax authorities take different approaches to the issue. In the United States part of the system permits the use of a W-8BEN form which is a certificate of tax status. This goes out of validity every 3 years. So overall, while investor's may view RAS regimes as more efficient because they do not involve long and complex reclaim processes, they are not devoid of complexity, particularly if one is dealing with large numbers of investors spread across the main markets. Management of documentation becomes a major issue.

Simple RAS systems generally require simple documentation. These can vary from presumption to documentary. In the presumption scenario the custodian can presume the eligibility for treaty rate based solely on very basic information such as the address of the investor. As the name suggests, a documentary regime will require specific documentation to establish treaty benefits. These may be required in advance, on a regular basis (e.g., Spain) or at the time of each payment. However, they are all simple in their application. Meet the simple rule and obtain the relief.

The problem generally with withholding tax, as with many other areas of financial services, is that the potential revenue streams and benefits are so great, that they attract highly competitive and commercial behaviour. This behaviour is most often aimed at reducing the transactional administration cost of processing. The bodies capable, through size of reach, of putting such systems in place, whilst great, are not all encompassing. The result is that some tax authorities, notably the United States, have devised RAS systems to apply in a certain set of circumstances. Some commercial groups, notably DTC, have also worked to a limited extent with tax authorities to make systems more efficient through the use of advanced technology and process analysis and simplification tools. However, none has yet managed to harmonise all the jurisdictions together with a single methodology which would be the utopian ideal for reducing costs and providing best value to investors.

DEPOSITORY TRUST COMPANY (DTC)

I've mentioned that one of the dimensions of complexity was whether a jurisdiction was reclaim or relief-at-source-oriented or a combination of both or, in fact, whether there was any treaty. The fact is that the issue of custody, once the preserve of custodians, is increasingly being entered, on a selective basis, by other firms who see specific added value opportunities, usually based either on the scale of the operations and customer base, or on the information they hold.

Many of these utility systems were originally designed to enable STP and therefore have at their core, the twin philosophies of automated response and minimisation of transaction costs. Having implemented these systems however, provides anchor points for other custody processes to be automated to varying levels of success.

One of the most successful is the US utility, The Depository Trust Company – DTC, which has over 600 participants. Originally only active in the United States, DTC has increasingly adopted a global approach and now counts participants outside the United States. Its objective when established was to provide a depository management utility for American Depositary Receipts or ADRs. An ADR, from a tax operations perspective, is effectively a security type where a single ADR actually represents a number of underlying ordinary shares. This central utility effectively managed the holding of underlying non-US securities by US beneficial owners through the issuance of a "receipt" security, held by DTC's nominee company, each representing a number of the underlying shares. This meant that DTC established an enormous information base and capability focused on just one element of the custody process.

In recent years, DTC's globalisation strategy has meant not only that its reach has increased, but also that the investment it has made in infrastructure and systems has enabled it to negotiate value added services on behalf of its participant base. These participants would otherwise not have the individual size to leverage major policy changes in tax authorities.

As the reader will have understood by now, in order to be able to benefit from relief at source, firstly, the jurisdiction must accept RAS procedures. Secondly the beneficial owner or his agent, must submit documentary evidence of entitlement. The DTC has negotiated with tax authorities to permit relief at source to be claimed without the need for documentary evidence to be supplied. This does not mean that documentary evidence does not need to exist. It does. DTC's participants have agreed to guarantee both to DTC and to the tax authorities that, for each relevant income event, proper, valid documentation does exist. The agreement between DTC and tax authorities gives the latter the right to audit any event of participant of concern, the ultimate penalty of course for the participant is that he will have his membership of DTC revoked if he has failed to meet the requirements of the agreement. This system is called the Elective Dividend Service or EDS, provided to participants under the DTC brand name TaxRelief^{SM}.

This relief-at-source regime is still, in the background, not without its idiosyncrasies. For example, while EDS used to be in place for Germany, it was actually a process of post payable refund. The EDS process for Switzerland looks like relief at source, but is actually a very quick refund process. This is because there's a delay of about three weeks between the pay-date for the ADR and the pay-date of the underlying shares.

Further, Israel and Japan under EDS are only eligible for debt issues and not, as are all the others, for dividend income. Since this system is very efficient, albeit not ubiquitous in scale or scope, it's worth giving a more detailed description here, not just of what the system is, but also the benefits that the system has for its various stakeholders.

DTC's Tax Relief℠ (TaxRelief) makes it possible for DTC participants to benefit from at-source or accelerated treaty or tax-relief arrangements set up with various countries' tax authorities or issuers. Participants can certify electronically the share quantities of their record date positions at DTC that are entitled to receive a particular distribution exempt from foreign tax, at a reduced rate of withholding or at the non-treaty rate withheld based on beneficial owner eligibility. TaxRelief is designed to accommodate appropriate withholding tax rates and offers an efficient alternative to filing manual, error-prone paper-based reclaim forms.

For example, if a participant has a position of 10,000 shares of an ADR in its DTC account on record date, the participant, based on its records as to who beneficially owns the share making up its position, might certify over its computer terminal that 8,000 of those shares are entitled to the favourable treaty rate at-source. The balance of the 2,000 shares would be paid out at the higher statutory rate. After receiving payment from DTC, the participant would make one payment representing both the dividend and the at-source benefit to each customer, simplifying participant processing, tax reporting and record keeping.

Tax Relief supports all international DTC eligible security types including ADRs, global shares, equities and fixed income securities for which arrangements have been set up with either the respective countries' tax authorities or issuers. It is used to obtain at-source or accelerated treaty relief benefits for US and other treaty partner residents on securities issued in Canada, Estonia, Finland, France, Germany, Indonesia, Ireland, Israel, Japan, Korea, the Netherlands, Norway, Russia, Spain, Sweden, Switzerland and Uruguay.

TaxRelief is accessed by participants via DTC's EDS, a service capability within its proprietary operating system. Elective Dividend Service is a powerful and effective tool that delivers important benefits for foreign taxing authorities, DTC participants, investors, paying agents, depository banks, issuers and DTC. Elective Dividend Service is able to handle a wide range of circumstances and/or requirements of foreign taxing authorities.

Benefits for foreign taxing authorities include the following:

1. Participants are contractually bound by certain terms and conditions with respect to beneficial owner documentation, audits, reimbursements of under-withheld taxes and prohibition from use of the EDS system;

2. Taxing authorities can specifically prescribe the beneficial owner documentation that participants must retain;

3. Taxing authorities can establish the criteria under which participants can be prohibited from the use of the system if a participant fails to cooperate with an audit or is deemed by the foreign taxing authority to have abused the EDS procedure in respect of tax relief on a specific security;

4. DTC enforces the reimbursement from a participant of under-withheld taxes discovered under audit by foreign tax authorities;

5. If a participant refuses to cooperate with an audit, or deliberately or recklessly fails to comply with documentary requirements, DTC has the authority to ban the participant from using the system for other securities issued from the same country of origin in the future. Because participants can derive such substantial benefits for themselves and their customers by using the system, banishment constitutes a severe sanction that effectively deters non-compliance

6. The system can also facilitate withholding tax relief for non-US investors that hold securities with DTC participants and that are eligible for withholding tax relief under an income tax treaty. This can also reduce the number of reclaims processed by a foreign taxing authority.

Benefits for participants and their customers (beneficial owners) are given below:

1. It increases the speed and accuracy of the refund procedure which supersedes the need for paper-based reclaims;

2. It eliminates or lowers transaction costs that otherwise decrease dividends and therefore return on investment;

3. Participants find it easier to continue to obtain at-source relief through the system, a system they now use for other foreign securities, rather than employ new or different procedures for securities issued from another country or foreign issuer;

4. The system's cut-off date for elections (could be as few as 2 days prior to dividend pay-date) gives participants additional time to determine customers' entitlements and to ensure that customer records are in order;

5. Electronic certification over EDS rather than hardcopy reclaim form submissions creates a secure electronic record at DTC that limits errors, and is less susceptible to theft, loss or tampering;

6. For relief at-source payments, participants and their customers receive simultaneous payment of the dividend and associated tax relief in one transaction;

7. For accelerated refunds, participants receive their customers' tax-relief entitlement in a single transaction through DTC's normal cash settlement system;

8. It reduces the steps required and decreases the time-period between withholding and the post-payment refund which if ownership changes frequently, reduces the risk of errors and makes correction and reconciliation easier;

9. It eliminates or reduces the possibility of payment of a single dividend in two payments in two different tax years, which may raise home country tax reporting and payment problems for the beneficial owner and its custodian;

10. It reduces foreign exchange risk;

11. DTC participants prefer the system to most other methods to secure withholding tax relief because it is significantly less expensive to use than a traditional paper-intensive reclaim procedure; and

12. The widespread applicability of this procedure has provided an opportunity for participants to standardise and automate their operating procedures, and thereby reduce costs.

Benefits for paying agents/depository banks are:

1. Paying agents/depository banks receive only one report to paying agent from DTC, rather than potentially hundreds of handwritten reclaim forms from participants which makes the process more efficient for the paying agents/depository banks;

2. It is easier and more efficient for paying agents/depository banks to reconcile allocation amounts; and

3. it eliminates the need for issuers/paying agents/depository banks to issue and mail/deliver potentially hundreds of individual checks to participants.

Benefit for issuers is:

1. Investors may be more inclined to purchase non-US securities if they are able to receive their entire tax-treaty benefits at-source or via an accelerated refund without offsetting costs that decrease yields. This may potentially give non-US corporations access to more working capital, which could increase their productivity and enhance their growth.

In summary, DTC's service provides an efficient modern electronic system to replace an inefficient manual tax reclaim process. Yet it provides tax authorities with the assurances, tools and remedies necessary to insure that qualified investors obtain tax-treaty benefits. Significant benefits are realised by foreign taxing authorities, participants and their customers, paying agents, depository banks, issuers, which is why the system is accepted throughout the financial services industry to secure withholding tax relief on DTC eligible securities.

As I mentioned in the opening to this chapter, systems like this do indeed increase simplicity and drive down costs as well as improve returns for investors. The problem is that in the scramble to gain revenue from the development of these systems, there ends up being more than one party attempting to gain the high ground. DTC certainly seems to have a frontal position, but DTC's system is not applicable to all countries and not to all types of income.

The situation is made even more interesting when, on the one hand an advanced system like DTC's is simplifying the way in which the rules are interpreted, while on the other hand some governments seem to be making equal progress at making the rules ever more complex. One such is the US 1441 NRA Regulations, the so-called QI Regulations, which I will describe next.

US SECTION 1441 NRA REGULATIONS (QI)

The United States is one of, if not the largest market for inward investment. It therefore holds a special place in any withholding tax book because its system of treaties and procedures will have a massive effect on most investors and most financial intermediaries. Equally, as I've mentioned already, the principles of this jurisdiction, in terms of relief at source, are being reviewed by the European Union as the preferred model for a combined regime across the European Union. It is therefore vitally important that readers obtain a clear grasp of this system including its advantages and disadvantages.

Originally issued as Treasury Decision (TD 8734), the full text of these regulations can be found in the US Federal Register 62 FR 53387-53498 dated 14 October 1997.

Generally, a foreign (non-US) person is subject to US tax on their US sourced income. Most types of US source income received by a foreign person are subject to US tax at the rate of 30%. A reduced rate, including exemption, may apply if there is a tax treaty between the foreign person's country of residence and the United States. US persons of course are liable to tax on their US income under the normal rules and rates for domestic income tax.

The term "NRA withholding" used on many occasions in this text actually refers to withholding required under sections 1441, 1442 and 1443 of the United States' Internal Revenue Code. Generally, however, and for the purposes of this book, NRA withholding describes the withholding regime that requires 30% withholding on a payment of US source income. Payments to all foreign persons, including non-resident alien individuals, foreign entities and governments, can be subject to NRA withholding.

For institutional investors, these regulations may have a very significant impact, particularly in the administrative overhead they will have to endure or additional costs from custodians who comply on their behalf. There are also severe and important issues of confidentiality and penalties that investors should know about if they derive income from the United States.

This system has already been cloned to a limited extent in both Ireland and Japan. Many of the world's tax authorities are looking at this step by the Americans very closely as it may, if successful, show the way for the structure of more relief-at-source regime developments in the future. Investors, who would otherwise balk at the complexity of these regulations, should therefore have a broad understanding of the intent of the United States, the impact of the regulations on them in tax terms and more fundamentally the operational impact that compliance has for them and their custodians.

These regulations have already had a major impact on all non-US investors and financial firms who derive income from US investments. They are a kind of relief-at-source system, with a capital RAS! They have imposed:

1. extensive complexity in administration,

2. onerous documentary requirements,

3. stringent reporting and cash deposit deadlines,

4. complex audit procedures, and

5. severe penalties for non compliance

The essential rule of the regulations for payers is as follows:

> Withhold tax at 30% unless you can reliably associate the payment with documentary evidence, valid on the date of payment, that the payee is entitled to a different rate of tax.

This simple rule belies a much more complex process. First we must differentiate between US payers – withholding agents, and non-US payers who will either be qualified or non-qualified intermediaries (QIs or NQIs). We must also place them in context, in a chain of investment distributions which start with the announcement of an impending distribution.

So, in summary, the United States is an Advanced Relief-at-Source System (ARAS). Its history is founded on concerns of the US Congress about problems with the then existing refund system, in particular abuse of treaties by US persons.

The system requires all foreign firms dealing with US source income to be either contractually tied in to the IRS as Qualified Intermediaries or otherwise by default, to be Non-Qualified Intermediaries. The former can protect the confidentiality of their client's identities in return for

1. prompt payment,

2. commitment (under penalty of audit and fine) to obtain and maintain adequate documentation about all their clients down through to the beneficial owner

3. prompt submission of reports 1042 for non-US persons and forms 1099 for all US persons

Prompt payment is made, within the regulations, subsequent notices and importantly in operational terms, according to the amounts calculated to be due to the Treasury and reference to separate documents provided by the Treasury and Martinsburg Computer Center. The larger the aggregate payments due from a QI, the shorter the period between income event and required deposit.

Appropriate documentation is now routinely provided under Know-Your-Customer (KYC) Rules. The IRS receives and, after analysis, approves (or not as the case may be) any particular jurisdiction's KYC Rules. Most often, to avoid liability, QIs routinely require a form W-8BEN, a self-certification form, as their proof of identity. The IRS sees these two methods as complementary and certainly does not see W-8s as a replacement for application of KYC rules.

Prompt submission of reports is assured by a combination of late submission financial penalties, threat of loss of QI status and, on the positive side, a requirement for forms to be submitted electronically if over a certain number. Forms 1042 and 1042-S represent filings on behalf of non-US persons and Form 1099 represents a filing for a US person. Further discussion of each of these areas is provided later on in this chapter.

Those firms not signing up to the US regulations are still required to make payments, however, details of their clients down to beneficial owner level must be given into the hands of a competent QI or withholding agent (by definition a competitor). The penalties for non-compliance for NQIs are more onerous than for QIs.

Figure 5.1 shows an overview of the issues that flow from the four core processes that are encoded into the 1441 regulations. Each of the different elements of the process has different issues associated with it. Some of these issues, while conceptually quite small, can have a major effect. For example, from an operational perspective a QI may choose not to apply an account designation flag (to indicate that they are acting as a QI for a particular account). This has no operational effect. However, if the QI subsequently fails a Phase II audit, any extrapolation of tax and fines due, may end up being calculated on the total number of accounts rather than only those which were designated as QI accounts.

The IRS, following various consultative discussions with withholding agents and prospective QIs, issues a range of update documents each year.

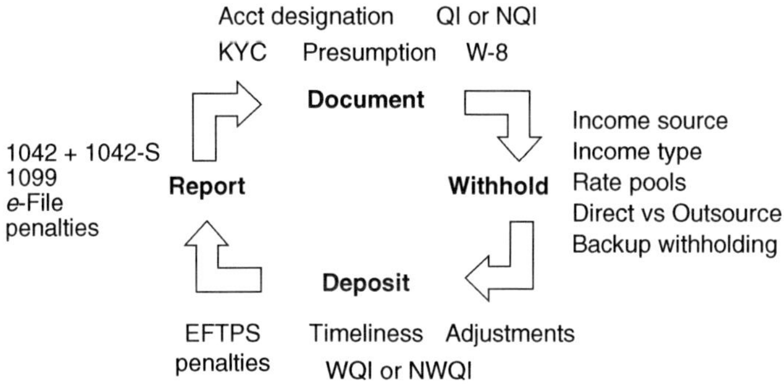

Figure 5.1 Overview of QI processes

Source: Author.

These are either Revenue Procedures (Rev. Proc.), Announcements or Notices. The most important documents for a custodian, and also for an investor to be aware of are:

Rev. Proc. 2000-12 – This revenue procedure contains three important elements:

- Guidance
- Application procedures
- QI agreement

The revenue procedure provides guidance for those eligible entities for entering into a qualified intermediary (QI) withholding agreement with the IRS under Section1.1441-1(e)(5) of the income tax regulations.

Section 3 of the procedure provides the application procedures for becoming a QI. Section 4 of the procedure provides the final QI withholding agreement. The objective of the QI withholding agreement is to simplify withholding and reporting obligations for payments of income (including interest, dividends, royalties and gross proceeds) made to an account holder through one or more foreign intermediaries. This procedure also establishes that the IRS will *not* enter into a QI withholding agreement that provides for the use of documentary evidence obtained under a country's KYC rules if it has not received the know-your-customer practices and procedures for opening accounts and responses to 18 specific questions listed in the revenue procedure.

Publication 515 – This publication, updated each year, includes integrated updates provided previously through interim Notices. The advent of the regulations was a time of great uncertainty. The custodial community was both cynical about the likelihood that the regulations would ever be promulgated or concerned over the costs of implementation. They were also confused by the complexity of the regulations and, given the nature of the industry, many had outstanding questions about how the regulations would affect them, their clients and in particular the specific profile of their investment vehicles and jurisdictions. The IRS themselves became aware of several areas of the regulations which, in the light of new comment from the industry needed urgent clarification or guidance. This was achieved with Notices. One for example provided interim relief to QIs who had been unable to put in place appropriate computer systems technology to meet their obligations. The particular notice required any QI who wanted relief from some of their obligations to set out an official statement of their position and warrant that their application for relief would be followed by compliance in due course. From the IRS perspective, some Notices were designed to reflect the difficulty the IRS perceived in getting financial firms to sign up to the QI status. The ability of the IRS to get significant numbers of financial firms to sign up to these regulations was critical and some concessions were made as incentives to move the process along. This included a provision that allowed firms who signed up before a certain date, to be exempted from the requirement to report to the IRS on a countryby-country basis. The number of QIs who signed up on the eve of the promulgation the regulations was just five. However, the target the IRS had was certainly in the hundreds and low thousands and this, to a large extent, has now been achieved.

In more recent Notices, the IRS has also moved its position on the provision of documentary evidence from NQIs. The regulations originally stated that, for an NQI, documentary evidence had to move at the time of the income payment to demonstrate to a competent authority (e.g., withholding agent), that the payment could be reliably associated with valid documentation. This was clearly unworkable in the industry and a change was made to allow the withholding agent to withhold at a rate advised by the NQI and that documentation must still flow, but at the end of the year. This just moved the problem on and concentrated it into a smaller time frame. Publication 515 updates the guidance on withholding for the current year.

IRS – INTENT VERSUS REAL IMPACT

The IRS's real intent was, and is, to ensure that it was able to detect abuses of treaty predominantly by its own residents.

In the run-up to promulgation, the investment management community saw the operational impact as everything from being invasive to an example of unacceptable extraterritoriality by the United States.

The process that was eventually implemented established the idea of a contractual relationship between the IRS and the investor or the firm acting on his behalf. This created the concept of a Qualified Intermediary or QI. Basically, the IRS contracts with QIs so that the QI agrees, subject to independent audit, to "know" about its customers and their income from the United States. In this way, the IRS is not burdened with the information. They rely on the QIs to maintain this information in the knowledge that the penalties imposed by the contract and the audit requirements gave sufficient control.

Any investor or firm not signing up to the contract to become a QI is by definition a Non-Qualified Intermediary or NQI.

Let's be clear about this in strategic terms. If you, as an investor don't have any interests in the United States and don't derive any income from the

United States, the regulations simply don't apply to you and the issue of status is irrelevant.

As one of the largest investment markets in the world however, it's unlikely that many of the financial services firms, institutional investors, mutual funds, pension funds, custodians, and so on, with their diversified portfolios (generally between 9 and 13 countries), will have failed to invest in the United States.

A summary of the operational issues raised by these regulations follows:

Scope – *All* non-US financial institutions wherever they are in the world, who handle payments sourced in the United States must accept either Qualified (QI) or Non-Qualified (NQI) Intermediary status. The latter is the default status for any firm not signing up to QI status.

Impact – The results of this are that the QIs

- sign a contractual agreement directly with the IRS,
- agree to document all clients through to beneficial owner,
- segregate client accounts and pooled accounts to avoid excessive withholding,
- are recommended to join the US Electronic Federal Tax payment System (EFTPS),
- send reports to the IRS either manually or electronically through Martinsburg Computer Center (MCC), and
- agree to independent audits on performance to contract.

Terminology and relationships explained

IRS The IRS is actually a division of the US Treasury. However, the Treasury department responsible for receiving tax payments, FMS Treasury tends to act entirely separately from the body that receives tax reports. So, in simple terms, QIs and withholding agents make tax deposits to the US Treasury using the Treasury's appointed agent bank, BankOne. These deposits are made either using a coupon book, or more likely either electronically through the US Federal tax Payment System (EFTPS) or via a QIs-nominated US Withholding agent where it maintains accounts. At the end of the tax year, the same QIs or withholding agents must make a report to the IRS of the tax paid during the year. It's only at this point that the IRS is in a position to compare tax paid with tax reported and make any judgments of under- or over-payment. The methods and mechanisms for each process are different and only combine once a year, from the perspective of QIs.

EFTPS

Electronic Federal Tax Payment System is the US domestic tax payment system used by US persons for the most part. It allows taxes to be deposited to the Treasury electronically. US domestic tax payers have the option, if the amount of tax to be deposited falls below certain levels, to deposit taxes "manually" using a coupon book and a cheque. Above those minima, and for the most part foreign entities will fall into this category, electronic deposits are mandatory. I mentioned earlier that there are two broad categories of firm, QI and NQI. Within the QI category, there are two subcategories – Withholding and Non-Withholding QI – "WQI" and "NWQI" respectively. A withholding QI has agreed not only to maintain documentation but has also agreed to accept "primary withholding responsibility". In this case, a WQI would normally be expected to credit funds to the US Treasury through its membership of EFTPS, directly. A NWQI on the other hand, has agreed primarily to maintain documentary evidence and advise a US withholding agent of the amounts that need to be remitted to the US Treasury. In these circumstances, the NWQI does not *need* to be a member of EFTPS, since the actual payment will be made by its US withholding agent, the funds of course debited from the QIs account held with the withholding agent.

KYC is the acronym for Know Your Customer. Most commonly associated "in country" with money laundering rules, in these regulations, KYC rules are used to help the IRS know that a foreign financial entity has KYC rules that enable it to know the identity of its customers to an agreed level of quality.

Martinsburg Computer Center (MCC) is the centre which is responsible for receiving reports (not deposits) from QIs and withholding agents. Typically these are Forms 1042, 1042-S and 1099. The Center provides guidelines for foreign entities to submit these forms electronically each year.

General issues

When compiling the regulations, the IRS did not, even though it was engaging with the financial services community, ask for any specific guidance whose object was to reduce paperwork or operational risk. The community itself responded in a fragmented way. Because many, if not all, of the firms involved are competitors, the advice given to the IRS in the consultative stage of the process, was coloured by each firm's particular way of approaching the issue and its level of automation. The result was a set of regulations whose impact was major. In this section, we'll cover many of these operational impacts. Remember that this is not an exhaustive explanation of the regulations. It's an analysis of the regulations with particular emphasis on the operational issues that the regulations raise for custodians. I've explained these issues, including some historical context, primarily so that custodians entering or thinking of entering into the US market can have some better understanding of key operational difficulties they may face, and that investors can understand the issues with regard to the confidentiality and security of their investment information and have some perspective to be able to ask intelligent questions of their custodian about their abilities to comply with sophisticated regulatory structures. Figure 5.2 gives the reader an overview picture of the difficulties the financial services community faces when dealing with these regulations. Some of the detail is explained later on. In the figure, I have outlined one particular thread in order to help demonstrate the complexity. The thread shows the relationships upward from a NWQI on the fourth level of the diagram and also the relationships downwards taking particular account also of the types of customer likely to be involved. In fact, any particular

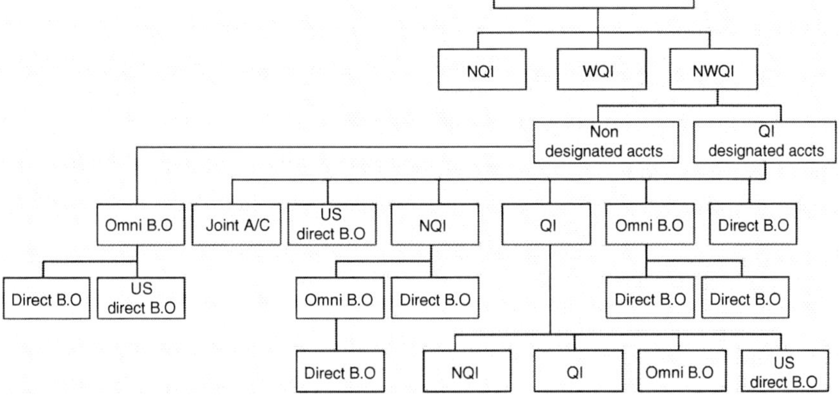

Figure 5.2 Investment chain structures

Source: Author.

financial firm, depending on a number of factors may follow a different thread.

1. Reading from the top down each level:First, we have to deal with two subsets of government generally referred to under the single term IRS. The area that is responsible for taking reports (IRS) and the second responsible for taking the money (Treasury). At the Treasury, payments over a certain amount must be made electronically, through EFTPS, otherwise payments can be made manually. Similarly at the end of the tax year, if the number of forms to be submitted exceeds a certain number (250) you must file these electronically via the Martinsburg Computer Center, otherwise you can file in the mail. The Treasury wants its money as fast as possible and sets time frames based on the amounts concerned. Unsurprisingly, the greater the value of the tax, the faster it must be deposited. The reporting on the other hand is usually done once a year, and for QIs who signed up before 31 December 2001, they avoid country-by-country reporting. Others may not be so lucky.

2. Both these entities deal with Withholding Agents and QIs directly. In the diagram, the withholding agent appears simply because there is a NWQI below on behalf of whom the withholding agent will be making deposits of tax to the Treasury. The key to remember here is that the Withholding Agent is responsible for depositing tax with the above on behalf of NQIs (who have no contractual relationship with the IRS) and those QIs who have not adopted primary withholding status. So where this thread shows a NWQI, there may be other firms using the Withholding Agent who are non-qualified intermediaries.

3. So, below a Withholding Agent are QIs and NQIs. Looking at the QIs, these are formed of two main groups, those who withhold and therefore send tax directly to the Treasury – Withholding QIs (WQI) and Non-Withholding QIs (NWQI) who accept the responsibility of being a QI but have a withholding agent to pay the actual tax on their behalf to the Treasury.

4. The Non-withholding QI at this level represents the majority of mainline custodians and global custodians. Most QIs have currently elected for non-withholding status and will either have a direct relationship with a QI above them or with a withholding agent. We must now turn about face and look downwards into the chain to see how a QI's operations are affected by the regulations.

5. Looking at the NWQI, he will have two main areas of concern: first, his relationship with other financial firms who may be either QIs or NQIs; second his own accounts. As you may imagine from this single thread and also the global nature of the custody sector, there probably will be a number of QIs and NQIs at this level reporting in to the NWQI.

6. Following the thread, looking at his own accounts, in order to avoid massive, but needless administration, he must segregate his accounts in to those for which the QI regulations and agreement apply and those where they do not. The QI agreement applies only to those accounts designated by the QI for which the QI is acting in that capacity. Ironically, this may seem a simplification which cuts down the number of accounts for which additional documentation is required. This is true, however it's useful to remember that the rules on audit require that, in order to assure compliance, an auditor will need to look at the NQI-designated accounts in order to make sure they've been properly set up and aren't contaminated with QI account information.

7. Looking at the accounts for which the firm *is* acting as a QI, these again must be segregated into those accounts representing US persons deriving US source income and those which do not. As back-up withholding on a US person is 28%, the rules establish that in an account with more than one person, the whole account must be taxed at the highest rate applicable to any one member. So having a US person in the same account as a non-US person will cause the non-US person to be taxed at 30% even though they may be eligible for a lower rate.

8. Now looking deeper, at say the non-US accounts of NWQI. We're doing this because, for the vast majority of custodians, the largest proportion of their customer base will be, from the US perspective, non-US persons. (It's perhaps enlightening to put this all in context at this point, as we are so far through the thread of responsibility, that the original reason for these regulations was and is to find those US persons identified here in the account structure). So, in the case of non-US persons, we find that he must still, from an administrative purpose, differentiate between those accounts which represent direct beneficial owners and those which are more properly described as flow through entities for example, partnerships. This is where the impact of sweeping up the issues of limitations of benefits clauses and hybridised entities is felt. The need to identify flow through entities is in place to ensure that a US person is not hiding in an otherwise opaque type of account.

9. That brings us at last to the lowest level. For the direct beneficial owners, the NWQI can document these directly fairly easily in the same way he has in the past. The regulations however say that the firm can no longer document the flow through entity at, for example, the partnership level, because there may be US persons somewhere in the partnership. So each flow through entity must be documented down to its ultimate beneficial owner – however deep that goes. This is known as the sub-accounting problem. There have been several clarification cases brought by a number of QIs mainly based on clarifications of the status of certain account types, mainly in the Trust area.

Simple really! The primary issue is that this program is dynamic. Not all financial firms are signed up as QIs and the QI program continues to receive applications. In operational terms, rather than design special systems to deal with many thousands of foreign financial firms who would, for the first time, be dealing directly with the IRS, the IRS essentially required foreign firms to sign up to existing US internal systems.

Identification

An example of this occurs right at the beginning of the process. Foreign financial firms applying for QI status are each issued with an identifying number, their QI number. This is actually issued by the United States as an Employer Identification Number (EIN), because it [The IRS] uses an internal existing agency to manage the numbering sequences for the return of tax forms, hence the actual term used is a QIEIN number. Many foreign firms are initially very confused as they clearly aren't employers in the United States at all. This may seem like a small issue. However, it's indicative of a larger problem faced by the IRS and as a result by many foreign firms. They don't always have English speaking personnel at the point where these regulations have effect and even where they do, the recipients must remember that the structures being used are usually US domestic structures. These regulations themselves run to over 800 pages, in English.

KYC Rules

At core, as we've found, the IRS' intent is to eradicate treaty abuse. The sine qua non of this need is the requirement to know precisely who it is that is deriving income from the United States. The IRS determined, quite correctly, that each jurisdiction had already done more or less work in this area in their own efforts to avoid money laundering. The basic premise was to ensure that the nature of whoever opened an account with a financial firm was known. Several high profile cases of regulatory authorities imposing massive fines on custodians in the 90s, for failure to keep accurate client records, stand testimony to the rigour with which governments wanted this issue addressed. More recent political events, notably 9/11 have done nothing but increase governmental eagerness to engage in anything that will increase knowledge of who owns money and who is moving it.

The IRS decided to use these individual KYC rules as a benchmark. They considered that if a jurisdiction had sufficiently good rules and controls, they could properly contract with a financial firm in that jurisdiction. The supposition was that if there was a failure under the QI agreement, the contracting firm would already be facing a far worse situation with their own regulators. Of course, in addition, it meant that the IRS did not have to create any new investigatory or compliance structures to monitor the efficacy with which QIs met their obligations.

The result is that the IRS will not enter into a qualified intermediary (QI) withholding agreement that provides for the use of documentary evidence obtained under a country's KYC rules if it has not received the KYC practices and procedures for opening accounts and responses to 18 specific questions listed in their revenue procedures. As at January 2009, the following countries in Table 5.1 have complied, submitted and have had their KYC rules approved by the IRS.

In most cases, the banking association of each country concerned has co-ordinated the responses to the 18 questions and to the application process in general. The full text of the attachment can be found in Rev. Proc, 2000-12.

What's of interest here is that the ability of a custodian to be a QI is dependent on jurisdiction. If a jurisdiction has not had its KYC rules approved, then it does not matter what the custodian wants, there can be no QI status in that country.

Documentation

At the core is the debate about what level documentary evidence was required. Don't forget that a QI can retain this documentary evidence confidentially through its contract with the IRS. An NQI must submit that documentation to a body which has IRS approval – that is, a QI or US withholding agent.

Generally, the IRS will not allow documentation to be accepted unless the documentation has been obtained directly from the account holder.

The documentation generally has to be obtained before any payment is made and the 30% withholding rule applies unless the payee is a US person or has documentary evidence of eligibility for a lower rate.

Table 5.1 Approved KYC jurisdictions

Andorra	Chile	Israel	Singapore
Anguilla	Colombia	Italy	Slovenia
Antigua	Cyprus	Japan	Spain
Argentina	Czech Republic	Jersey	St Lucia
Aruba	Denmark	Korea	Sweden
Australia	Estonia	Luxembourg	Switzerland
Austria	Finland	Liechtenstein	Taiwan
Bahamas	France	Malta	Turks & Caicos
Bahrain	Germany	Monaco	UAE
Barbados	Gibraltar	Netherlands	UK
Belgium	Greece	Netherlands Ant.	Uruguay
Bermuda	Guernsey	Norway	
BVI	Hong Kong	Panama	
Brunei	Iceland	Poland	
Canada	Ireland	Portugal	
Cayman Is.	Isle of Man	St Vincent	

Source: www.irs.gov

The standard of knowledge required by the IRS is that a QI cannot assume the documentation is valid and, if it has reason to feel that it may not be valid, it must apply the 30% rate.

The documentation issue is inextricably linked with the issue of "presumption rules". These rules apply when a QI cannot reliably associate a payment with valid documentation.

Presumption rules

If a withholding agent, QI or NQI cannot reliably associate a payment with valid documentation, they must apply certain presumption rules or they may be liable for tax, interest and penalties. If they comply with the presumption rules, they aren't liable for tax, interest and penalties even if the rate of withholding that should have been applied based on the payee's actual status is different from that which was presumed.

The presumption rules apply to determine the status of the person paid as a US or foreign person and other relevant characteristics, such as whether the payee is a beneficial owner or intermediary, and whether the payee is an individual, corporation, partnership or trust. Withholding agents, QIs and NQIs aren't permitted to apply a reduced rate of NRA withholding based on a payee's presumed status if, in actual fact, documentation is required to establish a reduced rate of withholding. For example, if the payee of interest is presumed to be a foreign person, a QI cannot apply the portfolio interest exception or a reduced rate of withholding under a tax treaty since both exceptions require documentation.

If the withholding agent relies on actual knowledge about a payee's status and withholds an amount less than that required under the presumption rules or doesn't report a payment that is subject to reporting under the presumption rules, they may be liable for tax, interest and penalties. They should, however, rely on their actual knowledge if doing so results in withholding an amount greater than what would apply under the presumption rules or in reporting an amount that would not be subject to reporting under the presumption rules.

I'm not going to give chapter and verse detail on these rules because, as I've said before, this is not a tax manual, it's about operational impacts. For those who do want a reference to the relevant sections of the regulations on this subject, Table 5.2 below provides guidance.

Suffice to say that, whilst the issue may seem simple from the viewpoint of existence or otherwise of documentation and its corollaries of default and reduced withholding, the presumptions rules sit amidst this matrix. While they may appear to provide some middle ground, in most cases they

Table 5.2 Referents to the QI regulations

For the presumption rules related to:	*See regulation section:*
Payee's status – general	1.1441-1(b)(3); 1.6049-5(d)
Effectively connected income	1.1441-4(a)(2)
Partnership and its partners	1.1441-5(d)
Estate or trust and its beneficiaries or owner	1.1441-5(e)(6)
Foreign tax-exempt organisations (including private foundations)	1.1441-9(b)(3)

Source: Author.

do not. For investors, the question for their agents is whether their withholding is being performed based on actual documentation or on presumption rules.

Penalties

There are a range of penalties that apply to QIs, NQIs and of course investors themselves. Investors in particular should be in no doubt of the intent and will of the IRS. The following appeared as the first item in a list of the 12 most common, illegal scams on the IRS web site aimed at the very people who are the target of 1441 NRA regulations:

> **Offshore Transactions.** Some people use offshore transactions to avoid paying United States income tax. Use of an offshore credit card, trust or other arrangement to hide or underreport income or to claim false deductions on a federal tax return is illegal.
>
> Through April 15, the IRS is offering people with improper offshore financial arrangements a chance to make things right. Eligible taxpayers who step forward will not face civil fraud and information return penalties. A taxpayer involved in these schemes who does not come forward now, however, will be subject to payment of taxes, interest, penalties and potential criminal prosecution.

The liabilities for penalties can be summarised as:

Under-withholding or Over-withholding – Over-withholding, as one might imagine, is less of an issue from the IRS viewpoint than under-withholding. In fact, given the complexity of the rules themselves and the concern of QIs to avoid any remedial liability to investors, it's far more likely that over-withholding will take place than under-withholding. If a QI has a number of NQIs below it, if the QI has any feeling that the NQI may not have adequate documentation in place to later substantiate a claim of treaty rate benefits, the QI is likely to impose a 30% withholding rate and let the NQI prove otherwise. Under-withholding is more of a concern for the IRS of course simply because it won't get all the tax to which it is entitled. The audit procedures for the QI agreement are very complex, but the important issue for QIs is that, at audit, compliance is essentially established by sample tests of accounts. The IRS's intention is that if under-withholding has taken place to a significant extent in the testing, then the QI will be required to make a payment. However, that payment is to be calculated not by determining the actual amount of under-withholding across the whole account base of the QI. No. It will be calculated as an extrapolation of the test results.

Late or inappropriate methods of filing – In particular, the IRS is keen to encourage electronic filing of tax information reports as well as electronic payment of taxes. The former is done through the Martinsburg Computer Center where filing can be done on magnetic media to a specified layout. The latter is done through EFTPS, the Electronic Federal tax Payment System. The rules say that, based on the amount of tax a QI is due to send to the Treasury, electronic filing may be mandatory and there are fines that can be imposed if this is not followed.

What is not commonly understood or remembered by custodians is the degree to which liabilities fall on themselves either as QIs or withholding agents, as well as their clients. The regulations are clear that failure to withhold tax properly renders the withholding agent *and* the client liable to tax, interest as well as any other applicable penalties.

For NQIs the problem is compounded. The situation is that NQIs have more onerous communications responsibilities that flow from the fact that they have been unwilling or unable to enter into an agreement with the IRS which would otherwise afford them some protection. Therefore, they are more likely to face communications and taxation principles which cause errors. Whilst the IRS is forgiving of small errors in such a complex regulatory structure, it is most unforgiving when errors are found to be endemic.

The difficulty that withholding agents had in the first year of the regulations was that they were required to deal with both QIs and NQIs (although some notable exceptions took a business decision only to deal with QIs as a business risk prevention measure). The regulations state that "in no case should a withholding agent withhold more than 30% of the total amount paid". This causes a problem, particularly when dealing with NQIs. The compliance requirements are so complex that it is likely that some firms will be in material non-compliance either deliberately or by accident. Now this can cause a risk management issue. So the issue of whether an investor's US source income is administered directly or indirectly through a NQI becomes crucial for both investors and custodian/QIs particularly in terms of the method used to mitigate the risk inherent in dealing with US income through effectively and unapproved, but regulated intermediary. The above of course has not taken into account the fact that, if penalties were applied, there may well be an internal case against the financial firm through its own regulatory structure. The essence of the message is that the regulations are constructed in such a way as to provide serious disincentives to financial firms and investors deriving US sourced income through a NQI.

When it comes down to the actual penalties and liabilities for any given omission or failure, the rules can be complex, so QIs must apply some significant technical resource to mitigating their risk.

As noted above the penalty for under-withholding is an extrapolation of the amount under-withheld found in an auditor's sample across the entire account base. This was mitigated in 2002 under Rev. Proc. 2002-55 which on the one hand allowed QIs to submit to spot check auditing of accounts on the one hand and deferred the application of the extrapolation concept to Phase II of the audit process.

Failing to file reports to the IRS carries a number of risks and the Treasury proposed in its Blue Book publication in 2009 to increase fines significantly for non-compliance. Failure to file 1042-S forms carries a fine of $30 per form (if corrected within 30 days) capped at $250,000 and $60 capped at $500,000 if corrected in more than 30 days but before 2 August. Failure to file after 1 August in a tax year carries a $100 per form fine capped at a mere $1.5m. If the failure is due to intentional disregard, the fine is $250 per form.

Making deposits also comes under the IRS and Treasury scrutiny. To paraphrase, if the withholding tax due is less than $200 annually, then payment can be made annually. If the withholding tax due is between $200 and $2,000 in any month, payment must be made within 15 days of the month end. If the withholding tax is more than $2,000 in any quarter month period, then payment is due within 3 banking days of the end of that quarter month period.

Finally, there's a wonderful sentence in Publication 515 that is pretty much self-explanatory. It reads:

> If you [QI] fail to withhold and the foreign payee fails to satisfy its US tax liability, then both you [QI] and the foreign person are liable for tax as well as interest and any applicable penalties. ... If the foreign person satisfies its US tax liability, you [QI] may still be held liable for interest and penalties.

Audits

It is through independent audits that much of the compliance to these regulations is administered. The latest guidance on this issue can be found in Rev. Proc. 2001-66 and Rev. Proc. 2002-55 at the IRS web site and also in the consultative document 2008-98.

Basically, an auditor will perform certain benchmark tests on aspects of the QI's activities under its QI agreement. If, for example, on audit a withholding agent is found to have under-withheld on some transactions, the determination of the amount of tax due to the IRS is based on an extrapolation of the scale and scope of under-reporting across all the QI accounts managed by the QI. This of course removes the costly necessity of checking each and every account, but could potentially leave the QI open to a very large liability. The process of course does provide for a QI to appeal a decision and provide its own basis for calculation of the actual amount due in such a circumstance. But of course this is a two-edged sword. If the QI has manifestly failed to manage its business effectively such that it ends up in significant under-withholding, it's likely that the cost of appealing the decision successfully to the extent that the auditor or the IRS agrees with its subsequent calculation is unknown, but the cost of performing the calculation itself to support the appeal may be large in its own right. Many QIs in this situation, and I'm not aware of any to date, are more likely to shut up and pay up I suspect.

Integration to the financial services business model

All of this has of course to be integrated into the way that most banks operate between each other in terms of the communications principle and how they structure their businesses. The most powerful integration tool is the SWIFT network which has most banks as members or users. SWIFT is described in more detail elsewhere, however, the message types that SWIFT have developed, to an extent, address the 1441 NRA issue. SWIFT messages can be used to notify parties, instruct for payments of withholding tax and also transmit withholding-rate pool information between QIs and withholding agents. In addition, more recent innovations include SWIFT messages to allow lists of beneficial owners to be transmitted electronically as well as an electronic version of a W-8BEN. In structuring the latter, the most important aspect was to replace the original signature required by the IRS. This has been done, not with a digital certificate (the level of advancement of the world's different financial institutions isn't homogenised to that extent), but with a simple text-based data packet. The issue is to make the signature data a standard capable of being used either in a SWIFT message or any other ISO15022 compliant message form. The signature data itself comprises of the tax identification numbers and country location of both the financial firm which holds the original paper document and that of the subject of that document. This is information which any financial firm worldwide must hold if it is to be a credible financial intermediary. The fact that it's a simple data packet allows all levels of firm to use it – it's the lowest common denominator.

The audit procedure has gone through two sets of major changes since 2003. The original guidelines were refined in 2005 after consultation both with the major audit practices as well as the financial firms subject to the audit procedure. See Rev. Proc. 2002-55. Investors should be aware of these issues to have a clear picture of just how much work their custodian is required to do in order to manage their account. There are three phases to the audit procedure. A QI who successfully completes Phase I, which is effectively a basic fact-finding exercise focused on documentation review, spot check and the completion of certain specific procedures, may not have to undergo Phase II or Phase III. If the IRS is unhappy with the results of a Phase I audit or has reason to be concerned, it can require a Phase II audit. A Phase II audit is more detailed and is termed "follow-up fact finding". This will be basically where the auditor needs to go into more detail, particularly in those areas of concern to establish whether the QI is in compliance or not. If this Phase II audit is failed, the IRS can require a Phase III audit which is euphemistically called "An Audit meeting with QI", where the IRS will discuss directly with the QI, its concerns over Phase I and II of the process in regard to the QIs compliance with its agreement.

There have been five main areas of concern for both custodians and auditors alike. Rev. Proc. 2002-55 gives a fairly detailed overview of these areas and also, importantly gives specific instructions for auditors to follow when auditing a QI. The five areas, which the reader should note are only summaries for general feel, are:

Waivers – The issue that many QIs had was that whilst they accepted that they must abide by the principles of the QI agreement, the actual amounts of withholding tax involved, for them, was relatively low. Therefore the cost of undergoing an audit, on top of the cost of complying was thought to be excessive. So the IRS had allowed four waivers, which, in the latest revenue procedure, have been extended. What's important to note here is that the waivers are not automatic, they must be applied for, and approval is not necessarily automatic.

- If the QI has a reportable amount of less than $1,000,000 a request for a waiver of audit can be filed. The level was originally $250,000.

- If the QI has a reportable amount of more that $1,000,000 but less than $4,000,000 *and* has already been audited in the preceding year, he can apply for a waiver of the external audit. This rule was originally based on the number of accounts in Notice 2001-66.

- Reconciling Forms 1042-S and 1099, which is a requirement for the preceding two waiver opportunities, has been lessened. Variances are allowed within "reasonable" limits.

- If a QI has a substantial internal audit staff and engages in an annual internal audit in these matters, based on the tests and checks that internal staff feel are appropriate, the QI can request a waiver of the external audit. This rule used to require a more rigorous internal audit procedure.

Scope – Some of the procedures that were included in the Phase I audit have now been deferred to the Phase II audit. The accounts at the QI that are subject to audit have now also been changed from those that receive reportable payment, to those that receive reportable amounts. Also, the review of withholding-rate pools, under-withholding and reporting have now been amended to be based on a spot check basis rather than a full sample.

Sampling – The number of accounts that an auditor should sample is reduced from 1368 to 321 and the analysis for under-withholding is changed to a "spot check" basis. This latter is important in conjunction with the following change in projections.

Projection – The problem here was that the original guidelines had the analysis of under-withholding based on a sample. The level of under-withholding found in the sample would then be projected or extrapolated to the entire account base. This is clearly something the QIs wanted to avoid. This has now been changed so that the Phase I audit now only contains a spot check and any under-withholding found results in the repayment just of the spot check under-withholding. However, QIs should not feel relieved too soon. The projection concept has only been moved to Phase II.

Internal audit – There used to be a certification process in place if a QI had an internal audit staff. The change now means that a QI's external auditor that uses internal audit staff and internal audit reports is not required to certify that their use hasn't affected the accuracy of their reports.
The above changes took place in 2005. In 2008, the IRS released a consultation paper 2008-98 which had, amongst other areas, proposed changes to the audit rules. Since the consultation period ended after the manuscript for this book was complete, at the time of writing, I do not know whether any substantive variation has been decided to the proposals. Therefore, in this book, I can only describe what those proposals were and the effects they would have if implemented "as is". From an audit perspective, the IRS proposed that, while the audit frequency would remain the same – twice in each six year contract cycle – each audit would have two parties involved, one of whom would have to be US resident. Additionally, each auditor would have to take joint and several liability for the audit. In practical commercial terms this means that each of the two audits would have to be undertaken by two auditors acting in concert. The liability issue leads me to believe that the US-based auditor would want to undertake its own audit before taking liability so, even though there may be advantages to an audit in concert, to all intents and purposes, including cost, there would be two audits, twice in the cycle.

Technical issues

Apart from the issues raised by Figure 5.1, Figure 5.3 provides an alternative way of thinking about the processes.

Withholding-rate pools

Prior to 2001, most US withholding agents held pools on behalf of their non-US custodians. However, these were very simple, basically treaty account or non-treaty account. Post 2001 however, the issue became more complex. Not only were there a range of withholding rates that could apply, those rates could apply differently based also on the income type received by the recipient. In other words, while one rate might apply to one kind of income, another might apply to a different kind of income, so the account held by the withholding agent could no longer be simple.

What the reader must be clear about is the difference between a rate pool and pooled accounting. The rate pool is the grouping of income into similar rates of withholding. The technical issue this raised is that, prior to these regulations, most custodians held only two types of account, treaty and non-treaty to define how an account would be treated for tax purposes. Post regulation, the custodians needed to describe their accounts in terms of the numerical withholding rates, for example, 0%, 15%, 30% as well as define the income type to which the withholding applies – in effect a matrix.

Pooled accounting is a mechanism by which the IRS allowed a significant reduction in paperwork for QIs and withholding agents. Forms that would otherwise be submitted for each underlying beneficial owner between a QI and a withholding agent were replaced by the same form

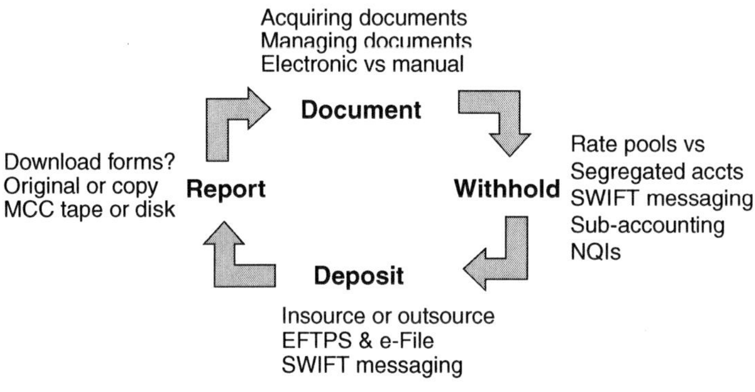

Figure 5.3 General issues of QIs

Source: Author.

allowing reporting based on the pool of withholding rather than its constituent elements.

Effectively, when an income event hits a withholding agent, if it's dealing with a NWQI or an NQI, it needs to know how much to withhold. Its problem is that it doesn't know anything about the underlying beneficial owner status. The QI agreement allows the QI to protect the identity of its underlying beneficial owners because that information would obviously be of a competitive nature for its withholding agent (also a bank). So, instead, maintaining the confidentiality of its clients, the QI must aggregate together into "pools" all the beneficial owners who are affected by the income event. Once it has this data, it can transmit it to the withholding agent as a withholding-rate pool statement. On the other side, on receipt, the withholding agent now knows how to calculate the amounts to withhold and remit to the US Treasury. From a technical standpoint, this caused a great deal of stress to QIs who were more familiar with structuring their accounts into "treaty" and "non-treaty". The rate pool statement of course inter-reacts with (i) the fact that the QI's account base and client holdings will be in a constant state of change as buys and sells are made and (ii) the aggregation of data must take into account the sub-accounting issue described below which flows from the inclusion of limitation of benefits, hybridised entities, and so on described earlier.

Sub-accounting

Sub-accounting is the term given to the issue raised by the very object of the regulations. If the IRS is to be comfortable that the foreign financial community is able to pick up a US investor in its client base, this means that many of the client structures and vehicles previously created under preceding regulatory structures have documentation and accounting problems that could spiral out of control in administrative terms for a custodian.

As an example, take a foreign (i.e., non-US) partnership with one hundred members. Assume that each of these in turn is a partnership with, let's say 50 members each and let's say that there's one US person in one of these latter partnerships. On 31 December 2000, the top level partnership could have been documented with one form, thus providing all the members and sub-members potentially with treaty-rate benefits. On 1 January 2001 and since then, the custodian dealing with this partnership would need to obtain and maintain in validity 5,000 documents demonstrating that, at any time an income event occurred, each of the recipients was entitled to the tax rate that was actually applied.

Technically of course this creates major problems for custodians, not least in the sheer volume of documentary evidence required and the subsequent manpower required to oversee and maintain its validity. Risk managers of course also had to assess what would happen if a document fell out of its validity and failed to be tracked. If an income event occurred during this period, in theory the recipient would receive income potentially at a tax rate they were not entitled to. Not so much of an issue if it happened only rarely, but in risk management terms the issue is more related to the potential weaknesses in the systems that can generate one failure and their ability to generate many more of the same. The former is not really going to worry the IRS and can easily be reconciled after the event. The latter is more serious and the penalties imposed by the IRS for under-reporting or underpayment are significant.

The other technical issue which needed to be addressed by the custodial community was that of separation of US persons from non-US in accounts where they had previously been mingled with others of similar numeric withholding rate.

The sub-accounting issue, when dealt with correctly, throws up the potential that there is, in one of the sub levels, not previously documented for tax purposes, a US person. There are several reasons why custodians must separate out US persons from non-US in their accounting structures.

First, the US person must be reported separately. A US person's income must be reported on a Form 1099 whereas a non-US person's income would be reported on a Form 1042. The problems raised by this are only varied in extent not type, by whether these forms are created electronically or manually. More importantly, a joint account must be taxed at the rate applicable to the highest rate of any person within it. So, in this example, an account with many persons eligible for treaty rate benefits, mixed with US persons, would be taxed at the highest rate applicable to any member, even though there are treaty beneficiaries in the pool.

The technical issues for custodian systems are significant. Not all financial firms signed up or have signed up to the IRS QI Agreement. Some, because they derive no US source income, and thus the regulations don't apply to them. Others are not signed up because they have chosen, for whatever reason to be a non-qualified intermediary (NQI). Still others are in jurisdictions where the IRS has yet to approve KYC rules. The result is that the regulations and the scale and scope of their application are an ever-changing scene. New firms are still applying to the IRS, applying jurisdictions will undoubtedly increase and firms which had heretofore not had any US persons or had no US source income, will enter the US marketplace. In all these events, a financial firm must decide its stance with regard to the regulations. The sub-accounting issue is one of the most technically difficult and most expensive to deal with whether systems are electronic or manual.

As the reader might imagine, the costs of complying with these regulations are not small and we have yet to see whether there will be a change to pricing policies from custodians.

W-8 series

Custodians are faced now with new account opening procedures in addition to KYC rules for anyone where income is expected from a US source. They must also now combine this with the volume issues raised by the sub-accounting problem. Many seek to minimise risk by adding the requirement for a self-certification with a form W-8BEN. Many custodians in the early days were confused and mistakenly believed that the W-8 was a replacement for the application of the KYC rules. This is not the case, but still, many custodians use the W-8BEN as a "catch all" solution.

A W-8 however brings its own issues. The validity of a W-8BEN is limited to 3 years following the end of the year in which it is signed by the beneficial owner. The exception to this is where the beneficial owner has a Tax Identification Number or "TIN" issued by the US government. Since this is not a common occurrence, many custodians have a document management issue to make sure that the W-8 remains valid. Remember, the regulations state that "at the time of the payment" a QI must be able to reliably associate the payment with valid documentation to establish the beneficial owner's eligibility for a lower withholding rate.

The other issue surrounding this documentary evidence is its volume and tendency to be replicated. It's a fact that many investors choose, for their own reasons, to funnel different types of investment through different custodians. So, it becomes likely that a beneficial owner will have to sign more than one W-8BEN if he is receiving US source income through more than one channel. Some of these W-8BEN's will of course only proceed directly to a QI where they will reside. Others however will be provided to a NQI. The NQI must provide these W-8s to a withholding agent or QI. The net result for US withholding agents is that they may be in a position of receiving multiple W-8s for the same beneficial owner – clearly not a sensible position. The number of W-8BENs that are in circulation because of this issue has been estimated to be in excess of 900 million.

There are actually four forms in the W-8 series.

- W-8BEN is a certification of Foreign Status of Beneficial Owner;
- W-8ECI is a certificate of a foreign person's claim for exemption from withholding on "Effectively Connected Income" that is, income effectively connected with the conduct of a business in the USA;
- W-8EXP is a certificate of a foreign government or other foreign organisation; and
- W-8IMY is a certificate of a foreign intermediary or foreign flow through entity

Issues for NQIs and withholding agents

For non-qualified intermediaries (NQIs) there really are two major technical issues. The NQI has not entered into an agreement with the IRS and therefore it has no protection to keep the identity of its account holders secret. The object of the regulations is effectively to allow that confidentiality for QIs in return for a contractual agreement and submission to audits, both of which underpin the IRS's ability to make sure its aims are being adhered to. For the NQI, this isn't the case. So the NQI must prove the eligibility of its account holders for every income event that takes place. The second technical issue is that an NQI must file a form 1042-S for each of its clients and one copy of this is sent to the IRS. Similar requirements apply for 1099 reporting. The NQI would typically receive a 1042-S form from its upstream QIs representing payments made to it at the omnibus (intermediary) level. All of its downstream reporting, copied to the IRS, would then need to reconcile to the received reports. Apart from the rather disturbing fact that I have yet to meet, in 7 years, an NQI who has met these regulatory reporting requirements, the number of 1042-S forms for NQIs, because they are at the beneficial owner level, are much more likely to trip the 250 form limit beyond which the reporting must be done electronically.

Here is where many NQIs fail to act. It is a common misconception that because no contract with the IRS is in place somehow the regulations do not apply. This is not correct. The QI contract merely creates specific obligations for an institution and grants certain benefits in return. All institutions receiving US sourced income on behalf of their clients are subject to the generality of the regulations.

Treasury issues

Electronic deposits (EFTPS)

The US Treasury also wants to make sure that deposits are made in a timely way. This is clearly best done electronically and, as with internal US corporations, the Treasury provides either payment by telephone, by coupon book or by electronic interface. For major foreign financial firms the first two of these would indicate a serious concern over professional conduct as well as risk. So most firms were, and are, encouraged to enrol in the US Electronic Federal Tax Payment System (EFTPS). Let's be clear, this was the system designed for and used primarily by US corporations and citizens to pay their US taxes.

The principle, which applies to most QIs, is that if the QI expects to pay over $200,000 in any one year to the US Treasury, this must be done electronically through EFTPS.

EFTPS offers three payment methods – ACH Debit, ACH Credit and FedWire – where ACH stands for Automated Clearing House. SWIFT messages were created to facilitate the payment process by EFTPS as most custodians are members of SWIFT but have never heard of EFTPS. Currently EFTPS has downgraded the importance of SWIFT in its advice to QIs. This is probably because most QIs are signed up as non-withholding. So their payments are being made to the Treasury on their behalf by their US withholding agent. The withholding agent being in the United States already has established means of paying withholding taxes that don't require SWIFT. As more firms sign up or convert into withholding QI status the SWIFT messaging facility will become more important as it will provide a well-documented and set-up message format for payment messages direct from the withholding QI. This probably needs a little more explanation.

Being a QI is one thing, and this is the primary way that custodians can keep the identity of their clients secret from their competitors. However, as a QI you have the option of taking up responsibility for primary withholding or of contracting that process out to a US withholding agent. This establishes QIs as either Withholding QIs or Non-Withholding QIs. The former make direct payments to the US Treasury (even though this will be via their US bank accounts). The latter do not make direct payments but rely on their US withholding agents to establish the withholding amounts and make the payments for them. Many QIs, unfamiliar with US internal payment practices, and not without a certain degree of sales activity from the withholding agents themselves, effectively outsourced the payment of taxes to their US withholding agents. So many payments are not made by QIs directly to the Treasury, but are paid by a US withholding agent on their behalf. Irrespective of the route taken, the responsibility for the timeliness of payments still falls on the QI concerned, and thus it is a critical management factor to be able to monitor US withholding agents payments.

Making deposits in a timely way

So, now we've dealt with how QIs and NQIs can make payments, we should spend a little time looking at when payments must be made. In general terms US tax payments can be made using a coupon book and even over the phone, but these methods are far more suited to the US domestic situation than that of international banking where the sheer volume and requirements for traceability and electronic commerce mean that the ACH or FedWire systems are more appropriate. If a foreign payer (QI or NQI) is liable to pay more than $200,000 in tax, the requirement is that this must be done electronically. However, this is not the only constraint. The regulations provide that the amount expected to be deposited in any one year is inversely proportional to the length of time available to make the deposit. This is the simple way of stating the case. The actual words are more complex and, as one has come to expect, the terms vary depending on the type of income received. In my view, this is one of the largest drivers for QIs and NQIs to use the services of withholding agents for this purpose, simply because the expenditure necessary to meet these obligations would be excessive.

So, for investors, it is clear that any assessment of the efficacy of their custodian must include an assessment of the whether they receive US source income, and if so, what systems and processes, including payments to the US Treasury, they have in place to ensure withholding is kept to a minimum. All these issues and processes, whether Treasury or IRS must be considered in the light of the penalties available to the IRS for any substantive non-compliance, an issue described in the preceding section.

IRS reporting issues

Electronic reporting (MCC)

If a QI or NQI is due to file more than 250 of any one type of document for example, 1099 or 1042-S, then this must be done electronically via the Martinsburg Computer Center. This is not *making* tax payments. This is *reporting* payments. Even if less than 250 forms are to be filed, the IRS and MCC recommend electronic filing anyway. This also is a critical question for QIs and NQIs and for their investors. Apart from the fact that an investor dealing with an NQI is at a greater inherent risk than if he is dealing with a QI for his US source income, the method of reporting can compound the situation and it is certainly best practice for a foreign financial firm deriving US source income, to report electronically as well as pay electronically.

The process involves applying for permission to file electronically on a Form 1149 which must be submitted to Martinsburg Computer Center. The relevant publications which provide further details of how electronic filing is made are Pub. 1120 for Forms 1099 and Pub. 1187 for Forms 1042 and 1042-S.

Forms 1042, 1042-S and 1099

The reporting issue is complex. Basically forms 1042 and 1042-S represent tax reports for non-US persons in the same way that W-8 series forms are for status certification of non-US persons. Forms 1099 (which are segregated by income type, e.g., 1099-DIV) are for US persons, in the same way that the W-9 series of forms is for status certification of US persons. That would be simple in normal circumstances as it represents the beneficial owners. However, we must overlay the contractual benefit of confidentiality and the communications principle to this situation. So, the W-8 series includes Forms W-8IMY as an example which allows a QI to keep its account holders secret thus allowing it to provide a withholding-rate pool table (thus allowing the withholding agent to do his job).

An non-US investor dealing with a NQI and who derives income from US sources may well receive a form 1042-S once a year showing the levels of income and withholding that have been applied. If the investor is dealing with a QI however, he will not necessarily receive those forms.

I've mentioned that the IRS, in late 2008, issued consultation document 2008-98 and if promulgated, this would mark a substantive and significant change in the rules. One of these, already described, is the proposed change to the audit rules to require two auditors per audit, each taking joint and several liability. The second are the proposed changes to the fines applicable to failure to file correct reports, which, if promulgated would establish a maximum fine of $1.5 million. The Treasury predicts revenue from fines exceeding $300 million in the period to 2018. Given a fairly static QI/NQI ratio, it's clear that the IRS expects to be levying these penalties whereas in the past it has been loathe to do so, preferring compliance through self-interest, if not self-regulation.

The IRS does review the results of periodic audits of QIs and it's clear that some of these proposed changes are directly preparing the community of non-US financial institutions for a more aggressive approach.

One area of the 2008 proposals not mentioned so far, is that relating to material failures. If we consider that the changes to the audit rules represent the IRS making sure that its measuring instrument is accurate enough and that the increase in penalties is making sure that the incentives for good performance exist, then what is missing is a set of clearer guidelines on what is meant to happen between these two issues.

The proposals include a new concept, that of a material failure. This concept and its detail is drawn directly from the US Sarbanes–Oxley Act. Essentially it requires a subject firm to establish appropriate levels of control to ensure that the firm is compliant. Once the concept of controls is established, the natural follow through are procedures to make sure that people with appropriate authority are involved and that any material failure is reported in a timely way. This describes, long form, what the proposals suggest. Each QI and NQI would need to appoint someone in the firm with appropriate executive authority to act. In my experience, many firms have QI-responsible staff at junior operational level, but few if any at all at C-level. Once the authority is established, the firm must establish a set of controls to (i) prevent, (ii) detect, (iii) deter and (iv) correct any material failure that could or does occur. Most, if not all of these controls do not exist in most firms today. As such they will represent a major cost for QIs and NQIs as will recruiting and training executives with sufficient knowledge to act intelligently to reports.

These controls, once in place, would require a process of reporting called a Notice of Material Failure to be issued once anyone in the chain became aware of such a failure. For NQIs, this represents a major turn-around. At present many are not in compliance with the regulations and fail to file reports at all based on the idea that the IRS is way too busy to figure out every last reconciliation between an upstream 1042-S and the lack of any downstream 1042-S forms against which to reconcile. The new proposals would require NQIs (and QIs) to proactively disclose any non-compliance as a material failure.

Taking all these into account, I believe that, even if moderated by the consultation process, the intent of the IRS to tighten up compliance is clear and unlikely to be diverted. When the FISCO and OECD groups consider the practical aspects of an advanced relief-at-source process as part of a combination regime, it will be critical for them to consider that the cost savings delivered through harmonisation of existing process between members, may be offset in whole or in part by new processes, such as those described above, that do not currently exist in the EU or OECD markets.

It's also absolutely critical to remember that the US is *not* a relief-at-source jurisdiction. It is a combination jurisdiction. It's very easy for practitioners to look at 1,200 pages of regulation on relief at source and forget that there are mechanisms both within the regulations (offset) and outside (long form claim process) that round out the jurisdiction. Due to the complexities and non-compliance currently endemic under these regulations, there are very large sums of money that have been taxed at 30% where the beneficiary is entitled to either a treaty rate or an exemption. This could be because of non-compliance at the institutional level, documentary failure at the beneficiary level or because of the account structures in between.

JAPAN QUALIFIED FINANCIAL INTERMEDIARY SYSTEM

Intent

The Japanese Government promulgated these regulations in order to increase foreign holdings of Japanese Government Bonds (JGBs). To that extent the system is far more limited than that which applies from the United States inasmuch as it only applies to a very limited income type. Its intent is also different from the US authorities. Here the espoused intent is to encourage inward investment rather than eradicate abuse of an existing system.

Having said that, it is clear that the Japanese QFI system has many structural similarities, not least in name, to the US system.

History

Prior to 2001, Japanese regulations granted withholding tax exemption only to the portion of interest arising from JGBs that correspond to the period when JGBs were held by non-resident investors in the Bank of Japan (BOJ) book-entry system. Legislation was introduced in 2001 in Japan that would expand this withholding tax exemption to interest on JGBs to include non-resident investors that maintain custody of JGBs through global custodians. This was an important change for the mutual fund industry, since many mutual funds were unable to qualify for the original exemption. The previous law provided that individual non-residents of Japan and foreign corporations were exempt from Japanese withholding tax on interest payments on JGBs, provided certain conditions were met concerning how the securities were held. Some mutual funds were not able to meet those conditions while maintaining custody of JGBs through their global custodians. Figure 5.4 shows the structure of the withholding tax system for JGBs prior to April 2001.

The legislation, which became effective for interest payments made on JGBs deposited in the scheme on or after 1 April 2001, allows a non-resident investor, such as a US mutual fund, that uses a qualified foreign intermediary (QFI) or a chain of QFIs to maintain custody of the JGBs to claim the withholding tax exemption. The legislation requires global custodians to obtain QFI status, and requires the non-resident investor to submit documentation to the Japanese tax authorities (via the QFI and the local sub-custodian) that would entitle the non-resident investor to claim the withholding tax exemption.

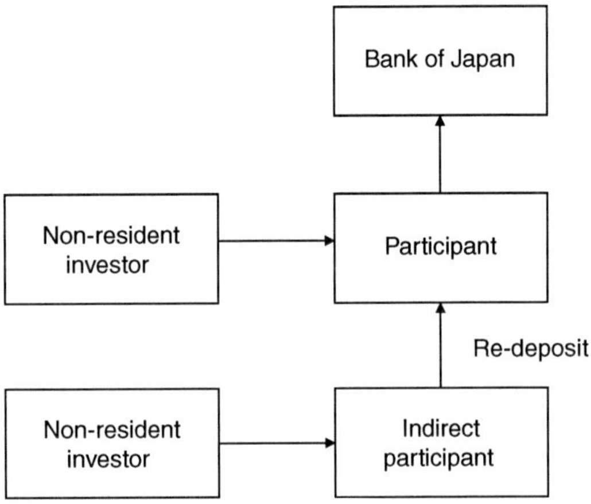

Figure 5.4 Historic system for Japanese Government Bonds

Source: Author.

Principles of the Japanese QFI system

1. To become a QFI a foreign financial firm must obtain approval from the Bank of Japan as a foreign indirect participant depositing JGBs with a participant or indirect participant (sub-custodian) in the Bank of Japan's book-entry system

2. The QFI applicant must also obtain approval from the Japanese tax authorities

3. QFI applicants must be resident companies of a state which has a tax treaty with Japan and which includes an article on exchange of information with Japan as the partner

4. If a foreign branch of QFI wishes to act in a QFI capacity, the branch office must also be in states with a tax treaty with Japan and which also must have an exchange of information article within the treaty

5. Non-resident investors must submit documentation to identify themselves as well as their ownership period and record of JGBs to the Japanese tax authorities via a QFI and sub-custodian

6. QFIs must keep book records and report information about holdings and records at beneficial owner (investor) level, to sub-custodians

7. QFIs must adhere to procedures and documentation prescribed and published in Cabinet Orders and Ministerial ordinance.

So from these seven principles, the reader can hopefully see the clear similarities to the US system. Exemption from withholding (i.e., 100% relief) can be gained only by

- submission of proper documentation;
- provision of agreements between foreign intermediaries and tax authorities;
- acceptable record keeping;
- adherence to rules; and
- only within jurisdictions with tax treaties (i.e., acceptable rules).

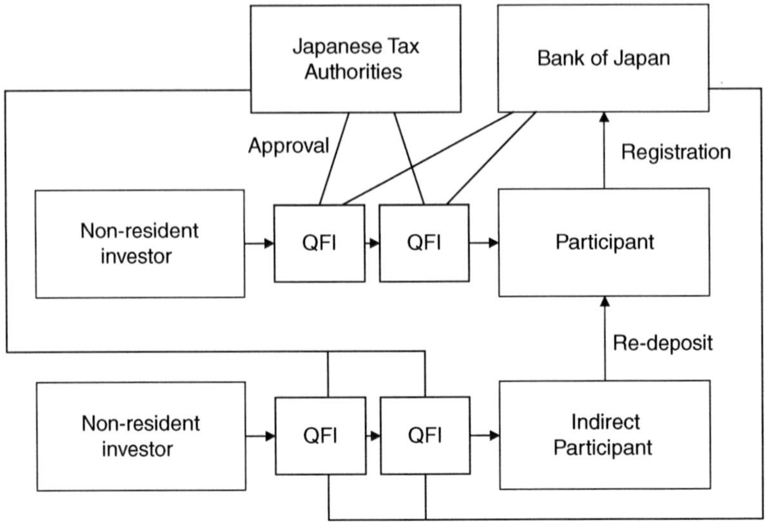

Figure 5.5 Japanese QI system

Source: Author.

Figure 5.5 shows the effect of the new regulations. The additional functional lines represent each QFI either alone or in a chain, needing to gain the approval of both the BOJ and the Japanese tax authorities. Each line will involve acceptance of the above principles and rules in order that foreign investors can gain the benefit of relief from withholding tax on the interest on JGBs.

IRELAND QI SYSTEM

So, the financial services firms around the world must act rather like the mythical two-headed god Janus. Their status and obligations are becoming more and more complex and these obligations vary depending on which way they are looking on behalf of their investors. The Irish followed the American example with a qualified intermediary system, although much less voluminous in content and depth, it has some significant differences from the American and the Japanese system. The Irish system is, like the US system, based on a domestic level of withholding which can be mitigated by documentation. There are currently about 30 financial firms signed up as QIs under the Irish system.

There are five significant differences between the US and Irish systems:

1. The tax rates are either fixed at the domestic withholding rate or are exempt. There are no bands of withholding or intermediary tax rates.

2. There is a possibility of a bond or guarantee required by the Irish QI against the risk of its failure to comply, where the US system has a regime of after the fact penalties.

3. The account structure required to operate the Irish QI system is much simpler and more related to pre-existing financial services structures that is, exempt and liable.

4. Tax information reporting is mandatory in the US scheme, but is by notice in the Irish scheme, that is, the guidance is given in the US regulations for 1042 and 1099 reporting which must occur each year. The Irish revenue on the other hand, will issue a notice if they want tax information reporting to be performed.

5. There exists a different entity type in the Irish regulations – Special Intermediary – for the purpose of dealing with ADRs.

The similarities are that both systems

- establish a matrix of income types and recipient types to whom the tax applies or does not apply;
- assume a default domestic level of withholding;
- allow documentation to mitigate the withholding level;
- require the withholding (exempt or liable) to be established at the time of the distribution;
- require documentation to a lower level than previously held by financial firms, that is, the identification of the real beneficial owner of income;
- require increased levels of automation; and
- require payment in specified time frames.

Most of the risks associated with the Irish regime are similar in nature to the US one. So, to that extent I'm not going to bore the reader with a replication of comments. Hopefully, having read the US description, the reader will be able to infer the risks and issues present in the Irish regime. It should also be interesting to see the parallels with the US regulations. Investors should consider for a moment, the difficulties faced by a custodian managing assets in a portfolio including the United States, Japan and Ireland where, for example, the custodian is in France. The custodian may well be an in-country agent for in-bound tax reclaims destined for the French tax authorities, a Qualified Intermediary under the US regulations (because he receives US source income for his clients), a Qualified Intermediary under the Irish regulations, for the same reason and also a Qualified Financial Intermediary with respect to Japanese Government Bond income. In each case, different documentary requirements apply, different withholding rates and methods of calculating and applying it and importantly different requirements for information reporting and audit compliance.

So, overall, the risk inherent for a custodian is less in the Irish QI regime than in the United States, simply because of the simpler structure, although Irish QIs can be required to put up a bond in advance. Also the costs associated with complying with the Irish regime are likely to be less as the differences to existing financial services practice are less. However, the absolute value of investments into the United States and Ireland are of course quite different which perhaps, to some extent, explains the scale of differences between the tow regimes.

Anyway, the following description of the Irish relief-at-source regime is provided with grateful thanks to, the Irish Revenue Commission for their help and information.

Firstly, and to make life a bit simpler, we must recognise that different terminology exists in each of these sets of regulations, but that the similarities in the words and phrases leave little doubt of the meanings.

AWA is an authorised withholding agent, that is, a firm that is authorised to make withholdings of tax on income. This is the same as a straightforward withholding agent described in the US regulations and in the general description of the tax reclaim models. Withholding tax in the context of the Irish regulations is dividend withholding tax, as opposed to the NRA withholding tax in the US regulations which applies to several more types of income. Qualified Intermediaries are the same in principle in the two models, although in the Irish model there is also the concept of a Special Intermediary. The tax authority, which is the IRS in the United States and Inland Revenue in the United Kingdom, is just termed Revenue here, for Ireland.

Principle

Dividends paid and other distributions ("relevant distributions") made by Irish resident companies are generally liable to a dividend withholding tax at the standard rate of income tax for the year of assessment in which the distribution is made.

The Irish resident company making the distribution is required to withhold the tax and pay it over to the Irish Revenue. However, the legislation makes provision for an entity known as an Authorised Withholding Agent (AWA) to act for the company making the distribution. If an AWA is involved, the amount of the distribution can be paid gross by the paying company to the AWA, who then takes over responsibility for applying the withholding tax rules.

The basic principle is that withholding tax must be deducted at the time the distribution is being made unless the company or the AWA has satisfied itself that the recipient is a non-liable person and is entitled to receive the distribution without the deduction of withholding tax. To this extent the Irish rules are the same as the US rules, in terms of the principle applied. The deposit rules are however much simpler. All withholding tax must be paid to Revenue by the fourteenth of the month following that in which the distribution is made.

Certain recipients of distributions are specifically excluded from the scope of the tax while certain other persons are entitled to an exemption. It should be noted that exemption is not automatic and must be established by means of an appropriate declaration of exemption, which must be completed by the applicant and accompanied by the necessary certification. Again the principle here is the same as the US regulations in that any lower withholding rate (i.e., exemption) that could be applied will only be allowed given the existence of appropriate documentation. The actual documentation, whilst simple in form, does however have more complexity in structure than the simple W-8BEN forms in the US regulations.

The legislation relating to withholding tax is contained in Chapter 8A of Part 6 of, and Schedule 2A to, the Taxes Consolidation Act, 1997. It was introduced in Section 27 of the Finance Act, 1999 and amended by Sections 30 and 59 of the Finance Act, 2000 and Section 43 of the Finance Act, 2001.

So, like the other relief-at-source regimes, there are different types of income and also different types of recipients that attract different tax treatments .

Types of distributions liable to withholding tax

Withholding tax at the standard rate of income tax applies to all relevant distributions made by Irish resident paying companies. For the purposes of the withholding tax legislation, relevant distributions are:

1. **Cash distributions.**

2. **Scrip dividends –** This is where a shareholder opts to take additional shares instead of a cash dividend in situations where the paying company gives its shareholders the option of taking either cash or additional shares. In such cases the shareholder who elects to take additional shares instead of cash is treated as if he/she received a distribution of an amount equal to the cash dividend which the shareholder would have received if he/she had not elected to take the shares. When this

happens the distributing company is required, when issuing the additional shares to each shareholder (other than a shareholder exempted from withholding tax) to issue a reduced number of shares instead of withholding a cash amount from the distribution. The paying company must then pay to Revenue an amount of withholding tax equal to tax at the standard rate of income tax on the cash amount which the shareholder would have received if he/she had not elected to take the shares instead of cash.

3. **Distributions in a non-cash form** – This is where a paying company makes a distribution, which consists of something other than cash (but not a scrip dividend). In such cases the paying company which makes the non-cash distribution to the shareholder (other than a shareholder exempted from withholding tax) is liable to pay to the Irish Revenue an amount of withholding tax equal to the tax which would have been payable on the distribution if it had been in cash and taxed at the standard rate of income tax. Furthermore, since no tax is actually withheld from the non-cash distribution the paying company is empowered to recover from each shareholder (other than shareholders exempted from withholding tax) an amount equal to the tax paid to the Irish Revenue in respect of that shareholder's non-cash distribution.

Distributions not liable to withholding tax

1. Distributions made to Ministers of the Government;

2. Distributions falling within scope of EU Parent/Subsidiary Directive;

3. Stapled Stock arrangements;

4. Distributions which are not liable to income tax in the hands of the recipients; and

5. Distributions made by an Irish resident company to another Irish resident company of which it is a 51% subsidiary.

Persons exempt from withholding tax

Exempt resident persons (excluded persons)

I won't go into detail on this section because this book deals with cross-border issues,that is, non-resident aliens. However, it's instructive to realise that such regulations can often, in order to address one type of issue, often have terms which relate to domestic residents too.

Exempt non-resident persons

Just for clarity, the term "relevant territory" used in the Irish regulations means a Member State of the European Union other than the State or, not being such a Member State, a country with which Ireland has a double-taxation treaty. Currently, Ireland has double-taxation treaties with 39 other countries, including 13 of the 14 other Member States of the European Union. Ireland does not have a double-taxation treaty with Greece but, as a Member State of the European Union, Greece is also treated as a "relevant territory".

The Irish QI system, as I've noted, gives exemption to certain types of recipient on dividend income. As with the US QI system, that exemption must be proved prior to receipt of the payment.

The following is a list of types of non-resident persons exempt from withholding tax:

1. An unincorporated body of persons, such as a charity or superannuation fund, which is resident for the purposes of tax in a relevant territory.

2. Individuals who are neither resident nor ordinarily resident in the State but are resident for the purposes of tax, in a relevant territory.

3. Companies resident for the purposes of tax in a relevant territory and which are not controlled by Irish residents.

4. Companies which are not resident in the State, which are under the ultimate control of persons who are neither resident nor ordinarily resident in the State, but are resident for the purposes of tax in a relevant territory.

5. Companies, the principal class of shares of which (or of a company of which it is at least a 75% subsidiary) is substantially and regularly traded on a recognised stock exchange in a relevant territory

6. Companies which are wholly owned by two or more companies, each of whose principal class of shares are substantially and regularly traded on one or more recognised stock exchanges in a relevant territory.

7. Parent companies in other EU Member States receiving distributions from Irish resident unlimited subsidiary companies in which the parent company holds at least 25% of the capital.

Before accepting that non-resident persons are exempt, the paying company, or AWA, must be satisfied that the person, if not a QI, is the person beneficially entitled to the distribution and has made the appropriate declaration of exemption with supporting certification to the company making the distribution. If the distribution is being paid to an exempt non-resident person through a QI or a chain of QIs, the declaration of exemption and supporting certification must be made to the QI from whom the dividend will be received.

Main participants and their obligations

Irish resident paying companies – An Irish resident paying company making relevant distributions is obliged to deduct withholding tax (at the standard rate of income tax which applies at the time the distribution is made) unless the company has satisfied itself that

1. the recipient is a non-liable person and is entitled to receive the distribution without deduction of withholding tax, or

2. the distribution is being made in the first instance to an AWA.

All withholding tax deducted by the paying company must be paid to the Irish Revenue by the fourteenth of the month following that in which the distribution is made. Payments must be accompanied by a return, which must be in an electronic format approved by the Irish Revenue. In exceptional circumstances, where the Revenue are satisfied that the paying company does not have the facilities to make a return in electronic format, they may authorise the paying company to make the return in writing in a form authorised by the Revenue. Again, there is a clear analogy here with the US regulations and in particular the structure for deposits. The US uses the EFTPS system and the Irish also require an electronic payment method as the default.

The paying company is obliged to retain all declarations and notifications received from shareholders and intermediaries for the longer of 6 years or the period ending 3 years after it ceased to pay distributions to the person who made the declaration or gave the notification to the paying company.

Company registrars. – Where company registrars handle distributions on behalf of quoted companies their obligations are similar to those of the paying companies.

Authorised withholding agent (AWA) – As noted already, the withholding tax legislation makes provision for an entity known as an AWA. The AWA can receive distributions from the paying company without the deduction of withholding tax regardless of whether the ultimate beneficiary is a liable or an exempt person. However the AWA then takes over the responsibility of the paying company as far as withholding tax is concerned. It must apply withholding tax, where applicable, when paying on the distributions to its clients, pay this withholding tax over to Revenue and make returns to the Revenue, in the same way as paying companies. An AWA must be authorised to act as such by Revenue.

Obligations of an AWA under the withholding tax scheme

An AWA must give notice in writing to each paying company, from which it is to receive relevant distributions on behalf of other persons, of the fact that it is an AWA. This allows those companies to make the distributions to the AWA without applying withholding tax. In the absence of such notification, the company must apply withholding tax to the distributions.

On receiving the distributions, the AWA must operate the withholding tax scheme as if it were the company making the distribution. Thus, the AWA must make the appropriate deduction of withholding tax when it pays on the distributions, or amounts representing the distributions, and must account for that tax to the Irish Revenue by the fourteenth of the month following that in which the distribution is made by the company.

Qualifying intermediary (QI)

A substantial portion of investment in Irish companies is made through an intermediary (e.g., bank or stock broking firm) or, indeed, through a chain of intermediaries. This is recognised in the withholding tax legislation, which makes provision for exemption at source in such cases provided the intermediary accepts an additional administrative burden. In order for an intermediary to receive dividends gross on behalf of non-liable clients, the intermediary must have entered into a "Qualifying Intermediary Agreement" with the Irish Revenue. In doing so the intermediary becomes a "Qualifying Intermediary" (QI) under the withholding tax legislation.

Criteria for becoming a QI

In order to become a QI, an intermediary must-

1. be resident in Ireland,

2. if not resident in Ireland, be resident for tax purposes in a relevant territory,

3. hold (or be wholly owned by a person who holds) a banking license in Ireland or in a relevant territory, or

4. be a member of the Irish Stock Exchange or a recognised stock exchange in a relevant territory, or,

5. be, in the opinion of Revenue, a person suitable to be a QI, and

6. enter into a QI agreement with Revenue and be authorised by Revenue to act as a QI.

QI agreement

Before an intermediary can be authorised to act as a QI it must enter into a QI agreement with the Irish Revenue. Under the terms of the QI agreement, the intermediary undertakes

1. to operate the withholding tax scheme (including the making of returns to the Irish Revenue) in a correct and efficient manner,

2. to accept any declaration or notification given to it in connection with the withholding tax scheme and to retain such declarations or notifications for the longer of 6 years, or the period ending 3 years after it has ceased to receive distributions on behalf of the person who made the declaration or gave the notification,

3. to exercise a duty of care and verification in relation to such declarations and notifications,

4. to make available for inspection declarations of exemption and notifications made to the intermediary in connection with the withholding tax scheme;

5. to provide the Revenue with an auditor's report on its compliance with the withholding tax scheme after it has been operating the QI agreement for one year and to provide further auditor's reports when requested to do so by the Revenue.

6. to allow for the verification of its compliance with the withholding tax scheme by the Irish Revenue in any manner considered appropriate by Revenue.

The agreement may also, in certain circumstances, require the provision of a bond or guarantee by the intermediary to protect the Exchequer against fraud or negligence in the operation of the QI agreement and the withholding tax scheme.

The Irish Revenue allows QIs to create and maintain two separate and distinct categories of funds or accounts known respectively as exempt and liable funds or accounts. In advance of a distribution being made, the QI can accept declarations of exemption from non-liable persons and notifications from other QIs and, at the foot of these declarations and notifications, notify the paying company in writing whether the distribution is for the benefit of non-liable or liable persons. The distributions for non-liable persons can then be paid gross by the paying company and will go into the QI's exempt account while the distributions for liable persons will go into the liable account.

Intermediaries operating through nominee companies

In some instances an intermediary can operate through one or more nominee companies and might want to have these nominee companies covered by the QI authorisation. While this is possible, it can only be allowed where the intermediary advises the Irish Revenue in writing of any nominee companies who wish to operate under the terms of the QI agreement. Such nominee companies also have to execute a power of attorney granting the principal full power to enter into a QI agreement with the Revenue on their behalf.

The QI authorisation will expire naturally after 7 years. This doesn't prevent the Irish Revenue and the intermediary from agreeing to renew, or enter into a new, QI agreement, nor does it prevent the Revenue from authorising the intermediary as a QI for a further 7-year period. However, the Revenue reserves the right to revoke a QI authorisation at any time if it's satisfied that the QI has failed to comply with the QI agreement or is otherwise "unsuitable" to be an QI.

Where revocation occurs, the fact that the authorisation has been revoked is published in "Iris Oifigiúil", the official Irish Government gazette. So, there's no hiding place for bad practice and investors have the opportunity to review these publications before selecting a custodian.

Obligations of a QI

A QI, which receives, on behalf of its clients, relevant distributions made by a company resident in Ireland, or amounts representing such distributions paid on to it by another QI, is required to maintain two separate funds or accounts in relation to such distributions and amounts, an Exempt Fund and a Liable Fund.

The Exempt Fund or account should include

1. excluded persons and qualifying non-resident persons who have made to the QI the appropriate declaration of exemption, and

2. other QIs who have advised the QI that the distributions, or amounts representing such distributions, to be paid on to them by the QI are to be received by the other QIs on behalf of persons in their Exempt Funds.

The Liable Fund is to include the remainder of the QI's clients.

A QI must notify the company making the distributions or, if the distributions are made through a chain of QIs, the QI (if any) immediately above it in the chain, by way of notice in writing, as to whether the distributions to be received by it from the company or the other QI, as the case may be, are to be received for the benefit of persons in its exempt account or liable account. The QI must keep its exempt and liable funds up-to-date and must notify the company, by way of notice in writing, of updates as often as may be necessary. The company must apply withholding tax to a distribution unless it has been notified by the QI that the distribution is to be received by the QI for the benefit of a person in its exempt fund.

Reporting

A QI is obliged to submit a return to Revenue when requested in writing to do so. This return must be made within the time specified, which won't be less than 30 days. When requesting a return, the Revenue may specify that they require only details of a particular class or classes of distributions relating to a specific period or they may request details of all distributions relating to a specific period. For example, details of all payments over £1,000 might be required or all distributions relating to a particular company or companies. A QI return must be in an electronic format approved by the Irish Revenue. Each return must contain in relation to the information sought by Revenue

1. the name and address of each company from which the QI has received distributions on behalf of its clients during the period specified and of each other QI from which it receives amounts representing such distributions on behalf of its clients;

2. the amount of each such distribution;

3. the name and address of the clients to whom the distributions were given by the QI; and

4. whether those clients were liable or non-liable persons.

Documentation

As mentioned earlier, exemption from withholding tax is not automatic and must be established by means of an appropriate declaration of exemption, which must be completed by the applicant.

This declaration has to be in a form approved by Revenue and, in the case of qualifying non-resident persons, must, where appropriate be supported by documentary evidence. This equates roughly to the US position of W-8BEN as the declaration and the application of KYC rules which would provide the supporting documentation. The supporting documentation is as follows:

1. A declaration made by a non-resident person (not being a company) must be accompanied by a certificate of residence from the tax authority in the country of the person's residence.

2. A declaration by the trustee or trustees of a non-resident discretionary trust must be accompanied by
   a. a certificate given by the tax authority of the country in which the trust is, by virtue of the law of that territory, resident for the purposes of tax, certifying that the trust is resident in that territory,
   b. a certificate from the trustee or trustees showing the names and addresses of the settlers and beneficiaries of the trust, and
   c. a certificate from the Irish Revenue indicating that they have seen the certification and have noted its contents. In this context it should be noted that the withholding tax legislation defines the term "beneficiary" in a wide manner. The term means any person who, directly or indirectly, is beneficially entitled under the discretionary trust, or may, through the exercise of any power or powers conferred on that person or any other person or persons, reasonably expect to become beneficially entitled under the trust to income or capital or to have any income or capital applied for that person's benefit or to receive any other benefit.

3. A declaration made by a non-resident company which is claiming the exemption on the basis that it is either
   a. ultimately controlled by persons resident for the purposes of tax in a relevant territory, or

b. a company, the principal class of shares of which (or of a company of which its is a 75% subsidiary) is substantially and regularly traded on a recognised stock exchange in a relevant territory, or
c. a company which is wholly owned by two or more companies, each of whose principal class of shares is substantially and regularly traded on one or more recognised stock exchanges in a relevant territory, must be accompanied by a certificate from the company's auditor certifying that in the opinion of the auditor it meets one of these criteria.

4. A declaration from a company claiming the exemption on the basis that it is resident for the purposes of tax in a relevant territory and is not under the control, directly or indirectly, of a person or persons resident in Ireland must be accompanied by
   a. a certificate given by the tax authority of the relevant territory in which the company is, by virtue of the law of that territory, resident for the purposes of tax certifying that the company is resident in that territory, and
   b. a certificate signed by the auditor of the company certifying that in the opinion of the auditor the company is not under the control, either directly or indirectly, of a person or persons who is or are resident in the Republic of Ireland.

Period of validity of exemption forms

Exemption declarations for resident (excluded) persons remain valid until such time as

1. the excluded person notifies the paying company or the QI that they have ceased to be an excluded person, or

2. the paying company or QI becomes aware, for whatever reason, that the person who made the declaration has ceased to be an excluded person.

Exemption declarations for qualifying non-resident persons remain valid for a maximum period of 6 years. This period of validity is determined by the date on which the relevant certificates accompanying the exemption declarations are issued. The legislation confirms that these certificates remain valid for the period from the date of issue until 31 December in the fifth year following the year in which the certificate was issued, thus providing for a maximum period of validity of 6 years if a certificate was issued on 1 January in a particular year. This is analogous to the US form W-8BEN albeit the validity period is longer. What's also interesting is the more extensive degree to which the declaration by a person is certified accurate by others, such as auditors and local tax authorities. This means that whilst obtaining the declaration will give the exemption required, obtaining the declaration in correct form for a custodian will be a more costly process. The US Form W-8BEN is a self-certification, whereas the Irish form is also a sort of self-certification, inasmuch as the person claiming the exemption is the one who ultimately signs the form, but the latter has third parties attesting to its accuracy.

The exemption declarations from *excluded* or *qualifying non-resident persons* can only be accepted where the declaration forms have been fully completed and signed and where the recipient of the declaration (paying company, AWA or QI) has no reasonable grounds to believe that the declaration (and any accompanying certificates) is not true or incorrect.

The sub-accounting issue

Where a distribution is to be made directly to an exempt shareholder by the company or by the AWA, the shareholder must provide evidence of entitlement to exemption to the company or the AWA. If the distribution is to be made through a QI, the evidence of entitlement to exemption must be given to the QI. That QI will then notify the company of the amount of the distribution to be received on behalf of exempt persons. Where a distribution is to be made to an exempt shareholder through a series of QIs, the evidence of entitlement of the shareholder to an exemption must be given to the QI from whom the shareholder will finally receive payment. In this case that QI will convey to the QI immediately above it, the amount to be received on behalf of exempt persons. That second QI will then convey details (of the amount of the distribution to be received by it which will ultimately be passed on to shareholders who are exempt) to the company. This is a critical issue. As with the US regulations, this requirement is the one that protects the identity of the beneficial owner/recipient from other financial firms in the chain who would otherwise be competitors of the firms below it. This chain approach applies through any number of intermediaries, provided that they are all QIs. If any intermediary in the chain is not a QI, withholding tax will apply. The only exception to this rule is American Depository receipts, to which special arrangements apply.

American Depositary Receipts or ADRs are one of a class of instruments known as Depositary Receipts. Other examples are Global Depositary Receipts and International Depositary Receipts. ADRs are US dollar denominated securities issued by a Depositary bank in the United States and representing ownership of non-US shares. A simplified procedure applies to ADRs which establishes a different kind of entity in the chain –

the Specified Intermediary (SI). In many respects an SI is similar to a QI but there are a number of significant differences. Among these are:

1. an SI does not have to be authorised by the Irish Revenue; and

2. an SI does not have to enter into an agreement with the Irish Revenue and accordingly doesn't have to provide an auditor's report relating to the intermediary's compliance with an agreement. However an SI does have to enter into an agreement with the QI (or with another SI if it receives distributions through them) under which it undertakes to supply the QI or the other SI, or, if preferred directly to Irish Revenue, returns showing details, such as name and address information and amounts of any distributions, or classes of distributions, which the Revenue has asked for. Such information has to be furnished by the SI within 21 days of the receipt of a notice requesting such information.

The Irish Revenue does reserve the right to revoke the right of an SI to be treated as an SI for the purposes of the withholding tax scheme if they're satisfied that the SI has failed to comply with its obligations with regard to the withholding tax scheme and particularly the obligation to furnish details such as name and address information and amounts of any distributions, or classes of distributions which Revenue has asked for.

Hopefully, no-one will now make the mistake of saying that relief at source is easy. The concepts are indeed logical and simple to understand. The consequences are far more complex.

CHAPTER 6

Long Form Claims

In contrast to relief at source, long form claiming takes place after the payment has been made to a client, net of statutory rate tax.

There are two types of long form claim:

- Quick refund
- Long form claim

QUICK REFUND

While a tax authority generally wants money as fast as possible, in some markets, the tax authority permits their withholding agents to aggregate payments of tax on distributions and make those payments at set intervals. This gives a commercial opportunity to the withholding agent as well as a benefit to the tax authority. In the former case, the withholding agent can put in place a "quick refund" product essentially providing a process to its customers whereby if they provide relevant documentation about the entitlement of one of their customers, they will make an adjustment to the tax amount accrued for payment to their tax authority and remit the funds back to their customer. The tax authority benefits primarily because in the absence of such a mechanism, the administrative load would eventually fall on them as a long form claim.

LONG FORM CLAIMS

This chapter provides a basic overview of withholding tax reclaims. It is not intended as a detailed guide, nor is it a "How to" manual. The complexities involved would fill two books at least. This chapter is designed to give the reader a basic understanding of the level of complexity involved, the scale of the problems faced by custodians in this area and enough understanding to enable the institutional investor to ask intelligent questions relating to his portfolio that will enable him and his custodian to provide the best possible return.

Figure 6.1 reminds us of the simple reclaim process using the taxation principle thread.

At the point where we most effectively join the process, links 1 through 4 have already taken place. The income event, in this case a corporate dividend, has been administered. The withholding agent, in the absence of information about the investor, has withheld tax at the maximum rate possible in order to protect himself from any financial liability and to meet his own domestic law requirements.

The custodian now realises that his investor has paid too much tax. This may seem like a simple act to describe. In practice, most custodians are dealing with a client base in the hundreds if not thousands, where the tax profile of each client is different, often in very subtle ways. This is why, traditionally, withholding tax has been a very expensive process to implement. Before Step 6 can take place in the process diagram, a number of factors need to be assessed including:

- The client's legal status may prevent or affect his ability to reclaim the over-withheld tax.

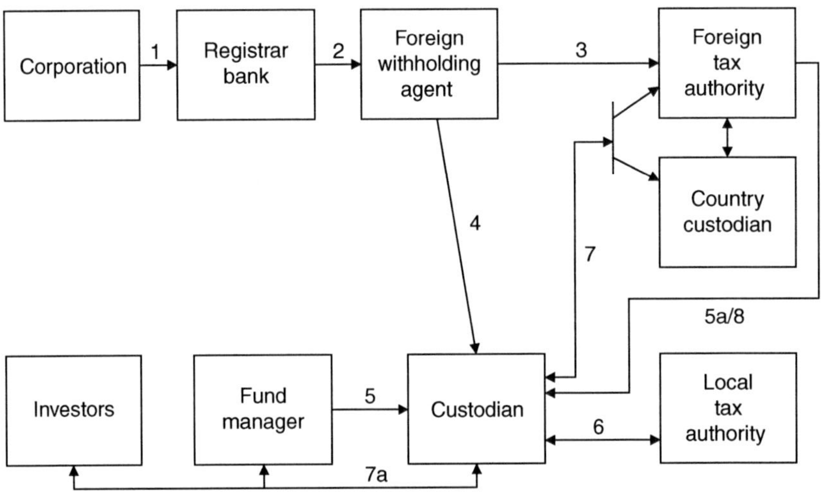

Figure 6.1 Overview of long form claim process

Source: Author.

- His documentation proving his status may or may not be out of date.
- The time delay between the sufferance of over-withholding and the date of the tax reclaim may mean the investor has fallen out of the statute of limitations.
- The type of income instrument may have special rules applying that change the amount of reclaimable tax.
- If the security was lent over the ex-date, there may be issues over who is entitled to the tax reclaim amount.
- The investor may not have supplied power of attorney to the custodian which will delay the process by an unknown amount of time.

All of these factors have to be weighed, for each and every income event, if the investor's best interests are to be served. Over-riding all of this of course, the DTAs themselves change from time to time, as do the procedures that the authorities use to implement the DTAs.

Steps 5 and 5a are both preparatory stages that a custodian must have in place prior to or in parallel with the core reclaiming process.

Step 5 in the process diagram represents the fund manager or investor providing information to the custodian and the custodian evaluating the availability of a tax reclaim.

Step 5a represents the custodian requesting from each tax authority and acquiring, a supply of the relevant tax reclaim forms. This raises a benchmarking process that should ensure that the custodian has sufficient forms for its expected volume of tax reclaims. Failure to do this will result in time delays which in turn will affect the custodian's overall performance against a benchmark of time to receiving the tax reclaim funds.

Step 6 represents the custodian requesting proof of domicile from the local tax authority that is, the tax authority in the country where the investor is resident for tax purposes. In order to do this, the custodian must have already identified the nature of the tax reclaim available. This is not because the local tax authority needs to know this information. It's because the most efficient way to expedite the process is to have a stamp from the local tax authority, citing domicile, actually on the tax reclaim form that the foreign tax authority receives. So the custodian, normally will complete the tax reclaim form as far as is possible, then send it off, usually by post, to the local tax office of the investor, with a covering letter requesting a stamp of authority to demonstrate that the investor cited on the form is indeed resident in the country for tax purposes.

Step 7 marks the stage when the custodian has received the tax reclaim form back from the local tax authority and he is free to send it to the foreign tax authority. It is usually from this point that most benchmarking takes place for the purpose of costing a contractual tax service. The most efficient method, at this stage, is for the custodian to have been given a Power of Attorney (PoA) to sign the tax reclaim form on behalf of the client (see **Step 7a**). This is a very fragmented process in practice. Some clients, whether from a control perspective, a monitoring perspective or simply because of internal risk management policy, may not provide PoA for this purpose. Step 7 in the diagram is a not a simple deposition to a tax authority. There are some tax authorities, most notably the French, where a tax reclaim is not recognised by a tax authority unless it has been delivered through an approved "in-country" agent bank. So the custodian or investor must know to which jurisdictions this rule applies and ensure that an appropriate relationship is in place with an in-country agent to file tax reclaims on their behalf.

Step 7a is therefore only applicable if PoA has not been given to the entity making the final tax reclaim. Given the chain structure of the custody process, this signature may have to pass through more than one set of hands, and be sent back through the same route, before the custodian is again in possession of a properly completed and duly signed valid tax reclaim form. However it is not uncommon, albeit not preferred by custodians, that signatures are required on forms by clients. Many clients who hold wide portfolios, but whose internal policies require a direct signature on such forms, may see many tax reclaim forms on a regular basis. It is questionable, whether these clients have the technical expertise to assess the reclaims adequately before signing and returning them to their custodians. It's arguable that if they had such expertise, they could have filed the reclaim themselves anyway. It's likely, I believe that many investors are signing these forms through policy without realising either the benefits of PoA or the risk attendant to effectively citing the details of a tax reclaim as correct without proper checking.

Step 8 represents a tax authority approving a tax reclaim under the appropriate DTA and remitting the refund to the applicant. This is most frequently done with an actual cheque in the post. Of course, if the reclaim was submitted via an in-country agent, the refund will follow a similar path back through the in-country agent to the investor or custodian concerned.

The last major change in withholding tax procedure was the advent of the Euro in 2001. Apart from the massive re-organisation of IT resource, tax authorities themselves had a hard task, re-designing tax reclaim forms to show Euro denominations. Other factors caused havoc in the changeover period, not the least the fact that different European countries changed their systems at different times.

Beneficial owners

A beneficial owner is the ultimate owner of the benefit in an income event. So, a private investor is also a beneficial owner. Different withholding tax rates can apply depending on the tax status of the beneficial owner and these must be researched in depth if the correct withholding and any reclaim is to be pursued successfully.

Documentation of beneficial owners is important because it's the primary documentation, usually obtained in the account opening process, that establishes how income is treated.

Financial instruments

There is clearly a range of financial instruments, income from which can be affected by withholding tax and these do change from time to time. It has to be said however, that the vast majority of withheld tax falls into the two categories of tax on corporate dividends and tax on royalties.

However withholding tax can also apply in certain circumstances to a variety of securities including ordinary shares, Government stocks, debenture stocks, convertible and bearer bonds, fixed term deposits, bank interest and unit trusts.

The role of sub-custodians

Sub-custodians play a vital role in the reclaim process and it's important for investors to be aware of this. Dealing with custodians who have not only a wide network of sub-custodians, but also where those sub-custody locations fit with the investor's portfolio, is an important element of the custody selection process. A global custodian may provide a globally based asset management and safe-keeping service but this is often underpinned by a network of smaller custodians who have specialist knowledge of their particular market or a particular area of the business. This is analogous to outsourcing, although not structured in the same way. A sub-custodian will provide in-country services which would otherwise be difficult or expensive for a global custodian to provide.

There are also some circumstances where an in-country custodian is also the route for a tax reclaim to be submitted rather a tax authority.

The role of investors

The investor only has a role in the relief-at-source or tax reclaim process if he has not derogated his responsibilities to a custodian under a PoA. The nature of the PoA granted is often an issue for investors as their financial affairs are complex and the requirements of internal policy (for institutional investors) and compliance may make it difficult for an investor to provide a blanket PoA to a custodian. Whilst abuse may be unlikely, since the custodian will have access to extremely sensitive information about the investor, it's more often the case that a limited PoA is given to a custodian with a remit solely to provide specific services. This limits the liability on both sides and makes operational compliance and thus risk lower.

Operationally, this is further complicated by the fact that many investors subdivide their portfolios in different ways. Some may wish to take direct responsibility for certain markets and outsource/derogate responsibility for others to the custodian. Again for reduction of risk and compliance, PoAs may be limited not just by the process empowered but also by the jurisdictions in which that process is derogated.

However, if no such derogation has taken place, the investor has the ultimate responsibility for ensuring that the information on any tax reclaim form is correct. The investor will be supplied with completed tax reclaim forms on a regular basis which he will have to sign and return to the custodian to facilitate efficient filing.

This area is one of the most aggravating for custodians. Investors, many of whom don't understand the process (or the tax itself), usually have other priorities (although I would hope that having read this book, the priority given to withholding tax reclaims would rise). Best practice would require that all parties recognise the scale of the value that a tax reclaim can represent (cf. Chapter 1) and make best efforts to facilitate the process. Unfortunately, investors often fail to make adequate provision of resources to deal with and turn around tax reclaims effectively. In my recent consultancy work I have often had to make note of the fact that a Service Level Agreement (SLA) should be just as much about what the investor is committing to as what the custodian is committing to. In many areas, investors can cause problems and indeed failures in the SLA, by not understanding the processes that custodians engage in and where they fit into the equation (hopefully this book will alleviate at least one portion of this problem). If the benchmark starting point for a tax reclaim is the income event notification, then, if the investor has not provided a PoA to the custodian, many days can be added to the process simply in order to get an investor's signature on the required forms. The benchmarking process described elsewhere, makes note of the fact that the benchmarking process should be directed, not just at the custodian but also at the investor who can materially affect the time taken to recoup funds for re-investment. The resources required include personnel with a combination of the knowledge to be able to assess accuracy to a given level and the authority to sign and return the forms to the custodian. The most common mistake of course, particularly for an investor new to the issue, is that he wishes to "see" everything. The only way this can be achieved in the tax reclaim arena is for no PoA to be granted, thus requiring all forms to be submitted to the investor. Whilst this solves the investor's hopefully temporary insecurity, it makes the investor liable for any errors. If the investor knows enough to make this judgement, he probably doesn't need the custodian for this purpose anyway.

The role of the investor is therefore much more effectively focused on establishing the level of competency of his custodian through detailed benchmarking. Having established the scope of competency, a properly constructed SLA should define how the custodian operates. The SLA will define, in turn, the exact nature of the PoA that is granted to the custodian. This is the way it should be done. Unfortunately, in practice, investors don't always perform this process and sign over too much power to a custodian in a generic PoA which can leave the investor exposed.

Certifying residency

As far as the foreign tax authority is concerned, it will only approve a reclaim or pay a reclaim, or indeed a relief-at-source application, if there is documentary evidence of the tax status of the beneficial owner.

In some cases the stamp on the reclaim form from the beneficial owner's tax office is sufficient. In others, in addition to this, supporting documentation is required. It is important to understand that citizenship of a country is not necessarily the same as residency for tax purposes and specialist advice may be needed to ensure correct forms are filed.

Responsibility for accuracy

Fundamentally, whoever is signing a tax reclaim form is accepting responsibility for its accuracy and truthfulness. If the investor has not given PoA to the custodian, then his custodian will be sending him completed tax reclaim forms for signature on a regular basis. This regularity can breed contempt and the investor/beneficial owner, must be very aware and very careful. They are not just signing the form in order that it can be processed. They are filing a legal claim under treaty regulation for a refund of tax.

The reality is that tax authorities have limited technology in place compared to custodians and it is entirely possible, given the volume of reclaims that are filed annually to some markets, for duplicate reclaims to be filed that is, two reclaims for the same single over-withheld amount. Clearly not an acceptable situation. In the absence of a PoA, the investor is responsible for making sure that not only is this particular reclaim correct in every respect, but also that it is the only reclaim filed for this particular purpose. This places great responsibility on investors, who may have withheld PoA for entirely subjective reasons.

Even when PoA is in place, this issue becomes moot. The wording on a PoA becomes extremely important, as does the wording of any other contractual document applying to this process, most notably the SLA.

If an investor has provided a PoA to a custodian, the custodian can complete the reclaim form *and* sign it. However the signature must be appended to the words "on behalf of". So, as you can see, the trace still goes ultimately back to the investor/beneficial owner. The degree of liability accepted by the custodian with respect to the accuracy of a tax reclaim is determined by the wording on the PoA and in the SLA. Legally, the issue goes to whether, in this respect, the custodian is contracted to provide "reasonable efforts" or "best efforts" in conducting calculations of validity, eligibility and value. In risk management terms, for the best interests of both parties, it is important to make the allocation of responsibility explicitly clear.

Service level agreements (SLAs)

Service Level Agreements do not usually address tax reclaim issues beyond defining whether or not such processes are offered, the markets in which they are offered, whether contractual tax is offered and the basic reporting on such activities that will be provided.

As seen in the last section, best practice in this area can be greatly improved by investors taking a more direct interest at the beginning of their relationship with a custodian. Chapter 12 on Benchmarking gives some good guidelines to the types of question and standards that an investor can ask of a custodian's tax operations department.

Also, as I've said already, I firmly believe that SLAs should be two way and that each part of the process should be understood by an investor to the extent that a custodian can show the investor how their actions can impact on the efficiencies of the processes involved.

The role of tax authorities

Tax authorities have two hats in the withholding tax process. From one perspective they are "local" tax authorities with respect to beneficial owners/investors resident for tax purposes in their jurisdiction. From the other perspective, they are "foreign" tax authorities receiving claims for refunds from foreign investors and custodians.

Proof of tax residency

For residents of their country, tax authorities provide proof of domicile for tax purposes. A custodian or investor who submits a completed reclaim form or a request for relief at source must ask their local tax office to stamp the form or provide some other documentation to attest that the subject of the tax form is indeed, as far as they are concerned, a resident of that country for tax purposes. This is basically what will establish eligibility for treaty rate benefits as far as the foreign tax authority is concerned.

Sources of reclaim forms

Tax authorities, in the main, process tax reclaims manually. That is they receive printed forms from custodians or investors. The source of these forms is usually, of course, the tax authorities themselves.

When the countries of the European Union each scrapped their own currencies and adopted the Euro, this caused a problem because all the tax authorities in those countries had their own forms all of which showed their previous domestic currency.

The opportunity to harmonise these forms across Europe was lost, which would have been a major step towards ultimately allowing an automation of these forms. However, each country did take a different approach to the provision of the many thousands of forms required by custodians and investors on almost a daily basis.

In particular of course, some custodians already had large stocks of these forms and decisions on what was to be done at the changeover weren't made clear until very close to the deadline.

Some countries allowed custodians to cross out and replace the domestic currency symbol with the Euro symbol, the pragmatic approach. Others required all previous forms to be used up first before they released new forms.

Whilst this is history now, it serves to highlight the fact that, however politically desirable harmonisation may be across Europe, its administrative systems, particularly in tax, are a long way behind in capability.

While the basic source of original forms remains the tax authorities, both internal IT departments and also external solution providers have not been slow to realise that being able to reproduce such forms from an electronic template, is a way of improving the efficiency of the process. This of course has to be done with the knowledge of the relevant tax authority whether directly or indirectly.

Receipt and assessment of reclaims

Although there is no network of linked tax authorities nor a unified system currently capable of transmitting and receiving tax reclaims, the tax reclaim forms are produced; they must still be delivered, once fully and properly completed, by normal mail. In relative terms this is a very small cost in the process. However, in operational terms it does include an element of risk both in the internal processing of reclaims through the post room and of course the larger risk that the reclaim will get lost somewhere between the custodian and the tax authority.

Custodians generally have a labour-intensive process to follow up filed reclaims, precisely because there is so little connectivity among tax authorities themselves, or between tax authorities and custodians. This labour-intensive process begins with the original filing. In a best practice environment filings would either be recorded on delivery or be followed up a few days after sending so that the client record could be updated.

Proof of identity

One of the keys to successful tax reclaims is the demonstration of identity. Fundamentally the tax authority in receipt of a claim for recovery of tax must be assured that the entity making the claim is who they say they are. This tends to be much more onerous in relief-at-source regimes (e.g., USA) since the tax authority will be granting relief from tax based on advance documentation that is, it will not have the cash. On the other hand, in a reclaim process, the tax authority already has the cash and so it can afford to adopt a different approach. In most cases proof of identity can take several forms. For instance, in order to have opened an account with a custodian, most investors, institutional or otherwise will have had to follow money laundering control regulations, known as KYC rules. These will include some evidence by the investor of their identity and particularly their status. There may also be room for a self-certification of identity. Finally, since the investor is undoubtedly registered with its own tax authority, this latter body can effectively certify that the applicant for a reclaim is known to them as a resident of their jurisdiction.

Proof of sufferance of double tax

Proof of sufferance is often a difficult area, which may seem strange to many readers. Of course the tax authority receiving a reclaim is facing several questions. Is the person making the reclaim the person they say they are? Did they actually receive the income they say they received and was tax actually withheld on that income as it is represented on the reclaim form? In most cases, particularly where, for instance, withholding agent and custodian are members of the financial network SWIFT, the custodian can use a SWIFT message to demonstrate that it has been advised by a withholding agent, of an income event on which tax has been withheld. More details of the SWIFT messages involved can be found in Chapter **9**. However, this can often be relied upon to demonstrate withholding. Apart from this the investor may of course be in possession of a hard copy dividend voucher which will show the details of the income and any tax deducted. This also can be used as proof of sufferance.

Finally, there is a level of trust that can be applied. If there is no other documentary evidence to hand, the custodian can produce on its own headed paper, effectively a statement of withholding to indicate to the receiving tax authority that the custodian knows that the income event has taken place and that recoverable tax has been deducted.

Powers of attorney

Powers of attorney are common in this area of back-office operations, although not ubiquitous. Most powers of attorney are strictly limited to the process of tax reclaims, and investors would not have it otherwise, nor for liability purposes would custodians. For good reason it is also sensible for investors to consider whether a PoA should limited in time as well as scope. If a service agreement is in place that has a fixed time-period, presumably so that the investor can negotiate a review or change at some agreed break point, then any PoA granted should be similarly limited in time. The PoA is used by a custodian to represent the claimant. Often this will not just be representation to a tax authority. As we have learned, there are many entities involved in this process. The best powers of attorney are thus limited in time to coincide with any time-limits on service provision, limited in scope to tax reclaims and also broad enough to give the custodian authority to deal with all the various entities they may come into contact with on behalf of the investor.

The PoA has two effects. The first is clearly to remove from the investor much of the onerous work involved in signing each tax reclaim form. The second is to allow the custodian to pursue the tax reclaim without further recourse to client contacts. Both are desirable as long as they are properly controlled.

Benchmarking

I've devoted a whole chapter to benchmarking later in this book. However, I felt it important to anticipate that chapter with some words on the tax reclaim process itself.

Investors have an absolute interest in this process not just as bystanders watching custodians process reclaims, but as we've seen, their actions can inhibit as well as enhance the efficiency of the process.

To that extent there are some particular areas of the process that attract risk and it's as well to have a clear picture of these as compliance officers and risk managers will also be paying attention to how well these issues are addressed. In particular, tax reclaims are one of the first areas where any failure to correctly identify certain aspects of an investor's profile, will appear.

Validity

Not all income events create taxable issues.

Figure 6.2 shows that, from the universe of all income events, the first filter that must be applied is whether the event is valid or not. In other words, on its own, is the income of a type which would normally fall within the definition of an income type which would attract withholding tax?

Establishing validity

Validity is a function of the income event and the treaty regulations covering the country of issuance and the countries of residence for which the custodian represents clients. An event is *valid* if, for the market m, a DTA exists which would create a withholding tax rate greater than the treaty rate for any income type I. This sets the scene for custodians or those processing reclaims.

The risk here is clearly that either some events will be thought to be valid when they are not or vice versa, resulting in either technically fraudulent reclaims or a failure to make reclaims when they are available. Actually in practice this risk is fairly small. Custodians are very good at establishing valid events and withholding agents, for the most part, are able to notify

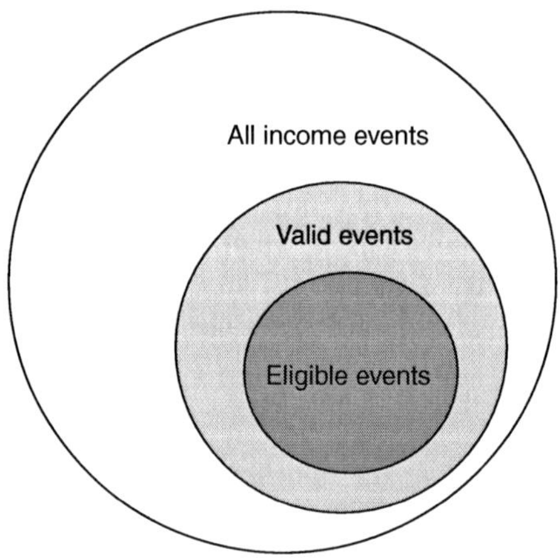

Figure 6.2 Validity versus eligibility

Source: Author.

correctly. There can however be problems associated with validity, particularly identifying where the income was technically sourced. This was highlighted at a conference recently when a US withholding agent asked how US source income could be reliably identified. True, in the vast majority of cases, the answer is obvious. Either the company is well known to be US and/or the security identifier is reason to presume a primary indicator of being US source. But there are occasions when the answer is not quite so clear and where, ultimately, the withholding agent and/or the custodian have to perform more research in order to establish their view of where the income is technically from. Clearly again the risk here is that one entity may view the set of research and come to one conclusion while another may come to a different conclusion. As I've said, this does not occur often, but it's as well from a tax perspective to have knowledge of the income source country as firmly identified as possible.

Eligibility

Once valid income events have been found, the key is to find those who are eligible to benefit from them. The flow from validity to eligibility is, for most custodians both automatic and usually electronic these days. The status of clients is usually documented manually but held electronically. The risk involved here is the way in which the client's manually documented status is transferred to an electronic medium. There is obvious potential for data entry error at this stage. Figure 6.3 shows the risk profile of this element of the process. This can be exacerbated by the continuing risk associated with *maintaining* correct documentation. Some forms of documentation are valid only within certain time-limits. If they are to be used as proof of eligibility, then the custodian concerned must make sure that their systems are capable of tracking document validity. If a client's data record is not updated, then, whilst in all eventuality the client's status has probably not changed, in a best practice environment, the compliance department should hold that the client's status is effectively "undocumented". Therefore there can be no eligibility for a treaty rate of withholding and thus no reclaim. This is found to a much higher degree in the US NRA 1441 relief-at-source regulations where documentary evidence rules are more strictly defined and applied. If a client's record is updated but is in error, the same risk would apply. The compliance function has the greatest interest in how these processes should work most efficiently and be monitored. The eligibility of a particular client is however not just dependent on status data. There are many other factors that may have a bearing on whether any particular client is eligible for a reclaim or not. Some are defined absolutely by their status while some are optional and may be selected by the client as a preferred instruction to the custodian. All are usually stored either manually or electronically. Where there are

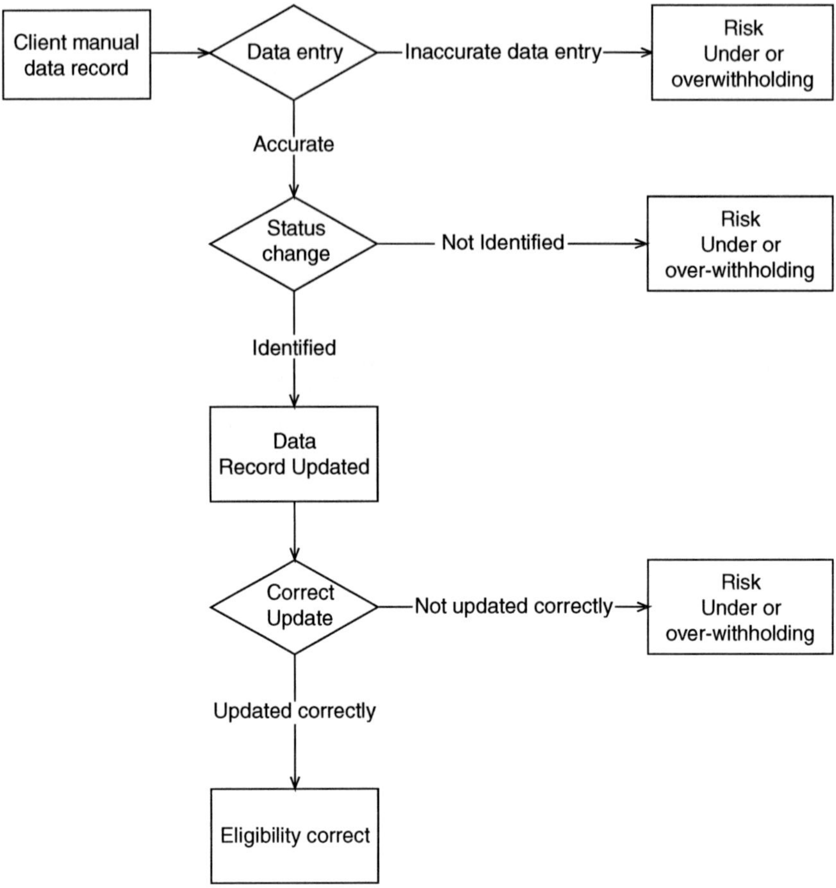

Figure 6.3 Risk profiling eligibility

Source: Author.

information elements held in both types of system, clearly the integration risk is highest with the likelihood that the manual information will be missed or inaccurately assessed.

Calculating value

Once valid income events have been applied to the custodian's client base to identify eligible recipients, the next stage of the process is to calculate the value of any reclaim. This is probably the simplest part of the process, being a straightforward calculation. It is also the most expensive to maintain. However this calculation is made, it is based on information about the client's status, the income event and the rates of withholding and treaty between the two countries concerned. Of course, from a custodian's viewpoint the set of permutations is limited to the scale and cope of his client base and their portfolio spread. Even so, the cost of researching and maintaining such information sources is not small. For those custodians employing third party software or outsourcing solutions, the information is often provided as part of the product or service offering and thus the cost and effort is spread across the supplier's entire client base for the most part. The risk in the process is clearly that the calculation may be incorrect. If the reclaim process is entirely internal, the liability will end internally. If there is an external element, say the provision of tax data, then liability may be attributable elsewhere depending on what and where the error was. A tax authority is likely to merely reject the reclaim as incorrect, after which it can be re-submitted in correct form, unless during the process, it crosses the statute of limitations. In most circumstances this will be a rare event.

Filling in forms

So, now we have a valid event, an eligible client with correct information and a correct calculation of the recoverable. The next stage is completing the tax reclaim form. These forms are actually relatively simple but appear very complex, are often multipart and usually, but not always are at least double language – the local language and English. Forms are completed either manually or electronically. By far the majority of custodians with internal solutions are still filling forms in manually. Conversely, those employing third party solutions either software or outsourcing, are almost always able to complete forms electronically and automatically. From a risk perspective, one would assume that manual completion is more risk prone than electronic. On the assumption that the electronic data is somehow more likely to be accurate than the manual, this is true. Compliance officers should risk assess the manual to electronic interface to establish the reality of this in practice. Either way, if the form, once completed, is incorrect in the smallest degree it is likely to be ultimately rejected.

Getting local tax authority approval

Having got this far in the process, the foreign tax authority is still not in a position to receive the reclaim forms. First, the forms must be sent to the local tax office of the claimant. Here, the tax office is asked to verify that the person named on the form as the claimant is indeed a resident of the local country concerned. There is little risk here, other than the usual loss of forms in the post or tardiness by the local authority to verify, stamp and return the forms to the custodian. From a protective position, the custodian should of course have retained copies of all documentation sent, so that the reclaim can be re-created if its lost.

Filing to foreign tax authorities

As has been said elsewhere, tax authorities themselves have something of a dilemma to cope with. Their primary function is to deal with tax affairs and the structure of withholding tax regimes. However, the existence of statutes of limitations also gives them access to an income source from those investors who fail to make reclaim submissions on time or make inaccurate reclaims which are not subsequently re-filed. A smaller proportion is accounted for by investors whose proof of domicile or other documentation is found to be invalid for the date of the income, in which case a withholding agent, if he's aware of such a lapse, must withhold at a higher rate.

As can be imagined from the relative amounts of over-withheld tax actually reclaimed, various countries around the world benefit from these failures to a very substantial degree.

Whilst quality assurance would of course be a natural element of any claim for the return of over-withheld tax, it is known that many tax authorities are particularly strict when it comes to assessing the validity of tax reclaims. It's therefore incumbent on the custodian to ensure that all the documentation provided, including the tax reclaim itself, is accurate and valid as at the date of the income event. This can affect relief-at-source regimes just as much as reclaim regimes. The US tax authorities require, as part of their QI Agreements, that if a QI is relying on a Form W-8BEN to self-certify its beneficial owner for treaty rate benefits, that W-8BEN has to have been valid on the date that the income was received. The problem for custodians is that W-8BENs are valid for 3 years after the year in which they were signed. This means a major administration operation consisting of cross-checking each income event for an investor as it occurs with the validity dates for the supporting documentation. Similarly in jurisdictions such as Spain, certificates of domicile must be lodged every 6 months in order to be able to claim benefits. In other jurisdictions fresh supporting documentation must be filed each time a reclaim is made. Needless to say, whilst this poses obvious problems for custodians, who have the potential for automation within their grasp or the ability to employ staff to do the job manually, tax authorities receiving this mountain of documentation from all over the world sometimes have difficulty managing rapid funds turnarounds.

Some tax authorities are however recognising that automation is good for business. Rapid returns of funds gives investors greater assurance and makes them more prepared to invest

The role of sub-custodians

Many of the global custodians, those largest custodial banks in the world, access local markets by appointing sub-custodians rather than set up operations of their own in each jurisdiction. This is the same effect as having a "specialist country desk".

Chasing for payment

This is one of the critical areas which is predominantly manual. Failure to perform it can significantly lengthen time to recoup funds. Many custodians have "country desks" which are staffed by people who know not only the language of the country they specialise in, but also the procedures and the people involved in the process. This is raised as a key benchmark. The length of time taken to recoup funds for each market is a standard benchmark which assumes no chasing of refunds after the tax reclaim has been submitted. There are therefore significant opportunities for custodians to demonstrate how their investment in people and systems can improve on this factor.

So, the basic reclaim procedure has seven main elements:

1. Pre-reclaim activity
   a. Notification of over-withholding
   b. Receipt and management of documentary evidence
   c. Establishing eligibility and validity
   d. Acquisition and maintenance of stock of tax reclaim forms

2. Reclaim process
   a. Completion and submission of standard tax forms
      i. To local authorities
      ii. To foreign sub-custodians (if applicable) or
      iii. To foreign authorities
   b. Chasing for payment

3. Post-reclaim activity
   a. Crediting client accounts

Variations to the basic process take two primary forms. The first is a variation by instrument type, the second by market. The latter is more extensive than the former simply because there are more markets involved and of course the political influences on those markets make variations more likely.

Of particular note, in terms of income type variations, is the process of DRs. Depositary Receipts are instruments that are often used to enable residents of a country who would otherwise be prohibited from owning shares in foreign companies, to do so. This doesn't stop anyone else from purchasing DRs. The DR is denominated in the currency of the resident's country.

So for example, an American Depositary Receipt (ADR) is denominated in US dollars. The DR represents a number of underlying shares in a foreign (in this example non-US) company. From a withholding tax perspective the variation to the process is that, for ADRs, the tax reclaim, if any, must be processed through the sponsor/issuer – for example Citibank, JP Morgan, Deutsche Bank and Mellon – ADR issues must go through them. The DTC, which is described in more detail in Chapter 5, has processes which support the underlying banks that sponsor and promote these issues.

There are a number of markets which have variations to procedure which can have a marked effect on the ability of a custodian to deliver good results.

Italy, for instance is renowned for taking sometimes up to 10 years to make tax refund payments, mainly because of the way in which it manages approvals and budgeting in the reclaim process.

Australia has dividends which can be "franked" or unfranked" which affects the availability of a tax reclaim or relief at source. The process is described here to show the type of effect and also the type of complexity that custodians must deal with on an every day basis. While we're on the subject of Australia, this serves as a useful point at which to highlight the application of withholding tax to other forms of income than dividends, which make up the majority of custodial work.

The Australian Tax Authority withholds over $1.43bn of tax from non-resident aliens. Of this, the following income types are represented:

- Interest 39%
- Dividends 22%
- Royalties 25%

The Tax Office (ATO) will provide a Certificates of Payment to non-residents whose Australian sourced income is subject to interest, dividend or royalty withholding tax.

A Certificate of Payment is a document issued by the ATO to non-residents (whose Australian sourced income is subject to Australian non-resident interest, dividend or royalty withholding tax) who require proof of payment to comply with their resident country's taxation requirements.

A Certificate of Payment will only be verified for those payees whose country of residence has a comprehensive double-taxation agreement with Australia.

The ATO will issue one Certificate of Payment per payee, per year, for each type of withholding tax. That is, only one Certificate of Payment will be issued for each total annual amount withheld for interest, dividend or royalty withholding tax.

Payers, in other words, custodians, request a Certificate of Payment for their payees, at the end of the financial year of the country requiring the Certificate of Payment. Most of the countries that have a double tax agreement with Australia have a financial year ending 31 December.

Before a custodian can ask the ATO for a Certificate of Payment for a payee, he must first obtain a request for a Certificate of Payment from the payee, the investor, for each year that a Certificate of Payment is required.

The next step, for the custodian, is to gather the following information:

1. the country of residence of the payee who requires a Certificate of Payment
2. the start and end dates of the financial year of that country
3. the name of the payee, and
4. the type of withholding tax applied. That is, was the amount withheld for interest, dividend or royalty withholding tax?

The custodian must also gather the transaction details for the financial year specified, including:

1. each amount subject to withholding tax by the payee,
2. the total annual amount subject to withholding tax by the payee,
3. each amount withheld and paid to the ATO,
4. the total amount paid to the ATO, and
5. the date each amount was paid to the ATO.

Franked dividends are payments made to shareholders or to holders of non-share equity interests on which the company has already paid tax.

Unfranked dividends have had no Australian company tax paid on them before they are paid to shareholders or to holders of non-share equity interests. If the dividend is unfranked, there is no imputation credit.

From 1 July 2001, certain interests which are not shares began to be treated in a similar way to shares for tax law purposes. These interests are called "non-share equity interests".

A dividend statement is sent to shareholders and to holders of non-share equity interests by companies to advise the dividend amounts and whether they are franked or unfranked, the amount of imputation credit and tax file number (TFN) amounts withheld (if any).

A distribution statement (also called a taxation statement) is sent to investors in managed funds or unit trusts. The statement can include unfranked dividends, franked dividends, TFN amounts withheld and imputation credits.

In Thailand, the nominee structure allows Thai beneficial owners to make their investments through nominee vehicles thus hiding their true identity behind the nominee. This, as we will see, is increasingly coming under scrutiny by tax authorities, particularly those that are developing advanced relief-at-source regimes where transparency to the beneficial owner is one of the building blocks.

Singapore and Malaysia share a similarity with the United Kingdom inasmuch as they have a system which permits an "imputation tax credit". This means that if there is withholding in one country at say 30% and the recipient in the United Kingdom is a 40% taxpayer, then, as far as his accounting goes, he can claim an imputation credit, effectively saying that he has already paid 30% and is therefore liable only for the difference, 10%. While this is all very well and good, one thing comes about. The imputation credit leaves the actual cash in the hands of the foreign tax authority, so the local tax authority, whilst giving the benefit of the tax already withheld to the beneficial owner, is not in possession of the tax concerned. This may be of more interest to the patriots who would prefer that if any tax is withheld, at least it should be their government that gets it and not some other foreign government.

These are just a few examples and, as with most things, by the time this book is read, some of these areas may have changed.

So, in this chapter we have learnt about the way in which tax reclaims are dealt with, some ideas on best practice, but most of all, the reader is probably more aware than ever before now, just how complex the activity of tax reclaims is. Indeed, there should be significant respect for the expertise of tax reclaimers generally. In the last part of the chapter we looked at some of the variants to the basic pattern. But to be honest, these vary both in time and in scale. It's much more important to understand the basic process and particularly the risks associated with it, than it is to apply knowledge of variations to your own particular circumstance. It does raise the question for investors that they should be aware of the level and depth of country-specific knowledge that is available from their custodian. This is not just about a simple form filling exercise.

CHAPTER 7

Optimisation Issues

So far we have discussed the basic threads of withholding tax, the essential principles. Along the way, I have referred to many variations to those essential principles to highlight the complexity of the issue. However, in a real world, highlighting such issues is not enough. As far as investors go, it's their money, so from a custodian's perspective, there is an imperative whether contractual or competitive, to ensure that operationally, such issues are identified and dealt with. There can of course be many solutions to these issues depending on their complexity. At one end of the scale, in addition to a basic tax reclaim/ optimisation service, a custodian may choose to add resource internally to create the ability to deal with complex scenarios. This will usually depend on the number of clients affected by variations of a particular kind. Equally however, custodians can and do decide that certain scenarios are just too complex and decide not to offer a service. Either that or they decide to unbundle the tax offering and are prepared to undertake complex claims, for a fee. Unbundling of fees is gathering pace amongst custodians, particularly as more complex scenarios are increasingly common, tax authorities require far more information and the spectre of increased regulation and tax information reporting can clearly be seen over the horizon. What was previously easily contained within a basis point fee model, will, I'm sure, move out into the value added service area in due course. The following are comments on some of issues that need to be optimised in any reasonable sized tax environment.

INCOME

Depositary receipts

Depositary receipts are a genre of derivative instruments that are, currently, extremely common. The most common are American Depositary Receipts or ADRs. Originally invented by JP Morgan, DRs are issued on a sponsored or unsponsored basis by a bank – a depositary bank – as a receipt in the classical sense, that represents a number of underlying ordinary securities that the bank holds on account. This is known as the "ratio". When seeking finance in the capital markets, one route that corporations (Issuers) can take, apart from issuing common stock or ordinary (ORDs), is to go to a depositary bank and have them issue DRs for their stock.

It is possible to issue a DR without using a depositary bank, although only very large issuers usually attempt this. Two examples are Alcon and UBS AG. These companies issue Global Depositary Receipts or GDRs. There are other types of DR where the prefix needed to create the acronym represents the market in which the DR is marketed, usually on the relevant exchange. Under this model, ADR is an American Depositary Receipt for a non-US stock for example, Nestle or Mannesman.

From a withholding tax perspective DRs have some peculiar properties. Since they do not represent stock issued in the country in which they are listed, they are not usually treated as income sourced from that country.

Tax authorities generally do not accept that DRs are securities against which a claim for entitlement under a treaty can be made. Hence the procedure for obtaining a tax reclaim or relief at source on a DR is different from that for other kinds of security. Essentially, the holder or their intermediary must, in addition to creating the relevant documentation for a reclaim, file that claim, not to the market, but to the depositary that issued the DR in the first place. For ADRs the depositary is one of the following: Bank of New York Mellon, Deutsche Bank, JP Morgan Chase or Citi. It is then the depositary's role to convert the claim at DR level into a claim at the ordinary stock level using the ratio, then process the claim. It's a mark of the complexity of this process that all four of these depositaries, over the period since 1992, have outsourced this obligation to a third party vendor, GlobeTax Services Inc., based in New York who therefore essentially acts as the market infrastructure for ADR tax reclaims.

There are other peculiarities of the ADR market. The Depository Trust and Clearing Corporation (DTCC) is a clearing organisation in the United States that has around 650 participant banks, predominantly US-based. On their behalf, DTC has negotiated special arrangements with certain markets, where relief at source is offered, and for certain security types. The arrangement allows investors, who hold foreign securities through ADRs held within a DTC account, to obtain relief at source in an efficient way without having to provide documentation up the chain. The DTC participant bank essentially warrants under penalty of audit and censure, that, for any position that it elects to be taxed at treaty rate, it has appropriate documentation of the beneficial owner to evidence an entitlement to the rate.

Finally, although this is by no means an exhaustive description of DR peculiarities, we must remember that filing claims on DR positions will normally take longer than claims on ORDs filed directly to the market. This is because there is an additional actor in the process – the depositary. Reclaim payments by depositories vary by market, but typically payments come in batches four times a year.

Reclassification

There are some types of investment vehicle, the most notable being Real estate investment trusts (REITs) who get to the end of a year having made distributions classified as dividends on which tax would have been deducted at the time. After year end, dependent on a number of factors, these entities have the opportunity to reclassify the income distribution to, say, a distribution of capital. This would not have been subject to withholding tax if it had been classified as such at the time. So, the net result is that an entitlement exists, but will only be known after the end of the tax year. In some markets, particularly the United States, this can cause major problems for custodians and investors. Because these markets operate a tax information reporting regime in parallel with the normal tax processes, not only will there be a claim against the tax authority, but all the tax information reporting that has been prepared and/or submitted will be (i) incorrect and (ii) will not reconcile to actual payments and classifications in custody systems. The US TIR system does allow for requests for more time to prepare information reports which does give some leeway for custodians to wait until reclassifications have occurred before issuing downstream reports. However, the reason that such deferments are usually requested is actually because the custodian needs that time just to do the basic work of creating the original reports. What's actually happening in the market is that reclassifications downstream are being ignored as too much work or are being charged as an additional fee to clients. It's important for custodians to assess the likely impact of reclassifications on their business and put appropriate processes in place to avoid the liability from a downstream client or other financial institution that clients are being financially damaged.

Interpretation of benchmarks

There is an extensive list of benchmarks in this book. However, in the market many custodians do not use these, preferring a more old fashioned simplistic set of criteria for judgement, if any are used at all.

An example of this is Recovery time. Each market pays back to claimants using a different model. In some markets of course such as France and, as we've seen previously, with ADRs, there are also market factors to contend with. However, there is available a market table showing the *average* market recovery time. Now most clients look at this table and assume that this is the length of time it will take to recover their tax starting from the point at which they were over-taxed – the pay-date – a completely reasonable assumption given the amount of money spent by banks on STP systems and also completely untrue. The benchmark for recovery is almost universally applied from the date that the claim is filed to the market that is, the date it leaves the custodian. This also would be reasonable (i) if the interpretation of the benchmark were made clear and (ii) if the preceding part of the activity between pay-date and filing date were very short.

As we'll see elsewhere however, even though this preparatory phase of claims filing is entirely within the intermediary's control, it is the least publicised because it is where there are more delays caused than any other part of the market process.

Intermediaries actually have extremely fragmented systems that have grown up over time and usually did not start out with a strategic design or purpose, but more of a tactical need.

I have seen custody reports that show backlogs of claims going back over three years worth over $17 million. In other words, there are claims that have not been filed yet (some of which will have gone out of statute of limitations), where the pay date was over three years ago. In these conditions, simplistic reporting and lack of use of benchmarks hides the reality of the process – an inefficient intermediary – and hides the effect on the client – lack of funds.

This is pretty counter-intuitive to the average client where the intermediary generates fees from the size of assets under management (AUM). You would think therefore (as a client) that it would be in the intermediary's financial interests to identify and process claims without a backlog in order to maximise both its client's income and its own. However, this is not the case. Withholding tax, for many years has been a back-of-back-office function, attracting little attention and even less investment mainly because no-one could figure out, other than by throwing people at it, how to make the process efficient. Those people, not only make mistakes but they work slowly and have a morass of paperwork to deal with.

Worse, the people in these functions know that they have a backlog. Internal reports often still show these amounts as "outstanding" claims that have some validity. Here are two vignettes that show the effect of allowing these backlogs to develop. First, the claim amounts are shown as outstanding even though there is little or no chance after so much time has passed that the claims will ever be filed at all. Think about it. If you have a department that's running like crazy to keep up with the current dividend season volumes and letting claims drop back into the backlog through a lack of capacity, what chance is there that those claims, after 3 years, will ever get compiled and sent? Very little. So, these claims should really be written off and the client made whole (it's not their fault their intermediary has a backlog and after all, it's actually their money). Second, let's presume for a moment that some claims from that far back do eventually get filed. When they arrive at a tax authority, they face a similar issue. The tax authorities generally are manually oriented and have the same kind of backlogs as the intermediaries (the difference is, they are the ones with the client's money). They take a pragmatic attitude, since they are also facing current claims from the current dividend season. They take the attitude "if you took 3 years before you even filed the claim, you can't be that concerned about the money", the net result of which is that, unless the intermediary makes a substantive effort (unlikely), the tax authority will not prioritise the claims over the current claims. The net result of that of course, returning to our original subject, is that the time cited as an average recovery time is an average because there are claims that take much longer than the average – guess which they are.

The use and interpretation of benchmarks therefore is critical. While individual benchmarks are important, it's equally important to recognise their limitations in the real world and their impact on other parts of the process, so that intermediaries and clients alike can have transparency on the subject of performance.

Eurobonds

A Eurobond is an international bond that is denominated in a currency not native to the country where it is issued. It can be categorised according to the currency in which it is issued. London is one of the centres of the Eurobond market, but Eurobonds may be traded throughout the world - for example in Singapore or Tokyo.

Eurobonds are named after the currency they are denominated in. For example, Euroyen and Eurodollar bonds are denominated in Japanese yen and American dollars respectively. A Eurobond is normally a bearer bond, payable to the bearer. The bank will pay the holder of the coupon the interest payment due.

The majority of Eurobonds are now owned in "electronic" rather than physical form. The bonds are held and traded within one of the clearing systems (Euroclear and Clearstream being the most common). Coupons are paid electronically via the clearing systems to the holder of the Eurobond (or their nominee account).

Eurobonds have historically been deemed to be exempt from withholding tax. However, in recent years things have changed. The tax authorities of an increasing number of markets including Estonia, Iceland, Ireland, Lebanon, Portugal and Spain are taking the view that an entitlement to exemption should be achieved by taxing the Eurobond in the first place and having a relief-at-source and/or long form process to obtain that entitlement, which would of course be 100%. At present around 5% of Eurobonds are taxable (Source: International Capital Markets Services Association – ICMSA).

Figure 7.1 provides a decision flowchart for a custodian who has clients with Eurobond income. This decision tree allows the custodian to establish whether or not it can meet the requirements of the Eurobond quick refund process and, if not, implement a long form process to ensure that their client is not disadvantaged. In the model shown in Figure 7.1, the custodian will use a third party service bureau to process any long form claims that are not paid under the quick refund or relief-at-source process.

The Eurobond market in terms of taxation is affected also by which market the Eurobonds are issued in. The most complex is Spain which is described here to exemplify the issue.

In the Spanish tax environment, under Spanish law, Eurobond Notes issued by a Spanish issuer are subject to withholding tax. No relief from this

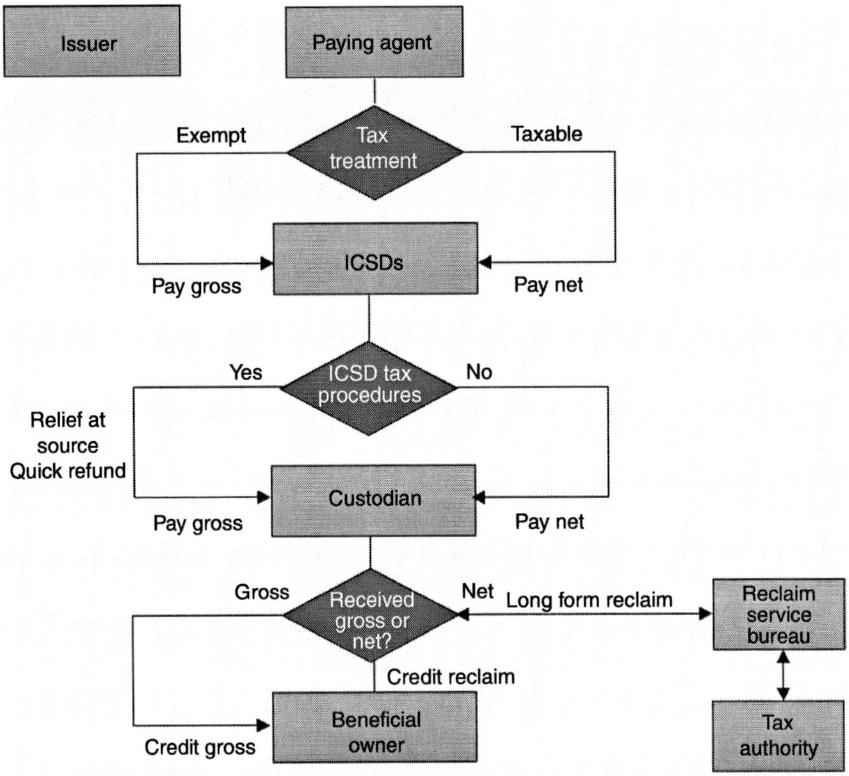

Figure 7.1 Optimisation for Eurobond income

Source: Author.

tax is available to investors who are either Spanish-resident or are resident in a jurisdiction deemed to be a tax haven. Since the ICSDs have a key role to play in Eurobond management, these firms manage the relief at source/quick refund process for the market, including Spain. The procedure required is based on the downstream custodians providing certificates of residency, known as Annexos, as the documentary evidence of an investor's entitlement to exemption plus the amount of interest received and details of the relevant Notes. The full procedure is shown in Appendix 4.

From a different perspective, as far as issuers of Eurobonds are concerned, the information that they should provide relating to the tax treatment of their instruments includes

- Taxable events,
- Availability of withholding relief,
- Eligibility criteria for relief,
- Documentation requirements and
- Holding restrictions.

What's important here is to avoid the presumption that Eurobonds are tax exempt. The answer is, as always, "it depends". Not only that but, even though tax is deducted, the ICSD's quick refund process is complex and has several quite tight deadlines. It is therefore likely, although the scale is unknown, that some Eurobond investors will be taxed, even though they think they won't be, that they may attempt to take part in the quick refund process but not be able to meet the deadline. In which case, the only route left for them will be to perform a long form claim either directly via their custodian or a third party.

Swedish redemption shares

Anyone, anywhere who has held Swedish equities may have received Swedish redemption shares (SRSs) which Swedish companies issue from time to time to their shareholders at a certain ratio and may have an opportunity to recover tax, irrespective of the existence of a double-taxation treaty. The SRSs are traded for a period of time on the open market and on a set date the SRSs are redeemed by the company for a pre-determined price.

If an investor sells the redemption shares out in the open market, there are no tax consequences. If the shares are held to redemption, and the holder is not a Swedish resident, then the entire proceed amount is subject to

Swedish withholding tax at whatever rate their account is set up to receive (statutory 30% or reduced 15%).

The Swedish Tax Authority (STA) ruled recently that for shares redeemed after 1 January 2005 a portion of the cost basis of the original shares are transferred to the SRS and that portion of the redemption amount is not subject to tax at all, so whatever was withheld from the "cost basis" portion is fully reclaimable.

The additional benefit here is that the beneficial owner does not have to be domiciled in a market which has a double-taxation treaty with Sweden in order to participate in the reclaim process. Since the withholding occurred on the total proceeds, there was an excess withholding no matter who was holding the shares, what will remain to be determined is the amount able to be recovered. This means that funds and investors domiciled in so-called "tax havens" like the Cayman Islands are also eligible to file claims on withholdings from SRSs.

The STA allows the investor to choose one of two ways to calculate the cost basis, a "default method" and a "actual cost method". The default method will calculate a set amount as the cost basis. *This method requires no back-up paperwork in order to reclaim, but is only beneficial if the shareholder had over a 400% return on the average purchase price or cannot piece together all of the trades adding up to the total position in the underlying security.*

To file using the actual cost method, the shareholder would need to compile all of the trades (buys and sells) including commission costs and calculate the average cost per share. The STA publishes for each redemption event, the percentage of the average cost that is transferred to the redemption share and that becomes the cost basis of the redemption share. In this method, the investor must provide proof of the trades. Actual trade confirmations are the best form of proof, but the STA has written that it may accept other documentation showing the buys/sells leading to the total position being claimed on.

So, again we see that, despite efforts to harmonise, individual markets can take actions that create complexities but that also create opportunities. Some of those opportunities would not be generally thought of to be valid if we maintained the original position that withholding tax entitlements are defined solely by treaties.

Residency

Some of the above are jurisdictionally specific issues, such as the Swedish situation. Others are more generic. This is one of the most difficult aspects of withholding tax – that there is no single rule set that enables an investor to know whether their custodian is doing the best job or for that matter, whether the custodian knows that it's doing the best job.

The point about optimisation is that it should be a strategic management issue *not* an operational issue. Senior management should be assessing the position of their firms with respect to their clients, taking into account as many variables as exist and making judgements about what resources are deployed, what kind of services should be provided etc. While some issues may be extremely complex, and therefore probably unwanted, at the operational level, the effect on the reputation of the firm and its client acquisition and management programs may require those difficult processes to be provided. I am very familiar with investors who choose specific custodians, and who move custodians, solely for the purpose of optimising tax services.

One more such is a generic issue – residency. As I've stated, tax residency, as opposed to domicile, is one of the main factors for establishing entitlements. It's often said that there are residencies that, because they are listed as tax havens or harmful jurisdictions, that tax optimisation is not possible. The usual example is the Cayman Islands. The lack of tax treaties with Cayman means that most practitioners will attach the "no action" notice to any investor who cites Cayman as a residency. However, "it depends". The fact is that certain types of entity can facilitate tax reclaims under double tax treaties on two grounds – first, if the entity can be treated as transparent that is, it's not a corporation and second, if the underlying investor is resident "onshore" in a jurisdiction that does have a tax treaty with the issuing jurisdiction. There are many millions of dollars that are therefore sitting in foreign tax authority bank accounts that should be in investor accounts solely because the investor chose to invest indirectly via a Cayman entity and did not realise, and nor did their custodian, that there was a way to penetrate the residency issue. This type of onshore/offshore linkage is called Master-Feeder.

Legal form

Critically linked to the issue of residency is that of legal form. As I noted immediately above with respect to Cayman, the residency issue could be penetrated if the investor was in an onshore environment where the treaty could be applied. However, in most cases, investors have a different legal form to the investment vehicle which they use to access the markets. So, the second rule of optimisation comes into effect, that investors and custodians must have a clear picture of how their particular legal form is structured in their own jurisdiction and how it is viewed by foreign tax authorities. It's the combination of the two that gets us closer to an optimised process.

Omnibus accounts for example, in some cases known as nominee accounts are not legal entities in their own right, although they are misnomered often into this category. An omnibus account is merely an account held at a custodian or broker or other financial institution that represents a grouping of underlying investors who, in their own right, may be omnibus in nature, flowing down through an account chain to the final ultimate beneficial owner.

Hedge funds on the other hand are entities with legal form. Unfortunately while the description would seem to be all encompassing, hedge funds that are US-resident tend to be legally structured as partnerships while European hedge funds tend to be structured more along the lines of a Unit Trust. Hedge fund as a term is actually more descriptive of a fund's investment strategy than of its legal status. It's also true that hedge funds tend to use prime brokers for their investment accounts rather than custodian banks. The nature of the structure makes a big difference to what and how entitlements can be obtained. For US hedge funds the matter will be determined on a jurisdiction-by-jurisdiction basis. The main concern is over treaty shopping (see below) and so most, but not all tax authorities view US hedge funds as partnerships where the entitlement is at the partner level, not the partnership level. Having said that, some tax authorities do allow some mitigation of what would be a most painful process if claims were actually to be filed at partner level. As long as the partners are known and their residency is the same as that of the fund which is claiming the entitlement, there are a range of alternative processes that are much easier to follow – if you know what they are.

Securities lending

Securities lending is an absolute minefield for withholding tax as well as its practitioners. In a securities lending environment the owner (lender) of shares will lend their securities to another entity (a borrower) under the terms of a securities lending contract which will determine the rights that came with the transferred shares. One of those rights will relate to any income that is paid while the shares are out on loan. While out on loan as far as the books of record of the lender and borrower are concerned, typically, the borrower will receive any dividends that are declared and distributed. Most securities lending contracts therefore provide, as is the natural concern of the lender, that any dividends received are passed on to the lender. However, the trail of documentation will show that the entity receiving the income will be the borrower. So, without some supporting documentation, the lender will have no way to reconcile payments received. The borrower will, through the broker, provide the lender with a "manufactured dividend". This is a payment from borrower to lender representing the amount that the borrower received. The question is – does the borrower pay the manufactured dividend net of statutory rate tax or treaty rate tax and if treaty rate, at whose entitlement rate?

Often the securities lending contract will define whether any tax is deducted and if so, what proportion is kept by the lender and what is kept by the borrower. The difficulty is twofold. First, very few of the practitioners in this area have any real knowledge of withholding tax and so make commercial decisions rather than informed decisions. Second, the problem is made more complex by the complex practice of series lending – where a borrower subsequently lends his borrowed securities out to a second borrower and so on. The lack of reporting in this area makes it almost impossible for good practice, let alone best practice to occur.

Let's however, suppose that the dividend paid was at a statutory rate of tax. There is therefore potentially an entitlement. The entitlement would normally belong to the borrower since they held the shares at record date. The base payment made by the borrower to the lender would naturally be the gross dividend minus the statutory rate of tax. If both parties (lender and borrower) are of different tax residencies and both are different from the jurisdiction of issue, there lies the problem. There are two scenarios. Both lender and borrower would have potential entitlements to a tax reclaim under their respective treaties. If the borrower's entitlement is greater than the lender's, life is simple. If the lender's entitlement is the greater life is difficult because he will be expecting a dividend minus statutory rate tax, but that will come with an entitlement to a certain amount of reclaimable tax. However, because he lent the shares, on record date, part of his entitlement value disappeared. Securities lending is a haven for what is termed tax arbitrage – managing one's investments specifically to gain a cash benefit from differential taxation rates. At the kind end of the spectrum this is viewed as good policy. At the other end, tax authorities are extremely suspicious of such activity and often ask more searching questions of claimants.

And that, in this scenario, is where the rub is. In a perfect world, a typical security lending contract would have a clause that allowed for a dividend to be repatriated to the lender minus an amount of tax that took into account the treaty entitlements of both parties minus the costs of actually filing the claim by the borrower. This is the key. The borrower must benefit and essentially his benefit is a slice of the administration costs expressed within his treaty benefit that goes back to the lender with his manufactured dividend. The issue then only becomes timing. If the borrower is supporting a claim based on his ownership of borrowed shares on record date, the payment of that claim might take years to realise. So another complex aspect of withholding tax in securities lending is when the payment of tax is made. Some contracts defer till the actual claim is paid, some pay both on the pay-date, and as such combine securities lending reclaims with contractual tax.

Table 7.1 Types of statute of limitation

Calendar year	Calculated as X years from the end of the year in which the income occurred
Tax year	Calculated as X years from the date of the issuing country's fiscal year
Pay date	Calculated as X years to the day from the pay-date of the income

Source: Author.

Statutes of limitation

Statutes of limitation or Time bars refers to the length of time following receipt of income which an investor has available in which to assert his right to an entitlement under any given treaty by filing a claim. The statutes vary by market and are of three main types. Obviously, such statutes only apply in practice to those jurisdictions that offer a quick or long form reclaim process. The fact that there are different types of statute of limitations is critical, in practical terms, only if an entitlement is not lodged until close to the entitlement limit. Unfortunately many investors as well as custodians and brokers do approach, and exceed, this limit because their internal procedures and resource management are not capable of keeping up with the flow of work during dividend seasons. The three types of statutes differ in the way they calculate the last day on which the entitlement exists.

It is clear from the above, that an investor or custodian who does not take into account the different types of statute for a given market can, inadvertently exceed the statute. If a claim is not filed within the statute of limitations the entitlement lapses and the money becomes the property of the relevant government.

Contractual tax

From an investor perspective contractual tax is the perfect solution to all withholding tax issues. Contractual tax describes a custody product that essentially allows the custodian to provide the gross income on pay-date. If there is a statutory rate of tax deducted from the payment received by the custodian, the custodian essentially makes the transaction whole again based on the entitlement of the beneficial owner. The beneficial owner benefits by having the gross income available immediately for re-investment. The custodian benefits by receiving a fee from the client for having essentially lent them the funds that made them whole.

There are some issues with this product however. First, the custodian has to price the service so that it makes a profit but does not lose out from any delay in reclaiming the funds it has already provided to the client. The degree to which the custodian can predict the recovery time, determines just how price competitive they can be. The smaller the number of claims, the lower the statistical base on data on which that calculation will be based and therefore the higher the risk that it will be incorrect. The custodian also has the problem that in order to recoup the funds, they must file a claim in the name of the beneficial owner – but he already has his money. So, in most cases, there are claw back clauses in the event that the beneficial owner does not support the claim in the most efficient way.

Tax authorities also have issues in optimisation. Their optimisation however, is aimed at reducing the likelihood of duplicate claims or fraudulent claims. In this case, technically, a claim made at the fund level when the custodian knows that the entity is transparent would be a fraudulent claim, since there would have been intent. Many claims are filed on the presumption that the claimant is opaque (claim can be filed at fund level) but tax authorities then judge based on the information that they have, that the claimant is transparent. This would not be a fraudulent claim since there was no intent. The difference is a fine line because the tax authority only has a limited amount of information on which to judge. Often the name of the so-called beneficial owner will provide a clue; for example, partnership or trust in the name or even the name of the jurisdiction such as Cayman inside the name of the claimant all are signs that a tax authority would expect a custodian to know and infer transparency or no entitlement because the jurisdiction is deemed harmful. On the latter, for investors it's quite common for accounts to have been set up years previously for specific reasons. It's useful to re-visit those reasons as the residency changes its status and treatment in the eyes of other tax authorities.

Crediting/offsetting the irrecoverable portion

It's very common at investor level, but unfortunately also very common elsewhere in the investment chain, that offsetting foreign tax against a domestic tax liability is an acceptable way to avoid double taxation. Apart from New Zealand, which specifically allows its residents to offset all of their foreign tax against their domestic tax liability, this view is generally incorrect.

In other words, if I have a domestic tax liability at 15% on my income which leaves me owing £10,000 to my tax authority; and I invested in a Swiss company and was taxed at 35% on Swiss investment income totalling £8,000, my calculation might be that I should provide £2,000 in tax to my tax authority. This is incorrect. The usual rule that applies is that the only portion of the tax that can be credited to a domestic tax liability is the *irrecoverable portion*. In the case of Switzerland and the United Kingdom for example, since the treaty rate is 15% currently, I am technically able to recover 20% from the Swiss government. So I am not able to credit the 20% against my UK tax liability.

Dividend washing

Dividend washing is the act of engaging in an activity of trading in shares between parties that leads to a net gain by both over a tax authority in terms of the amount of tax that the instigator of the trade would otherwise have been entitled to.

For example investor A resides in country B and investor C resides in country D. The investment target is country E. Country E has tax treaties with both countries B and D and has a statutory rate of 35%. Residents of country C are entitled to a treaty rate of tax of 15% on investment income from country E. However residents from country D are only entitled to a treaty rate of 25% on income from country E.

So, investor D buys shares in a company resident in country E. If he keeps those shares over record date, his dividend will be taxed at 35% and he will have an entitlement to claim back 10% from country E. However, in a dividend washing arrangement, investor D buys the shares and enters into an agreement with investor C. Under the agreement, investor C buys the shares from investor D just before record date and agrees to sell them back to investor D just after the record date. So, on record date the owner of the shares is investor C, who gets taxed at 35% but now has an entitlement to claim back 20% from country E. The parties agree to split the additional tax recovered between them. The net result is that investor C has gained financially just because he agreed to own the shares long enough to access the treaty benefits flowing from his legal status and residency in country D. Because he bought, then sold the shares back at an agreed price, he is otherwise unencumbered – free money. Investor D has essentially accessed a portion of the benefits of a treaty rate of tax to which he was not entitled, by reason of the stock transaction over the record date. So investor D gains financially over what he would have been entitled to if he had retained the shares long himself.

Needless to say, this model requires knowledge and counterparties who understand the principles involved. It also makes no sense for a private investor with minimal holdings. It makes more sense for institutions or investors who are capable of purchasing very large numbers of shares who can find counterparties who are prepared to engage in the practice.

This highlights one of the key issues for tax authorities that has been evolving over the last few years. The rules under which most tax treaties are written have been historically very black and white and relatively simple on this issue. If you hold the stock over record date, as far as everyone, including the tax authorities is concerned, you are the owner of the shares and entitled to the benefits of any treaty that might apply. So the practice of dividend washing is not, at the time of writing, illegal per se. However, many tax authorities are coming to view this activity in particular and the activity type (finding loopholes) of which it forms a more general part, as not in the spirit of the treaties they engage in.

The effect has been that tax authorities are taking a much more careful view of tax reclaims when filed. Many of the forms required are changing to include questions for investors about the reason for the ownership of shares and the length of time they have been held by the beneficial owner claiming the treaty benefit.

Of course, tax authorities have limited resources to deal with this kind of issue and the financial services industry has been very expert of late on the trading side in reacting to changes by finding new loopholes in treaties and processes. Tax authorities are now very aware of dividend washing and it's likely that their reaction will, over time, mean that the practice dies out.

Title versus ownership

As you can probably see, having a tax processing department as a custodian is not as simple as it looks.

There are a number of broker-dealers who have a very particular way of doing business that tax authorities definitely do not approve of. The issue is termed title versus ownership. In this scenario an investor will enter into an agreement with a broker to manage their investment purchases. The agreement, usually set under the legal jurisdiction of the broker, provides that the broker will be able to take shares purchased under instruction from their customer into their name. In other words they hold title to the shares. Under the agreement of course, any dividends paid on the shares will be paid to the broker's account and the broker subsequently pays the client.

In the same way as with securities lending, the client of the broker may have both a different jurisdiction and a different legal form to the broker itself. The terms of the contract will define what happens in terms of payments. The problem lies in the assumption made by the broker that they are entitled to file a claim on a payment made to them which is subsequently paid out to a client. The assumption is based on the belief that the contract jurisdiction and legal terms between themselves and their client must be both valid and respected by a foreign tax authority. Both are incorrect. In fact, a tax authority has a particular interest, under its treaties, to pay claims only to those investors who correctly are the ultimate beneficial owners of the income. The key word here is "ultimate". Tax authorities have long experience dealing with claimant entities which, on inspection, are deemed by them to be transparent. Such is the case here too. Tax authorities, in my experience, have only one question of a broker filing a claim on supposedly their security positions – Was there any third party who received a payment as a direct result of the payment being made to you with respect to these securities? If the broker tells the truth, they will be deemed transparent. The ultimate beneficial owner is the broker's client. The tax authority has no interest in a commercial contract outside their jurisdiction and again from experience, they give it no substance. This has tripped up a number of brokers, whose legal counsel insists that their interpretation is correct – right up to the point that they are fined. This is salutary for the whole industry where a number of practices exist which are against the principles of what the treaties are trying to achieve.

Protective reclaims

Most custodians, brokers and asset managers operate in a backlog situation. The volumes of claims that they must file and the very manual nature of the processes involved, mean that most have claims that were identified some time ago, but which, for lack of resource, have yet to be filed. This is usually because of a lack of internal knowledge and low efficiencies in document management. For those firms that are client acquisitive that is, they are bringing new clients on board regularly, this problem is exacerbated. They may take on a book of business which contains legal income on which claims may or may not have even been identified. The problem comes when either or both of these events occur close to the statute of limitations. The intermediary must either accept the consequences and not file the claim because it is technically not in a condition to file or they can file what is termed a protective reclaim.

A protective claim is a claim filed when the filer knows that the claim is not complete in some way. The claimant is leveraging the fact that once the tax authority confirms receipt, if the claim is filed before the statute, any lack of documentation can be tidied up after the event. The main thing is that the statute limit wasn't breached. There are a few issues here. First, you can only do this rarely and in certain markets. Typically, protective claims would only be filed if the claim value was large since the claimant is relying to a large extent on the goodwill of the tax authority. To avoid a simple rejection, it's also common that a protective claim is followed rapidly by a phone call along the lines of "please forgive me, I filed the claim and forgot to include ...".

At the end of the day, because the payment of these claims is at the discretion of the tax authority, there's nothing wrong per se with them. However, when I do see such activity in any large tax department, it sends out warning bells. My main concern is for the length of time the intermediary had the claim before filing it. As payment frequencies can be in the category of years, additional years going backwards, where the claim wasn't filed in the first place, merely add to risk and also devalue the investment performance of the client.

Treaty shopping

We've talked about title versus ownership and we've also talked about dividend washing. Both of these activities relate to the manipulation of the way that shares are bought and sold within a tax oriented environment. Treaty shopping on the other hand, represents an investor planning their own investments and engaging in essentially fraudulent activity in order to gain a tax benefit. The investor leverages a weakness in the documentation and KYC rules of a jurisdiction in order to set up an account with a custodian or broker. Having established an identity in that jurisdiction, the investor proceeds to invest cross border, but gains the benefit of a tax rate from his new jurisdiction rather than his real one. The example cited is usually of an American who rents an apartment in Paris. He provides his French utility bills as part of his account set-up and subsequently has a custody account with a French bank where he is deemed to be a French resident. Any investment income he receives to this account would be taxed as if he were a French resident rather than a US resident. Equally, any claims of entitlement he makes would be under the French treaties and not the US treaties. In all, he has essentially shopped around to find the most lucrative treaty under which to invest in a particular market, then set up an account to leverage that. So like dividend washing and title versus ownership claims which are not technically illegal but merely exploiting loopholes in a complex procedural structure, treaty shopping per se is also not illegal. What is illegal of course is the fraud perpetrated on the custodian or broker needed to set up the account.

Limitations of benefit

Finally in this chapter, I should mention Limitations of benefit (LOB). The US has the most limitations of benefit in its treaties. Limitations of benefit are what they sound like. If there is an activity or type of investor which is common enough to warrant it, a jurisdiction can place LOBs into specific treaties with other countries. The US has them in all its treaties. Other jurisdictions have LOBs in only some, dependent on their view of specific jurisdictions.

The key issue is that LOBs are usually extremely arcane and are typically buried in many layers of complex text within treaties. It is therefore very easy for investors and custodians to believe that they have an entitlement where in fact they do not. A good example is Irish resident unit trusts. If the trust is set up under UCITs III regulations, it will come under the LOB clause in the treaty with the United States. The LOB clauses have five "tests" all of which must be passed before the LOB has no effect. Most of this type of investment vehicle can pass four easily. The fifth is that the fund must be actively traded on at least two exchanges to be able to avoid the LOB. The problem in this case is that the funds, whilst they are listed on two exchanges, typically do not actively or regularly trade. If this sounds like a deep level of nit-picking – it is. My intention is to show how easy it would be (and is) to believe you have an entitlement. On the other side of the coin, tax authorities do not really sit there and research and perform the tests on every claimant. They are manually oriented and inundated with claims. So, it's entirely possible for claimants to claim when they are not entitled to and also for tax authorities to pay claims when they shouldn't.

A book listing all issues which could affect optimisation for investors and for intermediaries would be twice as long as this book. Those listed in this chapter are of the more practical orientation and designed to give the reader a feel for the types of issue that might be affecting them. Together with the chapter on benchmarking, which covers in more detail some of the measurable optimisation issues, I hope that the reader will have a more holistic view of just how complex this area of corporate actions is.

PART 3

Technology

Withholding tax has, historically, been the last to attract investment in technology. I remember well visiting a financial institution in 1996 shortly after entering the industry to find that the withholding tax department was in the sub-basement behind the filing cabinets using IBM PC ATs with little more than spreadsheets. This, while upstairs on the trading floor, the sight was of fields of the latest screens, usually three to a person. Withholding tax moved on of course in the intervening years, but not at the same pace as other parts of the custody environment.

Most of this lack of investment was due to the same reason that withholding tax generally was not an issue of great import – namely awareness. While investors were not aware of the issue and custodians did not have any of the precursors to automation, there was little initiative for change.

Some of the more forward looking firms of course did invest, both in people and systems, but these were remarkably few and far between. Since over 60% of withholding tax processes are manual and those manual elements are essentially outside the control of the custodian, there was little that custodians could do to improve efficiencies since any improvement usually meant more people and more manual systems. Equally, because of these constraints, the ability for third party software vendors to make any kind of impact, was limited to providing marginal improvements in processing such as the completion of forms from income data and calculated entitlements. Most, including the corporate actions platform vendors, restricted themselves to providing empty tax tables with basic, often incorrect, calculation algorithms, leaving the custodian to populate tables with manually researched data.

On the tax authority front, very little has changed. Most tax authorities still require paper forms and have manual systems for validating and questioning claims and payments. It is true that some movement has been made. Following an in-principle decision by groups of tax authorities to move towards greater automation, some have already implemented some process automation. This has, no doubt been fuelled by increasing concerns over money laundering, fraud and terrorism leading to a greater need to share investor information on the one hand and to delve more deeply into the increasing number of exotic investment vehicles that the financial services industry creates each year. Lastly, the pressure will increase as we move out of the first decade of the twenty-first century with what will be a completely different financial services model following the crash of 2008. That model will, as we'll discuss in a later part of this book, be characterised by more imposed regulation in place of self-regulation and more pressure on custodians to actively maximise investor returns. However, what's been achieved by tax authorities individually is, to say the least, fragmented. The opportunity for the different governments to work together to create a fully integrated global standard has been lost. The European Union has made some progress, again discussed elsewhere, but it's difficult to see how custodians can achieve major benefits when standardisation initiatives across the globe are all different, where they exist at all.

So, up to 2006, the industry had generally roiled along almost like a backwater which no-one wanted to visit, let alone spend money on. As you read this, most financial firms are aware on the one hand that withholding tax and its benefits are valuable in cash terms both for themselves and their clients *but*, and it's a big but, the volatility of the markets, uncertain levels of imposed regulation and their need to conserve cash on their balance sheets, mean that only radical or disruptive business models can deliver realistic solutions.

So, in the following three chapters, we will look at the strategic management of withholding tax for the twenty-first century in terms of the decisions, investments and results that can be expected from new technologies. We will also take a look at the whole subject of automating corporate actions and in particular, review the latest interim business model "virtual straight through processing" or V-STP as the precursor to a fully automated and standardised business process. Finally in this section, we will review some of the more common solutions available in the market today.

CHAPTER 8

Strategic Management

So, we know what both the problem and the opportunity are. The question that faces everyone in the investment chain is what to do about it. This question when asked in a financial services context almost always brings with it the issue of technology, but I believe that actually the challenge is in strategic management. A pencil is technology – and correctly applied is the proper response to some problems. Similarly at the other end of the scale, computing is technology. Its failure, if it can be said to have failed, is that the term IT has become synonymous with technology whereas it's actually just one portion of what technology represents – a way of identifying and dealing with problems.

To that extent, the problem for most investors and intermediaries is that the people who should know enough to make the resource decisions to address the issue, don't know enough to understand the scale or scope of the issue. The people who do know enough, are usually siloed (they don't know the full scope of the issue, just one or more parts of it) and they don't have the authority to make strategic resource decisions. The "technologists" and for this I bow to the multitude in terms of perception, the technologists that is, the IT department understand neither the strategic management issues nor the operational parameters of the problem to be able to create an effective solution, in a reasonable time frame, within a reasonable budget. In any event, IT is typically a reactive function. IT does not innovate per se in the corporate banking environment, it manages business projects allocated to it by others.

So, here's the problem for senior managers, given that withholding tax will continue to rise up the agenda as portfolio performance and custody fees decline and the tax recoverables become more material. In a world where the overall process is 60% manual, what are the solutions, what role can technology play in such an environment and how will those solutions be capable of evolving to meet increasing automation initiatives?

The response in current time is that technology is primarily a tool that custodians will deploy or purchase to minimise transaction costs, error rates whilst maximising efficiency and reconcilability. On the investor side, fund managers deploy technology principally to manage day-to-day trading business, but increasingly, to manage compliance reporting under all the different tax reporting regimes that apply to them.

As has been seen, the tax reclaim process, and indeed the relief-at-source process, as they currently stand, are capable of automation but as yet, and only in some instances, has any automation been applied to the process. In no instance is there yet a fully straight through processing (STP) approach available. That said, there have been some developments, most notably GlobeTax's work with SWIFT to provide a standardised tax reclaim service bureau which went operational in 2005.

Opportunities do exist for most custodians and fund managers to reduce costs significantly if further automation is applied. This will also provide shorter refund times and lower error rates. Automation can of course occur in several guises as outlined previously, but investors should ask questions to establish the degree to which technology, why and how its deployment has improved return on their investment more effectively and/or quickly.

It's interesting to note here, as a precursor to the chapter on benchmarking, that automation can have significant effects on processing speeds and efficiencies. One of the difficulties in an area such as this, where there are a multiplicity of solutions in use and also in the level of application to the processes themselves, is that benchmarks must be set on the basis of the lowest common denominator – which is a fully manual process. As will be seen, differing levels of automation can make some benchmarks almost irrelevant.

What is also important to recognise is that the issue is not just indirect for investment managers and other non-custodial financial firms. For pension funds, investment management firms, private banks and the like, if they are using a third party to process withholding tax affairs, there is a risk management issue. In order to assess the risk of whether one's custodian is reclaiming what you think he should be reclaiming, these firms must have tools available to be able to monitor the reports they will get from their custodians or outsourcing partners. In most cases, the SLA provides the basis for trust, but in others, for example pension fund trustees, there is clearly a need to be able to tell if the reclaim amounts filed are correct. So the investors effectively need to have knowledge of the calculation part of the process, even though they will not necessarily be filing reclaims themselves, so that they can compare custodial reports with their own income statements to be able to say confidently to their stakeholders that fund performance is being maximised. Having said that, if the larger global custodians or outsourcing companies are being used, there is less of an issue here as the job being done is more effective.

For financial services intermediaries therefore, there are four possible technology solutions available, noted below, each of which we will look at in more detail. Of course, which solution is most appropriate for any firm depends on several factors – their expected growth rate (if any), their attitude to risk, their philosophical attitude to automation solutions and of course their current position in technology and cash availability.

Buy – purchase a solution from a third party

Build – create your own solution

Bureau – purchase automated elements of the process from third parties

Outsource – partner with a specialist third party

BUY

Buying a solution to the withholding tax issue effectively means either buying computer software to automate some parts of the process, or outsourcing the issue to a third party supplier who may have automation in place. Since outsourcing has its own business dynamic, I have separated it out as a different solution even though it is technically "purchased" and therefore not in-house. From a purchaser's perspective outsourcing may well be effectively automating the process, certainly since, in an effective model income information would pass electronically to the service provider. So here we will deal with buying as it applies to computer software. There are a couple of third party suppliers of dedicated stand-alone withholding tax software – Web Services Integration Ltd and Global Operations & Administration Limited, both UK based. There are also a small number of corporate actions products which have some limited withholding tax functionality built in. The scope of such software varies greatly from information only systems usually offered by the larger global accountancy/consultancies through to more function-rich software that can include process management tools. At the end of the day, custodians must assess all options on a return on investment basis, which is in itself related to the number of reclaims or more accurately, as we'll see in a moment, the number of withholding tax events that are performed and the cost they would otherwise incur by doing the process manually.

Which option a firm decides to purchase depends on its current state of evolution and sometimes its status. Information software, often tax rates, leaves the purchaser with the difficult task of using the information in a practical operating environment. The more function-rich software can address both tax reclaim and basic and even advanced relief-at-source systems. From a financial perspective, most accountants will write down the cost of purchasing (usually licensing) such software over a number of years, usually four or five. The formula for calculating the cost of processing reclaims is given in Chapter 12 as:

$$\mathrm{CR} = \frac{D}{N}$$

where D includes S, the space cost, H, the human resource cost, V, the variable cost of reclaims and A is the cost of automation.

For a typical software purchase, "A" will itself be made up of a number of factors and be potentially variable as a result. So, for example in a typical software acquisition, the following costs could be expected:
Primary costs

- Licensing fee (often a one-off fee, but sometimes recurring)
- Maintenance fees (usually annual)
- Installation (single or multiple sites but usually a one-off cost)
- User acceptance testing (UAT)
- Upgrades (changes to operating system support and functionality)
- Updates (typically updates to data e.g., tax rates provided as part of the application)
- Customisations (ongoing costs of amending the product to fit specific internal needs)
- Training – systems (ongoing)
- Training – users (ongoing)
- Documentation – of changes to system
- Integration to existing systems (file connections, data sources, formats, standards etc.)
- Updates from legacy systems

Secondary costs would include:

- Vendor risk assessment
- Contract management
- Compliance assessment

- Employment costs
- Space costs
- Hardware and ancillary software costs

You might ask what use this formula would have for an investor or fund manager. Two issues are important. What the formula infers is that some costs are fixed, some are variable and occur regularly and others are variable but can reduce over time. As an example, when calculating A, the length of time over which the purchase of the software is written down, will mean that the effective cost per reclaim in the year following the last year of write-off will drop. The accrual for example may be over four years, so in the fifth year the cost per reclaim will drop by the amount of the annual write-off.

The second issue is that it's not just the custodians who buy such software or for that matter seek any of the technology solutions described in this chapter. Fund managers and investors are just as capable of, and sometimes responsible for, performing withholding tax reclaims as custodians. It's a commercial decision as to what gets included in a custody service agreement and what does not. Some pension funds and mutual funds do manage their own withholding tax affairs, others do it through custodians. What this chapter does is to begin to give fund managers and investors the tools to make that decision more intelligently by understanding the ways in which the various solutions apply to them.

I've already made the point that reclaim rates have been falling in general terms for several years and this would be a particular concern for many as a technology solution, even with variable costs of automation, will see a reduction in the volume of tax reclaims and therefore an increase in the cost per reclaim. By now the reader will spot this as a fallacy. The fact is that reclaim rates are indeed reducing but where the reclaim rate reduces the number of countries applying relief-at-source systems increases. Relief-at-source systems, even basic ones, require the similar amounts of information, document management and communication as do reclaims. Most software solutions have some element of relief-at-source processing management. So if the software isn't used for one process, it's likely to be used for the other and the volume is likely to stay reasonably constant.

BUILD

In other words "Do It Yourself". I've seen in my time levels of technology in this area that range from the quill pen, through the more common use of spreadsheets, to development of internal databases, like MS Access, to full-fledged mainframe systems, all aimed at internally automating the withholding tax process. The custodian can of course invest in an internal PC or mainframe build of a system and this is often seen as a good solution. It keeps knowledge and expertise internal and allows the custodian to convert specialist knowledge into a system that meets its own internal way of doing things. It also has benefits in that much of the information needed as source material for the process, for example, income data and client data, is usually already on such systems for use elsewhere in the firm's business. In addition, the custodian may have certain commercial practices that other firms are not party to and which it can uniquely automate therefore giving even more commercial advantage. However, internal builds by custodians have common problems and downsides. Budget, delivery time and efficacy are three, all of which may impact either the availability of solutions or their effectiveness or the cost per reclaim. Investors may not see the actual costs of this function from an internal build perspective because it's likely that these costs will be absorbed into bundled custody fees. It would of course be interesting if these were unbundled or charged separately because it would highlight the strengths and weaknesses of various custodial services offered. However, this is unlikely to happen and is not our direct concern here. What is worthy of note is the double edged sword of efficacy. An internal build has the strength that the custodian's special knowledge can be built in to the solution in a much more fundamental way, where a purchased solution would treat such matters as bespoke developments. On the other hand however, the purchased and outsourced solutions, in theory, have an upside benefit. That is that, to some extent, the purchaser is gaining the benefit of the third party's broader commercial experience of the area. It's also notoriously difficult to quantify the cost/benefit elements and return on investment for internal builds. In the last year, the financial services industry has been hit very hard and budgets for significant internal builds are difficult to justify. For a corporate actions function like taxation, even though it has moved up the agenda significantly, it still has some way to go. Internal build is, at present, by far the least favourable starting point.

Finally on build, particularly for those solutions which are internal to a department rather than official major build projects, custodians have to take into account the fact that people do move on. Built software is, after all, effectively a way of packaging knowledge in such a way that it can be extracted later. In other words, it de-sensitises the knowledge from the human holder. The problem is that the builders of such software have to make sure they have ways of keeping that knowledge current and also of keeping the way in which that knowledge was encoded for current retrieval also.

Build generally is a higher, and usually prohibitive, cost solution to the withholding tax issue, for all but the largest custodians.

BUREAU

For larger firms, buying or building are often certainly in the top three alternatives immediately considered because of the likely volumes of tax reclaims for which such systems will be used. The cost benefit equation is balanced in their favour. For smaller custodians and firms doing their own tax reclaims, recent changes have led to bureau-based solutions which provide partial relief from some of the problems associated with major builds or software purchases. Some aspects of the withholding tax process, as the reader is now well aware, are very difficult and can be extremely expensive, particularly if the custodian concerned processes tax events in the low hundreds or thousands per annum. Bureau offerings most commonly provide calculation of the value of a tax reclaim from a given set of data and some also provide form filling capability. The key to bureau offerings is to realise that the in-house cost is not eradicated as some parts of the process must still be undertaken internally. The benefit of these services is however that the custodian can apply a fixed and known cost per transaction for these very difficult elements of the process.

OUTSOURCE

It's very difficult to tell how prevalent this solution is. Business process outsourcing (BPO) is generally finding more and more favour in the financial services sector as internal processing costs escalate, margins narrow and the pressure to reduce staff count increases. However, the solution's opacity in the market is driven by the policies adopted by the senior management of the firms concerned. Simply put, in some instances, custodians do not want their clients to know that the process has been outsourced. They feel that in some way, outsourcing the function somehow diminishes their credibility as custodians and potentially provides a third party with sensitive client information. The contra to this argument is propounded by those who are happy to have knowledge of their outsourcing made (relatively) public. For these firms, the marketing benefits outweigh the downsides. They can cite reductions in unit costs by using an expert third party, rather than the costly in-house management. The information issue becomes a non-issue, for, to these custodians, it would not be in anyone's interests to have client sensitive information unprotected. So outsourcing providers spend a great deal of time ensuring such protection. BPO is thus seen and promoted as the "smart move". It puts the process in the hands of known and recognised experts, reduces unit costs and, because of their expert knowledge, ultimately ends with faster remittances. In the real world, both types of approach are present. The important thing is to ensure that someone is doing it.

Since the geologic-level traumas of 2008 in the industry, lay-offs in the tens of thousands have increased pressure to outsource, not just as a way to reduce costs. The problem is that as this number of people leave a firm, its "knowledge capital" is degraded significantly. Simply put, there may not be enough people left who know what they are doing to avoid increasing risk. This is highly ironic given that the reason for credit crunch lay in failures to assess debt risk in the first place.

Interestingly, the custodian ranked most efficient for tax reclaim services in Global Custody Surveys 2003–2007, with assets of over 62bn dollars, Union Bank of California, does outsource their tax reclaims. Smaller firms including small custodians, investment management firms, mutual funds, pension funds and so on often also see outsourcing as an excellent alternative to internal build or purchased software. This solution works simply because a third party has specialised in the process, developed its own tools to minimise the cost per transaction to the point where, as long as it's able to convince the client of its security procedures, the client can gain the benefit of that specialisation and actually reduce its costs. Further, this solution also removes internal staff costs and also the hidden costs of maintaining tax-rate information for what is a very niche part of the corporate actions process. Overall, the key to BPO is to ensure that the supplier does have appropriately tried and tested technology, has knowledgeable tax professionals on staff and in particular has good relationships with the various global tax authorities. Even more important of course is a record of successful tax reclaims, the greater in absolute volume, value, scale and spread, the better.

So, from an investor's viewpoint, when monitoring or selecting a custodian of assets, it's an interesting question to ask how withholding tax issues are approached and why. The answers will tell investors a great deal about how the custodian prioritises its own internal expertise and the withholding tax area generally.

A "global" custodian is likely to, and most have, internally automated some of the process, particularly with respect to researching and maintaining tax-rate information across a wide range of the variables we have already seen as applying to this area. They are more likely to have either built these systems into their own mainframe operations or purchased software for the purpose. This is usually based on the fact that the number of clients and the number of transactions per year warrants the expenditure/investment.

Second tier banks, custodians are in a grey area. The range of factors affecting how automation is leveraged in any firm means that the decision for these firms is very difficult. On the one hand, all these firms, quite rightly, aspire to growth and see themselves in potential competition with the larger custodians. There is often pressure therefore to act like a larger custodian. On the other hand, the volumes of clients and thus transactions may not make an internal build or purchasing either affordable or desirable. So there is no real pattern in how these firms approach automation. Some build internally, some purchase, some use bureaux and some outsource all depending on their internal view of their cost base and prioritisation of withholding tax.

The smaller firms, and also those who historically have not considered the area such as broker-dealers, are less likely to build internal systems and more likely to purchase skills coded into bureau offerings or more likely outsource their requirement entirely. This should not be interpreted as a negative approach or an implication of any kind of lack of commitment. In the macro economic cycle financial services is currently in its "back to basics" or "focus on core competencies" phase. This has naturally led to many aspects of the sector being outsourced to specialists. From the custodian's viewpoint this makes perfect sense. They can concentrate on their core competency and offer very high expectation levels in withholding tax services because they effectively have a firm who does nothing else but focusing in on returning value. It should not be forgotten that the existence of such outsourcing offerings also provides a fairly instant switch for operations. Internal builds of systems and their maintenance as tax regimes change are notoriously slow and very expensive, a fact that however indirectly, will reflect on custodial fees, whereas outsourcing companies tend to be smaller and more fleet of foot.

I have a set of six principles, which I call the six Cs of outsourcing, which help firms decide whether to outsource withholding tax and if so, what the key issues are to selecting a provider.

1. Competency
2. Complexity
3. Cost reduction
4. Compliance
5. Corporate governance
6. Competitive advantage

Competency

Best practice, let alone risk and liability mitigation, requires relief at source where available, to be obtained for the benefit of the client so he or she has maximum funds at all points in the investment lifecycle. Some countries, as we've seen elsewhere in this book, have accelerated recovery processes and, failing to meet the associated deadlines can result in up to a ten-year wait for your funds. Some security types, such as ADRs have no direct claim possibility, only indirectly on the underlying shares and through a sponsoring bank. Some investment vehicles are transparent to tax authorities and reclaims may be missed if confidentiality or refusal to disclose keeps broker income streams and client identities separate. Some methodologies are transparent to tax authorities, so brokers who claim title to securities may think they are entitled to treaty benefits, whereas foreign tax authorities will disagree and penetrate title to beneficial ownership. Some firms sell processes that, if followed, put FIs at significant risk. All this demonstrates the need for a provider who has extreme competency and deep knowledge. Outsourcing becomes logical because it's the primary focus of the partner and all of its expenditure is aimed at this one issue.

Complexity

There are 230 tax jurisdictions in the world, each may or may not have a treaty with any of the others, for the avoidance of double taxation. For each of these jurisdictions there are a number of types of investor and a number of types of income any combination of which can result in a different tax of withholding and treaty being applied. The date on which the income is distributed also affects the entitlement, and other factors increase the complexity further. The number of permutations is over 40 million. The in-house cost of recovery, for any fund with multiresidence members or for custodians with a broad client base, will be prohibitive compared to the number of likely claims that will be generated. A good outsourcing firm will succeed because its business model leverages economies of scale across the whole process. The largest outsource provider processes over 2 million claims a year – at that level, the focus on research and investment in processes buys a greater assurance of success compared to what could be delivered in-house.

Cost reduction

Outsourcing has a strong history of cost reduction. In fact it's usually one of the prime drivers to outsource. However, in withholding tax, as with other areas, there's no point in having cost reductions if you experience a reduction in other business factors such as market-perceived competence, scale and scope of offering. That said, there are significant cost savings to be had. Of course, outsourcing in its classical meaning is a product provided to custodians and brokers who need a service to remain competitive. The largest outsourcing firm in this area, GlobeTax, cites cost savings of up to 65%

using its V-STP process. In the current climate, such cost reductions are very attractive. The degree of cost reduction of course depends on the current status of a custodian's operation. A custodian who does not offer any service at all, will suffer no cost reduction at all, but will not benefit from the other advantages and be more competitive. It's also likely that while there are no cost reductions, this type of custodian won't be creating an inefficient system since they'll start essentially with a blank sheet. So their potential competitiveness will be increased. For those firms that do have existing functions, the decision to outsource usually starts with an outsource test of some part of their client base that they find most difficult. So cost savings will be phased. In the scenarios I've seen it's also true that it's rare for any financial firm to have a true idea of the costs associated with a given function. Adding up the IT costs, employment costs and space costs does not get you anywhere near the true cost. Most do not include critical contributions from research, legal, compliance, training, relationship management, postage and so on. Many firms actually calculate the "cost of a tax reclaim" and use the derived number as a lower threshold below which, in their estimation, the cost of reclamation is higher than the value that will be gained. Two problems with this. First, the calculation is invariably incorrect and too low. Second, the threshold is usually used by the institution as an excuse not to file a claim at all, as opposed to the more competitive track of reimbursing the beneficial owner for the reclaim entitlement. The net result is that the firm has not engaged in the cost of the claim but has benefited the client. It's also true that many people believe that tax reclamation is a "data processing" function. Their mentality therefore is that the cost of any given claim can be expressed in fixed dollar amounts. This is clearly not true, as the reader should by now, be able to fathom. The cost associated with any given entitlement depends on many factors and some claims will cost more to recover than others of the same value simply because of the market they happen to be in, or the type of beneficial owner concerned or the questions that tax authorities may or may not ask. Needless to say outsourcing enables such variables to be much more professionally assessed. At the end of the day, outsourcing is a valuable option to consider and may, if firms have not already done so, be used as an opportunity to properly cost out current activities thereby giving the outsource option a more clear opportunity to demonstrate its benefits in numerical terms.

Compliance

One of the biggest potential concerns of financial firms when it comes to (i) deciding whether to outsource and (ii) choosing which outsource supplier is the degree to which compliance issues can be addressed. This issue relates both to control procedures as well as regulatory issues that the banks may be subject to but which the supplier may not be subject to. At one end of the spectrum most suppliers are happy to undergo audits of compliance since it's in their interests to support their clients. These usually take the form of looking at controls on documentation, security of client data and of course the usual business continuity plans. What's going to be more concerning in the future is the degree to which firms will be able to meet the compliance requirements under tax information reporting. The US 1441 regulations require multiple levels of reporting across income types, tax-rate pools and also beneficial owner types. These reporting requirements, as in the US case, will become embedded either in the treaties or, more likely, in separate regulation. However, with Ireland and Japan already with similar (but not the same) tax information reporting requirements and FISCO suggesting the US model as the basis for the EU States, it's clear that financial firms will have massive overhead increases to be able to comply with each permutation of beneficial owner residency and income jurisdiction. In the past, these permutations were defined just by the residencies and the treaties that is, the applicable tax rates. In future these will just be the operational day-to-day characteristics. The end-of-year reporting could potentially add a significant administrative burden.

The tax information reporting element is further exacerbated by the general feeling that compliance will be achieved through audits and penalties. If the United States has its way, and the European Union follows suit, driven by reactions to the financial crisis of 2008, then for each jurisdiction there will be a treaty, regulation and contract. The latter will require oversight by two auditors with joint and several liability. The result will be a polarisation of firms into markets where they can justify the costs based on the mix of their clients' investments but still a massive increase in costs. It therefore starts to make more sense to outsource where there is a provider that can satisfy both the processing elements of relief-at-source and long form claims *and* the additional requirements of compliance to withholding tax regulation. It is far more likely that third parties will develop the resource needed at the global level since this will form part of their core offering and they can't really avoid the tax information reporting element of the new processes.

The issue of whether to outsource thus becomes a moot point where compliance is concerned. The ability of an outsource supplier to support a compliance processing requirement as well as a compliance to contract requirement will mean a cost for both parties, whichever does it. Equally, keeping such complex processes in-house, particularly for anyone who is not a global custodian, will mean much higher costs.

Corporate governance

The corporate governance issue in outsourcing withholding tax revolves around the benefit that can be gained from such outsourcing. The problem, as someone once said, is that people don't know they've got a problem until it's too late. If the financial crisis has done anything, we can only hope that one of the questions that rises up the agenda for business people is "what is it that we don't know?". Again the United States is the market that is, by default, pushing the rest of the world. Having said that, the rest of the world seems content to follow the principle and have a much higher "bar" for financial firms to meet in terms of expectation. The likely infusion of Sarbanes–Oxley type wording into new regulations on withholding tax and their subsequent proliferation will mean an increase in risk and liability for financial firms. Investors equally need to be aware of such potential risks to their portfolios as they will ultimately be the driving force behind any real actions.

The issue here is what I have consistently called "proportionality". There is a deemed or real expectation on behalf of investors that a financial intermediary has obligations to them that might not be explicit in contracts but derive more from the role that a financial intermediary performs. So, the question for investors is "tell me what I don't know". This has become a more vexed question in current circumstances now that the issues which gave birth to Sarbanes–Oxley in the United States have become global in scope with a lack of trust leading inexorably to an increase in regulatory oversight. We could posit some hypothetical situations that could, if raised to a large enough level with large enough consequences, mean serious risk and liability for financial institutions. We've already seen how the lack of controls in the debt market have reverberated around the world. And we already know from previous chapters that there is around $1.6 trillion of client money that's in the wrong place – and the financial firms know it in their back offices if not in their board rooms. If the combination of internal service level decisions leads to investors having an unrealised entitlement through the action, or lack thereof, of their intermediary – employed for the purpose of maximising investment return, and the intermediary either does not inform the investor, takes no action or implies that no action can be taken – this puts the financial institution at serious risk. In a Sarbanes–Oxley world, the result would have to be, under the regulations, a report of material failure direct to the board. For example, if a back office became aware that they had missed a relief-at-source process and thereby subjected their client to a long form claim process that would take years to realise, the client is now out of pocket for that period through no fault of their own. If a custodian has such inefficient processes and subsequent backlogs, that it takes 3 years after the pay-date before a claim is even filed, that then takes another 2 years to recover, the client has been out of pocket for 5 years, 5 unnecessary years again through no fault of his. If a client has significant ADR positions but the intermediary fails to claim tax back on the income from them, the client's entitlement still exists – it's their money – but the client is permanently out of pocket. If a non-qualified financial intermediary with clients with US sourced income fails to provide them with a 1042-S form and has taxed their income at 30% due to the omnibus structure of their superior accounts with qualified intermediaries – the investor has lost out until someone tells him there is a long form process *and* the intermediary is at risk of a significant (public) fine from the IRS of up to $1.5 million.

For small investors, there is no real case here, except at a class action level, which is highly unlikely. However, at the institutional investor level, where the amounts are more significant, these issues become extremely material. No fund manager wants to lose his or her job because they failed to know enough to ask intelligent questions of their custodians. Knowing this, any failures are likely to be followed through aggressively. When this sort of thing happened in the eighties and nineties, it was dealt with by the financial firms on a case-by-case basis, usually by making their complainant whole (i.e., repaying them their tax from their own pocket). This also meant that nothing ever really changed. It was essentially brushed under the carpet and operations continued as before. In this century, with all that's gone on, investors are both more sensitive and more vocal. The net result is that it's not a question of "if" any more, it's a question of when a material failure is going to be released to the street with all the reputational as well as fiscal damage that will follow for the offending institution. Ergo, any event of that nature will also have an effect on the institution's (probably) already fragile share price which in turn means that the issue is indeed one for the board room as a core corporate governance issue.

Competitive advantage

Finally in the six C's of outsourcing we come to competitive advantage. It has surprised me in the 12 years I've been in the business, just how little connection there is between front office and back office. In the training courses I run on strategic management in financial services, I use withholding tax as an example of this disconnect. The front office views corporate actions, and by inference tax reclamation, as a necessary evil. This is usually because at senior management level, they don't understand it. At relationship management (RM) level the expression of withholding tax is the number of complex documents the RM needs to get from a beneficial owner – so it's a pain, not a benefit. In the back office they see cash being put back into client's accounts as a direct result of their activity, but there's no way in the firm for them to get the value of that fact into a form that anyone else will listen to.

Apart from that basic disconnect, which doesn't necessarily argue for outsourcing as such, just better communications, the fact is that any competent outsource provider is likely to have a larger base of experience than an internal department. This has to be looked at two ways. First, most internal departments, while they may be doing a good job, are restricted in that their resource forms part of a larger budget constraint. So, naturally, they are more at risk in the ongoing day-to-day operations of coming across claims that are too small or too complex to process. Second, the object of having a competitive advantage is to increase business. With business increase comes a greater pressure on budgets and the ability to respond to new business, which may or may not fall into the same pattern as the tax processing an internal department is currently undertaking. On the other hand an outsourced service provider has as its core philosophies the need to make economies of scale while being able to have a completely scaleable business model. In addition, because of their scale of operations, they are probably already processing types of claim that internal departments have not yet come across. The net result is that outsourcing can provide an immediate competitive advantage since it applies the performance benchmarks and service levels of the provider with a much larger scale and scope of operation – to the purchaser. The nature of the tax process in this regard allows both white label and co-branded solutions to exist side by side, so firms planning to outsource can gain the best of both worlds.

I've given over a large section to outsourcing because I see it as a natural reaction by many firms to increasing cost constraints on the one hand and a realisation that it provides a zero cost method of improving fee income by improving the cash in its client's accounts. In comparison to other strategic options open to management, outsourcing is currently the most logical and generates the most up-sides for minimal and manageable risk.

Of course none of these strategic management options sits in a vacuum. Day-to-day processing must proceed and any decision to build, buy or outsource a tax processing operation has one-off costs associated with it and consequent risk. In such a complex area, building a solution for most firms is now unsustainable, even if they still had half the IT people they started 2008 with. The way in which specifications would need to change to encompass the volatility in the market would be too complex to keep up with and even parallel running two systems would cause significant problems. Buying solutions only puts a patch on the process since most solutions available require integration to existing systems, do not provide a full automation solution and they also suffer from a reliance on relatively small firms. Outsourcing does meet many of the fiscal needs of firms currently but does need to be managed carefully. The global custodians do offer their resource to other banks, which brings with it several confidentiality and disclosure issues and using an independent outsource provider requires careful assessment of control issues.

From a service level standpoint, given that withholding tax is now seen as a business differentiator in the market, doing nothing is not really an option other than one which will see business going out the door very quickly. That said, pricing and scaling of services becomes important so that new customers can be absorbed into systems without further expenditure. Knowing the kind of changes ahead (see Chapter 13), most custodians are now positioning themselves to both unbundled tax processing from their core custody offering into a value added service and to structure pricing to more accurately reflect the fact that tax processing is not data management. The market and other variables affect the workload involved in filing any claim. It's also true that most financial services brands have global reach but are supported, if at all, in one or two locations. The result is that even if you have an account at a major custodian, where that account is located will determine if you are even offered a tax service. This is particularly differentiated between the mature central European markets and say the Asia-Pacific markets. So, again, if we're thinking about strategic management, apart from unbundling (price), scale and scope of service (product) and how you connect the back office with the front office to maximise revenue opportunities (promotion), strategic managers also need to consider how connecting their various business units within the brand can strengthen their position and maintain loyalty in their client base (place).

If strategic management of this area was simple, everyone could do it and we wouldn't be faced as an industry with only a 7% success rate. It's clear then that the way in which senior C-level executives inform themselves of these issues and create successful strategies will be critical in future.

CHAPTER 9

Automating Corporate Actions

In this chapter we will be looking at the most obvious strategy to deal with low performance and manual processes – automation. As we've seen so far, on the market side, several elements of withholding tax can be and have been automated. Unfortunately, many more can be automated but have not been. The main reasons are that (i) there has been no concerted effort to automate and (ii) there has been no integration of standards, messaging and the will to use them and (iii) there are certain actors in the process that have either only automated to a limited non-standard degree or have not automated at all.

The main reason that efforts have only just begun to automate this area, despite regular calls for it and regular statements by the banks that it's at the top of their priority list, is that the elements that are most difficult to automate are those relating to the tax authorities.

Withholding tax is actually a subset of corporate actions, which in itself is a subset, usually, of income processing for most custodian banks and brokers.

Understanding and establishing effective taxation processes is all very well, but unless custodians are able to communicate in a secure, fast, efficient and consistent way, many of the gains made under one principle can be lost in others.

The three main areas that need to be addressed to be able to automate corporate actions are:

- Standards and messaging
- Documentation
- Electronic signatures

As we move towards a combination environment with document-based relief at source at its hub, it would be easy to believe that the only element necessary would be standards and messaging. With these in place, the documents would remain with the intermediary unless called for by audit, so the only automation required would essentially be an election by each custodian for that proportion of its position at a upstream financial institution or withholding agent, which could be taxed at a favourable rate. If the relief-at-source process worked as it technically should, the proportion of long form claims would be somewhat reduced, however, not by as much as some commentators have intimated. The problem is that many investment vehicles and account structures do not facilitate an election for relief at source, even though the underlying members may be entitled. The nature of the account structure often means that an omnibus account would be opaque to the payer and thus subject to a statutory rate of tax. This occurs often when a custodian bank has one omnibus account at a higher level custodian in which the assets of all its clients are aggregated. Only the lower level custodian knows the identity of these clients and so, at one level the tax rate cannot be applied on a relief-at-source basis because the lower level institution is never going to give away the details of its customers to another financial institution (competitor) – that's why they have omnibus accounts. The other occasion is where the account is omnibus structured not because of the custodian's business model but because of the investment vehicle itself for example, a nominee account. Taking both of these into account, the proportion of investors, who, even in a relief at source oriented model, would not be able to benefit from relief at source, is so large that the automation of messaging alone will be insufficient to solve the problem.

STANDARDS AND MESSAGING

SWIFT

SWIFT is the Society of Worldwide Interbank Financial Telecommunications. Established in 1973 by 239 banks across 15 countries they created a unified international transaction processing and transmission system for the banking community. They currently operate in payments, treasury, securities and trade finance areas.

Essentially SWIFT has two roles. Firstly, they are appointed by the International Standards Organisation to be the guardians of ISO standards for the financial services industry. Together with their members and users, they establish what kind of messages and data need to be sent between financial institutions. They then establish a message type (MT) to code the data in a standard format, currently to ISO15022, and publish the details so that the technology departments of the various financial institutions can adopt the message types to improve their business.

The second and equally important part of SWIFT's role is to provide a physical network across which these messages can be transmitted. It's important to recognise here that a message created under SWIFT's ISO standards does not *have* to be transmitted across the SWIFT network. Technically anyone sending a message electronically, for example by email, can adopt the standard format and, as long as the recipient knows that the message is of a particular type and to a particular standard, then they have the capability to "decode" the message electronically into their own systems. So, while SWIFT's physical network isn't *required* for the transmission of an ISO standard message, the SWIFT network has some advantages over other methods since it was designed specifically by and for the financial community, notably, from an investor's viewpoint, security of data and guarantee of delivery.

SWIFT is actually a not for profit organisation, a co-operative formed of "members", "sub-members" and "participants" who are co-owners of the business to a greater or lesser extent. SWIFT members are eligible organisations who hold a share in SWIFT. They include banks, eligible securities, broker-dealers and regulated third party investment management institutions (IMIs). Sub-members are constituted of organisations who are more than 50% directly owned or 100% indirectly owned by a full member. Participants include non-bank financial institutions who do not have voting rights but do have limited access to SWIFT products and services such as exchanges, central securities depositories and payment system market infrastructures. There are currently 7,900 members, sub-members and participants operating in 196 countries. It's also clear that this is not the full universe of financial institutions who might be engaged in the business of maximising an investor's portfolio. The reader should take note of the nature of this utility from the perspective that a custodian not part of SWIFT will need to explain how they communicate in the withholding tax (indeed custody) chain and how they guarantee security.

Risk and security

The issue of risk in getting withholding tax messages moved between the various parties can be summarised as follows. These are of course also generic issues for any financial intermediary. However, to understand the communications principle involved as well as the potential future developments in this area, it's important to understand just what exactly is backing up the process.

Confidentiality is vital from an investor's perspective and while automation is a valuable tool to reduce fees, it's also the main concern of investors in terms of where information about their investments and income is stored and to whom it is released. Since the communications principle effectively places this sensitive information into a domain outside the direct control of the financial intermediary, it's important best practice to understand the nature of the communication, the risks associated with it and the way in which best practice can be assured. Security, validation and authentication are key issues for SWIFT as for investors and custodians.

Security – In the SWIFT philosophy there are several areas where security is important when sending withholding tax messages:

- Security of access by responsible staff at the sending firm. This is most often either the withholding agent notifying a financial intermediary of an income event or an instruction from a custodian to a withholding agent with respect to the level of tax to which the beneficial owners is entitled.

- Security between the user and SWIFT which includes such issues as access control and encryption. The importance of this element cannot be overstated. This and security at SWIFT are the points at which sensitive information leaves the safekeeping of the custodian and is in the hands of a third party whilst it is delivered to its recipient.

- Security at SWIFT includes validation, storage, encryption and site security.

- Security between user and user is achieved with authentication using a database of identifiers called Bank Identifier Codes (BICs).

It is key to understand that SWIFT has no "added value" interest in the contents of a message per se. While they are fundamentally concerned with whether the content that leaves point A is the same as that received at point B, they are not interested in whether the message is about ten dollars or ten million dollars.

Validation – However, as part of the standards, it is vital that, having set the format of any particular message type, that the senders and receivers are able, where possible to have the content of messages validated. This does not mean establishing whether a corporate action is correct or not. It is more to do with making sure that the syntax of the message is correct. There are also areas of messages where, for any given code in one field, there needs to be a particular kind of entry in another, a sort of 'If... Then' validation. This kind of validation is performed by SWIFT to very strict standards which gives users the comfort that their individual operations do not need to replicate validation processes across the world's institutions, thus making them more efficient.

Authentication – Authentication is assured, as alluded to in my comments about security, by the presence and management of a database of unique identifiers. The two main categories are BIC (bank identifiers) and BEI codes (Business Entity Identifiers). Both have a similar structure providing a bank code or business entity code appended to a country code, a location code and a branch code. So people on the system can clearly and quickly (and securely) know who is sending and receiving messages as well as where they are.

Essentially, the service contract between SWIFT and its users means that the users must agree to be connected to the SWIFT system for at least seven hours a day. SWIFT themselves offer a "five nines" availability of their own system. In other words, they warrant that the SWIFT network will be available 99.99999% of the time. This means that, in most cases, as long as the recipient signs into the network, they are likely to get their messages in a few seconds.

The summation of this very complex system includes a number of internal checks and balances to aid reconciliation and identify the purpose of messages.

Standards

ISO15022. Again, in recent times, much has changed in ISO standards. By May 2003, all SWIFT users had moved from the old ISO7775 standard to the newly launched ISO15022 standard. I'm not going to go into a detail exposition of SWIFT message standards, nor of the detailed format of SWIFT messages themselves. However it is perhaps interesting and to some extent instructive for the reader to know the basics of how this important element of the communications principle is structured and delivered.
ISO20022. Even as ISO15022 was being implemented there were already groups working on ISO20022, the next standard. In this standard, the biggest difference is that messages are considered part of a business process. In this way, institutions can sponsor applications to ISO for entire business processes where some messages may already exist to support the process while others may need to be developed. In addition, existing messages may need to be amended in terms of the codes within the messages to help define new aspects of the business process.

Communications

FIN.

Financial Messaging (FIN), is a transaction-specific store and forward process. This means that messages are stored, then forwarded to recipients. In other words it's a batch process. SWIFT guarantees to deliver the message but has a time frame in which it can do so, sometimes up to 6 hours.

SWIFTNet

This is SWIFT's advanced IP-based messaging service. One of the difficulties in communications over the last few years has been the rate of change in available technology. Clearly a real-time messaging system has many advantages over a batch process, most notably of course time. The most invasive technology of recent times is of course the internet. The internet, which would otherwise be seen as a natural highway for the financial industry, suffered and still suffers from an inherent lack of security. It lacks security for two reasons: firstly, the technological issue of an open system and secondly, given the openness, the visibility. It's not only less secure to use the Internet, but the Internet attracts hackers almost like a candle does to a moth.

So, on the one hand we have SWIFT's FIN network, which is batch-oriented on the downside but extremely secure on the upside. The Internet, on the other hand, offers real-time processing capability on the upside, but lack of security on the downside. In simple terms SWIFTNet is the best of both worlds. It provides the security of the network, delivered with an Internet protocol, in real time.

So now that we understand the principles and concepts of SWIFT, without the technical jargon, what exactly is a SWIFT message like? Being electronic and having so many of them flying around the world, it's perhaps unsurprising that SWIFT messages are designed to carry the maximum information content in the smallest space. Effectively a SWIFT message is a data packet that is formed of groups or blocks of data. Each block has a different purpose and within each block there are a series of fields which the sender can populate with data. The data itself takes the form of codes to which both parties, being SWIFT users, have data dictionaries to enable them to effectively decode the messages.

Messaging for withholding tax

There are some specific messages that are currently used or available for use for withholding tax purposes, although there are still several areas where SWIFT messaging has yet to provide automated messaging solutions. This is not a failure of SWIFT nor of its members, but more a factor of the nature of the parties in the market and the degree to which they have the will and the need to automate, currently manual, parts of the tax reclaim process. The checks and balances I mentioned earlier are important, particularly in SWIFT messages because this is one of those areas where theory, as laid out in the DTAs can come up against practice. For a custodian performing many tax reclaims, it is difficult enough to keep track of the process. However, when for example some dividend rates change after their initial announcement or partial dividends are paid, the tracking and reconciliation process can mount to very expensive levels without a degree of organised automation and reconciliation.

The messages that apply most effectively to withholding tax are:

- MT564 – This message is a corporate action *notification*. It's used when a withholding agent wishes to notify a custodian of an income event, most commonly from a withholding tax perspective, a cash dividend. In many circumstances it is sent as a primary advice and another MT564 is sent when the event is confirmed. There are a variety of codes which can relate ultimately to the tax reclaim process including
  - DVCA – Cash dividend
  - CAPG – Capital gains distribution – distribution of profits resulting from the sale of securities
  - TREC – Event related to tax reclaim activities
  - TAXI – Tax instruction

- MT565 – This message is a corporate action *instruction*. As such the codes available are the same as those in an MT564. The message is sent by an account owner for example, custodian to an account servicer such as a withholding agent. The MT565 message, in withholding tax terms, would be the counterpart to an MT564 and indeed in the structure of a SWIFT message, there is often a linkage between an MT564 and an MT565 which aids traceability and reconciliation. If the notification goes one way, withholding agent to custodian, the MT565 goes the other way. So, in this example, the MT565 is the instruction sent by a custodian to a withholding agent. The theory is that for each payment, a custodian can instruct a withholding agent how much tax should be sent to the tax authorities, based on the knowledge that the custodian has about his client beneficial owner's tax status. The withholding agent does not normally know any of the details about the beneficial owner, as these are details kept very secret by the custodian. What happens in practice is that each client/investor of the custodian is pooled into a tax bracket. This may be as simple as two pools, treaty and non-treaty. It may also become very complex, as with the US regulations based on a matrix of different bandings of withholding tax level and income type. Various methodologies have been used by withholding agents, basically seeking to minimise the workload whilst maximising the confidentiality of their client details.

- MT566 – This message is a corporate action *confirmation*. This message can be used as proof of sufferance of over-withheld tax in some cases, since the message can include specific data about what income has been credited. This includes data under the following codes:

- GRSS – Gross dividend rate
- NETT – Net dividend rate
- TAXC – Tax credit rate
- NRES – Non-resident rate
- TAXR – Withholding tax rate
- WITF – Withholding of foreign tax
- WITL – Withholding of local tax
- FLFR – Fully franked rate (Australia only)

From these data, a withholding tax reclaim can be established and calculated when applied to other known facts about the beneficial owner's tax residency.

- MT567 – This message is a corporate action *status and processing advice*. It's used to advise the status, or change in status of a corporate action related event previously instructed or executed. In this message type the following codes have relevance in reporting event status:
  - AUTH – Sent to tax authorities – for tax reclaims, the event is pending because the reclaim is sent to the tax authorities.
  - VLDA – Valid for tax authorities – for tax reclaims, the event is pending, the event is valid for tax authorities.
  - INVA – Invalid for tax authorities – for tax reclaims, the event is invalid for the tax authorities.
  - REFT – Refused by tax authorities – for tax reclaims, the event is refused by the tax authorities.
  - TAXC – Amount of tax credit – amount of cash that is represented by taxes that have been previously paid.
  - TAXR – Reclaim of taxes – Reclaim of tax that was paid in excess of actual obligation.
  - TAXFR – Tax free amount – the amount of cash that has not been subject to withholding

- MT598 – This message is a corporate action *narrative*. The message is used to transmit complex instructions or narrative details and uses, together with more formal field structures, an 8,000 character field for such narrative – effectively a free text message. As usual with all these messages there is a code TREC to identify the message as related to tax reclaim activities.

  So, as we can see, SWIFT have provided a range of messages which have some, but not extensive or exhaustive application to the tax reclaim and relief-at-source processes described in the taxation and communications principles. These are excellent, if underused, messages in the custodial world, mainly because they have yet to gain acceptance in the community. There are also opportunities to make these messages more specific to the actual process. So for example, in an MT567, the code AUTH tells us that the event is at the tax authorities, this does not distinguish between a local tax authority providing proof of residency and a foreign tax authority assessing a filed reclaim.

- MT574 – One example of recent change relates to the US NRA Regulations Section 1441. As the reader now knows, there are two groups of points at which information about beneficial owners of US source income is transferred between financial firms.

  The first is either from an NQI to a withholding agent or from a QI to its US custodian. The message, MT574(IRSLST), is designed to provide information in the form of a list of to the US custodian or withholding agent to enable them in turn to place the beneficial owner into a pool with others who are able to claim the same rate of withholding tax under the regulations and treaties. The message is either sent once a year or once in a specified period (agreed between the parties) which may even be prior to each payment of a reportable amount.

  The second instance occurs because the regulations require that a form W-8BEN is provided by an NQI to a US withholding agent to demonstrate, in the absence of a QI contract between the NQI and the IRS, that, at the time of any payment made, the beneficial owner was actually entitled to the withholding rate applied by the withholding agent on behalf of the NQI. This is a classic example of pragmatism over theory. The regulations first provide that the W-8 must be an original with an original signature, although the IRS does allow an electronic W-8 between any two points (but not in a chain). SWIFT's own estimates were that over 900 million bits of paper would need to flow to meet this requirement. Apart from buying shares in FedEx, the solution was clearly to provide a mechanism for financial firms to move this information electronically. The message, MT574 (W8-BENO) provides all the data present on a W-8, with the signature replaced with the tax reference number or other identifier of the beneficial owner.

There are other message types which have some relevance, particularly in the FIN, store and forward network, although these have less relevance in SWIFTNet's real-time environment. In the FIN network, when a message is sent, the sender knows that the message will be sent, but only knows the delivery date and time within loose parameters. So some messages provide confirmation and reconciliation capability. In particular MT900 and MT950 represent cash balance messages (individual and end of day summary). An MT950 message is an end of day message which summarises all the messages that have been received during a day. On the one hand, these are clearly good practice to aid reconciliations between firms where the volume of messages can be very large. On the other hand, firms are well aware that each SWIFT message sent costs money and therefore it may be that, given the known identity of senders and receivers and the manual reconciliation processes that go on every day in custodian banks, some firms do not use these messages. That doesn't detract from the existence of, nor the relevance of, any automated method such as this to simplify the reconciliation process as a best practice policy.

DOCUMENTATION

The standards and messaging currently in place only deal with data. That data may be in the form of information about one party needed by the other in order to perform a process. To that extent, the standards and messaging are some way advanced. However, the really big issue in withholding tax automation is documentation. The type of documentation varies by market, the information on the documentation varies by market, most but not all markets require hard copy originals signed by the beneficial owner or their appointed agent. Where relief-at-source processing is automated, the documentation still has to exist in original format and be subject to audit.

So the difficulty for custodians lies in the fact that there is no common layout or format for a long form tax reclaim, and in relief at source there is no automated system to efficiently collate documents with the data they contain and provide audit access to the level that is likely in the next few years.

Since both a long form claim and a relief-at-source claim are based on (i) proof of residence, (ii) proof of legal form and (iii) proof of tax sufferance, we need some standard that applies to all these document types. We then need some standardisation which allows for each authority to request additional information dependent on the type of beneficial owner, which may also be documentary.

So, we see that there are fragmentary steps being taken to address some of the automation issues involved. However, since it's unlikely that a full automation model will exist within the next five to ten years, there needs to be certainly a custody solution that provides some relief from the manual processes.

ELECTRONIC SIGNATURES

However, even if we have standards and message types that allow for the transport of data and documents, and documents that have been modernised and standardised as far as possible, we still need to address the issue of signatures.

At this stage we do need to put this issue, again, in context. If the OECD, FISCO, CFA, ICG and so on manage to create agreement and a planned pathway to convergence to a relief at source/long form claim model, the complexities of account structures and the financial environment will still mean enormous numbers of financial intermediaries who are not in a position to benefit from that relief-at-source model due to the cost of compliance. There will therefore still be a major requirement for long form claims automation as well as the automation of those parts of the relief-at-source process that are new to practitioners – tax information reporting and audit support, both across a wide variety of markets.

That said, most documentation today has, as its sine qua non, the signature of an authorised person, financial institution or beneficial owner

V-STP

Once the reader has completed Chapter 13, it will become clear on re-reading this chapter that complete automation of the entire business process is some years away. Given that scenario, custodians and brokers face a major problem. In the face of global financial crises, how do they move towards STP in an efficient way. They could develop their own systems that parallel the manual systems but this will add an intolerable burden. Staff, already under pressure, will have to run both manual and automated systems while they evolve, over several years, in scenarios where most already suffer backlogs and lack of investment in people and resources. On top of that they will have to undergo audits of the new systems at an increased frequency, add and integrate new tax information reporting systems that don't exist in their manual systems. The problem is that while a custodian seeks to solve this problem from an internal perspective it's unlikely that there will be any short-term gain, quite the opposite, and in this context, short term may be ten years. The only solution available at present offers a pseudo automated way to minimise these interim costs. The problem is all the manual processes. If held internally there's no way to automate around them to create a smooth process. However, Virtual Straight Through Processing, as described below shows how one innovative firm has created a way to provide an automated process for custodians.

V-STP is a term which came to initial prominence in 2007. V-STP or Virtual Straight Through Processing is a term which described the confluence of three concepts which together provide a business model for financial institutions to automate the manual elements of a corporate action where the corporate action concerned is essentially manual.

V-STP was coined by GlobeTax and SWIFT and launched in September 2007 at a SIBOS convention in Boston. GlobeTax is an independent firm that provides outsource withholding tax solutions to the financial services industry and as such, it was well placed to create this solution. There are three elements to V-STP:

1. An outsource value proposition for the corporate action "value node";
2. Messaging standards for the transmission of data between counterparties and;
3. A computer network over which the data can be sent and received.

Of the two major financial messaging network providers, only SWIFT has so far delivered an operational V-STP model. Figure 9.1 shows how this works in practice.

From a custodian's perspective, the issue is that withholding tax processing is not capable of being automated. There are some parts that can be automated of course: the receipt of income data from withholding agents and the market, the calculation of entitlements for individual clients and even to a limited extent the preparation of the various forms needed. However

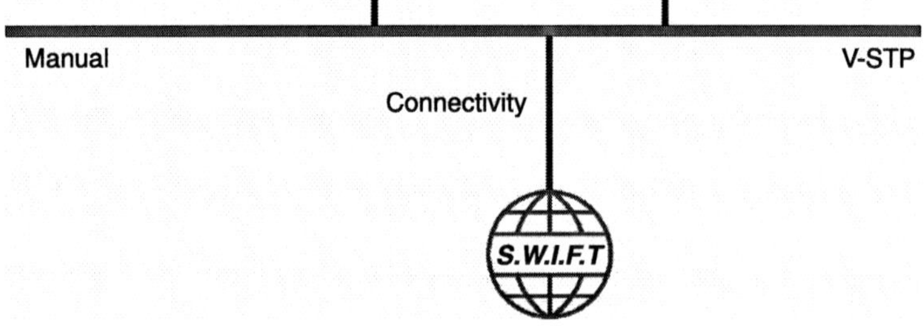

Figure 9.1 V-STP representational model

Source: Author.

overall, around 60% of the processes involved are still essentially manual. These include

- Tax research,
- Local certification of claims,
- Client certification of claims and
- Filing to foreign tax authorities

Most of these sub-processes are manual because they involve entities outside the control of custodians. The practice of using limited powers of attorney to replace client certifications is increasing, but there are still several jurisdictions where such powers of attorney cannot be used for this purpose. Most tax authorities process requests for certification and claims for entitlement manually and require paper-based forms with original signatures, both issues we will touch on later in this chapter. So, while these manual elements sit with the custodians, tax reclamation cannot be automated into an STP process. Traditional outsourcing would be a solution here except that traditional outsourcing would require custodians to send data in a number of potential proprietary formats, documentation of clients would still be manual and reporting would probably also be essentially either manual, ad hoc or both. The breakthrough occurred when the idea of using and developing ISO standard messaging to represent the whole business process flow and then use a secure network, already in existence, to move that data. This is essentially what ISO20022 is all about – developing business process standards rather than messaging standards. In this way, the messages have context and commercial meaning to their users.

Also key to this paradigm's success was that, while the way in which the elements were packaged was new, the elements themselves already existed. This served to offer a very low-cost transition from completely manual to V-STP.

Figure 9.2 reminds us of the overall tax process that custodians must engage in. All the processes marked in dotted lines are usually manual for the custodian. In a V-STP model, which we should remember can be applied to several types of corporate action, the first element is to select a provider or "value node". The characteristics of a value node provider are that they must

1. Have a commercially available and sustainable solution that meets the quality criteria of the custodian;

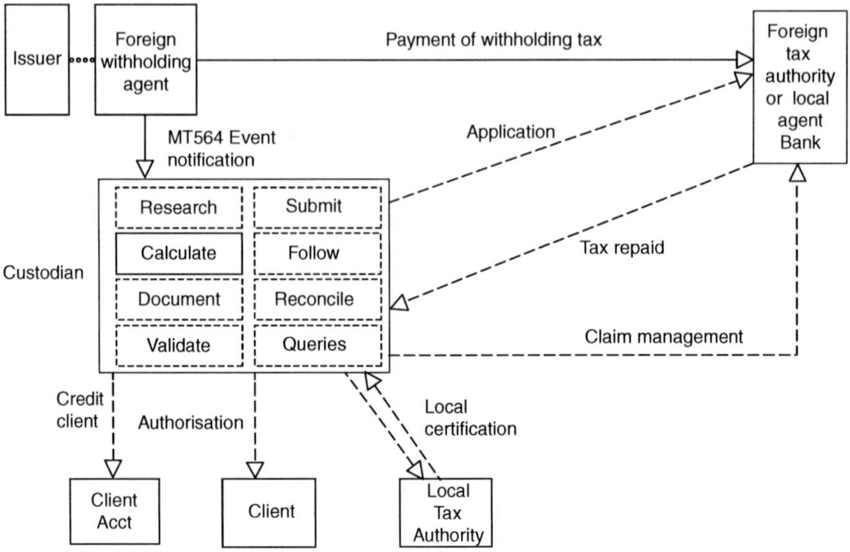

Figure 9.2 Tax reclamation before V-STP

Source: Author.

2. Be capable of packaging the data flows and other processes into a standardised form for the custodian; and

3. Be able to connect to the same computer network as the custodian in order to facilitate the data flows.

While there are many corporate action types, most of which are being investigated by firms such as Information Mosaic, Checkfree, GlobalClaimsFiling etc., the only firm providing a withholding tax reclamation solution that is V-STP is GlobeTax. Figure 9.3 shows the same tax reclamation process, but this time in V-STP flow and, importantly, from the custodian's perspective. Of particular note in this diagram is the fact that there are no dotted lines, no manual processes. TRSB is the value node offering of GlobeTax. GlobeTax essentially established themselves as a service bureau on the SWIFT network in 2005 giving them the ability to be on the same computer network as all their customers. They then packaged SWIFT product offerings and messages to deal with the various possible ways in which custodians might want to, or be able to send data to them. This included concepts such as standard category 5 MT message types in ISO15022, variations of these messages developed for other purposes, notably MT574(IRSLST) and MT574(BENO) and finally other tools such as SWIFTNet Mail, SWIFTNet Browse and FileAct. Put together GlobeTax had created a value node to which any

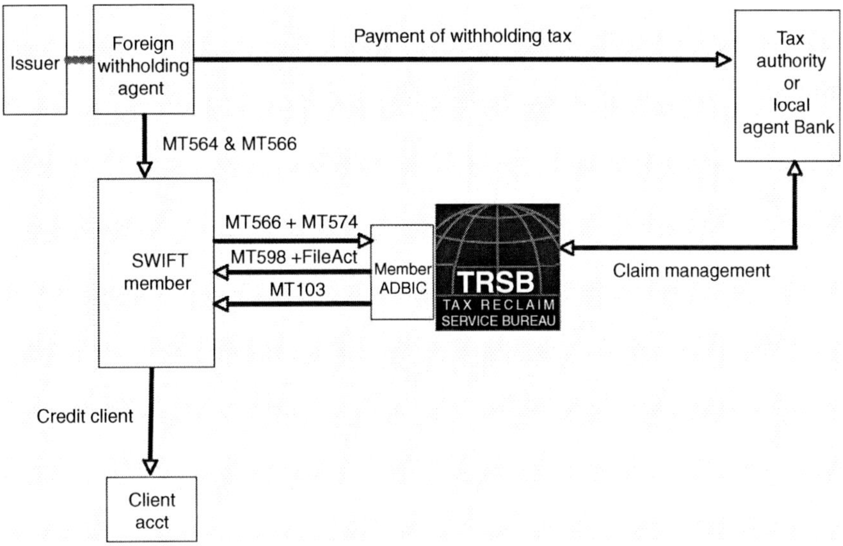

Figure 9.3 Tax reclamation after V-STP
Source: GlobeTax.

custodian could connect and a value node which could receive and send data in any possible combination of SWIFT tools that the custodian happened to employ.

In Figure 9.3, member ADBIC refers to the fact that, at that time, GlobeTax, even though a validated service bureau on SWIFT, could not have its own BIC address. The model was therefore developed on the basis that the custodian would apply for an additional destination BIC address or ADBIC, then assign the management of the ADBIC, which would be used solely for tax data, to GlobeTax.

The test of this model took place over three months starting in August 2007 with one of the top global custodians as the intermediary involved. Twenty client accounts were selected across six European markets. The tax reclaims for these clients were to be processed only using data provided over the SWIFT network. Whenever the custodian paid one of these clients, it would confirm the payment by sending an MT566 message to the client. The clients instructed the custodian to implement "duplicate reporting of MT566 messaging" which in effect meant that every time a payment was made by the custodian to its clients, GlobeTax received a copy of the message automatically. These messages were aggregated over each month of the test so that any reversals during the month could be reconciled out, then reclaims processed.

The results were clear. In the three months of the test, GlobeTax recovered over $104 million for the twenty clients. Of this, $44 million was recovered in less than four weeks from markets that would otherwise have taken the custodian (and anyone else) over 12 months to recover in. This exemplifies the first point I made earlier on. The value node supplier in a V-STP model can't rely on V-STP alone to be the wonder product. V-STP is a methodology not a product. In the case of this test, GlobeTax was already filing over 1.7 million claims a year with a 0% fail rate and often beat market average recovery times because of its proprietary processing methods and its close relationships with tax authorities. So, the $44 million represented

Table 9.1 Basic tax business process

	Request for data
	Tax data matrix
Announcement of income event (MT564)	
Downstream announcement of an income event (MT564)	
	Election of position for relief at source (cf. Withholding-rate pool statement)
	Request for certifications of residency
	Provision of certifications of residency
Confirmation of income event (MT566)	
	Request for breakdown of omnibus position
	Breakdown of omnibus position
	Request for certification of claim
	Request for foreign tax identification number
	Request for power of attorney
	Response to request for power of attorney
	Request for letter of authority
	Response to request for letter of authority
	Request for credit advice authority
	Response to request for credit advice authority
	Certification of claim
	Claim of entitlement
	Request for information supporting a claim
	Response to request of information supporting a claim
	Request for list of beneficial owners
List of beneficial owners (MT574)	
	Tax information report
	Processing advice
Payment of refund (MT102)	
Confirmation of payment (MT566)	

Source: Author.

not just good processing performance, but also at least $2.5 million in potential interest gains, if not re-investment values just by reason of having the money available early.

All the clients involved in the test were customers of a custodian with a branch network business. Many of the branches in this network already provide tax reclaim services, but some do not. So, clients with multiple accounts were at risk of receiving a fragmented offer depending on which branches in the network offered the service. The V-STP trial showed the potential for a simple, zero-cost solution that would allow all those branches to offer tax reclaim services to clients. They could either keep their own service or provide a parallel service by connecting to GlobeTax's TRSB value node. Since then, that custodian took the V-STP model for tax reclamation and rolled it out to its entire custody branch network.

Until such time as tax authorities become more technology driven in their processing methods as well as their standards, it's likely that V-STP, for custodians will become the predominant model for withholding tax processing for the next few years.

Despite V-STP as a methodology, the true automation of this part of corporate actions is not possible today. Efforts at harmonisation, as discussed in Chapter 13 establishes the principle that automation is a vital element of making the trading between markets more free.

Business process

The list in Table 9.1 shows some, but not all the elements that would need to be included into an automated process. Some of these are internal processes between FIs, some are between FI and client and others between FI and tax authorities. Even without harmonisation of process, the list below, if converted into messages would see existing systems revolutionised. The elements to the far left already exist. Those indented do not. This shows the scale of the automation, and thus agreement to standards, that faces the industry today.

CHAPTER 10

Solutions Reviews

There are a number of solutions and part solutions available in the market, some more applicable than others dependent on the nature of your business. Most are oriented on those firms, as opposed to individuals, that have volumes of potential entitlements that warrant expenditure on automation.

Similarly, the nature of these solutions varies depending on the particular issue that faces your firm the most. Custodians have different needs than brokers. Brokers have different needs than fund managers. For custodians, the main issue is the ability to process many entitlements, potentially from many clients of different residencies and different legal forms. The need is therefore more complete, all the way from tax research through to processing long form claims efficiently on behalf of your clients. That translates into a major business need. While withholding tax has not been seen as a competitive issue for custodians in the past, it's clear that there is pressure on multiple fronts for a more transparent benchmarking of the industry which will lead to a growth in the availability of solutions.

Even within the custody and brokerage community, there may be different needs, based on how the firm is structured and where it sees the major problem – is it the whole process or just, for example, filling in the forms?

For fund managers, especially highly regulated funds such as US mutual funds, there is a fiduciary and regulatory need to report accurately to stakeholders on the financial health of the fund. So the need is more of oversight – the ability to review investment income and establish whether there is an entitlement and whether anything is being done about it.

So, this chapter seeks to review some of the types of solution available and their advantages. Since the world of withholding tax is small, in some instances there are only one or two firms globally that provide a product or service in any given area.

INFORMATION PRODUCTS

At the start of all tax processing activities, irrespective of function, is the need for information. There are 234 tax jurisdictions at present. Taking all the possible permutations (54,522) and recognising that each may have a statute of limitations with each other of anything from 1 to 20 years (weighted average 5.2 years) and that, for a global custodian with a global client base, there could be anything up to 27 types of client and anything up to 10 types of income instrument subject to withholding tax, we arrive at the upper limits of scale for a tax product of 76,548,888 data points. Of course, the further away from a global custodian we move, in terms of need, the number of tax data points that need to be researched drops dramatically as each of the variables reduces. So, for a fiscally opaque fund, the residencies on one side of the equation drops from 234 down to 1, and so forth.

In addition, of the possible permutations mentioned above, many have a "null" result in that there are only around 5,000 treaties in force at present of the 54,522 possible. I'm often asked therefore whether this theoretical upper limit has any validity. My point is that unless someone does the research to find out that the result of any given permutation is a null, it could otherwise have a non-null result. In other words, you have to do the research in order to find out that there's no tax issue to address.

That said, there are a couple of providers out there

International Bureau of Fiscal Documentation (IBFD)

IBFD has extensive databases available on a subscription basis. The advantages of this type of information is that it is indeed extensive, including, often, both statutory and treaty tax rates as well as the text of the relevant treaties themselves. Sometimes the disadvantage can be the same – extensive data needs some preparation to manage and these databases include other taxes than withholding tax on investment income for example, capital gains tax. Secondly, the data in this type of database is, to a large extent, theoretical. In other words, it's an aggregated dataset, created from desk research and review of documentation such as the treaties. One of the problems with withholding tax is that, even with treaties as guidelines, as the reader will by now be painfully aware, the answer to any given situation is likely to be a combination of the theory plus custom, practice and even potentially case-by-case assessment. That said, IBFD is probably one of the most commonly used reference sources.

GlobeTax

GlobeTax has two products in its *e*-TaxData suite both of which are essentially different ways of looking at the same database. The database has

1.7 million data points which cover all the 234 jurisdictions. While the database does not currently have the full treaties in searchable form, most of the data points in it are not only aggregated from desk research but also have been used in real claims of entitlement in a live environment. *e*-Tax data Online is a subscription-based web site that provides a simple search engine allowing users to select variables such as country of residence, country of investment, years of income and beneficial owner type; and receive a response screen that provides statutory rates, treaty rates, market notes and custom and practice benchmarks such as average length of time to reclaim and statutes of limitation. Whereas IBFD is a researcher tool *e*-TaxData is a primarily a processor tool. While GlobeTax provides subscription services to the largest global custodians for the whole database, the firm has partners who provide access for financial firms with more narrowly defined needs in terms of scale and scope. The most notable are Exchange Data International and www.globalcustody.net both of whom provide access to the products on a "pay per click" basis, where GlobeTax markets, based on an annual subscription.

The other product in the suite is e-TaxData Distribution. From the same database, subscribers define the data set they need for their purpose. In a "pull" scenario, the subscriber sends a message requesting data. In the more common "push" scenario, the subscriber defines a set of rules which trigger a dataset being sent. Typically this might be "whenever the rate in a given set of markets changes" or "once a month". Distributed data can be delivered by any secure means including SWIFT.

Deloitte & Touche

Deloitte has a CD-ROM based tax database available which is quite extensive and easy to use. The interface is similar to other packages in that it is essentially a selector of variables.

CORPORATE ACTIONS PLATFORMS

Withholding tax is not truly a corporate action in the top level sense. A corporate action is the action of a corporation that results in an activity. So, for example a cash dividend, stock split or repo are all examples of corporate actions. Tax reclaims are activities that flow from the nature of given corporate actions. So, in the example, a dividend would be the corporate action and the results of that corporate action may be the activity of making a claim that the income was over-taxed. Most tax reclaim personnel are to be found in the corporate actions or income processing parts of financial firms. It's here also that a small number of software vendors are active, providing platform level software to receive, analyse and process these corporate actions. There is a whole industry that backs up these corporate actions vendors researching corporate annual general meetings and the like to analyse and create databases of "corporate actions". Once a corporate action event is received by a financial firm, it will need some way to assess and apply the corporate action to its clients in an automated way.

The degree to which withholding tax is functionally addressed in such corporate actions platforms is generally very low. The most common is a set of tables into which the customer must input tax rates. The functionality involved is also at a low level. Most corporate actions platforms perform only simple arithmetic on income events for example, statutory rate – treaty rate = claim. Of course, as the reader will now know, this is a gross oversimplification of the actual position of many beneficial owners, let alone markets where for example, there can be multiple statutory rates as well as multiple treaty rates. So, these corporate actions platforms, while excellent at their other tasks, tend to be very basic when it comes to tax processing. Users are left to obtain and input their own tax data and the calculations made may not necessarily reflect any given beneficial owner's true entitlement.

Some corporate actions vendors have recognised this weakness and are working with other commercial service providers to create links to more functionally rich services. Two good examples would be CheckFree, now part of the Fiserv, and Information Mosaic both of whom are looking at connectivity to outsource providers on an automated basis.

Stand-alone software

Corporate actions software of course is multi functional that is, it has a broad remit in the financial institution to implement all the activities required as a result of any given corporate action. There are however, a couple of firms that have specialised and produced stand-alone software dedicated to withholding tax processing.

It's educational to see how corporate actions vendors provide only basic functionality whereas dedicated software vendors provide a much more function-rich solution. It is interesting that in the 12 years I've been in the industry, no corporate actions vendor has thought it worthwhile to develop a more effective software module for this activity.

I mentioned earlier that complete automation of withholding tax is not currently possible due to the number of parts of the process (60%) that are manual and/or are outside the control of a financial institution. It's important to keep this in mind when considering stand-alone software. Such software can and does automate certain parts of the withholding tax chain, but importantly, not all parts. Typically a stand-alone software solution will contain tax tables (which in some cases the provider will populate and maintain for a fee), other tables, more extensive than that of a corporate actions vendor, for storing and maintaining client data and also algorithms to apply the tax table data to the client data for any given income event. Necessarily then, such systems must integrate to a host system – which may even be a corporate actions system – to receive income data (or have it entered manually). In some systems, in addition to purchasing tax data, the firms concerned will obtain, and automate the completion of, the relevant forms needed to make claims. It's important for purchasers to recognise that a tax authority may need to approve such an automated form for use on a caseby-case basis. They only have to accept their own originals.

The two most commonly found are Web Services Integration and GOAL.

The common trait amongst dedicated software providers is that they are, without exception, small firms, usually with less than £1m turnover. Until 2007, some of these firms could still claim to be absolutely focused on withholding tax, and thus have a specialisation benefit ("we do nothing else") that clients would count in their favour against the natural nervousness that large institutions have, especially in current circumstances, for engaging very small firms in critical areas. GOAL's acquisition of securities class actions firm Magenta One in February 2007 brought that specialisation era to an end. Being small is not of course, necessarily a bad thing. Smaller companies can react faster to market changes and therefore are usually the source of many innovations.

While they are continuously looking at different business models, the software firms generally still operate the standard industry model with an initial one-off license fee which provides the "rights to use" their proprietary code. In addition, users can expect to see a variety of fees being applied during the lifetime of the license, for example:

1. Annual maintenance fees;

2. Upgrade fees, to cover costs of migrating functionality to new operating systems;

3. Update fees, to cover costs of non-upgrade type changes to software;

4. Patch fees, to fix any bugs in the systems that aren't covered by maintenance fees;

5. Tax research fees;

6. Customisation fees, covering any changes to functionality that are unique to the customer.

Outsource providers

For custodians and brokers and private banks et al., all the above solutions have two major downsides – they all involve up-front costs that have to be amortised against variable claim volumes and none of them can deliver the holy grail of a completely automated solution.

Outsourcing on the other hand, as a business model, can provide a solution to both dependent on the service provider selected. Of the three outsource service providers, GlobeTax is by far and away the largest and most widely represented providing services to depositaries, custodians, brokers and beneficial owners. Acupay provides its services to issuers rather than directly to the market and currently, only has two such BBVA and Santander. GlobeTax's solution has two elegant features which keep it in first place. First, they operate a contingent fee model, so no-one pays anything until tax is successfully recovered. Secondly, they've been working closely with SWIFT and have developed an automated data model using SWIFT connectivity – dubbed V-STP or "Virtual Straight Through Processing". Since SWIFT is the most secure and already ubiquitous inter-bank communications mechanism, this model has many advantages.

GlobeTax's metrics and benchmarks are also impressive – a 0% rate since formation in 1992 and a zero backlog. When combined with a contingent fee model and V-STP data delivery, it's unsurprising that the firm is recognised as the leader in the field, processing nearly two million claims each year. It's also worth noting that they have also created a secure on-line documentation portal "eDocs" which, combined with V-STP for transaction data flows, means that they probably have the most automated withholding tax processing shop in the world at present.

As with any outsource solution of course, purchasers need to be aware of the advantages and disadvantages of the business model. Many firms in the last decade cited loss of control as a key reason not to outsource, but in 2009, with the global recession beginning to bite and many banks taking out entire layers of management and resource, outsourcing is again flavour of the month. Outsourcing, with an automated model does allow data flows to represent income transactions, status updates, reports and credits while automated documentation systems such as eDocs, allow the other elements of the process to be automated. From the custodian's perspective therefore, what used to be a manual, complex and error-prone job can be outsourced through controlled and standardised communications channels to providers who can then take on the manual processing elements using their focus to produce processing efficiencies that the customer could not have delivered internally.

Cost savings of up to 65% have been quoted, but where staff and resource reductions are possible, outsourcing also gets the subject matter into the hands of people for whom the activity is their sole reason for business. Increases in scale and scope of service have also been cited, as have reductions in risks associated with "misses" in the market. A "miss" is the occasion when a custodian knows that there is an entitlement but for one reason or another, fails to obtain the entitlement. Some misses are the fault of the beneficial owners for not providing adequate documentation, but many (too many) are from custodians with insufficient resources applied in an in-house business model.

Accountancy services

From the Ultra and High Net worth (UHNWI and HNWI) individuals, many don't use custodians or brokers for their tax reclaims. They use their accountants. There has grown up over the last few years a number of small accountancy firms that offer tax reclaim services. In the main however, their client volumes are low and they tend to be based in the market where their clients are resident. If the claims are low in volume, they may be very large in value. These firms will usually price either on a fixed fee basis or as a percentage of the amount claimed.

The larger accountancy firms of course provide similar services but usually to a very narrow band in their client base, leaving the larger volumes to the custodians or third party providers.

Custodians

Of course, apart from the software vendors, the above are organisations that provide services both to beneficial owners as well as financial firms acting on behalf of beneficial owners. If you're a fund manager or other type of beneficial owner, then the other category of "service provider" is your custodian or broker. Smaller beneficial owners, or those with minimal claim volumes will often use the services of their accountants.

Custodians provide a variety of tax services to their clients and, as described elsewhere, may either build, buy or outsource the business processes involved. However, as far as the market is concerned they are legitimate providers of services. Custody services generally are provided on a bundled fee basis calculated as a percentage of the assets under management. In the same way that GlobeTax's contingent fee structure leads to a natural motivation to provide high levels of efficiency (otherwise you don't get paid), the asset value fee model would seem to provide the same motivation. Since if tax is reclaimed it is usually put into the same account that generated the claim, thus increasing the value and hence the fees.

Some custodians also leverage the fact that they provide these services together with the fact that they are banks, to create specialist services such as contractual tax – effectively lending the beneficial owner the amount of the claim at the time of the original income and charging a fee. This service is described elsewhere.

The web site globalcustody.net has rankings of custody service providers and many of these include tax reclamation within their offering, albeit with only a few metrics for users to differentiate between providers.

Utilities

Increasingly we are seeing that the central securities depositories are beginning to offer services directly or indirectly to the market since they are usually the place where shares are held in accounts by custodians. The three most well-known would be the DTCC in the United States, Euroclear and Clearstream in the EU. All have different approaches and services, based on their markets, their clients and their expertise. In essence though, what they do is leverage their size and market position to negotiate special arrangements with tax authorities on behalf of their members.

In the United States, the Depository Trust and Clearing Corporation has, for some years provided its participants with a relief-at-source tool – the Elective Dividend Service or EDS. For participant banks in the DTC system who are predominantly US based, the DTC allows these banks to "elect" the proportion of their position in any appropriate security, to be taxed at either the favourable (treaty) rate or the unfavourable (statutory) rate depending on whether the participant has the appropriate documentation in its possession. This clearly makes it much easier for the bank to obtain relief at source for its clients, where available, without having to go through the standard documentation requirements. The downside for participants is that both DTCC and the participants are subject to a right of audit by the relevant tax authorities who have granted such special arrangements so that if there are any abuses of the system, action can be taken. The downside for the beneficial owners is that the EDS relief-at-source system is only available if they hold their shares at DTC through a participant bank *and* the income is from a specific set of markets *and* of specific types. So, it's not a one-size-fits-all and this describes the other utilities too. Their offerings are focused on "low hanging fruit" which tends to be in markets where they have a large client-driven interest. It's therefore not always certain what the expertise level is and what the most efficient route to a particular tax benefit may be.

The other type of utilities are those which focus on particular income instruments. The best-known would be Depositary Receipts or DRs. American Depositary Receipts are, for the most part, sponsored by one of four US banks (Citi, Deutsche Bank, Bank of New York Mellon and JP Morgan Chase) that purchase the underlying foreign (non-US) ordinary shares, package them up in groups and sell them to the market as the derivative instrument – an ADR. These utilities, because of the way in which the derivative is structured, must act as the first port of call for anyone holding an ADR who wishes to file the claim.

Claims on ADRs cannot, in theory, be filed direct to a tax authority because they are not deemed to be securities in that sense. So a claimant, whether beneficial owner or custodian on their behalf, would have to file the claim to the depositary first where the conversion from the depositary receipt to the number of underlying shares can be made and reconciled to the total DR position (so that there is no chance of an over-claim) and thence to the tax authorities, with the reclaim flowing back through the same route.

It's clear from all of the above that the number and type of solutions available is as broad as the number of variables that create such a difficult and complex industry. Some solutions are independent, such as GlobeTax. Others are either income type weighted, market weighted or methodology weighted. If you're a custodian, software or more probably outsourcing in current climate are the routes to compete effectively with other custodians. If you're an institutional investor, software tools and on-line research systems should help you understand the issues and help you evaluate whether you're getting a service and if so, how good it is.

Over all of this we must of course keep a close eye on the rapidity of changes occurring in the market and the degree to which any given solution is resilient (or comparatively resilient) to such change.

PART 4

Performance

In any complex process, the issue of performance does not take long to arise. In fact, considering that very complexity, it's amazing that the industry has so few benchmarks of performance. The key performance indicators seem to be (i) does the custodian offer a tax service and (ii) how long does it take to get money back from a given market. Both useful questions indeed, but woefully inadequate for an investor to know whether he's getting the best return on his investment both in the market and from his intermediary.

The reader will perhaps have some inkling of what to follow in this section of the book, having now a greater understanding of the complexities involved. Many of those complexities have such profound effects on investor returns that they should be measured in a consistent way across the industry. This would lead the way, not just for the potential of better understanding, not just a better return for investors but also the basis of a greater degree of competition in the custody market based on efforts to make processes more efficient through investment.

The base of all performance in this area is founded on good research and is in itself a benchmarkable element of the process. If we start with good information, we stand a much better chance of a good result because we are not just demonstrating an understanding of good practice, we are also implementing it.

CHAPTER 11

Market Reference Data

In withholding tax terms, market reference data relates primarily to the rates that will or have applied to any given payment, on the presumption that it's cross border. This may seem simple when we consider that essentially only two rates are of any importance. First is the statutory rate of tax, second is the treaty rate of tax. But as we've seen, for any custodian of any note, there will be a number of variables that affect these two figures as well as a wide variety of other factors that have to be considered before actually applying any of these rates.

In addition, the quality of information, tax being an interpretive art rather than a science, can make the difference between optimising income efficiently on the one hand and opening yourself up to liabilities and fines on the other. Liabilities from clients who have a right to expect custodians to know about such things (fiduciary duty) and fines from tax authorities if client records are not kept properly or if false claims are filed.

An efficient database would contain the following:

- Country of residence
- Country of investment
- Investment market type
- Beneficial owner type
- Income type
- Year of income
- Expected recovery time

- Statute of limitations

- Market-specific notes

Despite this seemingly simple matrix, the number of permutations is very large, in the order of 1.4 million. Smaller custodians with limited client types in their customer base or other similar mitigators will have a smaller database, but large nevertheless.

It's also true that, particularly with the increasingly exotic client types and investment instruments, it may not be obvious whether a treaty rate applies and if so, which one. It's quite common for different custodians to treat the same client type differently in their systems. While tax authorities remain predominantly manual, it's also quite likely that reclaims from both custodians would get paid – but that doesn't mean both are right, or that neither are right, just that the control systems are too loose and the tax authority has not made a clear enough determination. This is not to criticise tax authorities. They are the product of their history, which being manual and government-based means they will perforce be slow to change. It's also true that they have some difficulty keeping up with the much faster pace of change in the markets, so it's far more likely that a custodian, faced with an exotic new client or instrument type will treat it as similar to another client or instrument type for which there is clear precedent. Until each tax authority makes a more definitive determination, it's never certain whether a claim will be honoured.

So, most custodians follow a best practice rule that tax rates must (i) be efficiently researched and (ii) no tax rate used unless it is corroborated by at least two independent sources.

This raises four issues. The first is cost and the second is finding the sources, the third, inputting the data in meaningful form into your own database and fourth, keeping the data up-to-date as market conditions change and your client base profile changes.

There are basically only three ways to get research information. Either you deploy an internal resource to research each market, you use your sub-custody network to provide you with the information you need or thirdly, you buy the information from data aggregators out in the market.

INTERNAL RESOURCE

Many of the larger global custodians opt for this route because it ensures control over the whole research chain. The difficulty is that the resource required needs often to be multilingual and is quite scarce in the market. So, it's expensive to build up and maintain an in-house set of "country desks".

SUB-CUSTODY NETWORK

This is probably the most common. Most custodians with clients investing in specific markets will appoint a local sub-custodian with expertise in that market. One of the remits for the sub-custodian is usually to provide an information source back to the upstream custodian. This of course has its issues as well. While the sub-custodian may have market-specific knowledge of value, the superior custodian must have processes in place to make sure that information is provided in a proactive rather than reactive way and is of a consistent quality. To this extent both in-house and sub-custody networks suffer from the quality variances associated with changes in staff over time and the degree to which the information is interpreted consistently.

THIRD PARTY AGGREGATORS

There are a number of these firms in the market. They include, amongst others:

- GlobeTax Data Services
- International Bureau of Fiscal Documentation (IBFD)
- DataVenue
- Exchange Data International
- Kler's Financial Data Services
- Deloitte & Touche LLP

The resource deployed is only one facet of market reference data in this space of course. In recent time, as professionals have focused on withholding tax from an automation viewpoint, it has become feasible to provide market reference data in real time. Real time in this context merely means asking the following question: which is more efficient – to research all permutations of tax data in advance and keep it updated ready for the income event to which it applies *or* buy the data relevant to the income event at the same time as the income event, or even as part of the income event. Financial institutions acting as paying agents already do this to a large extent when making distributions of dividends or interest. They will deduct statutory rate tax from the payment under their domestic tax law and usually make reference to it in the payment for example, SWIFT message. What is less ubiquitous, but is becoming more so, is the change to buying a data file at the time of a payment or shortly afterwards which defines what any treaty rate would be for a given client type – so-called data distribution. The other alternative is to access.

These third party aggregators have some advantages over in-house solutions. Firstly, it's usually all they do, so it's in their interests to make reference data both standard and consistent. While they may suffer changes in staff, since all staff are oriented on this role, the effects are likely to be smaller. Some, but not all of these third party aggregators actually use their data to file reclaims in the market. Clearly data that has been used successfully for a given combination of client type and income type will be of a higher quality than that which has been obtained, for example, from a read-through of a treaty.

One other thing about third party aggregators is that they are more likely to come up with innovative ways to access data since it's at the core of their business model. One such example would be GlobeTax Data Services Inc. GlobeTax presents its data in two forms. The first is as a web site with a search engine allowing subscribers to query their database by selecting different sets of variables. The second is a data file, to a client's specification, provided via SWIFT's Data Distribution Service. Figure 11.1 and Table 11.1 show the query engine and a typical result.

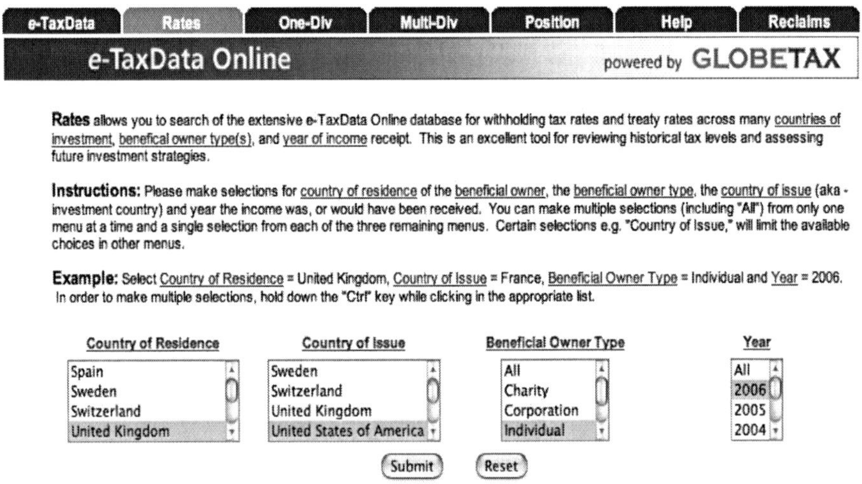

Figure 11.1 A typical tax reference database access tool

Source: GlobeTax Data Services Inc.

Table 11.1 A typical database query result

Residency	*Investment country*	*Beneficial owner type*	*Year*	*Statutory rate (%)*	*Treaty rate (%)*	*Extra rate (%)*	*Filling deadline*	*Expected recovery from filling*	*Notes*
United Kingdom	Australia	Individual	2006	30,000	15,000	0,000	10 years from the pay date	12 months	View notes
United Kingdom	Belgium	Individual	2006	25,000	10,000	0,000	3 years from February, 1 following the pay-date	24 months	View notes
United Kingdom	Finland	Individual	2006	28,000	0,000	0,000	5 years from the end of the year of the pay-date	6 months	View notes
United Kingdom	France	Individual	2006	25,000	15,000	0,000	2 years from the end of the year of the pay-date	12 months	View notes
United Kingdom	Germany	Individual	2006	21,000	15,000	0,000	4 years from the end of the year of the pay-date	10 months	View notes
United Kingdom	Spain	Individual	2006	15,000	15,000	0,000	2 years from the pay-date	14 months	View notes
United Kingdom	Switzerland	Individual	2006	35,000	15,000	0,000	3 years from the end of the year of the pay-date	18 months	View notes

Source: GlobeTax Data Services Inc.

ACCOUNTANCY FIRMS

The "big four" are the typical players in this space and they all provide varying levels of tax information. However, as commercial entities, you have to have an eye to the cost of information for the benefit you expect to gain.

TAX AUTHORITIES

Tax authorities of course have the ultimate, say, in terms of interpretation of the treaties that they are obligated to enforce. As such, they should be able to provide the best source of data. However, several issues flow from this source. First, except for a few, most do not proactively publish rates or changes. Some do not have English as their first or even second language. Some make a charge for any determination of rates. Above all, in the fast moving world of income processing, it may take some time to get an answer. Having said all that, for the real exotic cases, this may be the only way to get an answer.

So, while the buy side, funds etc. use data as a monitoring tool, custodians and other intermediaries use it for much more complex processing purposes ranging from establishing payment amounts as a paying agent through to using the data to assess entitlements. One of the major difficulties that all face is the degree to which the data can be systematised.

When I first came to this industry, I held the belief that the data space should be simple. The issuer would inform their agent of a distribution and, at statutory level anyway, should be able to advise the tax rate that would be applied, since this would be a function of the CFO's and Company Secretary's role. I quickly found that this is not the case. In fact, in making some announcements to the market about distributions, some issuers don't even specify the ISIN of the instrument they are making the distribution on. Sometimes, I have to wonder why the financial system works at all. So, if the issuer does not specify a statutory rate, the paying agent would need to do this. Now normally the paying agent and the issuer would be in the same market and hence both should know the statutory rate of tax to be applied. This of course is in current time. At this stage, we would not need to know historic tax rates within our database. If the market is a relief-at-source market, then below the paying agent, there will be a network of downstream custodians with clients of their own, receiving information and assessing it against their own tax databases by beneficial owner type and residency together with supporting documentation. From a data perspective, this is relatively easy to automate for those intermediaries who have simple or small client bases. For the global custodians it's a much bigger issue.

From an automation perspective, the first point at which a custodian will have sight of a statutory tax rate will normally be in a SWIFT MT564 message (announcement). These announcements will usually be integrated into a corporate actions platform, whether built or bought. If the corporate actions platform is a third party purchase, it will typically contain a set of fields to allow the custodian to input their research data. This is usually done manually.

Already we have research that's been done twice. Once by the paying agent and once by the downstream custodian. Of course, in these corporate actions platforms, the developers are not experts in withholding tax. The uninitiated will create a table with the capacity for one statutory rate per market (wrong), one treaty rate per beneficial owner type for that market (wrong) and the difference between the two being a claim entitlement (wrong). Such simplistic systems may work most of the time, but they are fundamentally flawed because they do not give any flexibility to deal with market variations. Given a limited capacity for data, the custodian's problem is that the data entered into such databases must first be researched. Most custodians have a "four eyes" policy in this regard. In other words data cannot be entered into such systems without first being cross-referenced and verified between two independent sources. Of course, none of the corporate actions platforms provide any functionality to perform such preparatory work. So a great swathe of research activity is necessarily manual, compiling information on a given data point, comparing and coming to a judgement on the particular variables that may or may not apply to a given beneficial owner. Having said this, it's quite common for different custodians to come to different conclusions about the applicable rate for any given type of beneficial owner in any given year. A good example would be an Irish resident fund. If set up under UCITs III, unless one reads the treaty and treaty notes within a database, it would be easy to suppose that the entity is entitled to claim against a treaty. However, in most cases, these types of fund are not entitled. So data alone is not sufficient and any data source must contain non-numeric information in such a way as to give enough information to pick this kind of issue up.

Moving on, once the payments have been made, many types of beneficial owner, particularly pooled vehicles, have either a fiduciary or regulatory duty to check that the income they receive is accurate for the conditions. So hedge funds, pension funds, mutual funds, and so on all have managers with a need to have access to both statutory rates and treaty rates as they apply to their investment vehicle for the markets in which they invest. It's here that often, the first signs of data degradation occur and more importantly the consequences. Investment managers acting on behalf of many funds use accounts at multiple custodians and brokers to effect trades in different markets. While this may be efficient at the front end, it's incredibly inefficient at the back end. In terms of tax services, they will almost certainly not be getting an optimised or integrated service. Some custodians will be providing different levels of service (see Chapter 12). Brokers typically do not provide these services at all. So as income flows into all these accounts, different amounts are deducted, sometimes due to differences of judgement, sometimes due to differences in service level. Unless the fund manager or investment manager knows of the potential problem, it's likely that there will be some significant shortfall in the fund's potential value.

This is a good opportunity for global custodians as well as the one or two third party specialist outsource providers who can both provide access to an integrated service. The global custodians can provide account facilities in all the markets, whereas an outsource provider can aggregate data from the various custodians and brokers to create a single data stream, much easier to optimise.

It also has to be said that much of the research into this market reference data is more complex than what it looks at first. There is no central source for information. The treaties concerned give structural context – in most claims, the specific treaty article that is being used to establish an entitlement is required on the claim form. However, it's the fiscal authorities that have information on statutory and treaty rates. These authorities used to be very open to providing written confirmation of rates to enquirers. However this is much less the case now. For exotic or complex beneficial owner types, it is very difficult to obtain a generic answer to a rate question. Most authorities will only answer a question as it applies to a specific named client. This makes general tax research even more difficult. We must also not forget the "it depends" principle. While almost all claims are based on a treaty, this is not the case in all circumstances. Some claims are based on legal statute. In some markets, as we've heard, there is a treaty but no process, while in others there is no treaty, but there is a process. These are not primarily operational issues. They are research issues.

Naturally, given all this complexity, it translates into cost. Most firms, of whatever type, try to minimise the scale and scope of their research to the minimum required to get the job done. For the fund managers this is relatively easy since they have a defined entity type and residency. For custodians the issue is more difficult. Not only do they have to research all the permutations of their existing client base and their investment markets, but also they must research all markets in principle. I was asked why this was so quite recently. The answer is, in order to know that you do not have an entitlement in a given market, I still have to do the research.

As the building block of all withholding tax issues, it's clear that the principles are simple – good quality data in an automatable form that is capable of ensuring that any given income event is taxed correctly and that any claim's scale is correctly identified. In practice, from issuer to custodian, the data can be inconsistent, incomplete and misleading. The best use of resource in any withholding tax reclaim environment has to be to get this function right at the highest quality. All else needed for optimisation follows naturally.

CHAPTER 12

Benchmarking

The reader by now has some grasp of the matrix of factors which can have an effect on the withholding tax issue and the subsequent value of a portfolio. In this chapter, I have taken each of the issues raised during previous explanations of withholding tax processes and tried to establish the kind of benchmark that might apply. I make no apology for repeating myself in terms of explanations behind some of these benchmarks. In my experience, the issues are many, complex and inter-reactive. For investors, and others, the more often an issue is explored, each time from a slightly different perspective, the more likely that a holistic picture will emerge.

This series of benchmarks could be used by

- an institutional investor to perform quality assurance on existing custodian's or internal departmental performance,
- a fund manager or custodian sales team to set and monitor benchmarks in order to establish a competitive advantage,
- an IT or other cross-functional improvement group to set project deliverables for an automation of withholding tax processes, and
- a board of directors to set minimum service levels for an outsourcing contract.

Part of the problem of benchmarking this process of course is that, in theory and to a certain extent in practice, several parts of the process, from any given viewpoint, are out of direct control.

Below I've given a summary table (Table 12.1) which shows how all these benchmarks can come together to create an overview of withholding tax issues. Following the table is a more detailed description of each benchmark,

Table 12.1 Benchmark indices

Code	*Description*
PE	Process Efficiency
PF	Proportion of Fails
ADP	Age Debt Performance
F	Fit
SR	Statute Risk
RAS	Relief at Source Efficiency
PoA	Power of Attorney Index
RT	Reconciliation and Traceability Index
B	Backlog Index
C	Capacity
CR	Cost Per Reclaim
ΔN	Reclaim rate
CB	Cost Benefit
TH	Threshold Index
CTI	Contractual Tax Index

Source: Author.

how they might be applied and what investors and custodians can learn from them.

Since there is no real set of benchmarks for this corporate actions area at present, rather than simply define the benchmarks in mathematical terms, I have taken a more discursive approach. This is to ensure that both investors and custodians are able to understand why I believe that a particular benchmark should exist and what factors affect it. The mathematical end point is still given both at the end of the discursive element and also in summary table at the end of the chapter.

PROCESS EFFICIENCY (PE)

This a simple additive formula with several elements. It is market specific and can also be aggregated to provide an average ranking. Because the profiles of many portfolios are different, this latter measurement is somewhat less useful than the market specific PE Index used in conjunction with the Fit Index (FI) defined later. The difficulty for practitioners is that there is likely to be a disparity of applied units in some of the measurements. The disparity exists because of the significant differences that can occur in different parts of the process, some can take seconds, whilst others may take months. For example, if a custodian has automated processes, the action of establishing validity, eligibility and value may be almost simultaneous and certainly not take days. However, the activity of communicating with clients and tax authorities most certainly takes days at the very least. So, for some custodians, several of the measures included in the benchmarking process will be so close to zero as to be effectively negligible. This does not mean however that they can be ignored because they are not negligible in all cases. On the one hand, there are many custodians who have not automated processes and who will take days, where others take seconds. Separately, even if the processes are automated and deemed to be negligible from a process efficiency viewpoint, these same elements each have a risk associated with them which must be considered. These then are the very benchmarks that can highlight custodians adopting less effective methods.

$$PE_m = \sum_{1}^{n} T$$

where T is the time taken in days for the process element n for the market m.

- $T1$ is the length of time taken for the custodian to be made aware of an income event, commencing from the pay-date. Usually this is an aggregate of the time taken from the issuance of a notification (e.g., a corporation announces a dividend, through a registrar bank to a withholding agent and thence to the custodian).

- $T2$ is the time taken in days for the custodian to establish the validity of the event, the eligibility of the event with respect to its client base and finally the value of the event to each of its eligible clients. Each of these elements has a corresponding risk associated with the way in which the custodian performs this activity, which are discussed later. While from an institutional investor's perspective, this time is only relevant for the particular investments he holds, it must be recognised that the custodian is acting for many investors. This measure is taken across all investors because the larger the number of clients, the more likely it is that the custodian will have efficiency business drivers in place to reduce the transactional cost of processing these three functions. $T2$ is an aggregate function in itself. $T2_m = (T_v + T_e + T_{val})_m$, where

  - T_v is the time taken in days to establish validity. As we've seen validity is a function of the income event and the treaty regulations covering the country of issuance and the countries of residence for which the custodian represents clients. An event is *valid* if, for the market m a DTA exists which would create a withholding tax rate greater than the treaty rate for any income type I.
  - T_e is the time taken in days to establish eligibility. Eligibility is a subset of validity. If, for any given valid income event there exist one or more clients to whom the event specifically applies for example, they have holdings in a particular security delivering a dividend or they are receiving a royalty on a license agreement subject to a DTA, then the event, from the perspective of the operational requirement, is both valid and eligible for further action.
  - T_{val} is the time taken in days to establish the value of the event to a client. Given that an event has been determined to be both valid and eligible, the custodian has a requirement to establish the value of the event. It is from this activity that all others flow.

- *T*3 is the time taken to assemble a tax reclaim. Again, *T*3 is an aggregate function. $T3_m = (T_f + T_d + T_s)_m$, where
  - T_f consists of the number of days required to obtain the correct forms.
  - T_d is the number of days required to acquire the specific data for each reclaim, enter it onto the form and quality check for errors and omissions.
  - T_s Is the number of days required to collate supporting documentation.

- *T*4 is the time taken to locally validate a tax reclaim. *T*4 is not generally market specific because all of its elements occur within the custodian or within the local jurisdiction. *T*4 consists of two additive, serial sub-processes. $T4 = (T_a + T_{lta})$, where
  - T_a is the time taken to obtain approval from the client. A signature is required on each tax reclaim form. If the custodian does not have power of attorney, this signature must be that of the client/beneficial owner. If power of attorney is vested in the custodian, the custodian may sign the form.
  - T_{lta} is the time taken in days for the tax reclaim form to be sent to the local tax authority and returned with a valid stamp.

- *T*5 is the time taken for the, now completed, tax reclaim to be sent for payment. This involves at least one and sometimes two steps. However, if there are two steps, as with France, where the tax reclaim must be submitted to a French sub-custodian who then files it to the authorities, the second step is usually opaque to the custodian from a measurement perspective. Therefore *T5* is measured in days from the date of posting by the custodian to the receipt of the tax reclaim.

- *T6* is the time required for the tax reclaim to be credited to the client's account. This is not as simple as it appears. Firstly, many authorities remit cheques rather than electronic payments, which therefore involves a clearance period. Secondly, if a tax authority remits funds covering more than one reclaim, funds cannot be credited to client accounts until a reconciliation process has identified how the sum received from a tax authority has been made up. Of course where the clearance process occurs in parallel to the reconciliation process, *T6* is actually just the larger of T_{cl} and T_{recon} Therefore $T6 = (T_{cl} + T_{recon})$, where
  - T_{cl} is the time taken to clear a tax reclaim payment.
  - T_{recon} is the time taken to reconcile a tax authority payment to a specific tax reclaim.

So, it can be seen that a process efficiency benchmark can be established. In mathematical terms of course, the custodian may take certain measures to minimise or even eradicate some of the elements described above. In which case these will drop to zero. In other cases, the time required for a particular part of the process is so small in comparison to other elements that it can be said to be immaterial to the process efficiency. This latter is important because, whilst the time required to perform an element may be insignificant, the effect of its failure can be extremely significant.

In the next section, we will look at the processes in more depth from a risk management perspective.

RISK MANAGEMENT BENCHMARKS

In this section we will look at some measurements that can be identified which either directly or indirectly point to greater or lesser confidence in custodial "attention to detail". Some of these benchmarks are obvious, some are less so. However, in a process with so many linkages and in particular where those linkages include external bodies over whom the custodian has little or no control, an error in any one element can cause the catastrophic failure of the whole process.

The basis of the risk management issue in withholding tax is to establish best practice and to measure performance against it. Some custodians will have minimised risk in this area of corporate actions in one or more ways . These include:

- Retention of staff with appropriate levels of skill, knowledge and experience together with back-up contingency and succession plans.
- Formalisation of manual processes to externalise the skills knowledge and experience of key staff.
- Automation. This may include in-house automation of elements of the process together with surrounding management tools to identify potential risk areas. Also included in this area would be the use of bureau systems where certain elements of the process have been automated by third parties and their value can be purchased as and when necessary.
- Outsourcing. This moves the whole process over to a firm that has demonstrable experience in the area. They may or may not have their own internal tools, however, their existence in the market, their pricing, the volume of tax reclaims they file annually and the level of success they have had, that is, their consistency, will reflect their capabilities.

Of course the final element in the risk management of this complex area is to assess the level of integration of the aforementioned elements. Custodians must decide the level of redundancy to incorporate into their systems to create resilient processes. To that extent, the institutional investor must pay attention not just to the individual benchmarks applying to the process elements described, but also to how the custodian integrates the different risk mitigation strategies together to create an efficient system.

From a contractual viewpoint, particularly if third party information or tools are being used, attention must be given to the nature of contractual liability and the measurements required by the custodian from his supplier.

So, with this background, the following risk factors may be benchmarked either by a custodian for internal management purposes or by an investor wishing to assess performance and risk.

Proportion of fails (PF)

This benchmark, PF, represents the top level measurement of risk management. Anecdotally, a tax reclaim form must be correct in every respect if it's to be validated by a foreign tax authority. Any error in calculation or indeed completion of the correct boxes on the forms will result in a rejection. It must be assumed to some extent that a custodian will have correctly completed all the preceding steps in the process before submission to a foreign tax authority, so the preceding steps themselves are less likely to cause a failure and are more likely to cause a delay. The difficulty with this approach from a risk management perspective is of course that the statutes of limitations overlay the process. If a delay is caused, if documents are lost in the post or other delays are experienced at one or more points in the process, there is a risk that the submission will fall outside statute. All these issues are separately benchmarked in this chapter. This is so that an institutional investor or custodial manager will have tools available to monitor and measure not just top level performance, but also some of the specific risk areas that go to make up the overall picture.

Proportion of fails is insensitive to the reason for the failure. It is highly likely that given the length of some statutes of limitation, sometimes years, a custodian with a failed reclaim or relief-at-source application, will have sufficient time to rectify the failure and re-file documentation to the appropriate authorities. The intention is that this measure should be applied to the originating event. To illustrate this, consider the following example. Of 1,000 income events resulting in tax reclaims, 30 fail on the first attempt, say because of an incomplete form, but are successful on the second attempt after remedial action. A further 30 fail completely. This could occur, for example if a custodian is applying a threshold system based on the administrative cost of reclaiming, this latter event might apply if the reclaim was for £100 and the cost of reclaiming is £80. The first failure makes the total cost of reclaiming, including the second submission, effectively £160 in order to get a £100 reclaim. However, from 1,000 reclaims PF in this example would be 60/1000 = 6%. It could be argued that the figure should be 3% because 30 of the reclaims were eventually successful. However, I would disagree with this on the basis that this latter interpretation fails to identify the problem in the system, which is its primary objective. At 3%, a custodian may consider this to be an acceptable level and take no further action. At 6% it's likely that a manager or someone will have to take notice and some action. The latter course is clearly best practice, the former is an example of using a benchmark badly and not using it to identify problems and improve business efficiency.

Of course, PF can only be measured with respect to an end point in the system. A reclaim which has been filed but not received or rejected cannot be included since, at the time of measurement, it's not known whether it has failed or not. This does not mean that such a reclaim will fall out of the benchmarking process, merely that it appears in a different benchmark set, a sort of "work in progress".

PF can be applied on a market-specific basis and also on an aggregated basis to all markets or even to a portfolio set.

$$PF = \frac{f}{\lambda}$$

where f is the number of failed events and λ is the total number of valid, eligible events which have either failed or succeeded that is, they must have reached an end point and not be "work in progress".

PF_m and PF_p would represent the same benchmark carried out for events only with respect to a particular market m or for portfolio of markets p.

It is clear also that, the lower the number of tax reclaims a custodian performs as part of his business offering, the greater the likelihood he will not have invested in risk mitigation measures as the cost will be deemed too high for the return. The consequence will be a higher level of PF. Indeed, in some cases PF as a ratio could exceed 1 even if not all reclaims ultimately fail. For example a custodian filing 30 reclaims a year may have 15 failures and a further 15 which fail then subsequently succeed, in which case PF = 1. This is where interpretation is important. The result highlights a problem. It could mean that all reclaims failed, but this is unlikely. It does mean that the custodian's processes and controls are well below best practice and must be addressed.

Age debt performance (ADP)

Age debt is a well-understood financial measure. This tool however, applied to this process, has two factors which must be used together to make the measure effective. Firstly, the standard age debt calculation places the receivable expected from the tax authority into a time slot for example, current, over 30 days, 1–3 months, over 6 months and so on. This is a good measure in itself and is useful in its own right for both tax departments and treasury departments as it is effectively a cash flow forecast statement.

Of course, another element that must be considered is the point in time from which the age debt measurement is made. Whilst the pay-date of a security would be an expected fixed point from an investor's viewpoint, many custodians use the date that the reclaim was filed to a foreign tax authority as their base point for calculation. This makes more sense, as, until that time, there is really no receivable recognised by a tax authority. Whilst the income event may be valid and the client eligible (so the client is legally entitled to a reclaim), the custodian creates the receivable through his actions in calculating the value of the receivable and processing the correct forms.

However, this is not the entire picture. Each market has variables which affect how and when payments are made. France pays twice a year. So, from this perspective the age debt benchmark gives no indication of when the receivable will actually arrive and the reader would have to know the profile of the French market to be able to intelligently interpret an aged debt or outstanding reclaims report from a custodian.

The second factor therefore is the *expected* age that the debt should acquire before payment is received. So for example, an age debt report showing £500,000 outstanding for 6 months from France is meaningless. If the events which created this reclaim value occurred more than six months ago, there is an issue to address as they should have been paid. If less than six months, irrespective of the date of creation of the event within that period, the reclaim is well within its expected receivable date and a custodian need not be concerned. As we have seen in the discussion on process management, particularly in the French market, it makes sense to hold French reclaims until close to the date of payment. This has the effect of making the payment period, and therefore the custodian, look remarkably quick. It also provides added time for internal quality control checks to make sure the reclaim is valid.

$$\text{ADP} = \text{AVE}\left(\frac{R_a}{R_e}\right)$$

where

1. R_a is the actual time in days from the date a reclaim is filed to the current day or date of payment and

2. R_e is the expected time in days for the reclaim to be paid starting from the date of filing.

The overall or average value of ADP is formed by attention to the market-specific values. In this way, a custodian or an investor can view not only a custodian's overall performance, but can also calculate performance for a particular portfolio spread based on *n* markets.

$$\text{ADP}_m = \left(\frac{R_a}{\text{R}_e}\right)_m$$

ADP calculated for the set of reclaims where payment has not yet been made is thus a good measure of whether a custodian is performing well.

ADP calculated for the set of reclaims where payment has already been received gives a good historical context to previous performance. A custodian may wish to establish this latter measure to assess the potential effects of investments in automation or outsourcing or demonstrate continuous improvement at a departmental or sales level.

Fit (F)

Fit is an important measure for investors. A custodian may have operations extending to many countries, for many types of income. Some of these, and the custodian's performance within them, are irrelevant to an investor whose portfolio does not include those areas.

Fit therefore is a measure of the degree to which the investor's portfolio matches that of the custodian. In many RFPs, this stage is both manual and laborious. Custodians spend much time extolling the virtues of their organisational structures and reach without making a measured statement of the fit between their activities and the needs of their customers.

Of course the fact that a custodian operates for example in a market which is not covered by a client's portfolio, does not mean that there is no benefit to be attributed to that fact. There will be a beneficial effect simply from the increased experience of world markets that flow from an extended market capacity. In addition of course, the investor may at some point decide to expand the coverage of his portfolio and selecting a custodian with a larger capacity than the investor's portfolio spread will then have its advantages.

Fit by markets, income types and client types are the three most important areas to consider. Fit by client types may seem strange but, any given "client" in this context may be representing a larger universe of sub-clients who may have a variety of statuses.

$$F = F_m \times F_i \times F_t$$

where

1. F_m is the fit in markets covered and is a percentage represented by the number of markets in the clients portfolio compared to the number of similar markets in which the custodian has expertise. It should be noted that this does not give any qualitative description of how good that market expertise is.

2. F_i is the fit in income types and is a percentage represented by the number of income types which the client will be receiving compared to the number of similar income types with which the custodian has experience dealing with.

3. F_t is the fit in client types covered and is a percentage represented by the number of legal entity types represented by the client compared to the number of similar client types with which the custodian has experience.

In all these cases, we deal with the word "similar". A perfect fit is of course 1. So if a client portfolio has 12 markets and the custodian deals with 20 markets, of which only 10 coincide with the client's markets, the fit is 10/12 or 83.3%.

The other calculation that can be made of course is the actual coverage of the custodian compared to the need of the client. In the above case this would be 20 markets covered divided by the matched need of 10.

So from a fit perspective, an investor can use this measure in two ways. The first as a measure of true quantitative fit to current need. The second as a measure of potential future fit.

Statute risk (SR)

The risk, in any process, occurs most when there is a defined moment or moments at which the possibility of success for the process becomes zero. In the tax reclaim process, this moment is the last day of the statute of limitations provided by the tax authority. Set by each country, once a tax reclaim fails to have been filed by this date, the value it represents effectively goes into the invisible earnings of the country concerned.

Given the reader's knowledge of the other and preceding elements of the process, it's not difficult to understand why, in the absence of significant automation or other resources, many custodians would struggle with a backlog of unfilled reclaims.

The measurement of the risk that a reclaim will cross the statute of limitations (SOL) barrier is defined by the length of time left between the end of the statute period and the current date as shown in Figure 12.1.

The risk becomes greater proportionately, the further back in the process the tax reclaim is at any given point relative to the end of statute date. As has been demonstrated, there are five preceding process elements. Statute risk is, in its most fundamental form a measure of the funds at risk in the process. However, the funds will either be paid or not paid, so the value at risk is easy to calculate. The probability that that value will be lost is a different matter. Again, SR, like many other benchmarks, is an aggregate measure which can be subdivided into market specific benchmarks. This allows individual SR elements to be compounded together to measure the SR for any portfolio p or any market m.

$$\mathrm{SR} = \frac{(T1+T2+T3+T4)}{(SOL)-Paydate}$$

$$\mathrm{SR_m} = \frac{(T1+T2+T3+T4)_m}{(SOL)_m-Paydate}$$

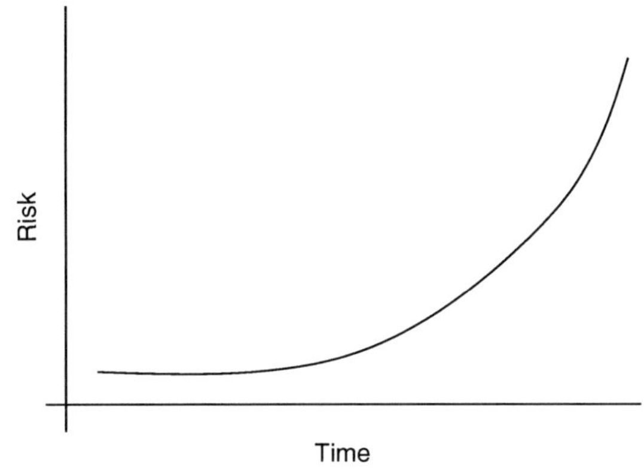

Figure 12.1 Statute risk

Source: Author.

$$\mathrm{SR_p} = \sum \frac{(T1+T2+T3+T4)_p}{(SOL)_p - Paydate}$$

where

1. *T*1, *T*2, *T*3 and *T*4 have the meanings ascribed earlier to the process timings

2. SOL is the number of days in the Statute of Limitations available for a reclaim to be filed

3. Subscript m and p represent the calculation performed on a limited data set by market m or portfolio of markets p

RAS efficiency (RAS)

There are a number of markets where relief at source is available. RAS efficiency measures the degree to which the custodian is processing in the most efficient way. Clearly, if documentation can be obtained in advance and maintained in a valid form, this will save the expense of proceeding through a reclaim process. There are three measures which fall into this category $\mathrm{RAS_m}$, $\mathrm{RAS_p}$ and $\mathrm{RAS_c}$ – measures of relief at source efficiency at the market, portfolio and client levels.

The issue is somewhat complicated because some markets offer relief at source, but only under certain conditions. So for example, Germany is a reclaim market, unless you happen to be a US participant in the Depository Trust Company (DTC). The DTC has negotiated special terms to allow its participants to benefit from a RAS system in Germany. So the RAS efficiency benchmark must reflect what the custodian is capable of treating as RAS internally and what is available to it from the market.

$$RAS_m = \frac{M_{ac}}{M_{av}}$$

where

1. M_{ac} is the number of markets where RAS is achieved. In this context M_{ac} is a measure of whether the custodian achieves relief at source on a majority basis. In other words, all other things being equal (i.e., documentation available and valid) does the custodian achieve relief at source for most of its clients?

2. M_{av} is the number of markets where RAS is available.

This measure, as with so many others can be used both at the "global" level as well as the portfolio level. So RAS_p would represent the RAS efficiency of a custodian at portfolio (not client) level with respect to a limited data set p, representing the countries in which the investor holds his portfolio. An example would be an investor with a portfolio of 15 countries. Relief at source is say, available in 5 of those countries, but the custodian only offers RAS in 4. At this level, the custodian's RAS_p efficiency is only 27% out of a potential 33%.

Of course there is another method of calculating and interpreting RAS. This is because in many instances the ability to obtain relief at source is dependent on valid documentation. So RAS_c can also be calculated by reference to the number of occasions on which RAS was actually achieved at the client level compared to the RAS that was theoretically possible at the time on that portfolio, if documentation was available and valid. The reader will see quickly that this is a sort of reverse way of measuring a custodian's ability to manage documentation. From a practical perspective, I prefer this method to a simple sampling system. The former is after all a sample whereas the latter is a direct reflection on the investor's ability to receive funds gross or with minimised withholding – in other words, achieve results. With such funds in place, the investor can re-invest or take the return, but at least he has the choice.

$$RAS_c = \frac{I_{ac}}{I_{av}}$$

where

I_{ac} is the number of income events in any one period where the custodian actually achieved relief at source and

I_{av} is the number of income events, for the same client and over the same period, for which relief at source was available in theory.

This may all look extremely complex. However the fact is that most custodians would be able to calculate this ratio electronically in a number of different ways.

PoA index (PoA)

There are a number of small factors that can affect the efficiency with which some of the process elements are administered. One such is powers of attorney. Without these, as has been described elsewhere, the process of a reclaim is extended because the custodian must obtain a signature on the form itself before sending it to the local tax authority for verification. Investors are of course extremely efficient at returning these forms, but delays can happen. The tax reclaim form is a statement and a claim for funds on a foreign entity. As such, from an institutional investor's perspective it's important that the form is thoroughly checked. A power of attorney, whether limited or not, vets such authority with the custodian. The difficulty for custodians of course is that the decision on whether a client provides a PoA rests ultimately with the client and the custodian can't be held completely responsible for not getting PoAs on every occasion. However, the PoA index does give an outside investor a feel for how the custodian's business processes are set up. A very high PoA index indicates that much streamlining and efficiency savings are possible. A very low PoA index implies that this custodian will have to engage in a great deal of potentially costly and time wasting communication with clients, some of which may be reflected in his custody fees. An index of around 0.5 indicates that the custodian has an even mix. However, this in itself may cause operational risk problems through having to operate effectively two parallel client document management philosophies at the same time.

$$\text{PoA} = \frac{C_p}{C}$$

where

C_p is the number of clients for whom the custodian has power of attorney with respect to withholding tax issues and

C is the total number of clients. To maintain consistency, this measure should be used with similar client bases for example, all those clients with cross-border assets under custody. Again, if necessary, because the industry is specific in several ways, to markets, portfolios and so on this index can be specified at any of the relevant levels. So from an investor's perspective, he would probably want to see the global position as well as the index as it pertains to his portfolio of invested countries.

Reconciliation and traceability (RT)

Reconciliation and traceability are two sides of the same coin. Increasing traceability permits easier and cheaper reconciliation in tax operations. Measuring reconciliations is an entire area of study in its own right that I'm not going to get into in detail here. However, from an investor's perspective what's important, in withholding tax issues, is

1. that reconciliation takes place,
2. that it's done in the most cost efficient (i.e., electronic) manner,
3. that it traps exceptions effectively
4. that in practice there aren't many un-reconciled items trapped, and finally
5. that all the trapped items are eventually reconciled.

Traceability is built into the above model. The very act of being able to identify, trap and reconcile items effectively means that the process must first be traceable.

$$\mathrm{RT} = \sum_{1}^{n} \frac{E_r}{E}$$

where:

1. E_r is the number of exception events identified and reconciled successfully and
2. E is the total number of exception events.

There are numerous variants of this index that could be defined. However, I think this one serves as a good start in the process. One can infer a great deal from the index which, in a best case scenario, would not be quoted as a percentage but as an actual ratio, in much the same way as blood pressure. In this way, the maximum amount of information can be derived. E, the number of exception events (as well as E_r) should be quoted on consistent terms. In this case, the events are those that are defined in the withholding tax process, whether it be recovery or relief at source. An exception event is basically a point in time where, with two points of communication, the data held by one point does not coincide with the other, where (in the case of quantitative data) it should in theory coincide either precisely or within a high confidence margin of say 90% to 95%. So for instance, in normal circumstances a custodian would have omnibus accounts with his withholding agent network representing the aggregation of all his underlying clients who hold cross-border assets. If the value at the withholding agent does not match the aggregated sum at the custodian, this would be an exception event. It would be reconciled by going through the client accounts to identify where the difference lies or, in the case of a very small divergence, the custodian may just make a balancing entry if the cost of researching minor items exceeds their inherent value. At the more basic qualitative level, if the custodian records that a tax reclaim form has been sent to a tax authority and subsequent follow-up finds the tax authority has not received the form, this would be an exception event. It would be reconciled either by finding the form or by re-issuing it. The absolute value of E gives an indication of how well the custodian's systems work together. The lower this figure, the better. E_r will always, hopefully, be lower than E and the degree of difference highlights how many events could not be reconciled within an agreed confidence limit.

Backlogs (B)

As has been said elsewhere, the nature of the tax process is that there are usually many more events in flow than there are resources to cope with them. The result is that many custodians have a backlog. This backlog can create a problem if the outstanding reclaims become likely to fall out of statute of limitations boundaries.

However, the statute risk calculation does not provide enough information, nor does the age debt tool. The first provides only a probability that failure will occur in the future based on the custodian's own benchmarking of his processes. age debt performance, ADP, gives a current picture at any one time for a given set of variables within the process – paid/unpaid, market, portfolio and so on.

Backlog however measures the differential rates between events being created and the rate that they are reconciled out of the process at the other end – the clear-up rate. This is also, of course, a measure of processing capacity.

$$B = I_c - I_r$$

where

1. I_c is the rate of creation of income events in any one time-measured unit and

2. I_r is the rate of reconciliation at the end of the process during the same time-measurement unit.

What can be seen is that *B* is a rolling measure. It could be stated at one point in time, but is much more useful if stated on a rolling basis. Again, *B* can be calculated per market, per portfolio and of course as an average overall. Figure 12.2 shows several aspects of the application of backlog benchmarking. Firstly, the creation of income events I_c is seen to peak twice during the year reflecting the two major "dividend seasons". The level of reconciliations I_r lags behind *Ic* representing the time taken for reclaims to be processed ($T1 + T2 + T3 + T4 + T5$). However, the peak rate of reconciliation is well below the highest rate of creation. This will mean that a steady backlog of reclaims will accumulate as the department's capacity is not high enough to meet peak demand. The failure to meet peak demand will be compounded further if the total capacity over the year is less than the total reclaim creation. In other words, if $I_c > I_r$, this may not be a problem *if* the statute of limitations for that country is sufficiently long *and* the reclaiming resource remains in place to absorb the backlog later in the year. If capacity is not sufficient to mitigate the effects of peak seasonal demand, reclaims may carry forward into the "to do" pile for the following year.

If *B* is always 0 or negative, this means that the peak capacity of the reclaim department is always greater than the peak demand that can be made of it and there should be no backlog. This does of course bring into question whether the custodian is overstaffed and custodial fees may be higher than necessary to maintain this service level. A more usual model is that at some points in the year, peak demand does exceed peak capacity

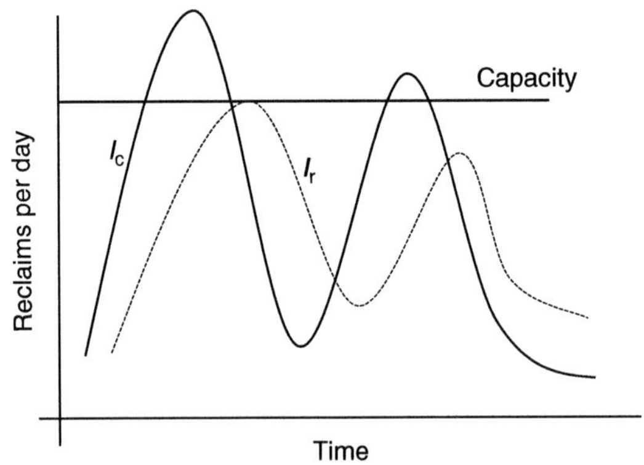

Figure 12.2 Backlog benchmarking

Source: Author.

and B is greater than 0 at some points and negative at others. At this stage, we need to look at annual capacity measurement to see whether the over-demand at one point in the cycle can be met at lower demand times.

Capacity (C)

Capacity $C = \int I_c - I_r$

This model assumes that at all points, the custodian has a fixed resource dealing with the issue. This is in fact the most common model, although how well this model is implemented is only visible once benchmarking such as this is employed to define the problem, or lack of it, more accurately. The reality is that many custodians have a backlog of tax reclaims. It can thus be inferred that the fixed resource model is being used but not particularly effectively. The other model that might be applied would be to have a fixed resource which is enriched at peak times so that the capacity of the custodian is always ahead of the demand and the resource is partially flexible. This latter model is not common, although custodians would see a benefit across many areas of departmental practice. A third alternative is to use the outsourcing model which effectively allows the custodian to move the benchmark to a third party, where there may be a contractual commitment say, to have issued relevant forms within a set period of notification of the income event. In any event, an outsourcing solution for custodians removes the relevance of backlogs as, commercially, outsource solutions providers would find it uncompetitive to have significant backlogs.

Cost per reclaim (CR)

Cost per reclaim is an important internal benchmark. It establishes the prerequisite data to decide whether a threshold value is appropriate from an operations perspective. It can also be used by custodians to establish whether an internal solution, purchased solution or outsourcing solution is the most effective approach to the withholding tax issue. The operations perspective may also be very different from the custody sales perspective as will be demonstrated in the next section.

Cost per reclaim, as the name implies, is an aggregation of all the fixed and variable costs involved in processing reclaims. It is rarely performed on an exhaustive basis and is more often "roughly" guessed at.

For those firms which have detailed departmental budgets and are cost centres, this figure may be easier to assess. One point to note here is that I'm unaware of any firm which currently holds its withholding tax department as a profit centre. However, it's clear that any withholding tax department worth its salt will be adding cash to its clients' accounts to a much higher value than its costs. Whether or not custodians have bundled or unbundled fee structures is irrelevant; it's clear that this activity should be priced into the custody service as it adds value and contributes directly to profit both for the custodian and the investor.

For those without a departmental budget or where the budget may be dispersed, I have provided a formula to assist.

$$\mathrm{CR} = \frac{D}{N}$$

where

1. D is the departmental cost $D = (S + H + V + A)$ where
   a. S is the space cost
      i. S = Area × (rent pm^2 + service charge pm^2)
   b. H is the Human Resource Cost
      i. H = Departmental base salaries × 2 as a rough guide to total employment costs (this figure is for the UK, other countries may have a different rough guide multiplier)
   c. V is variable cost of processing reclaims
      i. Number of reclaims in one budget year N × (cost of postage to client + cost of postage to local tax authority + cost of postage to foreign tax authority) + cost of telephone calls
   d. A is the cost of any automation that is applied to the process whether internal or external

2. N is the number of tax reclaims in one budget year. N itself is made up of course of the number of reclaims at each stage of the process. At each stage of the process a different level of cost will have been incurred. So for example at stage 1, there will have been no postage costs incurred. Rather than create a complex and effectively unwieldy benchmark by establishing a formula for N, I feel it is reasonable to calculate N as the number of reclaims which have passed stage 2. This is because, until this stage, there may not be a reclaim. After this stage there are reclaims and as such they should be counted, even though the reconciliation stage may not occur in the same budget year.

There are other costs and it's up to the reader to decide what level of cost modelling to perform. The elements above constitute the largest cost factors involved.

Reclaim rate (ΔN)

This measures the number of reclaims capable of being processed per day. As this is a long-winded process, it is identified by steps 1 to 4 in our model. In other words, in one day, given a number of income event notifications, how many can be completely translated into tax reclaim forms, correctly completed and waiting to be sent to a local tax authority. In an automated environment this number may be very large. In a manual environment it is likely to be an order of smaller magnitude.

$$\Delta \mathrm{N} = \frac{N}{W}$$

where

1. N is the number or reclaims in one budget year.

2. W is the number of effective working days in the same year

Cost benefit (CB)

This is basically a measurement of the effectiveness of the department.

$$\mathrm{CB} = \frac{\mathrm{Re}\,claimValue}{TotalDepartmentalCost}$$

For the internal department this is an excellent measure of the value that the department contributes to the firm. For the investor, this measure is a way of establishing a comparative basis of the return on investment the custodian is able to deliver.

Threshold index (TH)

A threshold is a double-edged sword for a custodian and an investor depending on its very existence and also the use to which it is put. In simple terms, a custodian may calculate in some way, the administrative cost of making a tax reclaim. In some cases, the custodian may not make such a calculation, but may instead infer that there is a base administration cost involved. Either way, the custodian sets a threshold in terms of the value of a tax reclaim. The principle is that reclaims falling at or below this threshold are not worth pursuing because the cost of administering the reclaim is larger than the value of the reclaim. There is one basic flaw in this argument. The reclaim value belongs to the client whereas the administration cost is borne by the custodian, who has other methods of spreading costs across its business.

The next factor to take into account when assessing a threshold value is whether the client loses money as a result. Some custodians will credit a client account with "below threshold" reclaims even though the custodian does not pursue the reclaim itself. This is clearly beneficial for the client.

Clearly the higher the threshold value, the more implicitly inefficient is the custodian as their applied administration costs are high. So, from a benchmarking perspective, we need a measure which shows the likelihood that any given portfolio will be affected by this value. The simplest way of course is to assess the average value of income event. However, this will only work to a limited extent because the value of the income event does not give a clear indication of the potential reclaim value, since this is affected by withholding rates and treaty rates. Instead, we look at the custodian. If a large proportion of reclaims in a custodian's possession fall below their self imposed threshold, there is a proportionate chance that the investors reclaims may also fall into this category.

Threshold Risk (TH) represents the proportion of events whose tax value falls below any given custodian applied level and which would otherwise be reclaimable or creditable to an investor's account.

$$\mathrm{TH} = \frac{T_{\mathrm{hx}} N_{\mathrm{h}}}{V_{\mathrm{al}}}$$

where

T_{h} is the threshold value
N_{h} is the number of reclaim events at or below T_{h}
V_{al} is the total reclaim value of all events

So, if a custodian has 200,000 income events per year whose total value is \$30,000,000 of which 50,000 fall below a nominal threshold of \$100, TH = (50,000 × 100)/30,000,000 = 0.16. A competing custodian who applies a lower threshold value, is likely to have a smaller number of events falling into this category, thus TH will be a smaller fraction. The use of the term "at or below" in this index, makes the calculation much simpler from a mathematical viewpoint (as otherwise a summation of each event and each value would be necessary). In addition, the use of this limiting factor gives an investor a view of the worst case scenario where all his hypothetical events are just under the threshold value and his portfolio would then receive the worst possible service (and value).

Contractual tax index (CTI)

In the same way that other indices can be modified to apply either to the whole market or to a portfolio of markets, the contractual index CTI can be calculated in different ways. Since contractual tax delivers the quickest gross funds to an investor, a high convergence between the investor's portfolio spread and that of the custodian is desirable. What this index does not do is make any assessment of the profitability of such an arrangement. Since custodian's prices for custodial tax must reflect their own efficiencies in the cost of financing as well as a profit margin, a convergence between the portfolio and the custody operation spread may not always be right for the investor.

$$CTI = \frac{C_p}{C_m}$$

where
C_p is the number of markets in the investor's portfolio which have matching entries in the custodian's spread and

C_m is the number of markets in which the custodian offers contractual tax

VEV index

Validity, eligibility and value index is a composite index and is most important in assessing a custodian's internal systems and procedures. It reflects the three stage internal process a custodian engages in after it becomes aware of an income event. The sub-indices which comprise the composite relate to the efficiency with which a custodian is able to

1. assess the validity of an event. The sub index here is the Validity index (**VI**) that is, at what speed can a custodian decide whether any particular income event is likely to generate a withholding tax reclaim or relief-at-source opportunity or not. This will be an assessment of jurisdiction (whether the jurisdiction is reclaim or relief at source) and whether the type of income is subject to withholding tax. VI can hold one of three values:
   a. 2 = a completely manual process based on knowledge held in paper form or in staff experience;
   b. 1 = partially automated through the use of common tools such as spreadsheets, where a matrix has been compiled against which the income event can be assessed. Since the knowledge has been externalised, it has also reduced the operational risk in the process as well as improving the ability of management to openly oversee the tool's level of accuracy and precision.
   c. 0 = completely automated where information about the income is held electronically and assessed electronically against information about jurisdictions. This value would also be used for outsourcing solutions.

2. Assess the eligibility of a particular income event/client pairing. The Eligibility index **(EI)** is a measure of how efficiently the custodian acquires, holds and manages information about its clients. This can range from a fully manual system through to a completely automated and integrated system. In this element of the process the custodian must acquire information from the client, usually from the account opening process under KYC rules, as well as documentation – irrespective of whether the client has issued a power of attorney. It must then assess, in the light of the validity of the income event, whether the particular client is eligible for further attention whether under relief at source procedures, reclaim procedures or other procedures (such as contractual tax). This will determine, under the communications and reporting principles, whether the client's account should be credited immediately (RAS or contractual tax) or at a later date (reclaim). Eligibility index, EI is ranged between 0 and 2 and is formed according to the following equation: EI = AF + SF, where
   a. Acquisition Factor (AF) is 0 for electronic and 1 for manual
   b. Storage and Retrieval Factor (SF) is 0 for electronic and 1 for manual. An example of an electronic system would include document imaging.

3. Determine, given validity and eligibility, the value of the event in tax terms to the client (independent of whether the regime is RAS or reclaim or the commercial rule is contractual tax). Value Index (VI) is 0 for electronic and 1 for manual. This factor models the way in which the custodian stores and manages information about the withholding tax rates that apply for any given combination of income event, date and type of client.

The range of values for VEV index is shown in Table 12.2.

These benchmarks represent ways of measuring processes. As such they can be used by anyone in the investment chain depending on the information available to them and their need. However, looking to the future, we must also have benchmarks that reflect the new paradigms for withholding tax. This means two new benchmarks: regulatory and audit compliance benchmarks. On the regulatory front, if each market requires end of year reporting like the United States, it seems likely that that reporting would be segregated by "foreign person's taxable income in a given market and resident person's income in a given market via a foreign account. In the United States this is 1042 reporting and 1099 reporting respectively.

In terms of the new audit paradigm that we've discussed, it's likely that each intermediary will need to be audited by each market of investment for compliance to its particular rule set. While harmonisation may be developed for processes, it's highly unlikely that audit rules will be the same. An

Table 12.2 Table of VEV indices

Validity index VI	*Eligibility index* EI		*Value index*	*Range*
	Acquisition *AF*	*Storage* *SF*		
0 – automated	0 – automated	0 – automated	0 – automated	0 – automated
1 – partial	1 – manual	1 – manual	1 – manual	5 – manual
2 – manual				

Source: Author.

intermediary facing two audits in a six-year period, as with the United States, compounded by 15 to 35 other markets, provides the possibility of an audit burden of up to 70 audits every 6 years. Even if the European Union could organise under one audit rule, the number of audits may decrease but each market will undoubtedly want slightly different information.

It therefore makes a compelling oversight case and also a compelling competitive advantage case, to have some measure of the degree to which any given institution meets its tax information reporting and audit obligations and to have these as published benchmarks.

PART 5

The Future

In previous years, this chapter would have been so much easier to write. Many times I've been asked for reports on tax reclaim activity by clients on a monthly or even weekly basis. My response is that weekly reporting is fine – if you like watching paint dry or grass grow. Withholding tax was one of those backwaters where everyone pretty much knew the problems, knew the insurmountable inertia that should be overcome for any significant change and the stupendous lack of awareness in the minds of the people who could ultimately make a difference.

In 2009, like so many things in the financial world, tomorrow will bring a new playing-field and we don't actually know what the rules of the game might be.

There is a general understanding that investment by the banks will be more constrained, so change may be more difficult to achieve through lower fund availability. On the other hand, we know that the failures of the industry in the last few years have destroyed trust in the wider economy and stricter regulation and penalties may force the financial service industry to invest. We know equally that investors, who were already on the edges of becoming activist in the general sense, are now looking down the barrel of a decreasing return, despite having entitlements form the good years still within their grasp. Their increasing knowledge of issues like withholding tax will only add fuel to the pressure on the financial services industry.

So, who knows what the future may bring? The following chapter and conclusions try to provide some small insight into the kinds of initiative that are in progress today and that may affect our industry in the next ten to twenty years.

CHAPTER 13

Regulation and Harmonisation

The woes in the financial world of 2008 have brought into extremely sharp relief, the contention between regulatory attitudes and industry practice. In the past, the financial world has been run on a rules-based system which, during deregulation, was loosened to a principles-based regulatory system by and large. In other words, each firm is deemed to understand the principles behind regulation, but how each reacts to that principle in a free market may be different. It's not difficult to see the knee-jerk reaction taking shape as I write this in early 2009, with rules-based regulation set to take centre stage. I re-read with interest, the FSA guidelines in the UK's intent to move towards principles-based regulation, as late as 2007. The FSA said in 2007: "Principles-based regulation means moving away from dictating through detailed, prescriptive rules and supervisory actions how firms should operate their business." It's difficult to see how, given intervening events, any tax authority will be able to resist demands for either a rules-based regulatory framework or at best a combination.

CORPORATE GOVERNANCE

I've been a champion over the last few years of the need for some further action from the issuer end of the investment chain. Essentially, we have to remember that investment is a chain. At one end is the issuer – the corporation that is in need of cash and decides on ways to attract cash. That might be by issuing and selling shares and/or it might be by issuing debt in the form of a corporate bond. Either way, the issuer has a vested interest in attracting money from investors. Like any good marketing plan, the effort you apply to get investors is most effective when it generates loyal investors, so you don't have to go through the cost of attracting brand new investors each time.

At the other end of the chain is the investor and between the investor and the issuer lies what can be a complex web of intermediaries – custodians, brokers, third party advisors, trustees, administrators and so on. Some of these have a fiduciary duty and some a contractual duty to act in the best interests of the investor. Some of the brokers, those who make markets for the issuer's products, have a fiduciary or contractual duty to act in the best interests of the issuer. However, I'd argue that in all cases, the best interests of the investor serve the interests of the issuer too.

Investors make money through two primary means when they invest in instruments like shares or bonds. They either make money on the difference between the buy price and the sell price and/or they make money by holding the shares long enough to attract dividend income. In the case of bonds, over a coupon payment date. So, my argument has always been that there is an inherent driver for issuers to look after investors. So why then do issuers continue to ignore the differential effects of withholding tax on their investors? Well, I have to say that it's the lawyers that are creating the barriers through a misplaced (and historic) assertion that "the tax affairs of investors are ... the tax affairs of investors". This outdated cop out gives the lawyers an easy way of avoiding a potential benefit for their customer's customer and also allows the issuers to point at the lawyers and say we can't or don't need to do anything. Hopefully, the changes to the structural framework of the financial services sector in the next year or so will remove this archaic thinking. I usually put the case in the following terms.

Suppose you have an annual general meeting and at it, there sit two major institutional investors. One represents a fund resident in one jurisdiction, the other a fund resident in a different jurisdiction. Both are investing in a firm resident in, let's say, Switzerland where the statutory rate of tax is 35%. The issue is that the treaty that governs each investor's entitlement to optimise their tax position is different. So, while both may get taxed at 35%, one investor knows that he can get 20% of that tax back, giving a net rate of just 15%. In a free market, it is reasonable, I accept, for the market to say that if the other investor does not know or can't be bothered to find out or does not take good enough advice – if he loses out, that's his problem. But this approach absolutely misses the point, and the opportunity.

As those investors sit there talking to each other, one finds out about the tax issue from the other. Now here we have to look at things from the investor's perspective. From the investor's perspective, the dividend distribution resolution at the AGM is essentially a statement by the board of directors about the company's desire to reward shareholders/investors for their loyalty that is, holding the shares long. It's reasonable to assume that when that resolution is passed, let's say at €1 per share, the intent of the board was to reward shareholders equally. In the current reactive environment, if I'm the investor that gets taxed at 35% and had no knowledge of the tax optimisation opportunity, I'm going to start questioning how much this company wants my money.

This isn't a legal argument, it's a marketing opportunity argument. The issuer doesn't *have* to give tax advice to its investors, nor does it *have* to take any liability. It merely needs to make a clearer statement of fact (a positive statement), as opposed to a disclaimer (a negative statement), so that its investors are fully informed of the facts relating to their investment. If they choose to ignore those facts, then that truly is up to them. The problem at the moment is that, as the reader should have understood by now, this area is so complex that it's very likely that an investor, even an institutional investor, may have little or no idea about the impact of their decision. Part of the problem here is "proportionality". Institutional investors do not usually take small positions in any stock. Hence the tax effects of any investment are likely to be significant.

I find it interesting that when I had conversations with fund managers in the last three or four years, the interest in withholding tax was difficult to engender. "the fund is experiencing 20%+ growth per annum – why would I want to spend effort in my back office generating an additional 2%?" was a typical reaction. In corporate governance, the same reaction has been prevalent. When times were good, it was just too easy to attract inward investment. There were frankly more investor funds available than there were places to put such funds – demand outstripped supply. Now however, I believe that both scenarios have changed. The pressure is now firmly on issuers to demonstrate value for money. Historically they have done that through earnings forecasts and dividend policies, drawing investors in to a potential buy–sell differential and/or dividend/coupon payment. With the market now at such low levels, CFOs and CEOs will need to be looking further afield to attract inward investment and yet there it is, sitting in front of them as it always was – it's just proportionately more valuable to them now than it once was.

Now, before I provide a packaged answer to where I think the future may lie from a corporate governance perspective, we have to overlay the investor perspective once again, in a real-world scenario. The fact is that, only the very largest institutional investors actually turn up at AGMs. Most of the time they engage proxy voting firms to vote on their behalf. Those proxy voting firms establish their product on the one hand as an easy way for large investors with large portfolios to manage their voting rights, but on the other, those votes are based on systematically designed "proxy voting policies" that both the issuers and investors buy into. This is generally packaged as corporate governance. So, if a company meets certain corporate governance criteria, established in proxy voting policies, the investor has an easier job of choosing which way to vote on any specific issue.

So the need exists at the issuer level, flowing from the more structured financial environment to offer better and transparently fairer value to investors. The need exists at the investor level, even more so now than at any other time, to find ways to optimise return on investment, which leads to higher expectations of intermediaries, but also now issuers too. The handle on delivering this value to these two ends of the investment chain lies in the proxy voting space and also in the offices of the CFOs.

A fuller description of the issue together with proposed policies for issuers and proxy voting companies is provided in Appendix 1. My view is that the concept of these policies was around two years ahead of its time when first propounded. The current economic climate also should feed the investor community with enough ammunition, if the regulators don't, to force issuers into a more proactive frame of mind.

REGULATIONS

Anyone who thinks that regulators won't impose stringent new regulations in the next twelve months, must have been on vacation to Mars during 2008.

There is however, still some tension between the various parties as to what to do, how to do it and what effects it will have. From the investor's perspective, given the perceived failures of both the banking and corporate giants in 2008, increased, rules-based, regulation is the natural response to the question currently being asked – what's going to come out of the woodwork next? It's already clear that investors around the globe are also the tax payers who will be footing the bill to bail out both the banks and the corporates. They are going to want their pound of flesh and it's going to be very difficult for regulators and governments to realistically withstand that pressure.

The issuers are of course in their own dire straits, whether they are directly affected by the global credit problem or indirectly by the global economic slow down, or both.

From a withholding tax perspective the issue is more complex, as one would expect. Currently the only tax authority to codify market practice into formal regulation is the US tax authority. Everywhere else the double tax treaties codify the principles of how two jurisdictions view each other, with the day-to-day practice of how that is implemented, left to each authority. This is why the withholding tax industry is so fragmented at present. It is likely, although not certain, that the approach of the United States to combine its double tax treaties with regulation of implementation will become a common model. That said, in Europe in particular there is also case law being developed that directly affects withholding tax issues. The issue is based on the principle in European law that no member state can treat its own residents any differently than it treats the residents of any other state in the EU. The net result is that a differential treatment of non-resident aliens and domestic residents by one country led to a decision by the European Commission that, in theory, ensures that any benefit bestowed on domestic investors for example, exemption from withholding tax, must be advanced to non-residents of EU member states.

So we see now that the term regulation is not really wide enough in scope to encompass the likely future impacts on custom and practice.

Outside the European Union and the United States there is little in the way of formalised regulation. Indeed, some of the precursor regulations that sit beside tax treaties such as data protection do not even exist in some markets such as India. Further east the situation in Asia Pacific, the evolution of the withholding tax industry is, in my estimation, about 2 to 5 years behind the more mature western European markets and the United States.

Lobbying and peer pressure groups

What worked in 1999, lobbying by individual institutions, won't work in the twenty-first century. There are a number of different groupings in the withholding tax and related worlds that readers should be aware of.

G30 is a group of thirty custodians who meet regularly to review issues unique to the custody world.

SWIFT has many levels and structures but is primarily concerned with setting and maintaining standards on the one hand and running its secure computer network for the transmission of standard messaging on the other.

ISO also has groups, organised by SWIFT usually, that look at different aspects of messaging and standards. Currently there are market practice groups, with an obvious remit to review and agree market practices for various aspects of messaging. There are also forward looking groups establishing new messaging standards, for example, I am part of the ISO 20022 Securities Evaluation Group that sits to review business process proposals to be implemented under the new standard.

Banking Associations have tended to be the main lobbying groups in the past. They face increasing complexity and pressure in the next few years and they are likely to be focal (if not vocal) in terms of either structuring rules or commenting on regulation.

Industry Associations exist in a plethora of abbreviations – SIFMA, ISITC, OECD, ICMA and ICMSA to name but a few.

FISCO is essentially a group of "experts" who have been brought together to look at the practical issues surrounding some of Giovannini's barriers.

One of the key issues is of course withholding tax. FISCO has produced two reports so far.

ICG is the Informal Consultative Group on the taxation of collective investment vehicles which was in turn formed by the CFA.

CFA is the Committee on Fiscal Affairs organised under the OECD.

Giovannini is a committee in the European Union which has been looking at harmonising the playing-field for financial services for some years. As far as tax is concerned, it was quickly realised that harmonising tax rates would not work, so efforts to remove the barriers outlined by Alberto Giovannini focused on getting harmonisation of processing model. While the deadlines for removal of the barriers have not been met, there are a variety of groups supporting his initial report.

MDPUG, the Market Data Practice User Group looks at the industry's requirements for that data mentioned elsewhere that is the start point for many corporate actions processing.

Experience of transitioning to regulation-based tax systems

In September 2008, the IRS issued Announcement 2008-98, a consultation document designed to address concerns about the way in which compliance to US 1441 NRA regulations is being made by qualified intermediaries.

The consultation ended in March 2009 and so, may already be at its next stage for readers of this book. Whether or not the proposals eventually take the form expected by the IRS will depend on the number and nature of responses to their consultation paper. However, it's useful to review the content, as originally proposed, not just for the actual changes themselves, but also as a measure of the underlying attitude of tax authorities to this kind of regulation. This is because, as we've already seen, the US model is the preferred relief-at-source model for Europe.

What the Europeans have to contend with is not just the complexity of having a document-based relief-at-source regime like that of the United States, but also the dynamics demonstrated by such a system. Since 2001, the very complexity of the regulations has led to a variety of exceptions (e.g., Home country rule), exemptions (e.g., portfolio interest) and other procedural amendments (e.g., requirements of NQIs with respect to W-8 documents) to be allowed by the IRS. Each of these was the result of pressure groups, usually custodians, whose individual client base dynamics gave rise to a particular difficulty in processing or documentation. The net result of all these disparate and uncoordinated requests was that the IRS has consistently given "relief" to certain groups. This in itself would be difficult enough for the industry to cope with, but worse, the IRS also provided these reliefs only for a specified time after which the rules would revert or be amended again. For QIs and NQIs alike, this has made the last 7 years an increasingly complex and costly exercise in compliance. For, any given QI has not only to meet the generalised needs of the regulations, but also has to consider and, if appropriate, make amendments to their systems and procedures which resulted from other QIs asking for and gaining temporary reliefs. Further, those QIs also had to contend with developing and maintaining new systems and procedures and also planning and implementation of systems to revert back to the original rules when the reliefs ran out.

In parallel to these efforts, the US Treasury makes annual proposals for changes to certain elements of the regulations that affect them. These are usually codified in the Blue Book. QIs who maintain vigilance at the IRS web site could be forgiven for missing the changes proposed in the Blue Book. In the 2008 Blue Book there were certain changes proposed to "tighten up" on the penalty regime that applies to QIs.

We will look at both sets of proposed changes in this section. It must be said that one or more of these proposals (and my discussion of them here) may, by the time this book is read, be irrelevant. I believe however that it's likely that most will go through, so both the content of the proposals and the principle of managing change they embody should, I hope, be relevant.

In essence there are two broad areas that the IRS wants to address in consultation paper 2008-98:

- Changes to the QI contract and
- New rules on audits

In the Blue Book, the US Treasury's main concern is to:

- Increase the penalties for failure to file tax information reporting and
- Increase the penalties for failure to deposit taxes on time.

2008-98

The QI Contract is the primary document that establishes the obligations of a qualified intermediary to the IRS and US Treasury, in return for which, the QI is able to protect the identity of its customers. The processing consequence of this contract, much abbreviated, is that a QI must withhold tax at 30% on FDAP income unless it has evidence, valid on the date that the payment is made, that the ultimate beneficiary was entitled to a different rate of tax. In order to protect its interests and have some level of oversight, even if only indirect, on the actual compliance of the QIs to this contract, the IRS requires the QI to undergo two audits during the 6-year term of its contract with them.

What has been increasingly clear from recent years and reviews of performance by the IRS is that QIs are not doing a particularly good job. From my own work with QIs it is very common that QIs do not allocate sufficient resources to the issue nor do they allocate enough authoritative resources. As I have said many times in training courses; the work you do to comply with these regulations must be taken in context both to the specific regulatory regime to which they apply *and* the fact that this regime is being used as the proposed model to be used in and between the 27 states of the European Union. So, it's unsurprising to learn that the changes to the QI contract relating to performance are focused on four issues:

- Prevention
- Detection
- Deterrence and
- Correction

If these terms look familiar together, it's because they are essentially the same as those used in another piece of regulation promulgated by the US government – Sarbanes–Oxley. So here we see, in part at least, the first reaction to the global financial crisis, which is to extend the same oversight controls that have been applied to US listed corporations and those non-US corporations that list on US exchanges in ADR form, to non-US financial institutions.

In particular, these four areas are enhanced by the IRS being concerned that, within any given QI, there are controls in place for each area and that the personnel charged with putting these in place and implementing the controls ongoing, have the authority commensurate with the implied requirements of the contract. Again, in my own travels, I have come across many a QI that has one, perhaps two, staff allocated to "QI" matters. Both would typically be either in the tax department or the income processing department, but critically neither would be of any significant seniority. I am at pains not to put words into the IRS' mouth at any point here, but I can see what (I think) they're getting at. In training courses I always start the course with a self-assessment of knowledge and experience on NRA 1441 matters. It's extremely common for there to be no-one on the courses above a 4 on a scale where 1 is no knowledge and 10 is complete knowledge. The other common factor I see is lack of experience. Many on my courses have only been in the role a few months and have no-one within the firm at any higher level. It's as if this is a "dead area". Everyone knows they have to comply but no-one wants the job. My other observation on these courses is the function of the people who attend – almost always operational staff, almost never compliance, almost never C or E level executives and almost never IT. This wouldn't be so bad if these firms did have people in these areas focussing on the issue, but it is clear that this is not the case. So I have some sympathy with the IRS here irrespective of whether I fully buy into their chosen solution.

So, in terms of prevention, detection, deterrence and correction, the requirement would be not only to have adequate controls in place to assure the IRS that potential failures have been identified throughout the whole lifecycle, but also to make sure that, if there is a failure, there are personnel identified in the controls who have sufficient authority to be able to implement a rectification. One of the other requirements in the proposals that flows from this four-point system, is that of a Notice of material failure. This is a very "Sarbanes–Oxley" statement. Under Sarbanes–Oxley (refer to *Sarbanes–Oxley – Building Working Strategies for Compliance*, by R McGill and T Sheppey, Published by Palgrave in 2007) the CFO and CEO of an impacted company must have adequate procedures and controls in place to notify them of any material failure in systems or controls that could affect the share price (aka investors) of the firm. Most Sarbanes–Oxley affected companies will be familiar with the concept of a notice of material failure because its inherent in most firms' response to the Act. So, the essence of 2008-98 is to propose the following key principles as changes to contractual terms:

1. Notice of material failure,

2. Authority of specific employees and

3. Controls to prevent, detect, deter and correct.

The question is, to return to my point earlier, if promulgated, will these be changes that are made across the board to both existing contracts and new ones, or just to new contracts following the 6-year renewal cycle? If the latter, this will be according to the norm delivered so far, but will then cause a contract management issue of enormous proportions.

That said, the second half of this tightening of controls and responsibility by the IRS needs to have some mechanism of oversight and here we see the second of the two main areas in context in 2008-98. The second area of focus is on changes to the audit process and procedure. These changes fall into three categories:

1. Evaluation of notice of material failure,

2. Oversight of non-US auditors by a US auditor and

3. Joint and several liability of auditors.

Clearly, the first element is a response to the requirement in the proposed change for there to be a process for notification of material failure. The audit rules change would dovetail to this requirement requiring auditors to evaluate (and report) the risk of a material failure within any QI.

The second issue is less transparent. There are very few auditors who are capable of performing a high quality QI audit. Most firms opt for one of the big three. However, the problem is, I suspect, that a foreign auditor auditing a foreign bank does not give the IRS enough direct control over the way that the audit and its results can be interpreted or normalised for the purpose of future regulatory changes. It's similar to, and may even have been affected by, the fact that there are changes going on with US withholding agents after their failure to live up to promises given relating to tightening up their procedures for dealing with QIs (by definition, a US withholding agent cannot be a QI, therefore cannot be under contract in the same way).

So, if adopted, the principle would be that a QI can employ an external (or internal) auditor as required by the existing contract, but it would additionally have to employ a US-based auditor as well.

The third element hinges on the second to create a potential minefield. The third element requires that where there are two auditors, one of whom must be US, that both auditors must take joint and several liability for the audit performed. In other words, where there is any legal case involved for failure to perform an audit correctly (and there are separate rules for auditors on how to conduct audits), both the US and foreign auditor must take joint liability (i.e., they can be sued together) and several liability (i.e., they can be sued separately). While I'm no legal expert I can't envision any circumstance where a US auditor will accept joint and several liability with a foreign auditor without essentially doing the audit themselves in parallel to the foreign auditor and charging a second fee. The net result of these proposals will therefore be to increase costs of compliance and the strictures of doing business with the United States as an investment market.

We now move on to the Blue Book proposals which, proposed in mid-2008, were to have become effective on 1 January 2009. There are really two interesting things about the Blue Book changes. The first is that the penalties exacted on the financial community for non-compliance will rise significantly. The second is that the projections made by the IRS of the income expected from applying those enhanced penalties will also rise in the period to 2018. The penalty changes are laid out below for reference:

	2008 Penalty	*2009 Penalty*
Tier 1: Failure to file TIR within 30 days of deadline.	$15 capped at $75,000 annually.	$30 capped at $250,000 annually.
Tier 2: Failure to file after 30 days but before 1 August.	$30 capped at $150,000 annually.	$60 capped at $500,000 annually.
Tier 3: Failure to file after 1 August.	$50 capped at $250,000 annually.	$100 capped at $1.5 million annually.

The IRS expects to receive income as follows based on these increased fines:

2009:	$10 million
2010:	$40 million
2011–2018:	$300 million

I'm curious about one thing. In my mind, the object of penalties is generally deterrence and not income generation. So I would expect to see penalty income projections dropping over time as the expectation of greater compliance (presumably through the operation of 2008-98 rules) increases.

In general terms, we now need to remind ourselves that these changes are occurring after 7 years of operation of these regulations and that these regulations are, in principle, the preferred option of the European Union for the relief-at-source element of a combined process approach to withholding tax.

So after 7 years, the regime, well-documented from day one is deemed to be working so well, that strictures for compliance are being increased significantly, oversight requirements are being ramped up and penalties for non-compliance generally doubled. When these regulations originally came out, technology expenditure was running at $5 tn a year. In the current climate, financial institutions are facing such a tough time that technology expenditure is dropping to "business critical only" levels. Staff cuts, ranging in the tens of thousands per institution, will remove a massive knowledge and experience base from many firms, which ironically will increase risk – which was the original reason for the financial turmoil in the first place.

I'm not sure that the IRS, or governments in general, have yet seen past the political knee-jerk of rules-based regulation as the panacea to financial crisis. It is clear that already fragile financial systems will be unable to cope with multilateral rules-based regulation, since capital will not be available for such projects. The net result would normally have been a concentration or consolidation of the industry into the very large and the rest. The very large will be able to withstand the violent turmoil and still invest for the future. Smaller players would either dis-invest in complex regulatory markets or outsource such services to their larger competitors. The problem that this gives us is that this model won't work any more when even, or perhaps especially, the largest players aren't stable or strong enough to weather the storm.

There's no doubt in my mind anyway that for the foreseeable future we will be looking at increasing regulatory structures centred on transparency and reporting with audit oversight. Custom and practice, currently not codified, will become codified into regulation or at least into published market practice in the same way that market practice is currently codified in the messaging community.

HARMONISATION

In discussing regulation, the essence of the argument was that a number of factors are now coming in to place which will see increasing regulation in the industry generally, some of which will almost certainly flow through and impact withholding tax.

We will take that trend for granted and look at the expected changes, collectively known as harmonisation. Harmonisation has been something of a dirty word in our industry mainly because we look for the negative outcomes – usually loss of jobs and loss of ability to compete. Certainly, the custody industry is always on a knife edge because the industry exists only because of the product and service differentiation between financial institutions. If we harmonise on any significant level, we, by definition, remove many of the differentiators that sustain the industry. At the same time, there is much within the withholding tax industry specifically that would lend itself to harmonisation and where the negative effects of such harmonisation would not be felt, because the changes would not affect a market differentiator. That's the pragmatic view, and it's based on the observation, over 12 years, that despite having many aspects which could be used as differentiators, custodians consistently see the withholding tax industry as a cup half-empty rather than a cup half-full.

The object of the exercise surely has to be to increase the amount of tax entitlements that are repatriated back to investors. Currently at only 7%, the rules, processes and complexities of the industry do not do investors any favours. Anything that allows more investors to increase their return legitimately will have a knock-on effect for the financial markets, freeing up capital that is tied up and unusable, for years in many cases, by being in tax authority bank accounts.

Equally, anything that allows tax authorities to meet their treaty obligations more efficiently and thereby encourage inward investment, will also free up capital and enhance the flow of capital around the globe creating a massive fiscal stimulus for many economies.

Harmonisation falls into five categories:

1. Tax rates

2. Process

3. Control and oversight

4. Standards and

5. Messaging

Tax rates

There is no doubt that over the last 20 years, tax rates have consistently been narrowing. The two key rates – statutory withholding rate and treaty rates have both been on a similar trajectory. In 1996 the gap between the highest and lowest statutory rate was 40%. Treaty rates similarly have been narrowing tending to a 15% level. The trend, if one were to apply a mathematical model to it, would be for a common statutory rate of around 20% to 25% and a treaty rate of around 15%. However, this global picture of a narrowing of rates does not mean that withholding tax rates will harmonise to the point where the issue ceases to exist or even be material. Even Giovannini and FISCO, within a European context recognised this when they analysed the market. The volatility of the markets in recent times has highlighted the need for transparency. As that transparency is delivered, tax authorities will undoubtedly be more circumspect about who is eligible for a treaty rate and what is required of them in order to get it. Equally, there are geo-political factors that affect statutory rates. The most common here are the needs of governments to fund care for ageing populations where there is little or no private care provision, for example China, and also the need to find ways to fund the massive subsidies being used currently to bail out entire industries fro example, US auto makers. The natural consequence will be an increase in personal and corporate tax rates globally.

The effect of this in the near future will be minimised as we go through the downside cycle of global recession. The number of dividends declared in the next 3 years is likely to be much smaller and the size of such dividends will also be much reduced where they do occur. Therefore the amount of tax deducted will be smaller and thus less material in terms of its absolute relationship to portfolio value. On the fixed interest side it's likely that the level of defaults on coupon payments will increase markedly.

Tax authorities are however, as we have discussed, under pressure both legally and under regulation, to treat non-residents in the same way as residents. This type of harmonisation of rates is likely to increase, but, considering the factors above, the harmonisation is likely to be a levelling upwards to higher rates rather than what was foreseen 5 years ago, of a levelling downwards.

FISCO and Giovannini's focus on process essentially leaves the path clear for individual states and jurisdictions in the European Union to maintain their own tax rates that serve the needs of those states. The United States has already set its statutory rate at the second highest globally and all other markets are tending to set their rates based on their needs with respect to trading partners and expected inflows of investment funds.

So, while there is a long-term trend which might be called harmonisation, the reality is that, for the foreseeable future, governments are going to be making tax decisions with respect to non-residents based on much more urgent short-term fiscal requirements and increasing paranoia about the transparency of inward investment in order to avoid the very problems such lack of transparency has caused in the past. Even with a downward trend, we will still see some markets increasing rates either across the board or on a selective basis. Harmonisation, as a term, does infer some form of guiding control – someone or some group is in control of a process called harmonisation with a defined objective, timeframe and method by which to harmonise. To that extent, harmonisation of tax rates is, to my mind, a bit of a misnomer. What's happening out there is a trend rather than a harmonisation. The effect may be the same, but the latter term better describes the visible facts as it reminds us that these changes are not a controlled thing.

Process

Currently, as I've described, there are several types of process available in the market today – relief at source, quick refund, long form claims representing over 95% of the available processes. But even within these genotypes the way in which the processes are constructed and managed is very different.

Harmonisation of process will significantly reduce costs and complexity for custodians and brokers which hopefully will increase the proportion of tax that is actually remitted back to investors. I think that with the US model already in place, if not operating efficiently, and the EU comparative model moving, albeit slowly, we can expect that within 10 years there will have been a significant trend towards a common process in many markets based on the availability of two opportunities in each market:

- Relief at source model, based on documentation of beneficial owners by intermediaries and the use of that documentation as part of a chain of custody up to the paying agent.

- Long form model based on filing tax returns or claims of entitlement to a tax authority.

Having said that, this only touches the tip of the iceberg. I don't see that the process model will become all that much more harmonised. The above would only require that some markets add a process to their existing processes. Those without a relief-at-source model would adopt one, probably based on the US model as Ireland and Japan have done. Those without a long form model would also need to adopt one. This might give some greater level of certainty for investors but the real issue is not at this level. Having a combined relief at source and long form claim model is all very well in principle, but in the absence of agreed standards and methodologies, each jurisdiction is well capable of, and I suspect will, implement those general principles in their own individual way. We've already seen in the European Union how this takes place with political factors allowing each state to agree to a principle yet have completely different ways of achieving them.

To me, this is just papering over the cracks and is similar to the conundrum of the way that the banks adopt an ISO standard for messaging as a principle, yet each implement the principle in a different way so that there really isn't a true standard, there's only a guideline.

Control and oversight

I do want to make some comments on the US control and oversight model as it's being used as a de facto default model. The concept encompassed by the US withholding tax model has been to take much of what would be custom and practice elsewhere and encapsulate it both into regulation and contract. Regulations, in this case being the Section 1441 of NRA regulations and subordinate to that, have their underlying procedures and processes encoded and controlled through the contract that the IRS has with foreign intermediaries – the qualified intermediaries or QIs.

This is actually the biggest change in the withholding tax system that has, or will take place in the next few years. In addition to creating a combination process model, the effect of bringing process into a regulatory and contractual framework has been the need to monitor how those processes are implemented given that the overall implementation means that the weight of responsibility for calculating and depositing tax fall not on the tax authority or the paying agent, but on a network of linked financial institutions. The net result is something that most of the world has not seen before in its historic withholding tax administration – oversight through tax information reporting combined with audits. It's true that in many cases tax authorities have or claim the right to audit financial institutions, particularly if they file large numbers of claims, but generally claims are assessed on a case-by-case basis at the time they are filed. The focus on the relief-at-source model as the primary element of the combined system means that tax authorities now expect most of the work to be done by the intermediaries.

With the principle of these comments I have no problem. My issue is that there is still a lack of cohesion and attention to detail. I do not doubt that any given system of administration must evolve to meet the changing needs of the market in which it operates. However, the US model has shown us that a great deal more thought needs to be put into the system before it is launched upon the world. In support of this view, I cite the numerous changes and challenges that the IRS has imposed and received on many aspects of their regulations. Of the more than 25,000 financial institutions in receipt of US-sourced income on behalf of their clients, only a small fraction have actually signed up to become qualified intermediaries, the vast majority remaining non-qualified. The "benefit" of being able to retain confidentiality of client identity within a QI context has clearly not been sufficient to convince most institutions to sign up. The complexity of the regulations is also a matter of concern. I come originally from outside the financial services sector and with a science background. On that basis, I know both intuitively and from experience that if you want to impose a system on others which primarily benefits you, to be successful it has to be simple, well-thought out and easy to implement.

The IRS has so far had to make many changes and interim reliefs available under the regulations as the industry lobbied through many separate uncoordinated groups, for amendments that gave them an easier ride – for their particular concerns. Its experience in the years since actual implementation has been a failure rate in tax information reporting, reportedly over 75%. Its latest consultation paper clearly evidences the issues that the IRS sees with the system they put in place in 2001: insufficient resource and priority applied by institutions, lack of understanding and failure to put adequate controls in place. What's interesting is that the European assessment that the US model was the one which was most appropriate for the relief-at-source part of a combination model, was made before the latest consultation paper was issued and so, current thinking does not include, potentially, enough provision for control and oversight. The problem is that once such added controls and oversight procedures are embedded, the cost benefits of having a standard approach are not only entirely lost, they are swamped by the added cost of compliance experienced by the financial institutions. In other words, the answer is not to add more controls and more penalties and more oversight. The answer is to go back to basics and create a system that is simple and efficient. That way the controls needed will be lower but equally effective, the oversight required will not be as burdensome and the investor will not be disadvantaged by having the threshold of relief being increased due to the added costs of processing for intermediaries.

As it stands, I believe that the US system will become over-regulated in the next two years and more financial institutions will find the cost of being a QI too high for the benefits delivered. More QIs will not renew their agreements and therefore become NQIs. Those that maintain QI status will narrow to only the largest firms, and investors truly seeking the benefits of relief at source without getting disclosed will move accounts to these firms. The NQIs, being the vast majority of financial institutions and who already in many cases do not comply with the regulations either through lack of understanding of their obligations or failure to apply sufficient resource, will unbalance the integrity of the system to such an extent that it stands a good chance of becoming unworkable.

I do believe that the combination system is a good one and the concept of a QI is also a good one. I don't believe we have either at present.

Standards

Standardisation is also not as simple as it first looks. While related to the issues of harmonisation, we already know that there are many factors involved in assessing entitlements in withholding tax. Yet there are several of these factors that no-one has talked about, many of which would make life much easier in terms of understanding. Some of these are described below.

Standardisation of beneficial owner types

Currently, each tax authority treats different kinds of beneficial owner differently. Similarly, many custodians categorise beneficial owners differently and also give them different names. There is currently no simple centralised list of types of beneficial owner as there are, for example, standardised lists of countries, currencies and their accepted abbreviations (ISO).

Standardisation of statutes of limitation

These have been set and changed historically but with no real relationship to any commercial or investment factors. If there was a standard statute of limitation either by trading bloc or globally, there would be much greater certainty from an investor and custodion viewpoint, which would translate into reduced costs and higher remittances.

Standardisation of forms

Again, each jurisdiction has different forms. These vary by year and by income type and by beneficial owner type in many circumstances. They also have different questions and warranties required. Having said that, on analysis, there is a core of data required by all, albeit the forms are designed domestically so the core data location is not standard. The application of xml tags to core form data would help and/or an agreement by tax authorities to a common global standard for core data with some mechanism for permitting different requirements by state to be included.

Standardisation of claim types

Linked to the forms issue, some markets allow only one claim item per form. Some allow only as many claims as will fit onto one printed form. Others allow one claim form to have a schedule of claim items to be appended to the claim. Clearly these variations must be encompassed by custodians as they are processing, but a standardisation that allows a common approach, whichever that might be, would remove one level of complexity. Obviously, the most efficient for the market, and therefore indirectly for tax authorities, is a claim that allows multiple items to be claimed at one time for one beneficial owner.

Standardisation of assessment

This is an area that is almost never considered. Most of the discussion of standards revolves around them being the precursor or pre-requisite to messaging. However, for any given type of claim or beneficial owner, tax authorities can take different views on what information is necessary before a claim will be valid. Some require lists of underlying investors within a pooled vehicle, others do not. Again, a standardised approach per beneficial owner type, even if it were on the lowest common denominator level, would be helpful.

Standardisation of remittance time

Currently each tax jurisdiction takes a different length of time to remit claims. Most of these differences and the time taken flow from the fact that tax authorities are still processing claims predominantly manually and according to their own resource deployments and project management skills.

It could be expected that any degree of automation within tax authorities would deliver a much more certain expectation of cash flow for investors, which in turn would then be available for re-investment.

Messaging

Without standardisation, messaging cannot make sense. However, it is messaging that actually is the key to automation and reducing costs to the point where that 7% can be increased. Essentially the industry needs a level of standardisation plus messaging that allows for a clear definition of the variables of claims to be codified and for claims to be submitted and assessed in an automated way.

Having said this, there is currently no-one working at an advanced level on what messaging might be required and within that, what the data dictionary and tags might be. Happily at least the new ISO 20022 process is present to be able to create such a codification if a body with sufficient claims volume to cover the whole market should emerge. The issue for the industry is that if a combination model is adopted, the number and type of messages will increase not decrease. There will need to be some automation and messaging related to tax information reporting and there will still need to be messaging related to relief-at-source elections between intermediaries in a chain of custody. There will also need to be messages relating to long form claims.

One of the key issues is to identify the different parties in the process to make sure that they all have some way in which to fulfil their roles in an automated environment. At present there are one or two tax authorities notably Germany, Switzerland and the Netherlands which have some degree of automation. However, this automation is of completely different types and not to any standard either in form or delivery mechanism. It's relatively easy to identify within the commercial chain, some of the parties fro example, issuers, paying agents, custodians, ICSDs, tax authorities. Others are not so obvious – administrators, fund managers.

One of the difficulties is that we have so far failed to get much automation in place within a simplified system which does not include the concept of qualified intermediaries. As tax information reporting and audit oversight are added, the concept of automating withholding tax expands to need to take these new functions into account and so new actors emerge as necessary elements – auditors, separation of tax authority treasury operations (cash) as opposed to information (reporting). This is evidenced by the 1441 NRA methodology which separates the movement of cash to the US treasury from the delivery of reports to the IRS. This also creates new potential standards and messaging which even the actors themselves, being more manually minded, have not thought of – for example the automated reconciliation of tax information reports to one agency with tax deposits to another part of the same agency, all integrated with audits of performance and documentation standards.

So, we may infer that while harmonisation and even standardisation may seem laudable concepts with obvious benefits, the delivery of these concepts is nowhere near as simple as might first be thought. Even the bodies that are looking at such issues tend to focus on only some of the issues. Other issues seem insurmountable based on past experience – the concept of all markets adopting a common form format for example, will be difficult to implement without a forum where tax authorities can discuss such issues, as a group, with the financial services community as a whole. The fact that even the most obvious harmonisation concepts will need at some point to be ratified by national governments gives cause for concern as these have no history of effectively coming to such conclusions. One of the more positive aspects of this issue would be to hope that governmental ratification remains at the highest level in terms of accepting the principle of combined processing, then leaving the details of how that principle is to be delivered to some over-arching financial oversight council. To that extent there is some hope derived from Giovannini's success on the European playing field although much of that still has to be physically delivered.

The big questions that flow from concepts like harmonisation are discussed below.

When? It's clear from all the players that the expectation is of a long and winding road, over many years, to harmonisation of process model. No-one, including me, thinks it's a bad idea. There is however a great degree of scepticism about what might happen along that road. It's obvious that the longer the road, the more likely it is to come across traffic jams, or side roads that will divert or slow us from the course. As we've seen, part of the problem is that even with a harmonisation concept, delivery can be interpreted in different ways. The US interprets "electronic" as a magnetic tape cartridge delivered with accompanying hard copy forms; the Germans in their DTV system interpret electronic differently as do the Dutch. The Swiss currently interpret electronic as a bar code on a paper-form. So, my estimation is that without actually starting further back in the process to harmonise understanding of what is meant by key concepts, the road will not only be long, it may be never ending since we would end up with an electronic system where we have replaced lots of different paper with lots of different data files.

We have also to contend with the fact that we are going to be either in recession or slow recovery for several years, during which the concept may be agreed, but the implementation and its associated costs will be far down the priority list.

What's it going to cost? This question has to be taken in conjunction with the question "what are the benefits". I'm sure that by the time FISCO publish their paper on the potential benefits and cost saving that would flow from harmonisation of process, it will be clear that there are financial benefits both for investors and for intermediaries. However, I believe that the cost of implementation, including as it must do, the parallel running of both paper and automated systems for some years as well as the hidden costs of developing the messaging standards and implementing them, will be both high and likely to be significantly underestimated. In the current climate, this is one of the key problems. Already, we are seeing estimates of technology spend, previously at $1 tn a year, being radically cut back. That's without taking into account the effect of tens of thousands of lay-offs where it is almost certain that some will suffer the "baby out with the bathwater" and find themselves without the skill base to implement what was agreed.
Who is going to pay?If we're all agreed that it's going to take a long time and it's going to cost a lot of money, those factors alone should not preclude the aim being valid, nor from the industry making the investment. One of my key issues however is whether the issue of who pays impacts on the core objectives of the initiatives. I've already noted that one of the issues that face intermediaries is that the cost of filing a claim may be either higher than the value of the claim itself or so close to it that the claim is not commercially viable. This leads most intermediaries to have a numeric threshold of claim value, below which, no claim is filed and, by inference, the entitlement of their customer is ultimately lost (or donated to a foreign government as I prefer to say). The average threshold is around $200 currently. So, now consider that intermediaries, for the OECD and/or EU markets, have to invest in new systems in parallel to existing ones for several years and also create new functionality to deal with tax information reporting issues as well as accept audit costs from up to 35 markets. When these costs are estimated and included into the threshold equation, its likely that the "cost per reclaim" will rise steeply and therefore the result will be that more investors will lose out as a greater proportion of their tax becomes too costly for the intermediaries to file on their behalf.

Now of course, the new system is based on a primary relief-at-source process, so that cost per reclaim, it could be argued, would only apply to a smaller number of events as a greater proportion of events would fall into the relief-at-source segment. Not so. At present, one of the difficulties of all the proposals is that they have to make simplifications in order to identify individual threads of efficiency. Having a relief-at-source methodology only works for those investors whose primary investment vehicle is capable of being an "ultimate beneficial owner" or where the structure of their accounts as ultimate beneficial owners with their intermediary is not omnibus in nature. These are two different issues which are extremely commonplace in practice. So, even with a relief-at-source mechanism in place based on intermediary documentation of their customers, there will be enormous numbers of investors who still fail to have tax deducted at a favourable rate simply because of the way that their investment vehicle is structured or their accounts are structured. All of these will fall back into a long form process it's true and for those markets that don't have a long form process at present, this will present an additional benefit, but it still means that the threshold issue will be keenly felt. We run the risk of spending enormous amounts of money on creating more efficient processes only to see that the net effect is to dis-intermediate more investors from their entitlement.

What do we get in the interim?This is a very vexed question because it has so many facets and several of these depend on the order in which things are agreed and done. We must also take into account that this is not a global initiative. It may take in most, if not all the mature markets and thus hit the 95% level, but from a systems and operations viewpoint, even 5% has to be handled in some way. The problem is that that 5% is actually in emerging markets some of which for example China, will become not only mature very quickly but also supplant some of the existing mature markets in the league table of importance to the investment community.

It's likely that agreement will be based on a broad set of principles and an understanding that moving towards standards and automation is a laudable objective with clear benefits. There may or may not be some expectation of time. Based on the success rate with Giovannini's barriers so far, any time expectation should be taken with a pinch of salt. It would not surprise me to see timeframes in the realm of 10 to 20 years.

However, once agreed in principle, most market players would want to start on the detail of creating standards. This pre-supposes an acceptance of certain key principles, one of which is the creation of electronic forms to represent what is currently done with paper. In the new areas of tax information reporting, we may have the benefit of learning lessons from the implementation of the US 1441 regulations to create a truly simplified and seamless reporting system.

The good news is that these changes would fit nicely with ISO 20022 principles and it's to be expected that an ISO 20022 Business Process may be the best development method to centralise all the necessary threads. This would allow, for example, the creation of business process messages for both intermediaries and tax authorities, the creation of xml marked-up documentation, including tax treaties and regulation so that such documents can be handled efficiently in automated systems while still being available in traditional formats. This would also allow the centralised design of tax information reporting and tax reclaim forms so that each state is permitted to maintain some freedom on their own internal processes.

The tax authorities of course, aside from the fiscal compliance functions of government, are a key to this harmonisation. While the EU may have members that agree in principle to such harmonisation, that's a very long way from having the buy-in from the fiscal authorities at state level where the current practices and customs are embedded in years of manual processing. Unless and until they are provided with solutions that help them, it's unclear whether the existence of standards or the acceptance of a single form would make any real difference. So governments are going to have to spend significant amounts of money too to meet these objectives or the industry is going to have to facilitate this in order to gain the benefits of automation on their side of the fence.

What kind of automation is possible? This is actually not just what's possible but what's feasible and what should be done. There are three levels here. If the tax authorities agree to harmonisation and if they agree to a good enough set of principles for example what we mean by automation, then certainly the industry is poised to deliver standardisation of messaging between issuers, paying agents and custodians. Some of these messages already exist and some do not. Where they do exist, for example MT564 and MT566, they may need to be updated to take account of the interim development period as well as the final expectation. SWIFT's main difficulty on this front at present is that current message types are not used in the same way between users, even where there is a standard. Anecdotally, if you take a hundred SWIFT users and ask them to send a single confirmation of a dividend payment, you'd get a hundred differently formatted messages. The response to this complexity for other corporate actions, rather than enforce the standards more rigorously as purists like me recommend, is to create the Event Interpretation Grid (EIG) where types of corporate action can be interpreted within the standard to minimise variations of interpretation which lead to the difference in formatting. SWIFT's StaQs product also supports this principle by providing a benchmark for messages that is, senders and receivers can flow test messages through StaQs to measure how closely the message format meets the standard. Of course, this business process does give the opportunity to have some greater strengthening of the standards particularly where messages have yet to be created. A close definition of the messages, so that interpretation leading to different formats is more difficult, will or should be a core focus.

So, automation at the intermediary and issuer levels should be relatively straightforward albeit complex. These institutions are already committed to using standards and automation and have the mind set to achieve STP. The problematic area is automating between tax authorities and financial community. Since tax authorities have little or no automation currently and they are the source of the entitlement re-payments, they are the key to successful automation. What type of automation is likely to be open to debate. It's unlikely, for example, that, given ISO standard messages, that they will spend the money necessary to connect to the SWIFT network directly. Since claims will also still come from investors directly on paper, they will want some method which allows them to use both automated messaging and paper-based forms at the same time.

When it comes to current conceptions of automation, these currently fall short of the necessary level. While tax information reporting may replace the need for complex documentation flowing up the financial chain (unlikely due to the omnibus issue described above), long form claims and amendments to reporting require a channel between authority and intermediary that allows for requests for information and responses to those requests. Given a sufficiently wide base of research, it's reasonable to suppose that 80% of those requests could be organised into categories and standardised. For example, a typical question might be "please supply a list of underlying beneficial owners in order that we can process your claim". This request is very common. It's sent by a tax authority to a claimant (usually an intermediary on behalf of a client who is a pooled investment vehicle). The objective is usually to make sure that the investors in a pooled vehicle are entitled to the same treaty rate as that of the vehicle that is claiming the entitlement. So, there would obviously be a requirement to be able to respond with that list, which may emanate either from a custodian or may require a sequential message from a custodian to a trustee administrator to provide it. Currently that would be done with an MT574. However, in automating the process, we would also have to take account of what responses might flow from such messages and decide at what point the response could not be codified, categorised or automated and must therefore drop down into a manual process – all a basic part of trying to get as near STP as possible. An example of where this would occur would be if the response to the first message (a list of underlying investors) did not satisfy the receiving tax authority. There may be a second request for further information as one option. If the income event is a bond interest payment for example, the follow-up question might be to request a file that shows how long the pooled vehicle held the bond prior to the payment. Such questions are now also becoming more common on equities too with many tax authorities adding a "qualifying period" before treaty benefits can accrue to a holder. The objective here is not to pick up so-called treaty shopping but to make sure that the holder is not dividend washing. The final result of a such a message sequence between tax authorities and intermediaries could either be the agreement to pay that is, it's a valid claim, or a judgement that the claim cannot be accepted at pooled level and that claims must be individually filed at underlying level. This of course would kick off an entirely separate sequence of events with even more complexity.

At the other end of the cycle, tax authorities make payments on long form claims, the relief-at-source elements being taken care of by reconciling the intermediaries compliance to the documentation rules under audit to their tax information reports at year end. Typically tax authorities make payments manually at present which involves writing a cheque. Clearly, this could be automated too, as long as the tax authorities have some mechanism by which to instruct payments to be made electronically.

There are other issues with tax authorities that revolve around their needs in any kind of environment. Some control processes at tax authorities are very weak precisely because the processes are manual. For example, it almost impossible for a tax authority to detect a duplicate claim or to assess whether the sum of all claims falls within the possible global limit set by the authorised share capital of the issuer (in other words does the sum of all share positions across all claimants exceed the authorised share capital of the issue?). Equally, in the relief-at-source portion of the model, the proposed use of self-certification of residency and status by a beneficial owner is unlikely to be seen as strong enough to give a tax authority the confidence that there has been no fraudulent claim. Even the United States recognised this in 2001. Their documentary system allows self-certification, but only on the basis that they have approved the jurisdiction's KYC rules. In other words, they can accept a W-8 self-certification only because they know that the QI is subject to enforcement under a domestic set of regulatory controls.

It's very clear that, at some point, we reach the point of a diminishing return in terms of the investment that would need to be made in standardisation and automation. Who decides where that point is and what happens after that is open to question. Once they see the potential benefits, I'd expect the tax authorities to be pushing the community to automate to the maximum. They'll do this from the viewpoint of little practical experience of automation. The financial services community on the other hand with much more experience, may well decide that the point of diminishing returns occurs at a much earlier stage.

What effect will it have on the industry?John Everett, Head of Tax at HSBC said at an operations conference in London in January 2009, that he expected the effect to be a polarisation in the industry and I agree.

Think about it. At present, most custodians down to the second or even third tier, have to contend with the proposed FISCO/OECD type regime with respect to their client's US, Irish and Japanese investments. But, even at that level, the tax information reporting is different between the three, as are the reclaim models and audit rules. So, already, intermediaries are either having to design and build systems to cope with multiple regulatory compliance systems as well as custom and practice. Now consider that, even with standardisation, the likely result is that automation will only encode the ability of each EU and/or OECD market to adopt a common core with market-led variables in reporting and processes under a "combination regime principle". Intermediaries, instead of being able to reap the rewards of a common umbrella, will have to spend even more money to develop and manage automated systems by and between 35 markets. The investment cost will be enormous. The result will be that most will not do so but outsource to one of the global custodians or a third party outsource partner who specialises in such processing.

Does the political will exist?Crucial question. Some cynics have observed that the European Union and to a more limited extent, the OECD, at the highest levels, are prepared to agree to almost anything that sounds logical or common sense (and often even if it doesn't). This is because they know that at the political level, they can then claim to be a supporter. They do this because they also know that delivery is very different to commitment. We have only to look to such agreements at Kyoto and Maastricht to see how this works.

From a withholding tax perspective, we have to recognise that, in theory if things were different, all these changes could be implemented without a fundamental change to the way in which the principles are delivered. Currently withholding tax is codified under double tax treaties which are stand-alone independent agreements, even if many are to the OECD Model Convention. There is no regulation in place other than the one from the United States. So what gets done to meet the treaty obligation of one jurisdiction to another is achieved through custom and practice – which is why the industry is in the position it's in. In some rare instances it is also codified to a more limited extent in domestic law, Spain is a good example.

The object of the treaties is to encourage inward investment by removing the potential for double or punitive taxation. To that extent, each jurisdiction is really trying to meet those obligations. In the same way that one SWIFT standard message can be interpreted in a hundred ways, so the ways in which tax authorities interpret their treaty obligations differs. I have in the past been tasked on this subject with the observation that most tax authorities are more interested in keeping non-resident's tax money as long as possible since if unclaimed by the statute it becomes their money. If that were true, all markets would move to a long form model and not relief at source. When I spoke to the chairman of one major tax authority in 2004, he commented that many people attributed this "greedy" approach to tax authorities when in fact its not true. That particular tax authority employed over 500 people just approving domestic certifications of residency. They really wanted to meet their obligations as best as they could because they didn't want anyone pointing the finger and saying that inward investment was drying up due to implementation of tax policy.

In today's markets, we find that corporations are moving operating locations based on tax policy decisions of governments and there may be an increased pressure created by the global financial crises affecting all governments together with increasing domestic pressure from ageing populations which require greater and greater tax revenues from smaller and smaller working populations to support them. Billions, if not trillions are being injected by most governments into the financial systems in desperate attempts to stave off a global financial collapse. If that works, at least two future generations will be burdened with the debt that can only be repaid through tax.

In countries like China, the ageing population is not supported by the state in the same way as it is in, for example, the United Kingdom. However, as the country develops, the state is likely to have to put structures in place to do so, since its working population will be the foundation of its continued growth. The other foundation will be inward investment.

So, while creating a more even playing-field across the European Union and OECD markets makes sense, those same governments are already in desperate need of funds. Here then is the tension between the motivation to tax non-resident investors to increase available tax dollars while at the same time not wishing to over-burden the tax scenario and stifle the inward investment. For many years the model of using a tax treaty to establish a friendly attitude at governmental level while having complex rules that slowed up the process of repatriation of tax refunds was one which suited everyone since there was no automated alternative that removed the need for the model. Whether there will be political will at the fiscal authority level therefore to spend time and effort on systems that will ultimately reduce the tax-take of the jurisdiction at a time when it is vitally needed, is the $64,000 question.

Overall, harmonisation of tax rates would never work. Harmonisation of process is the best route. However, that route, once established, will be long and hard. Hopefully, if there is enough consultation, the industry does have the opportunity to create an entirely new landscape by taking the best of what we have, create new enforceable standards and business flows, engage with tax authorities in ways that deliver them benefits as well as investors and thereby deliver true STP. Unlike other areas of corporate actions, where the STP solution has grown out of other, less than perfect systems, with the concomitant legacy of old habits being perpetuated in new systems, withholding tax is so complex and so manual, that any really harmonised system has the possibility to start from scratch and where not possible, to reinvent itself to erase those old legacy problems.

Conclusion

One of the problems with writing a book such as this is not just trying to create a holistic picture of a very complex issue that gives value by making it easier to understand. It's also about taking a picture in time, knowing that the picture will almost certainly change and that, to give good value, the picture drawn must be not only holistic but also flexible enough to have longevity.

I have been a passionate advocate of withholding tax since I first heard about it in 1996. I could not then, nor do I now, understand how we managed to create a tax system that was so complex that it's almost impossible for it to meet its objective of creating a level playing-field. The events of 2008 and early 2009 plunged the world into a financial turmoil that will have major implications for both investors and the institutions that count them as clients. When we entered 2008, we were already expecting a higher level of regulatory oversight, which by early 2009 seems now to be an absolute given. In fact, the question is not whether the regulators will become more aggressive, it's what level of pain will be inflicted and what will be the result for intermediaries, already facing problems of liquidity and trust.

For withholding tax, there are some hopeful trends, as far as investors are concerned. Certainly there is more awareness of the tax itself and of its inherent unfairness. Equally, fiscal authorities are more sensitive to the ever more complex investment vehicles and financial instruments available. To counteract this they will undoubtedly want greater transparency and regulatory oversight.

However, the research still shows that 93% of the tax that is over-deducted will never get back into the hands of investors. This will cause great tension. Everyone accepts that a healthy global financial system must be based on the free flow of inward investment and that to facilitate that, we must standardise and automate with the objective of lowering costs for intermediaries where this is consistent with delivering higher standards of corporate behaviour and customer service. In this way, more of the over-withheld tax will be returned to investors and thus support rather than hinder a global economic upturn. However, the need to support global flow of investment will naturally be considered in parallel with governments' needs to meet the enormous debt burden being created to help minimise the length and severity of the downturn. Currently $1.6 trillion sits in tax authority bank accounts and it will be tempting to slow the standardisation and harmonisation processes down, when each year of delay releases over $200 billion of investor's money back to government.

We must also remember that the world is not just the European Union, the United States or the OECD. The emerging markets of today are the global leaders of tomorrow. Their tax systems are around 2 to 5 years behind the more mature markets. We must also remember that, even in the mature markets, the amount of experience of successfully working together and delivering a common solution is both rare and fragmented. So, we don't have a great historical record of success in such things and we should recognise that, while harmonisation of process to a relief at source and long form model is clearly a good principle, it will be a long hard road to travel.

It's difficult to see, for example, how anyone will invest in automated solutions without some form of standard. It's equally difficult however, in current financial climates, to see how anyone will invest in standards efforts without seeing that some form of automation is possible. Creating a generalised model at the highest level is a good start, but the real value lies beyond this. We must ensure that at jurisdictional level, we get enough common ground and core agreement to avoid a multiplicity of models that can each still claim to meet to high level objective. To that extent, the greatest work lies with the tax authorities whose manual processes and different attitudes to foreign investors are at the heart of the issue, second only to the work of the intermediaries to demonstrate that they are capable of documenting clients adequately and of investing in systems of control worthy of the trust of tax authorities. Until then, we are likely to see the conceptual simplification of the withholding tax industry through automation and standards, complicated with additional oversight and control mechanisms in the form of tax information reporting, reconciliation of tax deposits and audits. I suspect that it will be many years before these costly constraints will be eased. The net result will be that already financially constrained intermediaries will pass on additional costs of compliance to investors and that, even with a universal combination regime, the number of investors achieving relief at source will decrease in the short term rather than increase. The multiplicity of jurisdictional models will polarise the custody world with many of the smaller intermediaries outsourcing withholding tax as a necessary strategy to meet investor needs.

Ironically, as we move through the difficult times, dividend and bond income is likely to drop sharply and so the current receivables from tax optimisation should drop. We can learn a lesson from the agricultural world. Investors and their intermediaries should be mindful that the tax that is still extant is still recoverable, so even in the bad times, there can be good news. With an average statute of limitation of 5.2 years, there is still plenty of value to be gained by farming the good years of the past while the current crop yield is low; and planting the seeds of good practice for the future.

Harmonisation and standardisation are not the death knell of withholding tax as many have claimed in the past. Rather, they herald a rare opportunity for the investment, custody and tax communities to work more efficiently and create a larger whole than the sum of its parts.

APPENDIX 1

Withholding Tax and Corporate Governance

As returns for investors get ever narrower, the level of knowledge and activism, particularly in the institutional investment space, becomes greater. This white paper discusses the potential issues that face Issuers and in particular boards of directors of listed companies, as well as institutional investors and their proxies. As withholding tax becomes more "material" to the interests of these groups, it's expected that more rigorous policies will be required of Issuers.

International Withholding Tax
The Responsibilities of Issuers to Foreign Shareholders

A paper on corporate governance policy and best practice for senior executives

Author: Ross K. McGill

INTRODUCTION

In this white paper, Ross McGill examines what expectations shareholders and boards of directors should have of each other when it comes to distribution of dividends cross border.

Ross McGill is author of *International Withholding Tax – a Practical Guide to Best Practice & Benchmarking* and recognised global authority on practical and strategic aspects of cross-border taxation. He is Director of Marketing at GlobeTax Services Inc., specialist provider of withholding tax services to the global financial services community.

SUMMARY

When a board of directors submits a resolution to an Annual General Meeting for the distribution of a dividend, there is a reasonable expectation by all the shareholders that they will receive the value that the company intended them to receive. Yet, in reality this all too often does not occur.

Rapidly increasing volumes of cross-border share ownership is creating a two-class community of shareholders from the corporate perspective, resident and non-resident, which is likely to affect long term cross border investment strategies of institutional investors. Due to over-taxation at the point of distribution and failure by many in the investment chain to deal with the issue effectively, the latter may ultimately receive up to 35% less value from a corporate dividend than that to which they are entitled and which the board of directors intended that they receive.

While companies are not legally responsible for the tax affairs of their shareholders, they are responsible for maximizing share value and fundamentally interested in attracting and maintaining investment. This requires transparency and best practice as supported by Sarbanes–Oxley in the USA, Higgs in the UK and other governance frameworks in development across Europe. Their ability to attract investment is thus closely linked not just to their performance as a business but increasingly, their performance towards their shareholder's interests. It is therefore in the best interests of companies with cross border shareholders, to adopt transparent, shareholder friendly policies to encourage investment.

Shareholders are the net losers at present. The withholding tax industry is highly fragmented in its knowledge, application and consistency in the support of shareholders. Shareholders should place pressure on boards of directors, through the application of corporate governance policies and voting, to require such boards to:

know about the effect of withholding tax as it pertains to their non-resident shareholder base,

facilitate the education of their shareholders about the material effects of their decision to invest in the company and provide access to solutions which can mitigate any loss in return on investment that would otherwise occur.

BACKGROUND

Increasing international share ownership

There is an increasing trend in cross border share ownership at both individual and institutional levels. Where shareholders may have different legal status and also different countries of residence, this brings additional complexity to the board's ability to deliver shareholder value without adversely impacting one group or another.

It is reasonable for a shareholder, when investing in a company, to expect that the company's directors will deliver shareholder value in equal measure to all members to the best of its ability, irrespective of their status and residence, wherever possible.

Withholding tax

There are two methods whereby a company can deliver shareholder value. Increase in share price and distribution of dividends. In the latter case, a dividend distribution to a shareholder can be significantly impacted dependent on the legal status and country of residence of the shareholder.

In cross border distributions, the withholding agent bank of the company concerned must remit a proportion of the dividend in tax to its local tax authority. The rate at which such tax is levied - The Withholding Rate – is applied generically without favour.

Double-taxation agreements (DTAs)

Double-taxation agreements, where they exist between pairs of countries, provide for a "Treaty Rate" of withholding tax, usually lower than the withholding rate.

While the treaty rates agreed between pairs of countries may give an entitlement to a lower rate of tax, recipients must provide evidence of entitlement in order to access such rates.

Where shareholders are registered there is a higher likelihood, although not certainty, that through the registrar, any manager of the shareholder's assets will have sufficient information to either have the lower treaty rate of withholding applied at source, or failing this, be able to recover the difference between the higher withholding rate and the lower treaty rate, remedially. For bearer shares, there will be no easy record of the status or residency of the shareholder, so a remedial tax reclaim is the only solution, if it is applicable.

Statutes of limitation

Many tax jurisdictions in which issuers have their corporate residency provide time-limits during which claims for tax can be filed. Most foreign shareholders will be unaware of these Statutes.

Statutes have two effects. The first is to provide the ability for the shareholder to go back in time over previous dividends distributed by the company and file for recovery of any over-withheld tax. The second, on an ongoing basis, provides time for the shareholder to file any claim.

Most shareholders have very little knowledge of domestic, let alone foreign tax law and regulation. In this instance it is best practice and should be policy, for the directors of issuing companies to make their shareholders aware, not just of the issue of withholding tax, but also the impact of Statutes of Limitation both historic and ongoing.

The practical effect

In a typical example, a US investor in a Swiss company will have 35% of their gross dividend deducted at source by the issuer's withholding agent bank and held by the Swiss tax authorities. If the US investor is a pension fund, they are actually entitled to the whole 35% back from the Swiss government. Even if not, they are still entitled to 20% back under treaty. This is bad enough and unacceptable if it is being missed. What compounds the situation is that, in this example, as is typical of several countries, the US investor would still be entitled to recover this level of tax for each and every one of the three previous years since the end of the year in which the original dividend was paid.

The question is, on the one hand, should the company, to sustain its reputation as a good investment vehicle, make the US investor aware that his investment returns will be 35% lower than he expects as opposed to other domestic shareholders, or, on the other hand is it up to the issuer to know such things as a matter of course. While short-term thinking would result in the latter course of action, there is no doubt that those companies that adopt a more proactive approach to getting the best for their shareholders, will attract and retain investment more readily.

It will not be long before the effects of Sarbanes–Oxley and of Higgs stimulate governments to add regulated requirements on issuers to deal with cross border impacts on investors thus underpinning what should currently be best practice.

The custody chain

Ownership of shares is rarely a simple process in terms of safekeeping of assets and management of investment income. A variety of firms can be, and often are, involved in the process. Complexity is caused as institutional shareholders do not arrange ownership and thus management of shares in any one company and also hold different parts of their portfolios through different intermediaries or custodians. In other cases, complexity is caused by the commercial relationships between custodians themselves who, in order to provide a cost effective service in several countries, contract with other custodians to provide subsidiary or country based "sub-custody" services.

Thus, when companies elect to distribute dividends to shareholders, there can be several intermediaries in between the withholding agent representing the company and the final recipient (shareholder).

While it is clearly in the interests of such custodians to both know of the issues facing shareholders who do not reside for tax purposes in the same country as the issuer (non-resident shareholders), the degree to which custodians actually have knowledge of withholding tax and implement such knowledge varies widely.

There are currently no industry wide policies to guide boards of directors as to the selection of custodians such that they may be assured of a proactive approach to withholding tax and thus the best treatment of their shareholders.

Many shareholders, particularly institutional shareholders, use intermediary custodians as asset managers, however, while estimates vary, it is clear that only a fraction of over-withheld tax on investment income is ever recovered.

Responsibility to know

Custodians and intermediaries

With only two exceptions, no organisation in the custody chain has direct responsibility to advise shareholder's on their eligibility for lower taxation rates unless the organisation has contracted to provide such advice or where they have, for marketing or commercial reasons, a motive to offer such advice.

The two parties who do have a direct interest are the shareholders themselves and the board of directors whose direct responsibility it is to perform the wishes of the shareholders.

There is debate as to the legal position of many custodian intermediaries in this context. Both companies and shareholders rely on intermediaries in many ways as "experts" whether direct or indirect, explicitly or implicitly. There are many shareholders who still have a valid entitlement to recover over-withheld tax on investment income received cross border, who will never receive it, never have received it in the past, and will, without action, continue not receiving their entitlements in future. The question is, to what degree should a shareholder or company expect their financial agents to tell them what they don't know and to what extent is there an implied duty on the intermediary as the "expert" to at least make the parties aware of the significance of the issue, if not provide a solution.

It's clear that there are two issues here. First is the implied duty as a deemed expert to bring an issue to the attention of the parties concerned. The second is to actively do something about it. The latter is clearly a commercial issue based on whether the intermediary has the requisite skills, knowledge and experience to recover this tax on behalf of its clients, in the face of competition from other intermediaries who do have such an appetite.

Even in the absence of specific contract terms in this regard, the company and its directors may reasonably assume a level of responsibility on the part of their custodian(s) as the "experts" in the field. However, this assumption has no legal precedent – yet. Given the truly enormous scale of the issue for the larger institutional investors, including mutual funds and hedge funds, it may not be long before losses in un-recovered tax accrued over many years and an intermediary custodian who has failed to educate or facilitate a solution, may be placed before a judge to decide whether there is an implied or fiduciary duty at custodial level, irrespective of contract terms.

Companies

All governance related law and regulation stand testament that directors are being held increasingly accountable in regulation and law, for failures to meet the expectations of shareholders. So it would seem reasonable to expect that a board of directors with an international shareholder base, would ensure that they were aware of any material issue that might affect their shareholders. Withholding tax, in this context, is clearly such an issue.

Companies often argue that the personal status, residence and tax affairs of shareholders are their own business. However, the issue of responsibility to know centres on the expected level of knowledge of issues such as withholding tax and the degree to which such knowledge, and its impact, is disseminated.

Because the effect of withholding tax is so significant and so material, neither shareholders nor directors can in future avoid knowledge and action.

From the company's perspective there may be an implied duty on directors, and particularly directors with financial expertise to at least advise those who have parted with cash in return for membership of the issuing company of the implications of such ownership. Those companies with a diverse and widespread shareholder base may also consider it prudent to go beyond educating their shareholder base about the existence of such issues and seek to provide positive methods to assist their members minimise the tax liability which has resulted from their investment in the company.

SUMMARY DISCLOSURE GUIDELINES

The issue of recovering tax from tax authorities is extremely fragmented and inconsistent. The problem for companies and for their shareholders is that no-one in the direct chain of investment is making the scale of this issue sufficiently open or clear. This means that there are shareholders unaware of their entitlements and companies unaware of the potential downside risk from their differential treatment of resident versus non-resident shareholders.

This could be avoided and brought to public awareness through the forced disclosure of some basic facts by both companies and by institutional shareholders e.g. mutual funds, pension funds etc.

A company should disclose:

1. the proportion of total shareholding held by non-resident persons segregated by country of residence and by status of beneficial owner

2. at annual general meeting, as supporting documentation to dividend resolutions, the effects of withholding tax on non-resident shareholders, by country of residence and status, detracting from the gross dividend declared

These disclosures will ensure that companies make all shareholders aware of the non-resident taxation issue at an early stage so that they can take action on its recovery.

A fund should disclose:

1. the proportion of its assets held cross border and the income derived therefrom, segregated by country of investment;

2. whether the fund is eligible for relief at source and if so, whether such relief at source has and is being maintained on income received;

3. whether over-withheld tax has been, or is in the process of being recovered and the proportion this represents of the total recoverable tax

4. the proportion of asset value represented by recovered tax

These disclosures will enable members and trustees of a fund to establish both the scale and scope of the withholding tax issue it faces and also the performance of the trustees in maximising fund value on behalf of its members.

SUMMARY POLICY GUIDELINES FOR COMPANIES

Prior to such disclosures, there are policies that companies could adopt to demonstrate their support for their international shareholder base. These principles and policies will ensure that effective education takes place and that the two most interested parties have the knowledge and tools at their disposal to maximise their investment, reputation and governance.

Principle

- Boards of companies with an international shareholder base should ensure or facilitate, as far as is practicable, that shareholders not resident in the country of incorporation, are, as far as practicable, not disenfranchised from the intent of the board in declaring any particular dividend value, by virtue of their non-resident status.

Policies

1. No shareholder will be disenfranchised from any portion of value delivered to him by the company by reason of his residency in a country different to that of the company's incorporation.

2. The Board of Directors will adopt one or more strategies to enable shareholder value to be maximised:
   a. Education – to provide greater awareness of the impact of cross border investment strategies for shareholders;
   b. Facilitation - to provide access to shareholder solutions for provision of relief at source or recovery of over-withheld tax
   c. Where facilitation takes place by the board, the commercial terms on which such facilitation takes place will, wherever possible be contingent on the success of any tax recovery for shareholders and free of cost to the company.
   d. Where withholding tax is newly addressed, the board will ensure they and shareholders are made aware of any Statutes of Limitations that apply to their company's shareholders by reason of its country of incorporation and ensure that appropriate remedial measures are taken to make shareholders aware of any historical value recovery entitlement and provide access to solutions for its recovery.

PROXY VOTING POLICIES

Many shareholders use proxy voting firms to vote their shareholdings at annual general meetings. Such proxy voting is enacted under policy guidelines issued from time to time by these firms. Below is are examples of Global Proxy Voting guidelines as they might be affected by residence/non residence issues.

Allocation of income

1. Vote FOR approval of the allocation of income, unless:
   a. the company has made no arrangements to facilitate the recovery of over-withheld taxes for shareholders who are not resident in the country of incorporation.

Mergers and acquisitions

1. Vote FOR mergers and acquisitions, unless:
   a. the impact on earnings for shareholders is unequal on the basis of the residency of the shareholder.

Shareholder proposals:

1. Vote AGAINST proposals that
   a. limit the company's business activities or capabilities, result in significant costs being incurred with little or no benefit or where shareholder earnings would be impacted unequally based on the country of residence of the shareholder

CONCLUSION

Over $200 billion of tax is withheld each year by foreign governments on cross border investment income. Compounded by Statutes of Limitations, the extant over-withheld tax in the possession of governments rather than those to whom it belongs, is likely to be well over $1.2 trillion at any one point.

Whilst intermediaries have a purely commercial interest in whether a shareholder's return on investment is maximised, the company and shareholder directly have most to gain, and lose. It's their money.

It's likely that in future, company boards of directors will come under increasing market-led pressure from more educated and aware non-resident institutional shareholders, to adopt corporate governance policies that more actively support their investment strategies and do not adversely impact them in comparison to their domestic counterparts.

Given the potential for a 35% difference in return between investing domestically and cross border, the absence of such corporate governance policies has the capacity to significantly affect international investment and portfolio planning. Corporate reputation, which is the public face of governance principles, is increasingly important in many ways and failure to address it could easily make or break such reputations and with them shareholder value.

Its also likely that firms interested in the management of corporate governance including proxy voting companies will include global policy guidelines with respect to withholding tax, that protect the interests of non-resident shareholder groups. To that extent, large companies may be forced to adopt active strategies in advance rather than be forced to do so by shareholders at an annual general meeting.

While in the near future this is likely to be market-led, in the longer term governments may take a more active interest and in addition to Double Tax Agreements that merely define entitlements, add regulatory requirements to ensure that between companies, intermediaries and shareholders, someone is properly tasked with the responsibility to make it happen.

APPENDIX 2

OECD Model Tax treaty (2008)

Many of the more recent treaties that form the basis of entitlements between jurisdictions are based on a model convention developed by the OECD. Some, such as the US treaties have additional clauses to deal with limitations of benefit (LOB). However, as law and practice evolve so the model treaty is updated. The latest, published in November 2008 by the OECD is reproduced here for reference.

MODEL CONVENTION WITH RESPECT TO TAXES ON INCOME AND ON CAPITAL

SUMMARY OF THE CONVENTION

TAXATION OF INCOME

TAXATION OF CAPITAL

METHODS FOR ELIMINATION OF DOUBLE TAXATION

Article 23 A Exemption method

Article 23 B Credit method

Chapter VI

SPECIAL PROVISIONS

Article 24 Non-discrimination

Article 25 Mutual agreement procedure

Article 26 Exchange of information

Article 27 Assistance in the collection of taxes

Article 28 Members of diplomatic missions and consular posts

Article 29 Territorial extension

Chapter VII

FINAL PROVISIONS

Article 30 Entry into force

Article 31 Termination

TITLE OF THE CONVENTION

Convention between (State A) and (State B) with respect to taxes on income and on capital

PREAMBLE TO THE CONVENTION

1. States wishing to do so may follow the widespread practice of including in the title a reference to either the avoidance of double taxation or

to both the avoidance of double taxation and the prevention of fiscal evasion.

2. The Preamble of the Convention shall be drafted in accordance with the constitutional procedure of both Contracting States.

CHAPTER I

SCOPE OF THE CONVENTION

Article 1

Persons covered

This Convention shall apply to persons who are residents of one or both of the Contracting States.

Article 2

Taxes covered

1. This Convention shall apply to taxes on income and on capital imposed on behalf of a Contracting State or of its political subdivisions or local authorities, irrespective of the manner in which they are levied.

2. There shall be regarded as taxes on income and on capital all taxes imposed on total income, on total capital, or on elements of income or of capital, including taxes on gains from the alienation of movable or immovable property, taxes on the total amounts of wages or salaries paid by enterprises, as well as taxes on capital appreciation.

3. The existing taxes to which the Convention shall apply are in particular:
   a. (in State A): ....
   b. (in State B): ....

4. The Convention shall apply also to any identical or substantially similar taxes that are imposed after the date of signature of the Convention in addition to, or in place of, the existing taxes. The competent authorities of the Contracting States shall notify each other of any significant changes that have been made in their taxation laws.

CHAPTER II

DEFINITIONS

Article 3

General definitions

1. For the purposes of this Convention, unless the context otherwise requires:
   a. the term "person" includes an individual, a company and any other body of persons;
   b. the term "company" means any body corporate or any entity that is treated as a body corporate for tax purposes;
   c. the term "enterprise" applies to the carrying on of any business;
   d. the terms "enterprise of a Contracting State" and "enterprise of the other Contracting State" mean respectively an enterprise carried on by a resident of a Contracting State and an enterprise carried on by a resident of the other Contracting State;
   e. the term "international traffic" means any transport by a ship or aircraft operated by an enterprise that has its place of effective management in a Contracting State, except when the ship or aircraft is operated solely between places in the other Contracting State;
   f. the term "competent authority" means:
      i. (in State A): ....
      ii. (in State B): ....
   g. the term "national", in relation to a Contracting State, means:
      i. any individual possessing the nationality or citizenship of that Contracting State; and
      ii. any legal person, partnership or association deriving its status as such from the laws in force in that Contracting State;
   h. the term "business" includes the performance of professional services and of other activities of an independent character.

2. As regards the application of the Convention at any time by a Contracting State, any term not defined therein shall, unless the context otherwise requires, have the meaning that it has at that time under the law of that State for the purposes of the taxes to which the Convention applies, any meaning under the applicable tax laws of that State prevailing over a meaning given to the term under other laws of that State.

Article 4

Resident

1. For the purposes of this Convention, the term "resident of a Contracting State" means any person who, under the laws of that State, is liable to tax therein by reason of his domicile, residence, place of management or any other criterion of a similar nature, and also includes that State and any political subdivision or local authority thereof. This term, however, does not include any person who is liable to tax in that State in respect only of income from sources in that State or capital situated therein.

2. Where by reason of the provisions of paragraph 1 an individual is a resident of both Contracting States, then his status shall be determined as follows:
   a. he shall be deemed to be a resident only of the State in which he has a permanent home available to him; if he has a permanent home available to him in both States, he shall be deemed to be a resident only of the State with which his personal and economic relations are closer (centre of vital interests);
   b. if the State in which he has his centre of vital interests cannot be determined, or if he has not a permanent home available to him in either State, he shall be deemed to be a resident only of the State in which he has an habitual abode;
   c. if he has an habitual abode in both States or in neither of them, he shall be deemed to be a resident only of the State of which he is a national;
   d. if he is a national of both States or of neither of them, the competent authorities of the Contracting States shall settle the question by mutual agreement.

3. Where by reason of the provisions of paragraph 1 a person other than an individual is a resident of both Contracting States, then it shall be deemed to be a resident only of the State in which its place of effective management is situated.

Article 5

Permanent establishment

1. For the purposes of this Convention, the term "permanent establishment" means a fixed place of business through which the business of an enterprise is wholly or partly carried on.

2. The term "permanent establishment" includes especially:
   i. a place of management;
   ii. a branch;
   iii. an office;
   iv. a factory;
   v. a workshop, and
   vi. a mine, an oil or gas well, a quarry or any other place of extraction of natural resources.

3. A building site or construction or installation project constitutes a permanent establishment only if it lasts more than twelve months.

4. Notwithstanding the preceding provisions of this Article, the term "permanent establishment" shall be deemed not to include:
   a. the use of facilities solely for the purpose of storage, display or delivery of goods or merchandise belonging to the enterprise;
   b. the maintenance of a stock of goods or merchandise belonging to the enterprise solely for the purpose of storage, display or delivery;
   c. the maintenance of a stock of goods or merchandise belonging to the enterprise solely for the purpose of processing by another enterprise;
   d. the maintenance of a fixed place of business solely for the purpose of purchasing goods or merchandise or of collecting information, for the enterprise;
   e. the maintenance of a fixed place of business solely for the purpose of carrying on, for the enterprise, any other activity of a preparatory or auxiliary character;
   f. the maintenance of a fixed place of business solely for any combination of activities mentioned in subparagraphs a. to e., provided that the overall activity of the fixed place of business resulting from this combination is of a preparatory or auxiliary character.

5. Notwithstanding the provisions of paragraphs 1 and 2, where a person — other than an agent of an independent status to whom paragraph 6 applies — is acting on behalf of an enterprise and has, and habitually exercises, in a Contracting State an authority to conclude contracts in the name of the enterprise, that enterprise shall be deemed to have a permanent establishment in that State in respect of any activities which that person undertakes for the enterprise, unless the activities of such person are limited to those mentioned in paragraph 4 which, if exercised through a fixed place of business, would not make this fixed place of business a permanent establishment under the provisions of that paragraph.

6. An enterprise shall not be deemed to have a permanent establishment in a Contracting State merely because it carries on business in that State through a broker, general commission agent or any other agent of an independent status, provided that such persons are acting in the ordinary course of their business.

7. The fact that a company which is a resident of a Contracting State controls or is controlled by a company which is a resident of the other Contracting State, or which carries on business in that other State (whether through a permanent establishment or otherwise), shall not of itself constitute either company a permanent establishment of the other.

CHAPTER III

TAXATION OF INCOME

ARTICLE 6

Income from immovable property

1. Income derived by a resident of a Contracting State from immovable property (including income from agriculture or forestry) situated in the other Contracting State may be taxed in that other State.

2. The term "immovable property" shall have the meaning which it has under the law of the Contracting State in which the property in question is situated. The term shall in any case include property accessory to immovable property, livestock and equipment used in agriculture and forestry, rights to which the provisions of general law respecting landed property apply, usufruct of immovable property and rights to variable or fixed payments as consideration for the working of, or the right to work, mineral deposits, sources and other natural resources; ships, boats and aircraft shall not be regarded as immovable property.

3. The provisions of paragraph 1 shall apply to income derived from the direct use, letting, or use in any other form of immovable property.

4. The provisions of paragraphs 1 and 3 shall also apply to the income from immovable property of an enterprise.

Article 7

Business profits

1. The profits of an enterprise of a Contracting State shall be taxable only in that State unless the enterprise carries on business in the other Contracting State through a permanent establishment situated therein. If the enterprise carries on business as aforesaid, the profits of the enterprise may be taxed in the other State but only so much of them as is attributable to that permanent establishment.

2. Subject to the provisions of paragraph 3, where an enterprise of a Contracting State carries on business in the other Contracting State through a permanent establishment situated therein, there shall in each Contracting State be attributed to that permanent establishment the profits which it might be expected to make if it were a distinct and separate enterprise engaged in the same or similar activities under the same or similar conditions and dealing wholly independently with the enterprise of which it is a permanent establishment.

3. In determining the profits of a permanent establishment, there shall be allowed as deductions expenses which are incurred for the purposes of the permanent establishment, including executive and general administrative expenses so incurred, whether in the State in which the permanent establishment is situated or elsewhere.

4. Insofar as it has been customary in a Contracting State to determine the profits to be attributed to a permanent establishment on the basis of an apportionment of the total profits of the enterprise to its various parts, nothing in paragraph 2 shall preclude that Contracting State from determining the profits to be taxed by such an apportionment as may be customary; the method of apportionment adopted shall, however, be such that the result shall be in accordance with the principles contained in this Article.

5. No profits shall be attributed to a permanent establishment by reason of the mere purchase by that permanent establishment of goods or merchandise for the enterprise.

6. For the purposes of the preceding paragraphs, the profits to be attributed to the permanent establishment shall be determined by the same method year by year unless there is good and sufficient reason to the contrary.

7. Where profits include items of income which are dealt with separately in other Articles of this Convention, then the provisions of those Articles shall not be affected by the provisions of this Article.

Article 8

Shipping, inland waterways transport and air Transport

1. Profits from the operation of ships or aircraft in international traffic shall be taxable only in the Contracting State in which the place of effective management of the enterprise is situated.

2. Profits from the operation of boats engaged in inland waterways transport shall be taxable only in the Contracting State in which the place of effective management of the enterprise is situated.

3. If the place of effective management of a shipping enterprise or of an inland waterways transport enterprise is aboard a ship or boat, then it shall be deemed to be situated in the Contracting State in which the home harbour of the ship or boat is situated, or, if there is no such home harbour, in the Contracting State of which the operator of the ship or boat is a resident.

4. The provisions of paragraph 1 shall also apply to profits from the participation in a pool, a joint business or an international operating agency.

ARTICLE 9

Associated enterprises

1. Where
   a. an enterprise of a Contracting State participates directly or indirectly in the management, control or capital of an enterprise of the other Contracting State, or
   b. the same persons participate directly or indirectly in the management, control or capital of an enterprise of a Contracting State and an enterprise of the other Contracting State, and in either case conditions are made or imposed between the two enterprises in their commercial or financial relations which differ from those which would be made between independent enterprises, then any profits which would, but for those conditions, have accrued to one of the enterprises, but, by reason of those conditions, have not so accrued, may be included in the profits of that enterprise and taxed accordingly.

2. Where a Contracting State includes in the profits of an enterprise of that State — and taxes accordingly — profits on which an enterprise of the other Contracting State has been charged to tax in that other State and the profits so included are profits which would have accrued to the enterprise of the first-mentioned State if the conditions made between the two enterprises had been those which would have been made between independent enterprises, then that other State shall make an appropriate adjustment to the amount of the tax charged therein on those profits. In determining such adjustment, due regard shall be had to the other provisions of this Convention and the competent authorities of the Contracting States shall if necessary consult each other.

Article 10

Dividends

1. Dividends paid by a company which is a resident of a Contracting State to a resident of the other Contracting State may be taxed in that other State.

2. However, such dividends may also be taxed in the Contracting State of which the company paying the dividends is a resident and according to the laws of that State, but if the beneficial owner of the dividends is a resident of the other Contracting State, the tax so charged shall not exceed:
   a. 5 per cent of the gross amount of the dividends if the beneficial owner is a company (other than a partnership) which holds directly at least 25 per cent of the capital of the company paying the dividends;
   b. 15 per cent of the gross amount of the dividends in all other cases. The competent authorities of the Contracting States shall by mutual agreement settle the mode of application of these limitations. This paragraph shall not affect the taxation of the company in respect of the profits out of which the dividends are paid.

3. The term "dividends" as used in this Article means income from shares, "jouissance" shares or "jouissance" rights, mining shares, founders' shares or other rights, not being debt-claims, participating in profits, as well as income from other corporate rights which is subjected to the same taxation treatment as income from shares by the laws of the State of which the company making the distribution is a resident.

4. The provisions of paragraphs 1 and 2 shall not apply if the beneficial owner of the dividends, being a resident of a Contracting State, carries on

business in the other Contracting State of which the company paying the dividends is a resident through a permanent establishment situated therein and the holding in respect of which the dividends are paid is effectively connected with such permanent establishment. In such case the provisions of Article 7 shall apply.

5. Where a company which is a resident of a Contracting State derives profits or income from the other Contracting State, that other State may not impose any tax on the dividends paid by the company, except insofar as such dividends are paid to a resident of that other State or insofar as the holding in respect of which the dividends are paid is effectively connected with a permanent establishment situated in that other State, nor subject the company's undistributed profits to a tax on the company's undistributed profits, even if the dividends paid or the undistributed profits consist wholly or partly of profits or income arising in such other State.

Article 11

Interest

1. Interest arising in a Contracting State and paid to a resident of the other Contracting State may be taxed in that other State.

2. However, such interest may also be taxed in the Contracting State in which it arises and according to the laws of that State, but if the beneficial owner of the interest is a resident of the other Contracting State, the tax so charged shall not exceed 10 per cent of the gross amount of the interest. The competent authorities of the Contracting States shall by mutual agreement settle the mode of application of this limitation.

3. The term "interest" as used in this Article means income from debt-claims of every kind, whether or not secured by mortgage and whether or not carrying a right to participate in the debtor's profits, and in particular, income from government securities and income from bonds or debentures, including premiums and prizes attaching to such securities, bonds or debentures. Penalty charges for late payment shall not be regarded as interest for the purpose of this Article.

4. The provisions of paragraphs 1 and 2 shall not apply if the beneficial owner of the interest, being a resident of a Contracting State, carries on business in the other Contracting State in which the interest arises through a permanent establishment situated therein and the debt-claim in respect

of which the interest is paid is effectively connected with such permanent establishment. In such case the provisions of Article 7 shall apply.

5. Interest shall be deemed to arise in a Contracting State when the payer is a resident of that State. Where, however, the person paying the interest, whether he is a resident of a Contracting State or not, has in a Contracting State a permanent establishment in connection with which the indebtedness on which the interest is paid was incurred, and such interest is borne by such permanent establishment, then such interest shall be deemed to arise in the State in which the permanent establishment is situated.

6. Where, by reason of a special relationship between the payer and the beneficial owner or between both of them and some other person, the amount of the interest, having regard to the debt-claim for which it is paid, exceeds the amount which would have been agreed upon by the payer and the beneficial owner in the absence of such relationship, the provisions of this Article shall apply only to the last-mentioned amount. In such case, the excess part of the payments shall remain taxable according to the laws of each Contracting State, due regard being had to the other provisions of this Convention.

Article 12

Royalties

1. Royalties arising in a Contracting State and beneficially owned by a resident of the other Contracting State shall be taxable only in that other State.

2. The term "royalties" as used in this Article means payments of any kind received as a consideration for the use of, or the right to use, any copyright of literary, artistic or scientific work including cinematograph films, any patent, trade mark, design or model, plan, secret formula or process, or for information concerning industrial, commercial or scientific experience.

3. The provisions of paragraph 1 shall not apply if the beneficial owner of the royalties, being a resident of a Contracting State, carries on business in the other Contracting State in which the royalties arise through a permanent establishment situated therein and the right or property in respect of which the royalties are paid is effectively connected with such permanent establishment. In such case the provisions of Article 7 shall apply.

4. Where, by reason of a special relationship between the payer and the beneficial owner or between both of them and some other person, the amount of the royalties, having regard to the use, right or information for which they are paid, exceeds the amount which would have been agreed upon by the payer and the beneficial owner in the absence of such relationship, the provisions of this Article shall apply only to the last-mentioned amount. In such case, the excess part of the payments shall remain taxable according to the laws of each Contracting State, due regard being had to the other provisions of this Convention.

Article 13

Capital gains

1. Gains derived by a resident of a Contracting State from the alienation of immovable property referred to in Article 6 and situated in the other Contracting State may be taxed in that other State.

2. Gains from the alienation of movable property forming part of the business property of a permanent establishment which an enterprise of a Contracting State has in the other Contracting State, including such gains from the alienation of such a permanent establishment (alone or with the whole enterprise), may be taxed in that other State.

3. Gains from the alienation of ships or aircraft operated in international traffic, boats engaged in inland waterways transport or movable property pertaining to the operation of such ships, aircraft or boats, shall be taxable only in the Contracting State in which the place of effective management of the enterprise is situated.

4. Gains derived by a resident of a Contracting State from the alienation of shares deriving more than 50 per cent of their value directly or indirectly from immovable property situated in the other Contracting State may be taxed in that other State.

5. Gains from the alienation of any property, other than that referred to in paragraphs 1, 2, 3 and 4, shall be taxable only in the Contracting State of which the alienator is a resident.

Article 15

Income from employment

1. Subject to the provisions of Articles 16, 18 and 19, salaries, wages and other similar remuneration derived by a resident of a Contracting State in

respect of an employment shall be taxable only in that State unless the employment is exercised in the other Contracting State. If the employment is so exercised, such remuneration as is derived therefrom may be taxed in that other State.

2. Notwithstanding the provisions of paragraph 1, remuneration derived by a resident of a Contracting State in respect of an employment exercised in the other Contracting State shall be taxable only in the first-mentioned State if:
   a. the recipient is present in the other State for a period or periods not exceeding in the aggregate 183 days in any twelve month period commencing or ending in the fiscal year concerned, and
   b. the remuneration is paid by, or on behalf of, an employer who is not a resident of the other State, and
   c. the remuneration is not borne by a permanent establishment which the employer has in the other State.

3. Notwithstanding the preceding provisions of this Article, remuneration derived in respect of an employment exercised aboard a ship or aircraft operated in international traffic, or aboard a boat engaged in inland waterways transport, may be taxed in the Contracting State in which the place of effective management of the enterprise is situated.

Article 16

Directors' fees

Directors' fees and other similar payments derived by a resident of a Contracting State in his capacity as a member of the board of directors of a company which is a resident of the other Contracting State may be taxed in that other State.

Article 17

Artistes and sportsmen

1. Notwithstanding the provisions of Articles 7 and 15, income derived by a resident of a Contracting State as an entertainer, such as a theatre, motion picture, radio or television artiste, or a musician, or as a sportsman, from his personal activities as such exercised in the other Contracting State, may be taxed in that other State.

2. Where income in respect of personal activities exercised by an entertainer or a sportsman in his capacity as such accrues not to the entertainer or sportsman himself but to another person, that income may, notwith-

standing the provisions of Articles 7 and 15, be taxed in the Contracting State in which the activities of the entertainer or sportsman are exercised.

Article 18

Pensions

Subject to the provisions of paragraph 2 of Article 19, pensions and other similar remuneration paid to a resident of a Contracting State in consideration of past employment shall be taxable only in that State.

Article 19

Government service

1. a. Salaries, wages and other similar remuneration paid by a Contracting State or a political subdivision or a local authority thereof to an individual in respect of services rendered to that State or subdivision or authority shall be taxable only in that State.

   b. However, such salaries, wages and other similar remuneration shall be taxable only in the other Contracting State if the services are rendered in that State and the individual is a resident of that State who:
   (i) is a national of that State; or
   (ii) did not become a resident of that State solely for the purpose of rendering the services.

2. a. Notwithstanding the provisions of paragraph 1, pensions and other similar remuneration paid by, or out of funds created by, a Contracting State or a political subdivision or a local authority thereof to an individual in respect of services rendered to that State or subdivision or authority shall be taxable only in that State.
   b. However, such pensions and other similar remuneration shall be taxable only in the other Contracting State if the individual is a resident of, and a national of, that State.

3. The provisions of Articles 15, 16, 17, and 18 shall apply to salaries, wages, pensions, and other similar remuneration in respect of services rendered in connection with a business carried on by a Contracting State or a political subdivision or a local authority thereof.

Article 20

Students

Payments which a student or business apprentice who is or was immediately before visiting a Contracting State a resident of the other Contracting State and who is present in the first-mentioned State solely for the purpose of his education or training receives for the purpose of his maintenance, education or training shall not be taxed in that State, provided that such payments arise from sources outside that State.

Article 21

Other income

1. Items of income of a resident of a Contracting State, wherever arising, not dealt with in the foregoing Articles of this Convention shall be taxable only in that State.

2. The provisions of paragraph 1 shall not apply to income, other than income from immovable property as defined in paragraph 2 of Article 6, if the recipient of such income, being a resident of a Contracting State, carries on business in the other Contracting State through a permanent establishment situated therein and the right or property in respect of which the income is paid is effectively connected with such permanent establishment. In such case the provisions of Article 7 shall apply.

CHAPTER IV

TAXATION OF CAPITAL

Article 22

Capital

1. Capital represented by immovable property referred to in Article 6, owned by a resident of a Contracting State and situated in the other Contracting State, may be taxed in that other State.

2. Capital represented by movable property forming part of the business property of a permanent establishment which an enterprise of a Contracting State has in the other Contracting State may be taxed in that other State.

3. Capital represented by ships and aircraft operated in international traffic and by boats engaged in inland waterways transport, and by movable property pertaining to the operation of such ships, aircraft and boats, shall be taxable only in the Contracting State in which the place of effective management of the enterprise is situated.

4. All other elements of capital of a resident of a Contracting State shall be taxable only in that State.

CHAPTER V

METHODS FOR ELIMINATION OF DOUBLE TAXATION

Article 23 A

Exemption method

1. Where a resident of a Contracting State derives income or owns capital which, in accordance with the provisions of this Convention, may be taxed in the other Contracting State, the first-mentioned State shall, subject to the provisions of paragraphs 2 and 3, exempt such income or capital from tax.

2. Where a resident of a Contracting State derives items of income which, in accordance with the provisions of Articles 10 and 11, may be taxed in the other Contracting State, the first-mentioned State shall allow as a deduction from the tax on the income of that resident an amount equal to the tax paid in that other State. Such deduction shall not, however, exceed that part of the tax, as computed before the deduction is given, which is attributable to such items of income derived from that other State.

3. Where in accordance with any provision of the Convention income derived or capital owned by a resident of a Contracting State is exempt from tax in that State, such State may nevertheless, in calculating the amount of tax on the remaining income or capital of such resident, take into account the exempted income or capital.

4. The provisions of paragraph 1 shall not apply to income derived or capital owned by a resident of a Contracting State where the other Contracting State applies the provisions of this Convention to exempt such income or capital from tax or applies the provisions of paragraph 2 of Article 10 or 11 to such income.

Article 23 B

Credit method

1. Where a resident of a Contracting State derives income or owns capital which, in accordance with the provisions of this Convention, may be taxed in the other Contracting State, the first-mentioned State shall allow:
   a. as a deduction from the tax on the income of that resident, an amount equal to the income tax paid in that other State;
   b. as a deduction from the tax on the capital of that resident, an amount equal to the capital tax paid in that other State. Such deduction in either case shall not, however, exceed that part of the income tax or capital tax, as computed before the deduction is given, which is attributable, as the case may be, to the income or the capital which may be taxed in that other State.

2. Where in accordance with any provision of the Convention income derived or capital owned by a resident of a Contracting State is exempt from tax in that State, such State may nevertheless, in calculating the amount of tax on the remaining income or capital of such resident, take into account the exempted income or capital.

CHAPTER VI

SPECIAL PROVISIONS

Article 24

Non-Discrimination

1. Nationals of a Contracting State shall not be subjected in the other Contracting State to any taxation or any requirement connected therewith, which is other or more burdensome than the taxation and connected requirements to which nationals of that other State in the same circumstances, in particular with respect to residence, are or may be subjected. This provision shall, notwithstanding the provisions of Article 1, also apply to persons who are not residents of one or both of the Contracting States.

2. Stateless persons who are residents of a Contracting State shall not be subjected in either Contracting State to any taxation or any requirement connected therewith, which is other or more burdensome than the taxation and connected requirements to which nationals of the State concerned in the same circumstances, in particular with respect to residence, are or may be subjected.

3. The taxation on a permanent establishment which an enterprise of a Contracting State has in the other Contracting State shall not be less favourably levied in that other State than the taxation levied on enterprises of that other State carrying on the same activities. This provision shall not be construed as obliging a Contracting State to grant to residents of the other Contracting State any personal allowances, reliefs and reductions for taxation purposes on account of civil status or family responsibilities which it grants to its own residents.

4. Except where the provisions of paragraph 1 of Article 9, paragraph 6 of Article 11, or paragraph 4 of Article 12, apply, interest, royalties and other disbursements paid by an enterprise of a Contracting State to a resident of the other Contracting State shall, for the purpose of determining the taxable profits of such enterprise, be deductible under the same conditions as if they had been paid to a resident of the first-mentioned State. Similarly, any debts of an enterprise of a Contracting State to a resident of the other Contracting State shall, for the purpose of determining the taxable capital of such enterprise, be deductible under the same conditions as if they had been contracted to a resident of the first-mentioned State.

5. Enterprises of a Contracting State, the capital of which is wholly or partly owned or controlled, directly or indirectly, by one or more residents of the other Contracting State, shall not be subjected in the first-mentioned State to any taxation or any requirement connected therewith which is other or more burdensome than the taxation and connected requirements to which other similar enterprises of the first-mentioned State are or may be subjected.

6. The provisions of this Article shall, notwithstanding the provisions of Article 2, to taxes of every kind and description.

Article 25

Mutual agreement procedure

1. Where a person considers that the actions of one or both of the Contracting States result or will result for him in taxation not in accordance with the provisions of this Convention, he may, irrespective of the remedies provided by the domestic law of those States, present his case to the competent authority of the Contracting State of which he is a resident or, if his case comes under paragraph 1 of Article 24, to that of the Contracting State of which he is a national. The case must be presented within three

years from the first notification of the action resulting in taxation not in accordance with the provisions of the Convention.

2. The competent authority shall endeavour, if the objection appears to it to be justified and if it is not itself able to arrive at a satisfactory solution, to resolve the case by mutual agreement with the competent authority of the other Contracting State, with a view to the avoidance of taxation which is not in accordance with the Convention. Any agreement reached shall be implemented notwithstanding any time-limits in the domestic law of the Contracting States.

3. The competent authorities of the Contracting States shall endeavour to resolve by mutual agreement any difficulties or doubts arising as to the interpretation or application of the Convention. They may also consult together for the elimination of double taxation in cases not provided for in the Convention.

4. The competent authorities of the Contracting States may communicate with each other directly, including through a joint commission consisting of themselves or their representatives, for the purpose of reaching an agreement in the sense of the preceding paragraphs.

5. Where,
   a. under paragraph 1, a person has presented a case to the competent authority of a Contracting State on the basis that the actions of one or both of the Contracting States have resulted for that person in taxation not in accordance with the provisions of this Convention, and
   b. the competent authorities are unable to reach an agreement to resolve that case pursuant to paragraph 2 within two years from the presentation of the case to the competent authority of the other Contracting State, any unresolved issues arising from the case shall be submitted to arbitration if the person so requests. These unresolved issues shall not, however, be submitted to arbitration if a decision on these issues has already been rendered by a court or administrative tribunal of either State. Unless a person directly affected by the case does not accept the mutual agreement that implements the arbitration decision, that decision shall be binding on both Contracting States and shall be implemented notwithstanding any time-limits in the domestic laws of these States. The competent authorities of the Contracting States shall by mutual agreement settle the mode of application of this paragraph.1

Article 26

Exchange of information

1. The competent authorities of the Contracting States shall exchange such information as is foreseeably relevant for carrying out the provisions of this Convention or to the administration or enforcement of the domestic laws concerning taxes of every kind and description imposed on behalf of the Contracting States, or of their political subdivisions or local authorities, insofar as the taxation thereunder is not contrary to the Convention. The exchange of information is not restricted by Articles 1 and 2.

2. Any information received under paragraph 1 by a Contracting State shall be treated as secret in the same manner as information obtained under the domestic laws of that State and shall be disclosed only to persons or authorities (including courts and administrative bodies) concerned with the assessment or collection of, the enforcement or prosecution in respect of, the determination of appeals in relation to the taxes referred to in paragraph 1, or the oversight of the above. Such persons or authorities shall use the information only for such purposes. They may disclose the information in public court proceedings or in judicial decisions.

3. In no case shall the provisions of paragraphs 1 and 2 be construed so as to impose on a Contracting State the obligation:
   a. to carry out administrative measures at variance with the laws and administrative practice of that or of the other Contracting State;
   b. to supply information which is not obtainable under the laws or in the normal course of the administration of that or of the other Contracting State; 1 In some States, national law, policy or administrative considerations may not allow or justify the type of dispute resolution envisaged under this paragraph. In addition, some States may only wish to include this paragraph in treaties with certain States. For these reasons, the paragraph should only be included in the Convention where each State concludes that it would be appropriate to do so based on the factors described in paragraph 65 of the Commentary on the paragraph. As mentioned in paragraph 74 of that Commentary, however, other States may be able to agree to remove from the paragraph the condition that issues may not be submitted to arbitration if a decision on these issues has already been rendered by one of their courts or administrative tribunals.
   c. to supply information which would disclose any trade, business, industrial, commercial or professional secret or trade process, or information, the disclosure of which would be contrary to public policy (ordre public).

4. If information is requested by a Contracting State in accordance with this Article, the other Contracting State shall use its information gathering measures to obtain the requested information, even though that other State may not need such information for its own tax purposes. The obligation contained in the preceding sentence is subject to the limitations of paragraph 3 but in no case shall such limitations be construed to permit a Contracting State to decline to supply information solely because it has no domestic interest in such information.

5. In no case shall the provisions of paragraph 3 be construed to permit a Contracting State to decline to supply information solely because the information is held by a bank, other financial institution, nominee or person acting in an agency or a fiduciary capacity or because it relates to ownership interests in a person.

Article 27

Assistance in the collection of taxes

1. The Contracting States shall lend assistance to each other in the collection of revenue claims. This assistance is not restricted by Articles 1 and 2. The competent authorities of the Contracting States may by mutual agreement settle the mode of application of this Article.

2. The term "revenue claim" as used in this Article means an amount owed in respect of taxes of every kind and description imposed on behalf of the Contracting States, or of their political subdivisions or local authorities, insofar as the taxation thereunder is not contrary to this Convention or any other instrument to which the Contracting States are parties, as well as interest, administrative penalties and costs of collection or conservancy related to such amount.

3. When a revenue claim of a Contracting State is enforceable under the laws of that State and is owed by a person who, at that time, cannot, under the laws of that State, prevent its collection, that revenue claim shall, at the request of the competent authority of that State, be accepted for purposes of collection by the competent authority of the other Contracting State. That revenue claim shall be collected by that other State in accordance with the provisions of its laws applicable to the enforcement 1 In some countries, national law, policy or administrative considerations may not allow or justify the type of assistance envisaged under this Article or may require that this type of assistance be restricted, e.g. to countries that have similar tax systems or tax administrations or

as to the taxes covered. For that reason, the Article should only be included in the Convention where each State concludes that, based on the factors described in paragraph 1 of the Commentary on the Article, they can agree to provide assistance in the collection of taxes levied by the other State. and collection of its own taxes as if the revenue claim were a revenue claim of that other State.

4. When a revenue claim of a Contracting State is a claim in respect of which that State may, under its law, take measures of conservancy with a view to ensure its collection, that revenue claim shall, at the request of the competent authority of that State, be accepted for purposes of taking measures of conservancy by the competent authority of the other Contracting State. That other State shall take measures of conservancy in respect of that revenue claim in accordance with the provisions of its laws as if the revenue claim were a revenue claim of that other State even if, at the time when such measures are applied, the revenue claim is not enforceable in the first-mentioned State or is owed by a person who has a right to prevent its collection.

5. Notwithstanding the provisions of paragraphs 3 and 4, a revenue claim accepted by a Contracting State for purposes of paragraph 3 or 4 shall not, in that State, be subject to the time-limits or accorded any priority applicable to a revenue claim under the laws of that State by reason of its nature as such. In addition, a revenue claim accepted by a Contracting State for the purposes of paragraph 3 or 4 shall not, in that State, have any priority applicable to that revenue claim under the laws of the other Contracting State.

6. Proceedings with respect to the existence, validity or the amount of a revenue claim of a Contracting State shall not be brought before the courts or administrative bodies of the other Contracting State.

7. Where, at any time after a request has been made by a Contracting State under paragraph 3 or 4 and before the other Contracting State has collected and remitted the relevant revenue claim to the first-mentioned State, the relevant revenue claim ceases to be
   a. in the case of a request under paragraph 3, a revenue claim of the first-mentioned State that is enforceable under the laws of that State and is owed by a person who, at that time, cannot, under the laws of that State, prevent its collection, or
   b. in the case of a request under paragraph 4, a revenue claim of the first-mentioned State in respect of which that State may, under its laws, take measures of conservancy with a view to ensure its collection the

competent authority of the first-mentioned State shall promptly notify the competent authority of the other State of that fact and, at the option of the other State, the first-mentioned State shall either suspend or withdraw its request.

8. In no case shall the provisions of this Article be construed so as to impose on a Contracting State the obligation:
   a. to carry out administrative measures at variance with the laws and administrative practice of that or of the other Contracting State;
   b. to carry out measures which would be contrary to public policy (ordre public);
   c. to provide assistance if the other Contracting State has not pursued all reasonable measures of collection or conservancy, as the case may be, available under its laws or administrative practice;
   d. to provide assistance in those cases where the administrative burden for that State is clearly disproportionate to the benefit to be derived by the other Contracting State.

Article 28

Members of diplomatic missions and consular posts

Nothing in this Convention shall affect the fiscal privileges of members of diplomatic missions or consular posts under the general rules of international law or under the provisions of special agreements.

Article 29

Territorial extension

1. This Convention may be extended, either in its entirety or with any necessary modifications [to any part of the territory of (State A) or of (State B) which is specifically excluded from the application of the Convention or], to any State or territory for whose international relations (State A) or (State B) is responsible, which imposes taxes substantially similar in character to those to which the Convention applies. Any such extension shall take effect from such date and subject to such modifications and conditions, including conditions as to termination, as may be specified and agreed between the Contracting States in notes to be exchanged through diplomatic channels or in any other manner in accordance with their constitutional procedures.

2. Unless otherwise agreed by both Contracting States, the termination of the Convention by one of them under Article 30 shall also terminate, in the manner provided for in that Article, the application of the Convention

[to any part of the territory of (State A) or of (State B) or] to any State or territory to which it has been extended under this Article.

3. The words between brackets are of relevance when, by special provision, a part of the territory of a Contracting State is excluded from the application of the Convention.

CHAPTER VII

FINAL PROVISIONS

Article 30

Entry into force

1. This Convention shall be ratified and the instruments of ratification shall be exchanged at .... as soon as possible.

2. The Convention shall enter into force upon the exchange of instruments of ratification and its provisions shall have effect:
   a. (in State A): ....
   b. (in State B): ....

Article 31

Termination

This Convention shall remain in force until terminated by a Contracting State. Either Contracting State may terminate the Convention, through diplomatic channels, by giving notice of termination at least six months before the end of any calendar year after the year ...... In such event, the Convention shall cease to have effect:

a. (in State A): ....
b. (in State B): ....

Terminal clause

APPENDIX 3

FISCO Second Report 2007

The text that follows has been extracted from the full text of the FISCO Report 2007 and formatted for the convenience of this book. The full reports are available from the European Commission.

Readers should be aware that the footnotes to this report have not been reproduced here.

INTRODUCTION

1.1. General background of the FISCO Group

The EU Clearing and Settlement Fiscal Compliance Experts' Group (FISCO) was created in March 2005 following the Communication "Clearing and Settlement in the European Union – The way forward"[2]. The aim of this Experts' Group is to give advice on the removal of Fiscal Compliance barriers to the post-trading of EU cross-border securities transactions. The key issues considered by the FISCO Group are Giovannini Barriers 11 and 12 on withholding and transaction tax procedures respectively[3].

This FISCO Second Report on Solutions is based upon the FISCO Fact-Finding Study[4] on fiscal compliance procedures related to EU clearing and settlement, finalised in 2006. The FISCO Fact-Finding Study ascertained the many different fiscal compliance procedures that actually exist within the Member States. This diversity hinders the functioning of capital markets and raises the costs of cross-border settlement with respect to withholding and transaction tax procedures. The aim of this Report consequently consists of highlighting the main problems, analysing the advantages and disadvantages of possible solutions and, whenever possible, indicating solutions.

The present document has been produced by the FISCO Group in line with its mandate[5]. It is important to underline that the solutions proposed in this report are not aimed at any tax (rate) harmonisation, nor are they intended to affect the tax revenues in the Member States. The aim of the proposed solutions is solely to remove fiscal compliance barriers related to EU clearing and settlement and to make local fiscal procedures work more efficiently. – for investors and intermediaries alike. These proposed solutions will also lead to procedures which will be better adapted to the way financial markets operate.

FISCO is composed of 15 high-calibre experts, mainly from private bodies and the academic community. The Organisation for Economic Co-operation and Development (OECD) is represented as observer. To facilitate the work of the group, the Commission provides a Secretariat made up of a Chairperson, a Secretary and two experts. A list of the FISCO members, secretariat and observers is annexed to this report. The Commission services are very grateful to all the FISCO members and their organisations for making their time and expertise available for the purpose of the present report. The report, however, does not necessarily reflect the views of the organisations to which the FISCO members belong, nor the views of the Commission or its services.

All reports and other FISCO documents are available on the FISCO website: http://europa.eu.int/comm/internal_market/financial-markets/clearing/compliance_en.htm

The Commission will use the FISCO findings as a basis for discussion with the Member States in line with its established policy of prior consultation on tax issues led by Directorate-General Taxation and Customs Union.

1.2. The Giovannini reports

The first Giovannini Report of November 2001 identified 15 barriers to the integration of EU securities clearing and settlement systems. Two of these barriers (11 and 12) relate to fiscal compliance procedures. Barrier 11 relates to domestic withholding tax regulations, i.e. that foreign intermediaries cannot sufficiently offer withholding tax relief at source or only under the condition that they have a fiscal agent. Barrier 12 deals with national provisions requiring that taxes on securities transactions be collected via local systems.

The second Giovannini Report of April 2003 called for the following:

– all financial intermediaries established within the EU should be allowed to offer withholding agent services in all of the Member States so as to ensure a level playing-field between local and foreign intermediaries (Barrier 11); and – any provisions requiring that taxes on securities transactions are collected via local systems should be removed to ensure a level playing-field between domestic and foreign investors (Barrier 12).

A mandate was given to the EU Clearing and Settlement Fiscal Compliance Experts' Working Group (FISCO) to examine these issues and to propose more efficient alternative tax procedures where possible.

1.2.1. Overview – Giovannini barriers

The matrix below shows the progress reached so far and the expected forecasts on the 15 Giovannini barriers to the integration of EU securities clearing and settlement systems.

Giovannini Barrier	*Progress*	*Forecast*
1. Diversity of IT platforms/interfaces	• Common Protocol established by SWIFT, high level message gap analysis finished; detailed analysis under consultation	• Support for implementation started; full implementation anticipated only by 2011; potential major impact from TARGET2-Securities ('T2S') to be assessed
2. Restriction on location of C&S	• MiFID rules on choice of settlement location adopted; Code of conduct signed	• MiFID rules not sufficient but constitute a step forward; T2S expected to have positive impact on settlement level; • implementation of the Code of Conduct will provide additional possibilities on settlement and CCP clearing level; • attitude of national supervisors and regulators is important
3. Different rules governing corporate actions	• Multiple standards and recommendations for many corporate actions adopted and in	• 'Distributions' standards in implementation phase; reorganisations, general meetings and

	implementation phase; work to combine them in one set of rules is under way	transaction management standards under development; related legal and fiscal issues to be examined
4. Absence of intra-day settlement finality	• ECSDA standards adopted and largely implemented by CSDs	• Practical impediments for CSDs participants remain and are under consideration (with EPDA and ERC); major T2S impact expected

1.3. The FISCO Fact-Finding Study

The FISCO Group issued in 2006 a Fact-Finding Study (FFS) examining EU Member States' fiscal compliance procedures for clearing and settlement of cross-border securities transactions. The Study analyses how these procedures hinder the functioning of capital markets and increase the cost of cross-border settlement, particularly in relation to withholding and transaction taxes. The main conclusions of the FISCO FFS are as follows.

1.3.1. Withholding tax procedures

The country reports produced by FISCO demonstrate that withholding tax collection and relief procedures vary considerably between Member States and that different procedures often apply even to different classes of securities within the same Member State. In some cases, these variations reflect differences in the substantive withholding tax rules or particular concerns about tax evasion and avoidance. In most cases, however, different approaches are taken to the same practical problems for no specific reason and there is clearly room for rationalisation as regards many fiscal compliance procedures. The complexity and administrative costs resulting from these differences may lead investors to forego the tax relief to which they are entitled, and may discourage cross-border investment for the same reason. In the view of the FISCO Group, the optimal withholding tax collection and relief procedures should:

- have sufficient audit and enforcement possibilities for local authorities to ensure the proper collection of withholding tax;

- allow for the appropriate tax relief to be applied at source without excessive documentation requirements and without exposing issuers, intermediaries and investors to unnecessary risks and costs;

- work in an equally efficient way, irrespective of where securities are held or where transactions are settled (local versus foreign intermediary or CSD) and irrespective of the investment structure or settlement arrangements chosen by the investors and intermediaries (direct versus indirect access); and

- ensure equal treatment of foreign and local intermediaries.

None of the Member States have tax collection and relief procedures in place that meet all of the above criteria for all types of securities. Several cases have been identified where procedural tax rules de facto prevent foreign intermediaries from obtaining direct access to the local CSD, or at least do not allow them to obtain such access under conditions similar to those granted to local intermediaries.

Also, the procedural tax rules do not always take into account the fact that securities transactions may settle outside in the books of a settlement service provider established outside the country of investment. In some cases, the procedures that were identified apply equally to all parties involved. In other cases, procedural tax rules put foreign intermediaries and/or investors at a disadvantage compared to local intermediaries and/or investors and thus may constitute a violation of the EC Treaty.

1.3.2. Other issues related to withholding tax procedures

To give an additional description of the current situation in Member States as regards fiscal procedures relevant to the work of the FISCO Group, the following should also be highlighted:

The relief procedures for withholding taxes do not take sufficient account of the often multitiered holding environment. It is simply assumed that the market will organise the transfer of information and of documentation on the beneficial owner in paper-form up through the chain of intermediaries in order for the entity closest to the "issuer" or the issuer itself to be able to correctly fulfill its withholding tax obligations on behalf of the source state. The problems arising from this set-up are treated in Chapter 2, focusing on the withholding tax responsibilities on behalf of the source state. However, in addition to the source state withholding taxes, there may also exist an obligation to levy withholding taxes on behalf of the *residence state of the recipient (beneficial owner) of the payment, normally as a prepayment of the tax to be assessed later on the basis of an income tax return. If an intermediary were to be able to take on full withholding responsibilities, the market would have to be organised in such a way as to take into account not only the existence of a source state withholding tax, but also the possible existence of a residence state withholding tax.*

1.3.3. Transaction tax procedures

Currently, eleven Member States have some form of transaction tax on the transfer of securities. In most Member States, the responsibility to collect the transaction tax lies with the parties to the trade or their agent. Only very few Member States impose the responsibility to collect transaction taxes on securities transactions on the settlement service providers. Tax rules that impose tax collection responsibilities on settlement service providers do not always take into account the f act that securities transactions may settle in the books of several local or foreign settlement services providers and do not allow all of the settlement service providers to collect transfer taxes under similar conditions. This issue may put certain settlement service providers at a competitive disadvantage compared to others. These disadvantages may result from:

- the legal uncertainty of whether transactions settling in their books are subject to the transaction tax;
- the absence of a legal framework for such settlement service providers to collect transaction taxes on transactions that take place in their books, and pay and report this to the relevant tax authority;
- the denial of exemptions of transaction taxes, if transactions linked to the one for which exemption is requested are not settled by a settlement service provider with tax collection responsibilities.
- The requirement to appoint a fiscal representative discharging the foreign intermediaries' tax collection obligation.

1.3.4. Transaction tax procedures and market liquidity

From the literature examined, as well as the collective experience of the FISCO experts, it is clear that there is general agreement that the existence of transaction taxes does affect market liquidity. However, the extent to which liquidity is affected is difficult to determine and controversial. One of the key difficulties is that of isolating the effect of transaction taxes from all the other factors (including a particular country's political and historical context) which can influence market behaviour. The literature and observations from the different country experiences make it clear that liquidity is not the only attribute of a securities market to consider when looking at the effects of transaction taxes. Other important factors (including controlling volatility and transaction tax) play an important role here. Nevertheless, a number of countries have had adverse experiences related to transaction taxes and their effects upon liquidity, share price fluctuation and transaction execution methods. As a result, in some cases governments have decided to abolish their local transaction taxes or to grant very wide exceptions (e.g. Germany, Netherlands and Sweden). While the FISCO Group acknowledges that the tax authorities may have their own views on the value of transaction taxes and, in particular, their revenue-raising capability, the Group considers that, in the light of the collective experiences described above, transaction tax procedures are a matter which should be considered at EU level.

1.4. The FISCO Second Report on Solutions (SRS)

In order to provide solutions to the problems identified by the Fact-Finding Study 2006, the FISCO Group, in accordance with its mandate, decided to continue its work by producing this FISCO Second Report on Solutions (SRS) in 2007.

This FISCO Second Report on Solutions (SRS) mainly deals with withholding and transaction tax procedure issues and is structured by the categories of problems identified by the Fact-Finding Study:

The relief procedures which exist in Member States do not at present take sufficiently into account the multitiered holding environment. Notably, the responsibilities for collecting withholding taxes on behalf of the source state (in principle, the state of the issuer), are often put on an entity that is not connected to the beneficial owner / final investor. It is thus assumed that the market will organise the transfer of information and paper-based documentation relating to the beneficial owner up through the chain of intermediaries. In reality, this is costly and inefficient and may create confidentiality and data protection/privacy issues. These problems are addressed in Chapter 2.1–2.3 of this report. Some remaining issues related to withholding tax and relief procedures are described in Chapter 2.4. Chapter 3 of this report contains proposals connected to transaction tax procedures and the removal of Giovannini barrier 12. Chapter 4 provides a summary of the conclusions proposed by this report. Finally, the report includes two annexes. Annex I is a reference to European Court of Justice (ECJ) cases that are relevant to the matters discussed in this report. Annex II is a list of the Members of the FISCO Group. The FISCO Group considers that any proposal for the removal of barriers associated with the fulfillment of tax obligations and the taxing of securities transactions and preventing the establishment of an internal financial services market must abide to the following general principles:

- Respects the needs of the national tax administrations to receive all the necessary relevant information and does not result in any loss of tax revenues;
- Allows foreign intermediaries remote access to national clearing and settlement systems under the same conditions as local operators, without the level of tax obligations or their limited possibilities for action in this area constituting a barrier to entry for the free cross-border provision of investment services;
- Assures local intermediaries that the remote access of foreign intermediaries will take place on the basis of a level playing-field in terms of rights and obligations, so that the removal of the current fiscal barriers does not place them at a competitive disadvantage in terms of the level of responsibility assumed with regard to local tax authorities;
- Ensures that no intermediary will face any tax liability when shortcomings in the information provided or errors in the making of the corresponding withholdings are not the result of negligence or misrepresentation on the part of the intermediary. There also should be no liability in the case of negligence or misrepresentation on the part of others, particularly the owner of the securities.

The approximation of national laws in order to remove the obstacles to the exercise of fundamental freedoms can take different forms. When describing the different types of measures and proposals to solve the present problems related to Giovannini barriers 11 and 12, it is relevant to recall the Council conclusions on clearing and settlement taken at the ECOFIN Council Meeting of 28 November 2006. The Council concluded that the clearing and settlement of securities transactions is a key area for financial integration in the EU, where substantial progress needs to be achieved. The Council highlighted the urgent work to remove legal and fiscal barriers in the context of the Giovannini barriers. The Council recognised the strategic approach by the Commission based on self-regulation as an attempt to enhance competition and reduce costs for users of post-trading services.

In this context it should also be recalled that, on 19 December 2006, the European Commission adopted a Communication announcing a series of initiatives to promote better co-ordination of national direct tax systems in the EU. The aim is to ensure that national tax systems comply with Community law and interact coherently with each other. The initiatives seek to remove discrimination and double taxation for the benefit of individuals and business, while preventing tax abuse and erosion of the tax base. The Commission regards withholding taxes as an area where co-ordination of tax systems can prove particularly useful, notably in view of removing discrimination and double taxation and reducing compliance costs, and also to prevent inadvertent non-taxation and abuse.

The "box" below describes the policy and market development in the trading and post-trading field.

Policy and market developments in the trading and post-trading field

European securities markets are currently in transition. On the trading side, securities exchanges are merging in order to reap benefits related to economies of scale. This is illustrated by, among other things, the merger between the New York Stock Exchange (NYSE) and Euronext NV/SA, the London Stock Exchange and the Borsa Italiana/Milan Exchange Agreement, and the very recent tripartite agreement between NASDAQ, the Dubai International Financial Exchange Ltd and OMX management. On the central counter-party clearing side, scale economies are equal, if not more important, and as a result consolidation has occurred here as well, e.g. as illustrated by the 2003 merger between the London Clearing House and Clearnet SA to form LCH.Clearnet. As regards settlement, Euroclear has brought together four CSDs under its banner and is currently implementing a single settlement system. This consolidation process is the result of several forces. Some are market-driven, such as technological change. Other forces are policy driven, such as deregulation and liberalisation. As a result, long gone is the time when markets were national in scope. Today, the national border is an increasingly meaningless concept for describing a market. In observing these market developments, the Commission's regulatory approaches as regards trading and post-trading matters will have to evolve in order to continue to effectively promote the general interest.

Trading

Developments have been particularly rapid in the area of securities trading, where technological innovations have enabled a strong increase in trading volumes and a multiplication of trading methods and trading venues. To ensure that regulatory objectives of efficiency, safety and consumer protection were met in this new market place, the European Union has updated its securities trading legislation by adopting the Markets in Financial Instruments Directive (MiFID)9. The MiFID, being a Lamfalussy-type framework directive, is complemented by an implementing Regulation10 and an implementing Directive11. The transposition deadline for MiFID was 31 January 2007. Only a few Member States met that deadline however. Nevertheless, many Member States transposed throughout spring and summer 2007. The deadline for applying MiFID is 1 November 2007. MiFID will facilitate competition across borders and among different types of trading venue through a series of measures. For example, it abolishes the so-called concentration rule that allowed Member States to require trades to be executed on the main regulated market, i.e. the traditional stock exchange. Moreover, it creates a new category of trading venue, the MTF or multilateral trading facility that will be able to compete with regulated markets while being subject to a similar, but not identical, regulatory framework. To counter the risks to market quality associated with competing trading venues, i.e. fragmented liquidity pools, the directive sets up pre- and post-trade transparency requirements. It also puts in place investor protection rules such as order-handling and best execution rules and governance rules that ensure that firms engaged in securities trading are well organised. The Commission expects these measures to dramatically increase competition both across borders and among venue types. Ongoing initiatives, started already prior to the implementation date of MiFID, such as the initiative of seven investment banks to set up a competing trading venue (Project Turquoise), support that view.

Post-trading

While securities trading has rapidly become more global, the market infrastructures supporting trading venues have not followed suit. In Europe, post-trading infrastructures by and large continue to cater for national needs. As a result, while domestic transactions are handled in an efficient and safe manner, cross-border transactions are costlier and riskier. To address this state of affairs, market participants, national governments and the European Commission have all been trying to dismantle the various barriers preventing the emergence of post-trading arrangements that are better suited to serve today's more global markets. EU legislation plays a role in addressing these problems. MiFID grants investment firms rights of access to post-trading service providers in other Member States (Article 34.1). Article 34.2 grants investment firms a right to designate their settlement system subject to links being in place and supervisory approval. Article 34.3 grants post-trading service providers the right to refuse access on legitimate commercial grounds. Article 46 grants regulated markets the right to use clearing and settlement arrangements from another Member

State, stating that supervisors can only block such use if it is demonstrably necessary in order to maintain the orderly functioning of that regulated market. MiFID's Article 35 also grants similar rights in respect of multilateral trading facilities (MTFs).

However, in addition to MiFID, the European Commission is pursuing other regulatory approaches as well.

1. One way is to work with the market in order to dismantle the barriers preventing more efficient post-trading arrangements from materialising. Effort along those lines is being carried out within the context of the so-called CESAME group. This group brings together the Commission and market participants and is aimed at dismantling six industry-related barriers of the 15 so-called Giovannini barriers, of which the fiscal barriers dealt with by the FISCO Group and the legal barriers dealt with by the Legal Certainty Group form part.

2. Furthermore, in accordance with the conclusions of the Commission Evaluation Report to the Council and the European Parliament[12] on the Financial Collateral Arrangements Directive[13] (FCD), the Commission is considering proposing amendments to extend the FCD depending on the progress made in respect to the technical issues related to the use of credit claims as collateral.

3. Building on MiFID, the Commission in 2006 forged an agreement among trading and post-trading infrastructures to sign a Code of Conduct on clearing and settlement. The Code improves price transparency, and thus enables customers to compare different service offers more easily. The Code also improves access rights and interoperability between post-trading infrastructures. One has to keep in mind that MiFID does not provide market participants with the right to choose the Central Counterparty (CCP), nor does it cover relations among post-trading infrastructures. Therefore, the Code creates a framework governing such relations. The Code will also enable users to buy unbundled post-trade services. This will bring more competition to the market and hence improve efficiency. On 15 September 2007, the Commission reported to the Economic and Financial Affairs Council (ECOFIN) on the state of post-trading in Europe, notably providing an overview of the current status of the Code of Conduct, its views on dismantling the legal and fiscal barriers and on how to move the stalled negotiations on the draft CESR-European System of Central Banks (ESCB) standards, which are aimed at improving the

safety and soundness of EU post-trading arrangements. The report was favourably received.

While these initiatives aim at making national systems operate better together and hence enable competition, the European Central Bank (ECB) has recently proposed to set up and operate a central platform for securities settlement. TARGET2-Securities ('T2S') will centralise settlement activities, with euro-denominated securities transactions in the future being settled on a single platform managed by the Euro-system. If confirmed, it is likely to improve efficiency (higher scale, less duplication), dismantle some of the barriers outlined above and improve safety (it eliminates the need for central banks to outsource the management of cash accounts). On 27 February 2007, the Economic and Financial Affairs Council (ECOFIN) welcomed the ECB's efforts to improve the efficiency of EU post-trading services, stated that the full impact of the T2S project should be properly assessed and asked the ECB to report back to the Council as the project is further developed.

2. RECOMMENDATIONS WITH RESPECT TO WITHHOLDING TAX PROCEDURES

2.1. Introduction

In European Member States, withholding tax is basically withheld either by:

1. the debtor of the income, i.e. the issuer, or by

2. the – mostly local – intermediary through which the securities are held.

This withholding tax is levied at the national statutory rate of withholding tax. Under double-taxation treaties and also sometimes on the basis of national laws, this withholding tax rate can be reduced or eliminated. This reduction might happen through a refund after the payment of income has taken place or through at-source (i.e. at the moment the income is paid). The FISCO Group is of the opinion that relief at source is the preferred method because of the optimized cash flow it offers to investors.

Consequently, Chapter 2.2 below describes the rationale for, and how to shift, tax responsibility to facilitate relief at source (2.2.1–2.2.7), followed by Chapter 2.2.8 describing measures to simplify and harmonise the currently applicable tax relief-at-source procedures. Having stated that relief at source is the preferred relief method, there are several reasons why it should ideally be complemented by the possibility to obtain relief through an efficient quick refund and/or standard refund procedure:

– It may not always be possible for intermediaries to provide the withholding agent with the required information prior to the payment date, especially where securities are being traded near record dates;

– Market claims are generally processed by clearing organizations and central securities depositories in an automated way and can only be processed at one single rate (generally the amount representing the dividend net of withholding tax at the maximum domestic rate), in which case relief can only be obtained through a refund;

– Intermediaries may not always be in a position to offer relief at source (for instance because their legal status does not allow them to offer such a service or because their market share does not justify the investments in procedures and know-how to offer relief at source). Chapter 2.3 describes how current quick and standard refund procedures could be made more efficient. Some remaining issues related to withholding tax and relief procedures are described in Chapter 2.4. Chapter 2.5 describes the conclusions presented in this chapter.

2.2. Measures to increase the efficiency of at-source relief procedures

Relief at source can be granted only with the help of the entity (issuer or intermediary) that has a formal withholding tax responsibility. The rule of thumb for efficient tax procedures is that they take sufficient account of the way the markets operate. A problem is often that the prescribed relief procedures do not take sufficient account of the multitiered holding environment and often put tax collection responsibilities on an entity that is not connected to the beneficial owner / final investor and therefore assumes that the market will organize itself to transfer information and (paper form) documentation on the beneficial owner up through the chain of intermediaries. In reality this is costly and inefficient and may create confidentiality and data-privacy issues. The FISCO group is of the opinion that many of the administrative and efficiency problems identified in the FISCO Fact-Finding Study can best be resolved by allowing all intermediaries in the custody chain to assume withholding responsibilities or to take responsibility for granting withholding tax relief.

2.2.1. Why should withholding responsibilities be shifted?

The main goal of shifting responsibilities to intermediaries is to avoid the need to pass on paper-form certificates and beneficial owner breakdowns through the chain of intermediaries that intervene in the income distribution up to the withholding agent. In addition, the upward forwarding of client information may create problems of confidentiality. Conceptually one could imagine two ways to get rid of the onerous requirement whereby paper-form documentation must be passed on through the chain of intermediaries.

1. One solution is to abolish the requirement of paper-form certification and allow intermediaries to make use of modern technology to pass on beneficial owner information to the local withholding agent in electronic format.

2. Another solution would be to shift tax collection obligations, or, at a minimum, the associated responsibilities to allow for withholding tax relief at source to the (local or foreign) intermediaries that are closer (or closest) to the beneficial owner. The FISCO Group considers that these two solutions should be combined. The Group is of the opinion that allowing electronic certification does not, on its own, constitute a satisfactory solution, and this for the following three reasons:

First, even if intermediaries were allowed to pass on beneficial owner certificates in electronic format, tax-relief procedures would still be costly given the high volumes of information to be passed on through the chain of intermediaries. Experience shows that the cost of passing on and validating such electronic certificates is significant.

Secondly, electronic certification on beneficial owners does not offer a solution to the confidentiality and/or data-privacy issue. Confidential customer information could be disclosed to competitors in the chain of intermediaries. In addition, there is a possible problem regarding the Personal Data Protection Legislation at both European and national level.

Thirdly, practical experience with existing cross-border relief procedures shows that the procedures are often unworkable. At present, numerous countries provide relief at source for investors residing abroad. The rules of such countries generally stipulate that information about the investor, the securities concerned, the income payment expected, and a certificate of residence issued by the responsible tax office of the investor must be forwarded to the responsible withholding agent in the issuer country. The withholding agent must receive this form by the record date. As illustrated in the Fact-Finding Study there is often insufficient time between the dividend announcement date and the income payment date to allow the beneficial owner to provide the required certificates, through the chain of intermediaries, to the issuer prior to the income payment. For actively traded securities, transactions around the record date, and particularly after the date the application for relief at source is made until payment date, make it impossible to provide the upstream withholding agent with up-to-date information in time. Such problems and similar difficulties have occurred in practice in connection with the relief procedures for non-residents e.g. in the Netherlands, Portugal, and Hungary. Some procedures have even additional complications that make them unworkable when the information has to transit through a chain of intermediaries. The removal of the above obstacles will not be achieved by the sole use of electronic systems, but require that the possibility will be offered to shift part or all of the withholding responsibilities to an intermediary in the custody chain that has a direct link with the beneficial owner in such a way that the detailed beneficial owner information no longer needs to be passed on through the chain of intermediaries to the local withholding agents. This includes allowing for pooling of assets into tax-rate pools and passing on beneficial owner information electronically on a non-individual level for those (domestic or foreign) intermediaries that do not opt for a withholding responsibility. Obviously, these electronic systems could be compatible with "traditional" proceedings in the case of individual investors, or when formal requirements have not been properly fulfilled.

2.2.2. Which responsibilities could be shifted?

If the withholding responsibility is shifted cross-border to a (domestic or foreign) intermediary, there is always a bundle of duties or obligations that must be accepted and fulfilled by this intermediary. However, it appear s sensible – similarly to the US QI regime to allow an intermediary either to assume the full tax withholding responsibility, or not to do so, and instead just to act on an informative basis. In the latter case, the intermediary holding an omnibus account either provides withholding-rate pool information to his upstream intermediary or establishes sub-accounts with the upstream intermediary or issuer that is acting as withholding agent. The intermediary assuming full withholding responsibility shall be referred to hereinafter as "Responsible Withholding Agent". In contrast an intermediary without assuming full tax-withholding responsibility will be referred to as "Responsible Non-Withholding Agent" – in analogy to the US QI regime. Section 2.2.2.1 describes in more detail the responsibilities of a Responsible Withholding Agent. Section 2.2.2.2 describes the responsibilities of a Responsible Non-Withholding Agent.

2.2.2.1. The responsible withholding agent. The Responsible Withholding Agent must assume the tax-withholding responsibility "itself", i.e. the obligation to deduct and deposit withholding tax with the relevant tax authority of the issuer country. In connection herewith, the Responsible Withholding Agent must:

- Collect the prescribed documentation/information evidencing the owner's entitlement to receive the income payment at a reduced withholding tax rate according to an applicable tax treaty or a domestic relief provision;
- Archive the documentation/information obtained on the basis of which the withholding tax relief has been granted;
- Remit the withholding tax deducted to the tax authorities of the issuer country;
- File tax returns periodically with the relevant tax authorities of the issuer country (the tax return should be filed electronically; the data to be provided, the formats to be applied, and the deadlines for filing should be harmonized – as explained below);
- Be available, in case of a tax audit, to enable the relevant tax authorities to check compliance with the withholding obligations assumed;
- Be responsible, vis-à-vis the tax authorities of the issuer country, for withholding; however, such responsibility should be engaged only when the intermediary has not used "reasonable efforts"; and
- Be entitled to act as agent of the beneficial owner for refund purposes; this includes the possibility to set off tax amounts to be refunded against taxes to be remitted to the tax authorities.

The individual components of this field of activity must be based on harmonized procedures, ways and means within the EU. It is necessary to provide a level playing-field within the EU and to remove the existing obstacles resulting from the different and versatile conditions currently existing within the EU Member States. In order to reduce the onerous paper-based administrative burden, efforts should be made to replace paper-based communication, tax returns and deposit obligations by electronic means. In this respect, the Italian system may serve as a good example. At present, foreign intermediaries without a permanent establishment in Italy can opt to assume withholding responsibility, if they inter alia activate an electronic connection with the Italian Ministry of Economy and Finance.

The adoption of electronic systems would also be helpful for the submission, upon request, of the investor's documentation to the tax authority, for purposes of examining the investor's entitlement to tax benefits. The utilisation of existing systems would avoid setting up completely new installations, which would be costly, especially for smaller banks. To benefit fully from the electronic communication systems, messages used for transferring information should also be standardized. In some countries (such as Italy) it is a requirement to appoint a local fiscal representative if a foreign intermediary intends to assume withholding responsibility. This requirement, which was clearly identified in the FISCO Fact-Finding Study as an obstacle, must be abolished.

2.2.2.2. The responsible non-withholding agent. The responsibilities of a Responsible Non-Withholding Agent are similar to those of a Responsible Withholding Agent, but without the requirement to deduct and remit the withholding tax to the tax authorities. Instead it should be allowed to pass the tax-rate information on a pooled basis to the security issuer/agent or any upper tier authorized intermediary (A1) as appropriate.

If the information is provided to an upper-tier authorized intermediary that does not have tax deduction responsibility, this authorized intermediary is responsible for relaying that information to the next upper-tier authorized intermediary or the issuer, in conjunction with one of the methods outlined above (i) or (ii). The reporting to the upper-level intermediary then forms the basis for the tax-withholding by the intermediary/issuer with withholding responsibility.

2.2.3. How: Legal liability and reliance on "Good Faith"

In the national tax laws, there should be clear provisions regarding the liability of the withholding tax deduction and collection, as well as for collecting beneficial owner information that is passed on and/or reported to other intermediaries. No liability may be imposed on authorised intermediaries acting in "good faith". This should be the case both for beneficial owner information collection and for tax collection, if any. If foreign intermediaries may opt for withholding tax responsibility, this must be on equal terms and conditions, with respect to the applicable reporting obligations and legal liability, as for local intermediaries, in order to maintain a level playing-field and to prevent unjust competition. The legal responsibility for tax withholding and reporting, if any, should also be clearly regulated if this option is not utilized by a foreign intermediary. It should be emphasized in the law that there is an obligation for the beneficial owner to pay his or her own tax. The legal remedies to uphold the right to recourse any paid tax on behalf of the beneficial owner should also be closely monitored and reinforced. The Finnish system is a useful example to illustrate this point:

Neither the foreign custodian, nor the local account operator nor the issuer can be held responsible for unpaid taxes, if they have fulfilled their duties laid down in the tax law. The only person who can actually be held responsible, if the account operator and the issuer have fulfilled their obligations, is the beneficial owner. Consequently, the FISCO Group proposes that it should be clearly stipulated in the tax law that ultimate legal responsibility should not fall upon authorized intermediaries acting in good faith and following the prescribed forms for collecting "sufficient evidence" on the underlying beneficial owners. It is also the opinion and recommendation of the FISCO Group that some general rules and guidelines for all EU Member States should be implemented in this respect. There should also be some guidelines for harmonising the requirements of how long information or documents must be kept by intermediaries and/or withholding agents.

It should be possible to transfer funds to authorized foreign intermediaries in Member States (who cannot opt themselves for withholding responsibilities) net of treaty rates based on information received in "good faith". The liability of the Responsible (Non-) Withholding Agent should be understood as shifting the standard of care and the connected liability imposed on local intermediaries to foreign intermediaries and not to impose additional liabilities or a stricter standard of care on foreign intermediaries. This affects countries such as France, where the local intermediary remains legally responsible to the French tax authority in addition to the foreign intermediary. A local intermediary must be released from any liability to the extent such liability is assumed by the foreign intermediary.

This proposal is in line with the ISSA Tax Relief Model (see 2.2.8.5. below). However, in contrast to the ISSA model, an option between either assuming withholding responsibility or acting as Non-Withholding Agent appears more favourable than a strict system without any flexibility.

Moreover this proposal, in contrast to the ISSA model, allows for a Responsible Withholding Agent to act partly with primary withholding responsibility and partly without it. Such possibility for combining options is also offered in connection with the US QI regime. Different options are imaginable e.g. with respect to different types of customers or different income types. However, when an intermediary does not opt for withholding tax responsibility, the tax law should clearly state who actually will be legally responsible for the withholding tax collection.

2.2.4. To whom should the responsibilities be given?

As mentioned above, the main goal of shifting responsibilities to upper-tier intermediaries is to avoid the need to pass on paper-form certificates and beneficial owner breakdowns through the chain of intermediaries that intervene in the income distribution up to the withholding agent.

Depending on the type of income, two different models could be adopted to achieve this goal: One model "Model 1 – Dividend and Interest Income" imposes primary withholding responsibilities on the issuer or a local intermediary, with the possibility for other intermediaries to take on all or part of these withholding responsibilities. The other model "Model 2 – Interest Income" imposes withholding responsibilities exclusively on the person established in the source country who pays income for the immediate benefit of the individual beneficial owner in the same source country.

a. Model 1 – Dividend and Interest Income

b. Model 2 – Interest Income

2.2.4.1. Model 1 - Dividend and interest income. Under this model, primary withholding responsibility is imposed on the issuer, but each intermediary in the custody chain is given the option to take over part (in the case of a Responsible Non-withholding Agent) or all (in the case of a Responsible Withholding Agent) of the withholding responsibilities. The main advantages of this solution are that:

– Intermediaries can grant at-source relief without the need to pass on detailed beneficial owner documentation to the issuers or upstream intermediaries;

– At the same time, relief is only given on the basis of a proper identification of the beneficial owner and a verification of its entitlement to relief (even if such information about the individual beneficial owners is not necessarily passed on to the issuer or upstream intermediaries); and

– All intermediaries are treated equally: In order to ensure a true level playing-field amongst intermediaries, no distinction should be made between foreign and local intermediaries as regards the type of responsibilities they can assume or the conditions under which they can assume such responsibilities. Intermediaries that are not interested in offering relief at source services are not obliged to take on any responsibilities. In certain jurisdictions, however, the withholding responsibility is legally already imposed upon the last domestic intermediary closest to the beneficial owner. In such cases there will be no level playing-field within the EU if those intermediaries or CSDs cannot opt out from the responsibility. The FISCO Group recommends to provide for the option rather than for an obligation to assume all or certain withholding responsibilities. To realize the proposed solution it is required that: The legislation of Member States' that currently do not allow the local tax authorities to audit and/or enforce withholding obligations imposed on foreign intermediaries.

Smaller intermediaries may be discouraged by the compliance cost associated with the assumption of withholding or QI responsibilities in a large number of Member States. This could be addressed by:

i. harmonizing the withholding tax relief procedures among Member States; and

ii. foreseeing an efficient and fast standard refund procedure for those intermediaries that do not wish to take on the responsibilities to grant relief at source.

2.2.4.2. Model 2 – Interest income. In several Member States the withholding tax on interest payments does not really aim to be a revenue-raising tax on non-resident investors, but it merely serves a tool to ensure that resident non-corporate investors are effectively paying taxes on such income. Where this is the case for domestic source interest, an alternative solution to the one described above could be to impose withholding responsibilities exclusively on the person established in the source country, who pays income for the immediate benefit of beneficial owners that are individuals resident in the same source country.

If the local custodian is paying interest for the immediate benefit of a resident individual, it must apply withholding tax;

If the local custodian is paying the interest to an intermediary (in the pictogram the global custodian), it has no withholding obligations, even if the intermediary is holding the securities for a taxable individual investor that is resident in the source country. Some Member States already apply this principle today with respect to interest payments (cf. Germany, Austria, Luxembourg, Sweden). The main advantages of this solution are that:

It does not impose any new responsibilities on foreign intermediaries outside the country of the beneficial owner, and hence it neither imposes an additional compliance cost on foreign intermediaries nor does it require Member States to develop new rules or procedures to audit and enforce the obligations of foreign entities; and

Since withholding obligations are only imposed on the intermediary with a direct relationship with the beneficial owner, no beneficial owner information and/or documentation must be passed on between intermediaries.

The main disadvantage of this solution is that:

> It may allow taxable investors to evade taxes by hiding behind a foreign intermediary, since it does not require withholding agents to look behind the payee to which they are paying the income.

However, to the extent payments are made to EU resident intermediaries, the withholding or reporting obligations imposed by the EU Savings Directive on those intermediaries constitute a good safety-net against such potential tax evasion (cf. pictogram). In addition, the beneficial owner generally also has an unlimited tax liability in the residence country for all income and is therefore, in most cases, obliged to file annual tax returns and also pay his or her non-withheld taxes on the income.

2.2.5. On which legal basis should the responsibilities be assumed?

The legal basis for the proposed withholding tax relief procedures should be set in accordance with each Member States constitutional or similar provisions. It seems, however, desirable that the relevant (tax) authorities be given the authority to enter into agreements with foreign intermediaries regarding the assumption of withholding responsibilities by the latter on the basis of a model contract – similar to the US QI agreement. One can notice that the principle of contractual agreements is used more and more by the tax authorities and taxpayers for purposes of arrangements of applicable procedures. In addition to the mentioned US QI agreement, this appears typically to advance pricing agreements ("APA").

Moreover, in contrast to the QI agreement, not only foreign but also domestic intermediaries should be entitled to enter into such an agreement with their local tax authority. It seems highly desirable to develop a single model contract that would be used by all EU Member States. It would be logical that in the model preparation the industry's points of view are taken into account. To facilitate this, consideration should be given to the idea of creating a Consultative Group at EU level. The parties of such an agreement are the intermediary on one hand and the tax authority of the issuer country on the other. Technically it should be possible to enter into such an agreement by signing a "one-pager" that incorporates the various applicable terms and conditions, as amended from time to time, by reference. The conclusion of such a contract with a domestic or foreign tax authority should not be mandatory but should remain optional. Intermediaries should be allowed to opt for entering in such a contract on a country by country basis and preferably entitled to make use of the contract. vis-à-vis each downstream intermediary separately. It is expected that the business model adopted by the intermediary will have an effect on such decisions. Despite the fact that the principle of a contractual agreement is preferred to legal regulations, mainly due to the flexibility offered by such arrangements, some adaptations of the Member States' laws will be inevitable, for at least the following reasons:

Firstly, in many jurisdictions the withholding responsibility is reserved for those issuers or intermediaries that are residents of the issuer country. Accordingly, shifting the withholding responsibility abroad will require a change of the relevant laws;

Secondly, the recommended contractual agreement between the tax authority and the domestic and foreign intermediary will, for its part, require a legal basis under the law systems of many Member States. Generally it should be possible to establish such legal bases by way of ministerial regulations or decrees in contrast to formal laws issued by legislative bodies. Thus, the necessary legal adaptations within the Member States should be reasonably limited.

2.2.6. How to ensure audit and tax assessment

If the local tax authorities allow for the withholding responsibility to be outside the issuer country, they must also keep it under appropriate surveillance. The question is how such surveillance should be performed:

1. directly by the tax authorities of the issuer country; or

2. by the tax authorities of the relevant intermediary; or

3. by external auditors; or

4. by means of a cooperation of these institutions.

There is already some experience in the cross-border field of shifting withholding responsibility to intermediaries, granting relief at source and simplified refund procedure. That experience should be used for finding an appropriate solution.

Firstly, under the US QI regime, specific periodical audits have to be performed by external auditors, who submit their report directly to the local tax authorities of the source country, i.e. to the US Internal Revenue Service (IRS). The drawback of this regime is the cost attached to the involvement of external auditors.

Secondly, in contrast to the US QI regime, the Japanese QFI regime does not contain any audit requirements. Instead the foreign intermediary must have comprehensive documentation about the beneficial owner. Upon request, this documentation must be made available to the Japanese Ministry of Finance. Thus, under this regime, the surveillance by the local tax authorities is undertaken by an information system. The positive effect of this system is that it is not necessary to provide the documentation of all beneficial owners upfront to the local tax authorities, in contrast to a reporting system.

Thirdly, the mechanism of surveillance via the "Elective Dividend System" (EDS) of the US Depository Trust Company (DTC) should be taken into consideration. This procedure is a simplified collective relief at source or quick refund procedure applied by the DTC with regard to dividends derived by US residents from certain European securities. Under this procedure the DTC-participants notify the DTC of those positions of foreign-sourced dividends that are entitled to tax-treaty relief. The DTC sums up the positions received and submits a collective claim for relief at source or quick refund at the relevant foreign tax authority without disclosing the names of the beneficial owners. Under the DTC procedure, as agreed e.g. with the German Ministry of Finance, there is no periodical audit provided for. The German tax authority merely has the right to request from the DTC, within 4 years after the refund has been paid to audit the entitlement of the investors to benefits under the US / German tax treaty. In the event of an audit, the German tax authority turns to the DTC and informs them of the scope of the audit and of the investors to be audited. In turn, the DTC forwards the relevant questions to the US intermediaries involved. Those intermediaries then furnish proof of entitlement to relief on the basis of the relevant documentation, e.g. registers showing the names requested and certificates of residence issued by the US IRS (US "Form 6166"). The principal favourable effect of this method of surveillance is the absence of a complex and costly periodical audit, in contrast to the US QI regime. In this context it seems remarkable that some EU Member States, such as Italy, do not subject local intermediaries to periodical audits. Consequently, the submission of foreign intermediaries to periodical audits could be discriminatory, if local intermediaries are not subject to the same requirements In view of this, it appears rather doubtful whether there is any need for a compulsory periodical audit within the EU. Another favourable effect of the DTC procedure, and of the other procedures mentioned, is that they all, as far as possible, avoid disclosing the beneficial owners' names. From a level playing-field point of view, intermediaries should not be required to reveal confidential customer information to competitors, such as other intermediaries or banks, but only to tax authorities and third party auditors. In any case, where it exists, banking secrecy must be taken into consideration. Consequently, no other intermediaries should be involved in the audit procedures of a

Responsible (Non-) Withholding Agent. The FISCO Group recommends the following audit procedures:

It seems appropriate to involve both the tax authorities and external auditors in an audit, by means of co-actions. The task of the external auditor should focus on periodical systems checks, and the task of the tax authorities should focus on audit actions as the case arises. The decision must be made whether the tax authority of the issuer country or the tax authority of the relevant intermediary's country should be competent. It seems proper that the audit comes from the issuer country, as the revenue of that country is affected. The "distance" between the issuer country and the location of the Responsible Withholding Agent can easily be bridged by use of electronic systems. Moreover, it could be beneficial to involve the tax authority of the intermediary's country by way of mutual administrative assistance. In this sense, the principle of cooperation between (home/host) supervisors, which is based on MiFID, could be considered as an example for the cooperation between fiscal authorities in the case of cross-border operations. This could be appropriate for particular audit measures or in particular situations, e.g. in the event of adverse audit results.

The external auditors should perform systems checks, as opposed to random sampling of groups of investors, which inevitably would be quite comprehensive. Random sampling based on the "agreed-upon procedures" audit under the QI regime has frequently turned out to be a costly experience. The systems checks recommended should comprise:

– accurate keying of the investors into the intermediary's systems, i.e. customer data and required documentation procedures, whether the system guarantees that the conditions are met for the granting of benefits (such as proof of residence and systems residence codes);

– accurate keying of securities data held in custody and the income derived, particularly correct application of withholding tax rates – regular domestic / benefited domestic / treaty-benefited rate;

– accurate functioning and processing of payment streams of securities income, e.g. its classification and accruals;

– accurate tax deduction, amounts corresponding to correct tax rates, timely remittance.

Cost control should be kept in mind, as the profit margins arising from the securities custody business are rather small. Thus it appears reasonable that the external auditors can make use of the findings of the internal audit department of the intermediary. For this purpose, and as an example the instrument of the "securities account audit" ("Depotpruefung"), which is compulsory on an annual basis in Germany, could be used. This special audit rule provides for the securities custody business and the associated processing systems to be audited annually by an external auditor. The audit comprises the periodical reports of the internal auditors of the bank concerned. The external auditor has to file his statements in a report, which is submitted to the competent supervisory authority of the bank. Eventually Member States' existing audit requirements need to be matched to the requirements of the suggested systems check. The tax authority of the issuer country should be entitled to request such an audit report from the relevant supervisory authority, if the need arises. This right should also be subject to the time limitation of e.g. 4 years. The great advantage of such an audit procedure is that only one audit is performed and the findings could be presented to 26 other Member States. The corresponding audit methods of the relevant tax authority (i.e. the tax authority of the issuer country) should be composed of 2 elements:

– the entitlement to request the relevant audit reports from the competent supervisory authority of the intermediary; and

– verifying tax relief granted by requesting relevant information from the Responsible (Non-) Withholding Agent about the beneficial owners.

The beneficial owner information to be provided upon request should consist of:

– registers showing the names of the beneficial owners involved;

– self-certificates filed by the Responsible (Non-) Withholding Agent, i.e. copies or electronic versions; and

– know-your-customer ('KYC')-documentation as described in the prior section i.e. copies or electronic versions.

Such audits need not be performed periodically, but only as the case arises. The right to request the audit reports and such verification should be subject to a time limitation. As with the US DTC procedure in respect of some European countries, the entitlement to request an audit of the intermediary with Responsible Withholding Agent-status should be limited to e.g. 4 calendar years after the tax relief has been granted.

Apart from the audit methods mentioned, no additional action or even separate audit seems necessary. It should be carefully borne in mind that the industry must not become overburdened by audit instruments. In this context it should be noted that the European Banking Federation has criticized the "reconciliation" required under the US QI system. It is argued that this instrument imposes too great a burden compared to the benefits that might be derived from it.

2.2.7. How to ensure recovery of tax and related penalties

To recover withholding tax that has erroneously not been deposited with the tax authority or to recover penalties, the tax authority of the issuer country could have recourse to the "Council Directive 76/308/EEC of 15 March 1976 on mutual assistance for the recovery of claims relating to certain levies, duties, taxes and other measures", as amended by the Council Directive 2001/44/EC of 15 June 2001.

According to Article 2 of the Mutual Assistance Recovery Directive, it can now be used for the recovery of all claims related to tax on income and on capital interest, administrative penalties and fines, and costs incidental to these claims. At least theoretically, the Mutual Assistance Directive should allow a tax authority to recover the tax and penalties due from foreign intermediaries. However, there are apparently other reasons in the daily business practice that will avoid recourse to the enforcement methods of the Mutual Assistance Recovery Directive and make the Mutual Assistance Directive (77/799/EEC) the last resort.

The first reason is that the intermediaries which shall be authorized to assume withholding responsibility are financial institutions, i.e. a limited, specific group of economic institutions. Due to their daily business these institutions are aware of the sensitivity of dealing with other people's money. The experience under the US QI regime, which has been in force since 2001, i.e. more than 6 years, shows that even in the case of non-compliance with the QI Agreement, no recourse to legal enforcement measures has been necessary up to now.

The second reason is that the tax authority will always have the possibility to withdraw the status of the Responsible Withholding Agent. If such action is taken, it will immediately become public through daily business and will seriously affect the reputation of the intermediary heavily. It is therefore anticipated that intermediaries will want to avoid risking their reputation and consequently will avoid recourse to enforcement methods.

The Mutual Recovery Assistance Directive 76/308/EEC – When considering the possibility of applying the Mutual Recovery Assistance Directive, it must be observed that this Directive only relates to the taxes that are listed in Art. 2. The Directive consequently applies to "taxes on income and capital" (Art. 2(g)), including those levied by way of a withholding tax. It does not however apply to transaction taxes imposed on the sale, purchase, transfer or registration of financial instruments that require recovery assistance. The Directive stipulates several conditions (Art. 7), confirming mutual assistance with regard to the collection of taxes. The aim of this Directive is to provide assistance between tax authorities of different Member States, for the recovery of claims that remain unpaid. The provisions of this Directive – and of the implementing Directive 2002/94/EC – make it clear that the organisation of the Mutual Recovery Assistance is not adapted to direct contacts (and direct payments) between financial intermediaries and tax authorities in different Member States.

The Mutual Assistance Directive 77/799/EEC – The Court has repeatedly held that effectiveness of fiscal supervision constitutes an over-riding requirement of general interest capable of justifying a restriction on the exercise of fundamental freedoms guaranteed by the Treaty. In assessing the proportionality of national measures restricting these fundamental freedoms, the Court tends to take account of the possibilities offered by the Mutual Assistance Directive to check the tax situation of taxpayers. At the same time, the Court repeatedly underlined that there was nothing preventing the tax authorities concerned from requiring the taxpayer to provide such proof as they considered necessary in order to determine whether the conditions provided for in the legislation at issue had been met.

These considerations of the ECJ confirm that the aim of the Mutual Assistance Directive with regard to cross-border situations is not to replace the normal audit rules that each of the Member States applies within its territory. This Directive has been adopted in order to ensure that the Member States exchange information "concerning particular cases" (as confirmed in the 5th recital of the Preamble to the directive), where the national control and investigation measures – whose effect does not extend beyond national frontiers – are insufficient.

Consequently, this Directive only deals with collaboration between Member States' competent authorities. It does not provide for any communication of information by taxpayers or financial intermediaries to the tax authorities. Moreover, the Directive applies to taxes on income and on capital – as defined in Art. 1(2) – including withholding tax, but it does not apply to transaction taxes on the sale, purchase, transfer or registration of financial instruments.

2.2.8. Simplification and harmonisation of at-source relief procedures

Harmonisation and simplification of procedural issues cannot be completely achieved due to varying substantial differences in tax laws and regulations. Examples of such issues are differences in tax rates, in the allocation of legal responsibility for the withholding of tax, differences in timing of the withholding responsibility (payment date versus "pro rata temporis systems") and in procedural requirements. Such differences can only be solved by amendments to substantive national tax law provisions or tax treaties and will, in many cases, also require adjustments of national legal systems as well as tax laws. The FISCO Group finds, however, that the suggestions in this chapter may be used as a basis for the discussion of future harmonised EU Tax Relief Procedures. The suggestions below are based on the conclusions made in the FISCO Fact-Finding Study. In many countries there is a formal possibility of relief at source on payments, but since this may be conditional upon a tax residency proof for m or similar being furnished before the payment of dividends or interest, this system does not, in practice, allow any tax relief at payment. In other countries, even a receipt of a tax refund after a formal application is made difficult and sometimes a practical impossibility. The FISCO Group finds that such formal possibility is not sufficient and also that, in such countries, certain substantial tax law provisions may need to be amended in order to make relief at source effectively possible and to harmonise tax relief procedures within the EU.

The fact that withholding tax collection and relief procedures differ substantially between the Member States is a serious problem in itself. Intermediaries incur substantial costs to cope with these differences or may forego the relief to which their clients are entitled because of the costs attached thereto. To solve this problem, it is necessary that a harmonised withholding tax relief procedure be introduced. Consequently, the following features should ideally be harmonized for all EU Member States:

- timing of withholding tax deduction and of the remittance of the tax to the local tax authorities;
- reporting obligations;
- documentation requirements and validity period for documentation;
- statute of limitations for the introduction of refund claims;
- tax authority arrangements for processing refund claims;
- procedures for reviewing compliance by intermediaries with their obligations.

It should be noted that the ambitions of harmonisation and simplification with respect to forms and administrative procedures exist also in the recently adopted EU Directive on Services in the Internal Market, by the proposal of introducing a One-Stop-Shop in the Member States for non-domestic corporations and businesses, acceptance of forms from other Member States and the exchange of information.

2.2.8.1. Information delivery and proof of tax residency for tax relief. The Responsible Withholding Agent or intermediary must apply the correct tax rate, i.e. the entitlement to tax relief of each investor corresponding to his residence and the applicable tax treaty or domestic rules of the issuer country. According to the conclusions in the FISCO Fact-Finding Study, there should be no excessive documentation requirements as proof for the applicable tax relief. The currently customary certificates of residence that need to be issued annually by the responsible tax office of the beneficial owner could be abolished. This appears an appropriate step on the road to an Internal European Market. The FISCO Group recommends that the existing certificate of residence system, when applicable, should be replaced by self-certification of the beneficial owners. However, the experience under the US QI regime, and under the domestic US withholding tax rules, shows that even such a system can become rather bureaucratic and burdensome for intermediaries.

2.2.8.2. Self-Certification and Know-Your-Customer (KYC) rules. Self-certification will be the optimal way in future to receive the correct investor information, since the complexity of tax residency rules, tax treaties and - above all - the actual circumstances of the investors' presence and activities in a specific state are best known to the investor him-/herself. With respect to individuals it is often sufficient to rely on general know-your-customer rules (KYC) only. For corporate investors, or in special cases, for instance when the account file contains addresses in different countries, or when it is not clear whether the account holder is acting for his own account or not, it may be needed to request additional information to be provided. In this connection, FISCO has a preference that such additional information be limited to a self-certification. The collection of such self-certification should discharge the liability of the Withholding Agent. It is to be noted, indeed that several countries – such as e.g. Austria and Germany – currently apply only the KYC-rule for interest payments to non-resident investors. The KYC rules of these countries provide that a natural person opening an account with a bank has to identify himself by either his passport or identity card (with photo). Based on this document, the bank must determine the customer's full name, date of birth, place of birth, nationality, residence address, type number issue date, and issuing authority of the passport or identity card. Legal persons must be documented by extracts from public registers and/or copies of the certificate of incorporation or other organisational documents. These data must be archived by the bank together with a copy of the passport or identity card. Generally this means that, if the accountholder is identical to the beneficial owner within the EU Member States, it could in principle suffice that the Responsible Withholding Agent relies on the applicable KYC documentation of his country. However, as stated above, in certain circumstances, it may be desirable to also request a self-certification made under penalty of perjury. It would facilitate tax compliance if such self-certification should be standardised within the EU. If the statement made by an investor is incorrect, this may, in many jurisdictions be a criminal act. Based on the information provided, the CSD or the account operator can decide on a tax code with respect to each customer. The EU Tax Relief Procedure should be based on a common standard of information collection from beneficial owners. We propose that this common standard be included in a single document, valid in all the EU Member States, presented upon opening an account or deposit. When accounts are opened, such self-certification should also be able to be handled electronically in the future. There are intermediaries that only operate electronically on the internet. In such cases the customer should be able to identify themselves electronically. In certain jurisdictions, there are already ways for tax payers to identify themselves and file tax returns electronically, e.g. the US, Sweden, Finland and Germany.

2.2.8.3. Updating and passing on information. It should not be necessary to renew information or documentation on a regular basis e.g. year ly. Instead, it should be sufficient for investors to update information when changes occur. Such investor information should be subject to tax audits. Transitional provisions may, however, be necessary for old accounts. In the EU Tax Relief Procedure, authorized intermediaries without the status of being a Responsible Withholding Agent should be allowed to pass the tax-rate information to the security issuer/agent or any upper-tier authorized intermediary as appropriate.

This may involve:

i. segregation of assets into tax-rate pools on the books of the upper-tier authorized intermediary/issuer, or

ii. tax-rate breakdown of income entitlements arising on assets held in a single pool on the books of the upper-tier authorized intermediary/issuer in accordance with the tax rates applicable to the underlying investors.

Where the information is provided to an upper-tier authorized intermediary who is not a Responsible Withholding Agent, the authorized intermediary is responsible for relaying that information to the next upper-tier authorized intermediary or the issuer, in conjunction with one of the methods outlined above (i) or (ii). The reporting to the upper-level intermediary then forms the basis for the tax withholding by the Responsible Withholding Agent.

Intermediaries should be allowed to pass on information and withhold tax based on the reliance on information received in “good faith” between authorized intermediaries in the Member State, and provided that self-certification principles are respected. This should be done without the requirement to provide or receive evidence of the beneficial owners' tax residency ahead of each payment.

This model should be defined in EU guidelines and applied in domestic tax laws/guidelines, and be monitored and audited by local tax authorities.

2.2.8.4. Domestic investors. When pools are used it is necessary to take care of domestic investors holding securities through foreign intermediaries in order:

i. to be able to ensure that domestic taxes will eventually be paid;

ii. to prevent the deduction of withholding tax at the highest "non-treaty country" rates.

The need for withholding could be questioned here, since there generally are ways to collect taxes from domestic investors, who have an obligation to submit annual income tax returns. Such potential delay of cash flow for the tax authorities might instead be solved by imposing interest charges on payments after a certain time-limit. It could also be considered whether or not it may be possible to implement reporting obligations for the foreign intermediary. This must however be in consistency with EC law and principles.

2.2.8.5. The ISSA Model. The Group of Thirty, ("G 30") issued its report "Global Clearing and Settlement – A Plan of Action" in January 2003. In this report, Recommendation 8 considered, inter *alia, the need to automate and standardize tax relief arrangements.*

In 2004, a tax relief model was developed and proposed. The tax relief model was endorsed both by the G 30 and by the International Securities Services Association, ISSA, and was posted on ISSA's website in February 2005. The model, (hereafter named the "ISSA Model") based on optimal relief-at-source methodology, builds on existing technology and best practices and anticipates a phased implementation approach. The model is presently subject to review and comments by other industry groups and interested parties. The ISSA tax relief model is designed to fully satisfy the G 30 criteria by:

- standardizing tax relief arrangements;
- creating a platform that facilitates the automation of associated procedures and the electronic communication of associated data;
- providing each party involved in the tax relief process with an opportunity to minimize associated costs.

The ISSA Model is based on the optimal relief-at-source methodology. Accordingly, it envisages that appropriate tax relief will be secured on dividend and interest income arising from securities at the point of income payment and that it will not normally be necessary to file (electronic or physical) tax reclaim applications to secure this relief. Moreover, the model does not envisage any radical changes to existing practices and system capabilities. Rather, it largely builds on existing technology and best practices that are already used to secure tax relief in a number of countries of investment[24]. According to the model which builds on self-certification, investors complete a standardized declaration confirming their:

1. identity;
2. residence;
3. generic category (individual, corporation, pension fund etc.); and
4. tax relief eligibility.

If the investor fails to complete a declaration, the investor will not be entitled to any tax relief under the model. Instead, a tax relief may be claimed by the general refund procedures. According to the ISSA Model, the declaration is provided to the issuer/agent or any authorized intermediary acting for the investor (depending on the national legal systems of responsibility for the correct withholding).

2.2.8.6. Other "Best practices" building on a system of tax relief at source. As concluded in the G 30 report and in the FISCO Country Studies made in relation to the FISCO Fact-Finding Study, a number of countries already operate (wholly or partially) a relief at source tax system in a way that is essentially compatible with the ISSA Model, such as the AWA and QI systems in Ireland and US as well as the Japanese QFI system for bonds. Also certain Nordic country systems, such as the Swedish system and the newly reformed Finnish withholding tax system, make tax relief at source generally available. In these systems a relief at source is generally available based on pooling of assets into tax-rate pools in the books of the upper tier intermediaries. It also builds on self-certification and does not require that individual beneficial information passes through the chain of intermediaries ahead of the payment. In Sweden, tax relief can be obtained on payments to foreign intermediaries, but the withholding responsibility lies mandatory on domestic intermediaries only. Based on the fact that there are already systems in place in certain jurisdictions allowing for tax relief at source and that those systems are also often well-functioning for withholding tax collection, the FISCO Group proposes, in accordance with its findings, that a harmonised EU Tax Relief Procedure be implemented in order to create a level playing-field within the EU. The methodology of tax relief at source and the availability of using pooling of assets into tax-rate pool(s) combined with standardisation/centralisation of investor tax documentation and requirements, could provide a firm basis for streamlining and simplifying the current tax-relief processes in the EU Member States.

2.3. Measures to increase efficiency of quick and standard refund procedures

Even in a system with at-source relief as the normal and preferred method for applying treaty rates and even with a fairly long time-period before taxes must be forwarded to the tax authorities, there is still a clear need for efficient refund procedures. A supplementary refund procedure should be standardised throughout the Member States by using a similar form for application and by implementing a harmonised time-limit for the application of refund. Such refund procedures should consist of both a quick and a standard method.

2.3.1. Quick refund procedures: Time limit or offsetting possibilities for tax to be paid to local tax authorities

Late transactions near record dates and standardized procedures for corrections in withholding of taxes require a certain period of time before the tax actually has to be paid to the local tax authorities. In some countries many corrections can be administrated without the need for a formal refund application with the tax authorities due to the fact that the collectors of the tax (CSD and the nominees) have a certain amount of time before the taxes must be paid to the Tax Agency (e.g. 4 months in Sweden). Some "quick refund" methods in certain jurisdictions are also based on such concepts. The FISCO Group therefore suggests that the time limit for intermediaries and withholding agents to forward the taxes collected to the tax authorities be harmonised throughout the Member States and extended e.g. to 3–5 months. The cost of such deferred tax payment may often be compensated due to less administration and fewer costs for handling errors in reported and withheld taxes. In some countries the tax administrations have acknowledged this and therefore support the keeping of such extended time limits in national tax law. It seems however, that many countries today have shorter time limits for the payment of withholding taxes. As an alternative, if tax is collected on a current monthly basis, it might instead be possible to offset any tax corrections from tax payments during subsequent months.

2.3.2. Simplifications in standard refund procedures

The FISCO Group recommends the following simplifications in respect of refund procedures. One-Stop-Shop

Standard refund procedures should be centralized in each country to one tax authority or tax office only. As the refund procedure currently works in many Member States, the local tax office responsible for the area where an applicant lives, is liable for the "stamping" of forms confirming the tax residency of that applicant. If there are many local tax offices it can be very time-consuming to find the right office especially if intermediaries are involved and acting on behalf of many applicants.

One form – Standardised forms for application throughout the Member States should be implemented. It may be necessary to consider varying requirements in different tax treaties in this respect. However, such standardisation might build on the proposed beneficial owner declaration according to the model described previously. There could be, for example, certain boxes to fill in for different categories of tax payers (individual, corporation, pension fund etc). Standardised forms for tax-residency certificates used in all EU Member States should be introduced in order to greatly facilitate the refund procedures. Such forms must be able to be filed electronically.

One time-limit – The time-limit for a refund application should be harmonized throughout the Member States, e.g. 4–5 years after the year of distribution. This would assist investors in different jurisdictions, as well as intermediaries acting on behalf of their customers, to safely meet those time-limits.

2.4. Substantive rules that constitute a barrier

Countries where withholding tax is levied and/or relief from withholding tax is granted on a "pro rata temporis" or on a transaction-by-transaction basis raise particular problems which are described in section 2.3.1.2.1. of the FISCO Fact-Finding Study. One substantial feature of a "pro rata temporis" or "transaction-by-transaction" withholding tax on income from fixed debt securities is that the collection of tax is not postponed until the moment of the coupon payment by the issuer, but can take place immediately at the moment of the transaction on the secondary market. The problems identified in the FFS were twofold:

– In cases where only local settlement service providers or CSDs are allowed to collect the withholding tax, foreign settlement service providers that are holding the securities with a local CSD may be precluded or discouraged from settling taxable transactions on their own books. This is due to the fact that the local settlement service providers need to intervene in the settlement on individual transactions in order to be able to collect that tax. This problem could be resolved by allowing foreign CSDs or settlement service providers to assume responsibility for tax collection and relief, without needing to appoint a local fiscal representative, and thus ensuring a level playing-field between local and foreign settlement service providers.

– The remaining problem with such a tax regime is the fact that it requires complex and costly procedures to be developed to track all changes of beneficial ownership. This represents relatively high costs for foreign CSDs or settlement service providers, compared to local CSDs/settlement service provider s, as the development cost can only be spread out over a small number of players in the case of a foreign CSD. The FISCO Group is of the opinion that this latter problem cannot be resolved without touching on the substance of tax rules, and since the legitimate concerns of this group are limited to procedural tax barriers, this issue is not further discussed in this report.

2.5. Conclusions on withholding tax procedures

The withholding tax relief procedures which exist in Member States do not, at present, take sufficient account of the multitiered holding environment. The present procedures are therefore costly and inefficient. The FISCO Group is of the opinion that at-source relief procedures are the best method to improve the present situation because of the optimized cash flow they offer to investors. Many of the present administrative and efficiency problems can only be resolved by shifting withholding responsibilities to intermediaries, and by allowing all intermediaries in the custody chain to assume withholding responsibilities or to take responsibility for granting withholding tax relief. The withholding tax relief procedures differ substantially between the Member States. This is a serious problem, since intermediaries incur substantial costs to cope with these differences or may forego the relief to which their clients are entitled because of the costs attached thereto. To solve these problems, it is necessary that a harmonised withholding tax relief procedure be introduced. Even though relief at source is the preferred relief method, there is a clear need also for efficient refund procedures.

2.5.1. Conclusions on at-source relief procedures

2.5.1.1. Shifting withholding responsibilities. Many of the administrative and efficiency problems identified in the FISCO Fact-Finding Study can be resolved by eliminating the need to pass on detailed information on beneficial owners through the custody chain up to the local withholding agents. This can be best achieved by allowing any intermediary in the chain to either assume full withholding responsibilities or to take responsibility for granting withholding tax relief by sending pooled withholding -rate information to the upstream intermediary. This possibility would be enhanced by the abolishing of the requirement of paper-form certification and the permission to allow intermediaries to make use of modern technology to pass on beneficial owner information to the local withholding agent in electronic format and to allow the use of pooling of assets into tax-rate pools.

The Responsible Withholding Agent must assume the tax-withholding responsibility "itself", i.e. the obligation to deduct and deposit withholding tax with the relevant tax authority of the issuer country as well as collecting beneficial owner information that is passed on and/or reported to other intermediaries.

In national laws, there should be clear provisions of the legal responsibility of the withholding tax deduction and collection. Withholding agents or other intermediaries should only be responsible for non-compliance with their own obligations. No liability may be imposed on authorised intermediaries acting in "good faith". This should be the case both for beneficial owner information collection and for tax collection, if any. The concept of "good faith" should also be defined clearly in law.

Some general EU rules and guidelines for the concept of acting and relying on information received in "good faith" should be implemented. There should also be some guidelines for harmonising the requirements of how long information or documents must be kept by intermediaries and/or withholding agents.

It should be possible to transfer funds to authorized foreign intermediaries in Member States (who cannot opt themselves for withholding responsibilities) net of treaty rates based on information received in "good faith".

In some Member States' jurisdictions, the withholding responsibility is reserved for those issuers or intermediaries who are residents of the issuer country. Accordingly, shifting the withholding responsibility abroad may require a change of the relevant laws. However, the shifting of responsibility may be done on the basis of a contract. The recommended contractual agreement between the tax authority and the foreign or local intermediary will, for its part, require a legal basis under the law systems of many Member States. Such legal bases should be generally established by way of ministerial regulations or decrees in contrast to formal laws issued by the legislative bodies.

Involving both the tax authorities and external auditors in an audit, by means of co-actions is the option preferred by the FISCO Group. The audit of the external auditor should focus on periodical on-site systems checks. The tax authority of any issuer country should have access to the external auditor's report; they should also have the possibility to verify the tax relief granted by the Responsible Withholding Agent or the Responsible Non-Withholding Agent in individual cases. Besides the audit methods mentioned, no additional action or even separate audit seems necessary.

2.5.1.2. Simplification and harmonisation. An EU Tax Relief Procedure is proposed in order to facilitate the clearing and settlement of securities within the Member States by simplifying and harmonising the tax relief procedures. The EU Tax Relief Procedure should be built on a model allowing for the appropriate tax relief to be applied at source without excessive documentation requirements and without exposing issuers, intermediaries and investors to unnecessary risks and costs. The Procedure should work in an equally efficient way, irrespective of the location in which securities are held or transactions settled and irrespective of the investment structure or settlement arrangements chosen by the investors and intermediaries and ensure equal treatment of foreign and local intermediaries.

With respect to individuals it is often sufficient to rely on general know-your-customer rules (KYC) only. For corporate investors, or in special cases, it may be needed to request additional information to be provided. In this connection, FISCO has a preference that such additional information be limited to a self-certification.

The EU Tax Relief Procedure should be based on a common standard of information collection of beneficial owners, mainly based on self-certification by the beneficial owner. This common standard should be included in a single document, valid in all the EU Member States, presented upon opening an account or deposit. It should be possible to pass this document to authorities electronically, without the need for it to be renewed on a regular basis.

Intermediaries should be allowed to pass on information and withhold tax based on the reliance on information received in "good faith" between authorized intermediaries in the Member State, and provided that self-certification principles are respected. This should be done without the requirement to provide or receive evidence of the beneficial owners' tax residency ahead of each payment. This model should be defined in EU guidelines and applied in domestic tax laws/guidelines, and be monitored and audited by local tax authorities.

Besides the aim of tax relief at source in the EU Tax Relief Procedure, the proposed harmonisation and simplification of certain information collection of forms for self-certification, and of the refund procedures, is also a very important goal in itself. Although the complete EU Tax Relief Procedure is the primary proposal and goal of the FISCO Group, the harmonisation and simplification work in other respects such as harmonising forms and other procedural issues is also very important. This work – which is already similarly conducted by other groups and bodies, such as the IFA/OECD PATT Project and the Group 30 ISSA Model Project - could start immediately, preferably by forming an EU group to review these issues. This group should be composed of participants from interested Member States, and should include representatives from both private bodies and tax authorities.

2.5.2. Refund procedures

A supplementary refund procedure should be standardised throughout the Member States by using a similar form for application and implementing a harmonized time-limit for the application of refund.

One-Stop-Shop. Standard refund procedures should be centralized in each country to one tax authority or tax office only.

One Form. Standardised forms for application throughout the Member States should be implemented.

One Time-Limit. The time-limit for a refund application should be harmonized throughout the Member States, e.g. 4–5 years after the year of distribution.

2.5.3. Substantive rules that constitute a barrier

In cases where only local settlement service providers or CSDs are allowed to collect the withholding tax, foreign settlement service providers that are holding the securities with a local CSD may be precluded or discouraged from settling taxable transactions on their own books due to the fact that the local settlement service providers need to intervene in the settlement on individual transactions in order to be able to collect that tax. This problem could be resolved by allowing foreign CSDs or settlement service providers to assume responsibility for tax collection and relief without needing to appoint a local fiscal representative, and thus ensuring a level playing-field between local and foreign settlement service providers.

3. RECOMMENDATIONS WITH RESPECT TO TRANSACTION TAX PROCEDURES

3.1. Introduction

The Giovannini reports recommended the removal of any provisions requiring that taxes on securities transactions be collected via a functionality that is integrated into a local settlement system. Such provisions require foreign investors to link up with the local settlement system that operates the tax functionality and thus reduce the foreign investor's choice of provider for securities settlement. In its Fact-Finding Study, the FISCO Group concluded that two Member States impose a tax on securities transactions under which the responsibility for collection is imposed on settlement service providers: the UK, which charges Stamp Duty Reserve Tax (SDRT) on transactions in chargeable securities held in electronic form; and Ireland, which charges stamp duty (SD) on instruments which effect transfers on the sale of registered securities in Irish companies or equitable interests in Irish securities. Both UK and Irish rules require the entity that is approved as an operator of an electronic system enabling title to units of a local security to be evidenced and transferred under local securities legislation25, to collect the tax. So far, the only approved system under UK and Irish rules is Euroclear UK & Ireland Limited (former CREST).

The Fact-Finding Study focused principally upon whether the relevant rules of both countries allow all EU-based settlement service providers (including those that are not operating an approved system under UK and Irish rules) to assume tax collection responsibilities under equal conditions. The underlying view supporting that approach is that transaction taxes collected by settlement service providers do not reduce the choice of provider for securities settlement as long as all settlement service providers are allowed to ensure the collection of the tax under equal conditions. In this respect, the FISCO group concluded that, while the UK SDRT rules allow settlement service providers that are not approved as an operator of a relevant system, but are considered a clearance service, to enter into an election and account for SDRT as operators of a relevant system, the Irish stamp duty rules do not contain any specific provisions relating to transfers of interests in Irish shares within systems that are not a relevant system within the meaning of Companies Act 1990 (Uncertified Securities) Regulations 1996. Section 3.2 contains a summary of this issue and proposed solutions.

Since the FISCO Fact-Finding Study was presented, comments have been made that even if UK SDRT rules allow operators of a clearance service, within the meaning of Section 96 FA 1986, to enter into an election to collect SDRT, the rules do not contain a clear definition of who should be considered as such an operator of a clearance service. This may not ensure a level playing-field between settlement service providers that are, and those that are not, considered an operator of a clearance service. A more detailed description of this issue and proposed solutions can be found under section 3.3 below. Certain CSDs have expressed their concern about the fact that, even if the relevant rules allow them to collect transaction taxes and cater for a level playing-field between all settlement service provider, irrespective of the residency or legal status of the operator of the settlement system, the mere requirement for such CSDs to collect transaction taxes imposed on clearance service providers constitutes a significant hindrance for the efficient cross-border clearance and settlement of securities, and exposes the CSDs to considerable operational risk. This problem will be described in further detail in section 3.4.

3.2. The Irish stamp duty (SD) rules

The factual position is described in the FISCO Fact-Finding Stud. The crux of the problem is that Irish Stamp Duty rules do not really take into account the fact that securities transactions may settle in the books of several local or foreign settlement service providers which do not necessarily have the status of approved operators of a relevant system. This leads to the following issues:

– legal uncertainty as to whether transactions settling in the books of such settlement service providers are subject to Stamp Duty;

– the absence of a legal framework for such settlement service providers to collect transaction taxes on transactions that take place in their books and to pay and report this to the tax authorities; and

– the denial of exemptions of Stamp Duty, if transactions linked to the one for which the exemption is requested are not settled in a relevant system.

This issue may in the first place be important for the tax authorities whose concern is lost revenues. However, it may also put settlement service providers that are not approved as an operator of a relevant system at a competitive disadvantage. A possible solution would be for Ireland to clarify by legislation whether transactions in securities interest taking place in the books of a settlement service provider that is not an operator of a relevant system are taxable. Such legislation could provide that such transactions are not taxed26, in which case the issue disappears. However, such exemption would risk creating an uneven playing-field between approved and non-approved systems as well as an incentive for settling transactions in non-approved systems. Alternatively, such legislation could make it clear that transactions with securities interest in the books of non-approved systems are also taxable. In order to create a level playing-field in such cases, the legislation should also allow an operator of a non-approved system to collect the tax under conditions similar to those granted to operators of an approved system. It should be noted, however, that even if Irish rules were to foresee a level playing-field between approved and non-approved systems in this respect, the mere requirement to collect stamp duties on transactions in their books would constitute a significant commercial barrier for accepting Irish chargeable securities (cf. infra) and most likely not achieve the goal of allowing investors to choose the service provider they prefer for the settlement of their transactions.

3.3. UK stamp duty reserve tax (SDRT): definition of clearance service under section 96 FA 1986 (UK)

Under Regulation 4A of the Stamp Duty Reserve Tax (SDRT) Regulations 1986, operators of a "relevant system" under the Uncertificated Securities Regulations 2001 are required to:

i. give notice to the Board of Her Majesty's Revenue & Customs (HMRC) of each charge to tax arising in respect of transactions carried out through the relevant system; and

ii. to pay the SDRT due on those transactions.

The UK Uncertified Securities Regulations permit any person who satisfies requirements as to security, resources, practice and systems to operate a system under which shares in UK companies can be transferred through the system. So far Euroclear UK & Ireland Limited is the only system which is approved, but there is no national barrier to approval. Operators that are approved fall under the SDRT Regulations for such operator systems and must comply with the obligations imposed by the Regulations and, more particularly, Regulation 4A. The UK SDRT rules also foresee a specific regime for securities transactions settling in the books of settlement service providers that are not an approved operator of a "relevant system", namely the special regime for so-called "clearance services". Under this regime there is a 1.5% season ticket charge on entry into the system, but once into a clearing system the basic 0.5% charge on transfers is not payable. Under Section 97A FA 1986, the operator of a clearance service can elect that the clearing service charge does not apply, provided they enter into appropriate arrangements with HMRC under which they will account for the 0.5% charge arising on transfers within the clearance service. In practice, the clearing system that considers doing so needs to contact the HMRC in order to agree upon:

i. how SDRT will be accounted for, paid and reported to HMRC;

ii. how higher rates and relief are applied;

iii. appropriate audit information and material;

iv. how to deal with clearing service clients; and

v. the termination arrangements.

Once agreement on the above items has been obtained, the clearing system needs to document all the above items in a document – a so-called "97A election" which is then reviewed and approved by the Board of the HMRC. If the clearing system is not resident in the UK, the HMRC may request the appointment of a tax representative. HMRC in the UK provides some general guidance as to the issues on which they will require to be satisfied before agreeing to such an arrangement. These include things like compatibility with accounting for SDRT through Euroclear UK & Ireland Limited, ensuring all chargeable transactions are reported and duty paid, ensuring a flow of audit information which is accessible in the UK and the need for a non-UK clearance service to appoint a UK representative. Certain details of those practical requirements may be discussed with HMRC to ensure that no barrier is created by the imposition of local requirements such as maintenance of information in the UK and the need for a UK representative. The FISCO Group considers that the definition of a clearing system is unclear in relation to Stamp Duty Reserve Tax (SDRT) purposes, which may prevent a level playing-field between settlement service providers that are considered a clearing service (such as CSDs) and those who are not. One feature of the concept of clearance service as envisaged by the UK legislation seems to be the ability to internalise settlement. It has been argued that the ability to internalise settlement is not limited to CSDs. Any Euroclear UK & Ireland Limited member , for example, can settle a transaction on its own books without the need to forward settlement instructions to Euroclear UK & Ireland Limited, provided both contracting parties use the services of the same member. This is correct, but looking at the terms of the UK legislation, the higher rate charge applies where a person enters into an "arrangement" to provide clearance services and it is possible that one reason why Euroclear UK & Ireland Limited member custodian/nominees are not generally regarded as such is that they do not enter into such arrangements. It is likely that these kinds of movement occur where a client may have given an instruction to purchase and another instruction to sell and the custodian can generate a match internally rather than a case of actually setting out to provide that type of service. There may well be instances where these services are being provided without notifying HMRC or indeed accounting for the tax either at the standard or higher rates. It is certainly the case of transfers of beneficial ownership which are internalised and within the scope of the charge to SDRT at 0.5% under Section 87 FA 1986. There is a mechanism for reporting such transactions via Euroclear UK & Ireland Limited and for accounting for the SDRT due. This is known as a non-settling on account transaction (NCOAT). The Euroclear UK & Ireland Limited blue book gives an example of this (on page 39 of the blue book). The FISCO Group recommends that the uncertainty as to what a clearing system is for UK Stamp Duty and Stamp Duty Reserve Tax (SDRT) purposes be addressed by UK legislation or by HMRC, clarifying what the criteria are for maintaining that an organisation provides a clearance service. Such criteria would have to distinguish the situation of a clearance service from the functions that Euroclear UK & Ireland Limited perform, otherwise Euroclear UK & Ireland Limited itself would need to elect for the alternative 0.5% charge instead of the 1.5% charge on entry. There is a need for a coherent and consistently applied test for what is a "clearance service". The concept should not be applied in a convenient way by the tax authorities merely as a tool to enable them to collect a compensatory amount of tax whenever they envisage that, on future dealings, it may be practically inconvenient for them to collect the 0.5% dealing charge. If there is not a consistently applied concept, then there could be an argument that the legislation is being applied in a way which results in unequal treatment between settlement service providers.

3.4. Provisions requiring settlement service providers to collect transaction taxes as a barrier per se

Since the publication of the First FISCO Fact-Finding Study (FFS), several CSDs have expressed their concern about the fact that, even if the relevant rules allowed them to collect transaction taxes under conditions similar to those granted to any other settlement service provider, the mere requirement on CSDs to collect transaction taxes still constitutes a significant obstacle and creates operative risk exposure preventing them from accepting securities subject to such transaction taxes (and hence reduces the choice of settlement service providers for such securities). As a matter of fact, such a requirement will often not be compatible with the business model under which foreign CSDs operate:

– many CSDs do not have access to information on individual trades at the level of beneficial owners. This is due to the fact that the settlement instructions, that they are receiving from clearing organizations and their members, relate to netted transactions which result after the mutual obligations of the buyers and sellers trades are offset by the clearing organization. Access to such individual transactions at the level of the beneficial owners is a pre-requisite to ensure the collection of transaction taxes;

– not all CSDs have access to a cash account of their members, which prevents them from collecting the tax through a simple debit instruction to such an account. In addition, the maintenance of an IT-environment with the capacity necessary to compute, collect and pay transaction taxes is costly. The cost of developing such systems is economically relevant for a local provider. Compliance by remote settlement service providers, with the legislative requirements of the jurisdiction of incorporation of the company whose shares are traded, would mean that such service providers would have to build systems and incur expenses of compliance which they could not justify commercially.

The only logical recommendation which can ultimately be made to address the above, unless changes in local legislation or non-commercially justifiable changes in business model were made, would be not to impose the tax collection responsibilities on local settlement service providers. However, the FISCO Group acknowledges that it may be difficult to find an alternative tax collection mechanism that would give sufficient tools to local tax authorities to enforce the collection of the transaction tax, especially for transactions between non-resident counterparties.

3.5. Conclusions on transaction tax procedures

As regards Ireland, it is necessary to clarify the treatment of transactions in the books occurring in those settlement systems that are not an operator of a relevant system. At a minimum, the rules should cater for a level playing-field between all settlement service providers and between investors.

As regards the UK, it is necessary to clarify the definition of clearance system and the criteria used. Then it is possible to consider why some systems are regarded as meeting the definition and others are not. Again, the definition should result in a level playing-field amongst all settlement service providers.

In general, any regime requiring transaction tax to be collected by settlement service providers, even without discriminating as regards the legal status of residency of such a provider, will constitute a significant obstacle, dissuading or preventing foreign CSDs from accepting securities subject to such transaction tax. The SDRT gives comparable audit and enforcement powers to the relevant tax authorities to collect the tax (in particular for transactions between non-resident counterparties) however , it does not ensure a level playing-field between all settlement service providers irrespective of their residency or legal status, and it is not compatible with some of the business models for trading, clearing and settlement of securities transactions.

The only logical recommendation which can ultimately be made to address the above would be not to impose the tax-collection responsibilities on local settlement service providers. However, if the tax is maintained with settlement service providers, the FISCO Group could not identify another tax collection mechanism that would give comparable audit and enforcement powers to tax authorities and would ensure a level playing-field and compatibility with various business models.

4. CONCLUSIONS

4.1. Conclusions on withholding tax procedures

The withholding tax relief procedures which exist in Member States do not, at present, take sufficient account of the multitiered holding environment. The present procedures are therefore costly and inefficient. The FISCO Group is of the opinion that at-source relief procedures are the best method to improve the present situation because of the optimized cash flow they offer to investors. Many of the present administrative and efficiency problems can only be resolved by shifting withholding responsibilities to intermediaries, and by allowing all intermediaries in the custody chain to assume withholding responsibilities or to take responsibility for granting withholding tax relief. The withholding tax relief procedures differ substantially between the Member States. This is a serious problem, since intermediaries incur substantial costs to cope with these differences or may forego the relief to which their clients are entitled because of the costs attached thereto. To solve these problems, it is necessary that a harmonised withholding tax relief procedure be introduced. Even though relief at source is the preferred relief method, there is a clear need also for efficient refund procedures.

4.1.1. Conclusions on at-source relief procedures

4.1.1.1. Shifting withholding responsibilities. Many of the administrative and efficiency problems identified in the FISCO Fact-Finding Study can be resolved by eliminating the need to pass on detailed information on beneficial owners through the custody chain up to the local withholding agents. This can be best achieved by allowing any intermediary in the chain to either assume full withholding responsibilities or to take responsibility for granting withholding tax relief by sending pooled withholding -rate information to the upstream intermediary.

This possibility would be enhanced by the abolishing of the requirement of paper-form certification and the permission to allow intermediaries to make use of modern technology to pass on beneficial owner information to the local withholding agent in electronic format and to allow the use of pooling of assets into tax-rate pools.

The Responsible Withholding Agent must assume the tax withholding responsibility "itself", i.e. the obligation to deduct and deposit withholding tax with the relevant tax authority of the issuer country as well as collecting beneficial owner information that is passed on and/or reported to other intermediaries. In national laws, there should be clear provisions of the legal responsibility of the withholding tax deduction and collection.

Withholding agents or other intermediaries should only be responsible for non-compliance with their own obligations. No liability may be imposed on authorised intermediaries acting in "good faith". This should be the case both for beneficial owner information collection and for tax collection, if any. The concept of "good faith" should also be defined clearly in law.

Some general EU rules and guidelines for the concept of acting and relying on information received in "good faith" should be implemented. There should also be some guidelines for harmonising the requirements of how long information or documents must be kept by intermediaries and/or withholding agents.

It should be possible to transfer funds to authorized foreign intermediaries in Member States (who cannot opt themselves for withholding responsibilities) net of treaty rates based on information received in "good faith".

In some Member States' jurisdictions, the withholding responsibility is reserved for those issuers or intermediaries who are residents of the issuer country. Accordingly, shifting the withholding responsibility abroad may require a change of the relevant laws. However, the shifting of responsibility may be done on the basis of a contract. The recommended contractual agreement between the tax authority and the foreign or local intermediary will, for its part, require a legal basis under the law systems of many Member States. Such legal bases should be generally established by way of ministerial regulations or decrees in contrast to formal laws issued by the legislative bodies.

Involving both the tax authorities and external auditors in an audit, by means of co-actions is the option preferred by the FISCO Group. The audit of the external auditor should focus on periodical on-site systems checks. The tax authority of any issuer country should have access to the external auditor's report; they should also have the possibility to verify the tax relief granted by the Responsible Withholding Agent or the Responsible Non-Withholding Agent in individual cases. Besides the audit methods mentioned, no additional action or even separate audit seems necessary.

4.1.1.2. Simplification and harmonisation. An EU Tax Relief Procedure is proposed in order to facilitate the clearing and settlement of securities within the Member States by simplifying and harmonising the tax relief procedures. The EU Tax Relief Procedure should be built on a model allowing for the appropriate tax relief to be applied at source without excessive documentation requirements and without exposing issuers, intermediaries and investors to unnecessary risks and costs. The Procedure should work in an equally efficient way, irrespective of the location in which securities are held or transactions settled and irrespective of the investment structure or settlement arrangements chosen by the investors and intermediaries and ensure equal treatment of foreign and local intermediaries.

With respect to individuals it is often sufficient to rely on general know-your-customer rules (KYC) only. For corporate investors, or in special cases, it may be needed to request additional information to be provided. In this connection, FISCO has a preference that such additional information be limited to a self-certification.

The EU Tax Relief Procedure should be based on a common standard of information collection of beneficial owners, mainly based on self-certification by the beneficial owner. This common standard should be included in a single document, valid in all the EU Member States, presented upon opening an account or deposit. It should be possible to pass this document to authorities electronically, without the need for it to be renewed on a regular basis.

Intermediaries should be allowed to pass on information and withhold tax based on the reliance on information received in "good faith" between authorized intermediaries in the Member States, and provided the self-certification principles are respected. This should be done without the requirement to provide or receive evidence of the beneficial owners' tax residency ahead of each payment. This model should be defined in EU guidelines and applied in domestic tax laws/guidelines, and be monitored and audited by local tax authorities.

Besides the aim of tax relief at source in the EU Tax Relief Procedure, the proposed harmonisation and simplification of certain information collection of forms for self-certification, and of the refund procedures, is also a very important goal in itself. Although the complete EU Tax Relief Procedure is the primary proposal and goal of the FISCO Group, the harmonisation and simplification work in other respects such as harmonising forms and other procedural issues is also very important. This work – which is already similarly conducted by other groups and bodies, such as the IFA/OECD PATT Project and the Group 30 ISSA Model Project – could start immediately, preferably by forming an EU group to review these issues. This group should be composed of participants from interested Member States, and should include representatives from both private bodies and tax authorities.

4.1.2. Conclusions on refund procedures

A supplementary refund procedure should be standardised throughout the Member States by using a similar form for application and implementing a harmonized time-limit for the application of refund.

One-Stop-Shop. Standard refund procedures should be centralized in each country to one tax authority or tax office only.

One Form. Standardised forms for application throughout the Member States should be implemented.

One Time-Limit. The time-limit for a refund application should be harmonized throughout the Member States, e.g. 4–5 years after the year of distribution.

4.1.3. Substantive rules that constitute a barrier

In cases where only local settlement service providers or CSDs are allowed to collect the withholding tax, foreign settlement service providers that are holding the securities with a local CSD may be precluded or discouraged from settling taxable transactions on their own books due to the fact that the local settlement service providers need to intervene in the settlement on individual transactions in order to be able to collect that tax. This problem could be resolved by allowing foreign CSDs or settlement service providers to assume responsibility for tax collection and relief without needing to appoint a local fiscal representative, and thus ensuring a level playing-field between local and foreign settlement service providers.

4.2. Conclusions on transaction tax procedures

The FISCO Group recommends the following as regards transaction tax procedures:

As regards Ireland, it is necessary to clarify the treatment of transactions in the books occurring in those settlement systems that are not an operator of a relevant system. At a minimum, the rules should cater for a level playing-field between all settlement service providers and between investors.

As regards the UK, it is necessary to clarify the definition of clearance system and the criteria used. Then it is possible to consider why some systems are regarded as meeting the definition and others are not. Again, the definition should result in a level playing-field amongst all settlement service providers.

In general, any regime requiring transaction tax to be collected by settlement service providers, even without discriminating as regards the legal status of residency of such a provider, will constitute a significant obstacle, dissuading or preventing foreign CSDs from accepting securities subject to such transaction tax. The SDRT gives comparable audit and enforcement powers to the relevant tax authorities to collect the tax (in particular for transactions between non-resident counterparties) however , it does not ensure a level playing-field between all settlement service providers irrespective of their residency or legal status, and it is not compatible with some of the various business models for trading, clearing and settlement of securities transactions. The only logical recommendation which can ultimately be made to address the above would be not to impose the tax-collection responsibilities on local settlement service providers. However, if the tax is maintained with settlement service providers, the FISCO Group could not identify another tax collection mechanism that would give comparable audit and enforcement powers to tax authorities and would ensure a level playing-field and compatibility with various business models.

APPENDIX 4

Spanish Eurobond Relief at Source Procedure

GLOBALTAX PROCEDURES – TAX RELIEF PROCEDURE FOR SPANISH EUROBONDS

Issued by the International Capital Market Services Association www.capmktserv.com

Disclaimer: In view of the extension of exemption to Tax Havens residents the Spanish tax procedure for international debt instruments subject to law 19/2003 has been slightly amended (removing the Tax Haven references) and may need to be modified further once the scope of the changes and the new applicable requirements have been clarified by the Spanish Tax authorities.

Spanish Withholding Tax Procedures for international debt instruments issued by Spanish resident issuers subject to Law 13/1985, as amended by Laws 19/2003, 23/2005 and 36/2007, and under articles 59.q) or 59.s) of the Corporation Tax Regulations approved by Royal Decree 1777/2004, of 30 July 2004.

I. IMMEDIATE REFUND

As per the immediate refund procedure (procedure which complies with Spanish Law 13/1985, as amended by Laws 19/2003, 23/2005 and 36/2007, and under article 59.s) of the Corporation Tax Regulations approved by Royal Decree 1777/2004, of 30 July 2004), Spanish withholding taxes will be deducted and then, where applicable, immediately refunded on the same date (the "Immediate Refund").

The Immediate Refund Procedure is only available for or on behalf of beneficial owners which are eligible for relief from Spanish withholding tax where securities are held: (i) by/through Customers/Participants of the ICSDs which are a central bank, another public entity, or international body, a bank or credit entity or financial entity, including collective investment schemes, pension funds or insurance entities, resident in any OECD state (including Spain) or any country with which Spain has signed a double-taxation treaty, and subject to a specific regime of administrative supervision and registration; or (ii) by/through Customers/Participants which are not resident in an OECD country or country with which Spain has a double tax treaty and if the ICSDs issue an Annexo II or III (although the ICSDs have no general obligation to do so); and (iii) if such Customers/Participants have granted the ICSDs a power of attorney or other one-time certification to prepare and submit tax certification on their behalf. The ICSDs however reserve the discretion to amend the procedures described below.

1. Depending on the form of the notes, at least 20 Business Days before the income payment date or the Spanish International debt instruments' redemption or maturity date where such International debt instruments were initially issued below par (the "Payment Date") or as soon as possible if the information is not available before: The Depository notifies the ICSDs of such upcoming Payment Date and details of the event.

2. The ICSDs notify their respective Customers and Participants of an upcoming Payment Date according to their standard procedures and communication channels, specifying the certification requirements to be met to benefit from relief from withholding tax.

3. *Beginning as of the date specified in the contractual documentation between the ICSDs and their Customers/Participants:* The ICSD's Customer/Participant (as owner of the information) initiates the sending of provisional information on the beneficial owners which are eligible for relief and wish to benefit from an Immediate Refund. This information is collected by the ICSDs using electronic or other approved/authenticated channels of communication, amongst others SWIFT, tested telex, secured/approved email or mail. According to the contractual documentation between the ICSDs and their Customers/Participants, this provisional beneficial owner information must include, inter alia, the identity (indicating the tax identification code for Spanish residents), the address and tax residency, the position and the amount of income for each beneficial owner requesting an Immediate Refund and must not include beneficial owners which are residents of Spain and not eligible for tax exemption ("the Provisional Beneficial Owner Information").

4. The ICSDs' Customers/Participants are obliged to inform the ICSDs using the abovementioned communication channels of any change in the Provisional Beneficial Owner Information already provided, so that, in line with Spanish law as interpreted by the Spanish Tax Authorities (rulings dated 28 September 2007 and 31 January 2008), it is accurate at close of business on the business day before Payment Date ("the Record Date") (the "Final Beneficial Owner Information"). All such changes must be communicated to the ICSDs as soon as possible before or at Record Date close of business, but in the following two cases (a) and (b) the particular timetable set out below applies:

Case (a): any trade or transfer which takes place shortly before the close of business on Record Date which would result in a change in the Customer's/Participant's total position and would therefore lead to an incorrect claim for Immediate Refund;

Case (b): a change of ownership on the books of the Customer/Participant which takes place shortly before the close of business on Record Date and would have an impact on the information previously provided by the Customer/Participant on the beneficial owner(s) (whether reflected or not in the ICSDs' records).

In Case (a) and (b) above, the Customer/Participant must provide updated and accurate Final Beneficial Owner Information as soon as possible after close of business on the Record Date and in any event before 8:00 AM CET on Payment Date.

In addition to the contractual obligation of the Customer/Participant to update the Provisional Beneficial Owner Information, the ICSDs support their Customers'/Participants' reconciliation by monitoring that the sum of the positions reported in the Provisional Beneficial Owner Information by each Customer/Participant does not exceed its total position on close of business on Record Date.

Moreover, the ICSDs control that this sum of positions based on the Provisional Beneficial Owner Information remains in line with the total position of the Customer/Participant by automatically monitoring the settlement activity of each Customer/Participant which may affect its total position. The balances are continuously reconciled and any discrepancy, compared with the Provisional Beneficial Owner Information, is reported to the relevant Customer/Participant for action by using the most relevant approved communication channel (telephone, email if approved, SWIFT).

If provided in a timely manner updates will be processed upon receipt and included in the Immediate Refund request. The maximum withholding tax rate will be applied for every position or portion of position for which no

Final Beneficial Owner Information is provided by the above deadline or is provided on time but not reconciled.

1. *As from close of business on Record Date:* As mentioned in 4 above, the ICSDs process the Final Beneficial Owner Information (as updated by the Customer/Participant so as to be accurate at Record Date close of business) and control that the Final Beneficial Owner Information provided by each Customer/Participant is in line with its entitled position, and that no excessive Immediate Refund is claimed.

2. *As from close of business on Record Date and until Payment Date 10:30 CET*: Annexes I, II or III (depending on the beneficial owner status and status of the ICSD's Customer/Participant) are completed and signed by the ICSDs, as duly authorised representatives of their Customers/Participants by virtue of Powers of Attorney or, where appropriate, by the relevant ICSD in its own name, which Annexes will each reflect the Final Beneficial Owner Information, position and amount of income.

3. *On Payment Date at 10:30 CET at the latest:* The ICSDs transmit to the Depository electronically or by fax the final breakdown Cover Letter which includes the breakdown of the global position subject to tax and the position applying for Immediate Refund, a consolidated list of beneficial owners applying for Immediate Refund and copies of the relevant Annexes (each Annex including the relevant Final Beneficial Owner Information) duly signed and dated on or after Record Date at close of business (together "the Documentation"). According to the procedure agreed upon with the Paying Agent, the Depository will in turn transmit the Documentation to the Paying Agent, which can subsequently inform the issuer. If requested the ICSDs would endeavour to send a courtesy copy to the issuer.

4. *On Payment Date from 10.30 CET until 13:00 CET:* the Depository will i) check the good receipt of documents provided by the ICSDs against the breakdown cover letter (see §7) ii) reconcile the certificates with the global position and the position applying for Immediate Refund. If any discrepancy or problem is detected the Depository will immediately contact the ICSDs for urgent corrective action.

5. *On Payment Date 13:00 CET at the latest:* The Depository sends a pre-advice of funds (containing details of the amount and Immediate Refund to be paid) to the ICSDs based on the ICSDs' Documentation as checked and reconciled by the Depository (as per §8 above).

6. *On Payment Date for same day currencies (before the currency deadline):* The Depository sends to the ICSDs a pre-advice of funds (MT564 SWIFT message) which includes the Immediate Refund amounts, and pays the income and the Immediate Refund amounts respectively to the accounts of Clearstream and Euroclear with good value.

7. *On Payment Date for next day currencies (before the currency deadline):* The Depository sends to the ICSDs a pre-advice of funds (MT564 SWIFT message) for the net entitlement (taxed at the maximum rate) and pays the income respectively to the accounts of Clearstream and Euroclear with good value. On the business day following the Payment Date the Depository sends a second pre-advice of funds (MT564 SWIFT message) for the Immediate Refund amount only, and pays the amount respectively to the accounts of Clearstream and Euroclear with current value.

8. *As of the business day following the Quick Refund Deadline* (as defined in Section II.1 below): All the original Annexes relevant to the Immediate Refund and the original ones related to the refunds claimed after Payment Date or not processed for Immediate Refunds are sent together (but separated in two different packages) by the ICSDs to the Depository which in turn will deliver them to the Paying Agent and then to the issuer. The original Annexes should be sent to the Depository at the latest on the 15th calendar day of the month immediately following the Payment Date.

II. QUICK REFUND PROCEDURE

As per the quick refund procedure (procedure which complies with Spanish Law 13/1985, as amended by Laws 19/2003, 23/2005 and 36/2007, and under articles 59.q) and 59.s) of the Corporation Tax Regulations approved by Royal Decree 1777/2004, of 30 July 2004), Spanish withholding taxes will be refunded after Payment Date but before the relevant Spanish issuer is obliged to pay such withholding taxes to the Spanish Treasury (the "Quick Refund"). The ICSDs however reserve the discretion to amend the procedures described below.

Beneficial owners which are eligible for an exemption from withholding taxes and which have not obtained an Immediate Refund or a Quick Refund may seek a refund through the ICSDs from the Spanish Tax Authorities.

1. The below procedure refers to the Quick Refund deadline, which is currently 10:00 AM CET on the Business Day before the 10th calendar day

of the month following the relevant Payment Date ("the Quick Refund Deadline").

2. Customers/Participants which: (a) held positions or a portion of positions which were taxed at the maximum tax rate on Payment Date; (b) held these positions or portion of positions for beneficial owners (including themselves if applicable) which were eligible for relief from such Spanish taxes; and (c) wish to benefit from a Quick Refund should send to the ICSDs before the deadline specified by the ICSDs in their notification to their Customers/Participants (which in no event will be later than the Quick Refund Deadline) a list of beneficial owners, including their positions and amount of income according to the same requirements mentioned in the Immediate Refund section (thus providing Final Beneficial Owner Information which is accurate at close of business on Record Date).

3. *As of the Payment Date until the Quick Refund Deadline:* Upon receipt of the Final Beneficial Owner Information, the ICSDs will verify that the position for which the Customer/Participant claims a Quick Refund is equal to or smaller than the position which was taxed at the maximum rate on Payment Date for that Customer/Participant. If the reclaimed position exceeds the available position for Quick Refund the ICSDs will contact their Customer/Participant to request corrective action before the Quick Refund Deadline. The ICSDs will only send a Quick Refund request to the Depository for sufficient or reconciled positions. Depending on the status of the beneficial owner and the Customer/Participant, Annexes I, II or III will be completed and signed during the Quick Refund period – and no later than the Quick Refund Deadline – by the Customer/Participant or its legal representative (which may include the ICSDs acting under a power of attorney) or, where appropriate, by the relevant ICSD in its own name, each Annex including the Final Beneficial Owner Information and position for the Quick Refund.

4. *By the Quick Refund Deadline:* The ICSDs will transmit to the Depository – electronically or by fax – the final breakdown Cover Letter which includes the total amount for Quick Refund, a consolidated list of Beneficial Owners applying for Quick Refund and copies of the relevant Annexes (each with the relevant Final Beneficial Owner Information) duly signed and dated as of Record Date close of business and until the Quick Refund Deadline. Until the business day following the Quick Refund Deadline the Depository will i) check the good receipt of documents provided by the ICSDs against the breakdown cover letter (see §7) ii) reconcile the certificates with the global position and the position

applying for Immediate Refund.. If there is any discrepancy or problem, the depository will contact the ICSDs for corrective action. According to the procedure agreed upon with the Paying Agent, the Depository will in turn transmit the documentation to the Paying Agent, which can subsequently inform the issuer. If requested, the ICSDs would endeavour to send a courtesy copy to the issuer.

5. *As of the business day following the Quick Refund Deadline:* All the original Annexes relevant to the Immediate Refund and the original ones related to the Quick Refund are sent together (but separated in two different packages) by the ICSDs to the Depository which in turn will deliver them to the Paying Agent and then to the issuer. The original Annexes should be sent to the Depository at the latest on the 15th calendar day of the month immediately following the Payment Date.

6. *On the business day following the Quick Refund Deadline:* The Depository sends a pre-advice of funds (MT564 message) to the ICSDs for the total Quick Refund amount including the breakdown per reclaim. The Paying Agent pays in a single payment per individual ISIN the Quick Refund amounts respectively to the accounts of Clearstream and Euroclear with current value date for the benefit of the beneficial owners.

7. By the 19th calendar day of the month immediately following the Payment Date: The ICSDs will consider that the original Annexes sent have been received and checked by the Depository if no notification mentioning otherwise has been received by that time.

III. SUMMARY OF CERTIFICATION REQUIREMENTS

1. The information relative to the beneficial owners should be made available to the ICSDs by their Customers/Participants in accordance with the abovementioned procedures, communication channels and timetables, as completed/supplemented by the detailed notifications sent by the ICSDs to their Customers/Participants from time to time.

2. As per Article 44 of Royal Decree 1065/2007 of 27 July 2007, as interpreted by the Spanish Tax Authorities, Annexes can be completed and signed at the earliest at the close of business of the business day before Payment Date ("Record Date") until the Quick Refund Deadline, and must reflect the Final Beneficial Owner Information at close of business on Record Date.

3. Where securities are held: (i) by/through Customers/Participants of the ICSDs which are a central bank, another public entity, or international body, a bank or credit entity or financial entity, including collective investment schemes, pension funds or insurance entities, resident in any OECD state or any country with which Spain has signed a double-taxation treaty, and subject to a specific regime of administrative supervision and registration; (ii) such Customers/Participants have granted the ICSDs a power of attorney to prepare and submit tax certification on their behalf; and (iii) the Customers/Participants provide the ICSDs with the appropriate Final Beneficial Owner Information, the relevant Annexes I, II or III will be completed and signed by the ICSDs in the name and on behalf of their Customer/Participant. Depending upon when the Final Beneficial Owner Information is provided to the ICSDs and is reconciled, the ICSDs will submit such Annexes for Immediate or Quick Refund.

4. Where such Customers/Participants have not granted a power of attorney to the ICSDs, Annexes I, II or III (as appropriate) may be completed and signed by such Customers/Participants and submitted for Quick Refund.

5. Where Customers/Participants are not resident in an OECD country or country with which Spain has a double-taxation treaty, Immediate or Quick Refund is available only if the relevant ICSD, in its sole discretion, issues an Annex II or III for such Customers/Participants in its own name.

Certificates of Residence issued by the relevant tax authorities of the countries of tax residence of the beneficial owners must no longer be submitted for an Immediate or Quick Refund.

APPENDIX 5

Important Notice

Below is an example of a DTC Important Notice which advises US Participant banks of the opportunity to obtain relief at source on their holding position at DTC.

TO:	All DTC Participants	
FROM:	Citibank, N.A. ADR Department	
SUBJECT:	SK Telecom Co Ltd	CUSIP: 78440P108

RECORD DATE:	December 31, 2008
PAYABLE DATE:	**TBA**

SK Telecom Co Ltd has declared a taxable cash dividend subject to multiple tax rates depending on country of residence of the beneficial owners of the ADSs. In order for holders to qualify for a reduced rate of withholding tax pursuant to an applicable tax treaty, Participants must provide to **Citibank, N.A./GlobeTax**, the attached withholding certification regarding the beneficial owner of the ADSs as the Korean Tax Authorities require such information in order to establish entitlement to the benefits of the applicable tax treaty. **Additionally, under the ruling KukSeChung Jae 85-18, Participants now need to provide two (2) original certificates of residency <u>in English</u> from beneficial owners domiciled in Belgium or the Netherlands in order to receive a reduced withholding rate.** In the absence of sufficient proof that the non-resident holder qualifies for the benefits of a tax treaty, withholding tax will be at a rate of **22%.**

In order for a Korea domiciled ADS holder to receive the 15.4% (Individual) or 0.0% (Institution) withholding rate, a verifiable identification number is required:

Individuals - Passport/ Tax ID/ Resident Registration # are acceptable
Residence Registration # is a 13-digit number (6digits-7digits)

Institutions - Company Registration/ Tax ID #
Tax ID # is a 10-digit number (3digits-2digits-5digits)

A COPY OF THE FORM OF IDENTIFICATION MUST BE SUBMITTED ALONG WITH THE WITHHOLDING CERTIFICATION FORM.

Participants using the DTC EDS system agree that the following criteria have been met:

1. The Participant has determined that the beneficial owner of the shares (individual or legal entity) is a resident of a country with a current double-taxation treaty with Korea and is eligible for a reduced withholding tax rate.

2. The Participant hereby certifies that it will indemnify Citibank, N.A., (and its agents) for any liability Citibank, N.A. may incur as a result of reliance upon information provided by such Participant in connection with an EDS election, a claim for refund, or a failure to provide information requested by the Korean Tax Authorities as described in items 5 and 6 below. Citibank, N.A. shall not be liable for failure to secure the refund.

3. The Participant understands that Citibank, N.A. shall not be liable for any loss due to foreign exchange fluctuation.

4. The Participant agrees to immediately return to Citibank, N.A. any funds erroneously received as a result of an improper EDS election or refund claim. In addition, The Participant agrees to pay any interest, additions to tax or penalties thereon.

5. If requested by the Korean Tax authorities (directly or indirectly), the Participant agrees to provide Citibank, N.A. with beneficial ownership information regarding the depositary receipts such as the names, entire addresses, the countries of residence for tax purposes, their dates of birth, tax identification numbers or social security numbers, as well as the number of depositary receipts for which the reduced rate of withholding tax was certified, the rate that was applied, and any other information that may be reasonably requested. Such information will be provided within two weeks of the Participant being informed of the request.

6. Except for residents of Belgium and The Netherlands, Certificates of Residency are not required in advance of an EDS election. However, the Korean Tax Authorities reserve the right to request that a Certificate of Residency be produced to support the EDS election. The Participant agrees to provide any Certificates of Residency requested pursuant to item 5.

Please note that Korean law does not permit a non-resident holder to recover withheld tax directly from the Korean government even if the non-resident holder subsequently produces evidence that it was entitled to have tax withheld at a lower rate. All tax reclaims must be processed through the appropriate tax-withholding agent in Korea.

Participants can use the following tax chart to determine the beneficial owner's applicable tax rate. In order to certify for the country of residence and to apply for a favorable withholding tax rate for the beneficial owner(s), please input your election via the "EDS" system at DTC. In addition, please complete and return the attached certification to Citibank, N.A./GlobeTax as well as attach any required certification of residency documentation. A failure to return the attached certification (on company letter paper, with an original signature) and certificates of residency on a timely basis will cause the dividend to be paid less the maximum withholding rate.

If completed certifications are not provided to Citibank, N.A./GlobeTax on or prior to January 15, 2009, to support an "EDS" election, the dividend on your holdings will be paid at the maximum withholding rate.

NOTE: THE DEADLINE FOR CERTIFYING VIA "EDS" IS JANUARY 15, 2009.

ORIGINAL CERTIFICATIONS MUST ARRIVE IN OUR OFFICES BY JANUARY 15, 2009.

RELIEF AT SOURCE PROCESSING IS SUBJECT TO A TAX RECLAIM PROCESSING FEE OF $0.0035 PER ADS

POST PAY-DATE TAX RECLAIM PROCESSING IS SUBJECT TO A TAX RECLAIM PROCESSING FEE OF $0.005 PER ADS WITH A MINIMUM CHARGE OF $25.

For additional information on the certification process, please contact Jeanny Yang at Citibank, N.A./GlobeTax at 1-800-628-4646, and send the original certification to: Citibank, N.A./GlobeTax, 90 Broad Street – 16th floor, New York, New York 10004.

RECORD DATE: DECEMBER 31, 2008

Please refer to the following chart to determine withholding tax on dividend payments on Korean issues:

COUNTRY		*TOTAL TAX RATE (%)*
Republic of Korea	Institutions	0.00
	Individuals	15.40
Mongolia		5.00
Azerbaijan		7.00
Albania, Brazil, Bulgaria, Chile, China, Croatia, Czech, Hungary, Jordan, Kuwait, Lao, Lithuania, Morocco, Myanmar, Oman, Poland, Rumania, Russia, **Saudi Arabia**, Slovakia, Thailand, Vietnam, United Arab Emirates		10.00
Venezuela		11.00
Pakistan		12.50
Algeria, Australia, Austria, Bangladesh, Belarus, Belgium, Canada, Denmark, Egypt, Fiji, Finland, France, Germany, Greece, **Iceland**, Indonesia, Ireland, Israel, Italy, Japan, Kazakhstan, Luxembourg, Malta, Mexico, Netherlands, Nepal, New Zealand, Norway, Papua New Guinea, Portugal, Singapore, Slovenia, Spain, Sri Lanka, Sweden, Switzerland, Tunisia, Ukraine, United Kingdom, Uzbekistan		15.00
South Africa, USA		16.50
India, Turkey		20.00
Philippines		22.00
Malaysia	Labuan	22.00
	Others	15.00
Other Countries, Non-Certified holders		22.00

PLEASE NOTE: TAX RATES ARE SUBJECT TO CHANGE

To: Citibank, N.A. / Globe Tax Services
90 Broad Street 16th Floor
New York, New York 10004-2205
Phone: 1-800-628-4646 Fax: 1-800-633-4646

Re: Withholding Certification for **SK Telecom Co Ltd Cusip: 78440P108**

I / We the undersigned ______________________________
(contact name)

authorized representative of ______________________________ holding ADRs at
(DTC Participant name)

______________________ of SK Telecom Co Ltd Cusip: 78440P108, request
(DTC PTS number)

that the upcoming cash dividend payable to holders as of December 31, 2008, be paid at the preferential rate(s) indicated below or as provided on the attached shareholders listing.

Name of Beneficial Owner	Country of Residence	ADRs Held	Tax Rate	ID Number
				FOR KOREAN
				RESIDENTS AND
				INSTITUTIONS
				ONLY
PLEASE SEE ATTACHED (more than 7 Beneficial Holders)				

TWO (2) ORIGINAL CERTIFICATES OF RESIDENCY IN ENGLISH ARE REQUIRED FOR BENEFICIAL OWNERS DOMICILED IN BELGIUM, OR THE NETHERLANDS.

PLEASE ACCOUNT FOR ALL SHARES INCLUDING UNCERTIFIED / INELIGIBLE BENEFICIARIES AT 22% WITHHOLDING RATE.

IF THERE ARE MORE THAN 7 BENEFICIAL OWNERS PLEASE CALL JEANNY YANG AT THE NUMBER ABOVE FOR A PRE-FORMATTED SPREADSHEET. PLEASE RETURN THE DISK AND THIS COVER LETTER ON LETTERHEAD WITH THE REQUIRED AUTHORIZED SIGNATURES TO THE ADDRESS ABOVE.

I/We have determined that the beneficial owner(s) of the shares (individual or legal entity) is eligible for the preferential rates as stated herein and I declare that I have performed all the necessary due diligence to satisfy myself as to the accuracy of the information submitted to me by these beneficial owners.

I/ We hereby certify that I/We will indemnify Citibank, N.A., (and its agents) for any liability Citibank, N.A. may incur as a result of reliance upon information provided by such Participant in connection with an EDS election, a claim for refund, or a failure to provide information requested by the Korean Tax Authorities. Citibank, N.A. shall not be liable for failure to secure the refund. The Participant shall be liable for any loss due to foreign exchange fluctuation. The Participant agrees to immediately return to Citibank, N.A. any funds erroneously received as a result of an improper EDS election or refund claim. In addition, The Participant agrees to pay any interest, additions to tax or penalties thereon. This is not tax advice. Please consult your tax advisor.

x ______________________________
Authorized Signature of Holder or Owner

TEL: ____________________

____
Print Name of Signatory

FAX: ____________________

Further Reading

The following is a non-exhaustive list of ECJ cases that are relevant to the matters discussed in the FISCO report reproduced in Appendix 3.

REFERENCE TO ECJ CASES

Access to fiscal relief subject to different conditions – precluded

Svensson and Gustavsson in C-484/93, ECR (1995), p. I-03955, Para 19 (making the grant of housing benefit subject to the requirement of domestic residence – precluded);

Futura Participations in C-250/95 ECR (1997), p. I-02471, Para 43 (making the carry forward of losses for tax purposes, subject to the requirement that accounts must be kept in compliance with the relevant national rules – precluded);

Safir in C-118/96, ECR (1998), p. I-01897, Para 34 (filling the fiscal vacuum arising from the non-taxation of savings in the form of life assurance policies taken out with non-Swedish companies by introducing a special tax – precluded);

Société Baxter in C-254/97, ECR (1999), p. I-04809, Para 19 (preventing the taxpayer from submitting evidence for the expenditure relating to research carried out in another Member State – precluded);

Bent Vestergaard in C-55/98, ECR (1999), p.I-07641, Para 25 (preventing the taxpayer from submitting evidence for the deduction of the costs of training courses, taking place in another Member State – precluded)

Skandia in C-422/01, ECR (2003), p. I-06817, Para 56 (pension insurance premiums are deductible, still subject to the condition that the insurance company must be established in Sweden – precluded); and

Commission v Denmark in C-150/04 (judgment of 30 January 2007), Para 58 (the mere fact that a taxpayer makes contributions to a pension scheme taken out with an institution established outside Denmark cannot form the basis for a general presumption of tax avoidance or justify a fiscal measure which prejudices the enjoyment of a fundamental freedom guaranteed by the EC Treaty).

Non-justifiable restriction on procedural rights

Bruno Barra in case 309/85, ECR (1988), p. 00355, Para 17 (the citizen's right to enforce the repayment of amounts charged by a Member State in breach of Community law is the consequence and complement of his/her substantive rights);

Metallgesellschaft and Hoechst in joined cases C-397/98, C-410/98, ECR (2001), p. I-01727, Para 107 (restriction by the national public authority on a claim on the grounds that the taxpayer did not get involved in burdensome administrative proceedings to seek remedy first – precluded);

Fokus Bank in E-1/04 (judgment of 23 November 2004), Para 43 (in the absence of fiscal nexus, non-resident shareholders are denied procedural rights and cannot be a party to tax administrative proceedings – precluded).

Equivalence of the treatment accorded in different member states

Société Baxter in C-254/97, ECR (1999) , p. I-04809, Para 17 (national tax authorities are not prevented from benefiting from the harmonised company law directives on annual accounts);

Bent Vestergaard in C-55/98, ECR (1999), p.I-07641, Para 26 (the EC Assistance Directive can be invoked by tax administrations);

Skandia in C-422/01, ECR (2003), p. I-06817, Para 42 (the EC Assistance Directive can be invoked by tax administrations).

Index